UNDERSTANDING GREEN
CONSUMER BEHAVIOUR

Despite a century of intensive research into the human mind, our understanding of how people in everyday life actually make choices and solve problems is surprisingly limited. *Understanding Green Consumer Behaviour* recommends a fundamental reorientation regarding the ideas and methods which are applied in contemporary cognitive research.

Through the study of green, environmentally friendly consumers, *Understanding Green Consumer Behaviour* examines basic aspects of the working of the human mind. The book adopts an interdisciplinary approach drawing on insights from psychology and anthropology, as well as the author's own intensive field research. This comprehensive interdisciplinary framework allows the author to develop an understanding of the entire cognitive process, addressing such issues as: How do consumers develop 'meaning' regarding green products? How are such processes subconsciously structured by certain activities of the mind? How intelligent and successful are consumers in assessing the environmentally friendly attributes of products in daily life?

This book will be of interest to people studying business, consumer research, psychology, anthropology and environmental issues.

Sigmund A. Wagner is Lecturer at the Management Centre, University of Leicester. He holds a doctorate in social studies from the University of Oxford.

CONSUMER RESEARCH AND POLICY
Series editor: Professor Gordon Foxall
Distinguished Research Professor, Cardiff Business School

CONSUMER RESEARCH
Postcards from the Edge
*Edited by Stephen Brown, University of Ulster, UK
and Darach Turley, Dublin City University, Republic of Ireland*

CONSUMING PEOPLE
*A. Fuat Firat, Arizona State University West, USA
and Nikhilesh Dholakia, University of Rhode Island, USA*

UNDERSTANDING GREEN CONSUMER BEHAVIOUR

A qualitative cognitive approach

Sigmund A. Wagner

London and New York

First published 1997
by Routledge
11 New Fetter Lane, London EC4P 4EE

Simultaneously published in the USA and Canada
by Routledge
29 West 35th Street, New York, NY 10001

Typeset in Garamond by Keystroke, Jacaranda Lodge, Wolverhampton
Printed and bound in Great Britain by TJ International Ltd, Padstow, Cornwall

British Library Cataloguing in Publication Data
A catalogue record for this book is available from the British Library

Library of Congress Cataloging in Publication Data
Wagner, Sigmund A., 1966–
Understanding green consumer behaviour: a qualitative cognitive
approach/Sigmund A. Wagner.
p.   cm.
Includes bibliographical references and index.
1. Consumer behavior. 2. Green products. 3. Cognition research
(Psychology). 4. Intelligence (Anthropology). 5. Schema theory. 6. Knowledge
structures. I. Title.
HF5415.32.W34   1997
658.8′342–dc21   97–18704

ISBN 0–415–15732–3

For my parents and Evi

CONTENTS

CONTENTS

FIGURES

TABLES

PREFACE

This book is about knowledge and how we acquire and use it in daily life. It develops its arguments for green consumer behaviour. But this does not mean that other behaviours could not be explained through the insights and conclusions generated here.

In 1969, a global audience was watching live on TV man's first landing on the moon. When the Apollo space capsule with Neil Armstrong and Edwin Aldrin on board detached from the mother spaceship and started its descent to the lunar surface, this was closely monitored by ground control in Houston, Texas. Prior to the space mission, elaborate computer programs had been developed that allowed the ground control scientists to monitor closely the space mission of Apollo 11. Brilliant computer and astrophysical scientists had been recruited for that task. Much 'theoretical science' had been put into monitoring programs. An elaborate system of alarms had been established to warn of any danger to the mission and the astronauts' lives. Many variables had been covered in these programs; and manuals had been compiled to provide explanatory information on variables and alarm messages.

When Armstrong and Aldrin were approaching the lunar surface, a couple of minutes before touchdown, one of the monitors in their capsule suddenly emitted an alarm warning: 'Alarm 1201'. Immediate contact was made with ground control in Houston to check whether the mission should be aborted or not. In Houston, neither the guidance officer in charge, a young computer scientist, nor any of his colleagues knew what 'Alarm 1201' stood for, and there was no time to consult the manuals that had been compiled. A decision that would possibly affect the lives of the astronauts and the success of the mission had to be taken immediately.

What should the guidance officer decide? How should he solve this problem? What advice should he give to Armstrong and Aldrin? The later chapters of this book explain that the way the problem of 'Alarm 1201' was solved does not fundamentally differ from the way green consumers choose products in a supermarket.

ACKNOWLEDGEMENTS

This study into green thinking benefited greatly from the criticism and encouragement of my teachers, supervisors, examiners and fellow doctoral researchers at Oxford University. First of all, my thanks to Chris Cowton and to Maryanne Martin for their supervision and advice over the years. Many thanks go to Nick Woodward for introducing me to an anthropological view on human reasoning. I am similarly grateful to my examiners, Elizabeth Howard and Gordon Foxall, and their constructive approach. I am particularly indebted to Karl Homann and his group of researchers at the Catholic University of Eichstätt for their methodological insights into the nature of social science research.

For critically reviewing and commenting on the final draft of this study, I thank Robert Worcester from MORI, Elizabeth Nelson and Jerry Rendall from the UK Ecolabelling Board, and Martin Charter from the Centre of Sustainable Design. My sincere thanks also go to the interviewees, the many consumers who willingly talked about their shopping habits, and the executives who shared their views on green consumers with me. Extra thanks to Dennis Pimm and Florian von Brunn for helping with some of the 'sampling'. Last but not least, very special thanks to Evi, my family, and my friends here in England and back home for always being there!

INTRODUCTION

This book is about cognition – the way we think, know, understand and learn. It is the much revised outcome of a doctoral research project at the University of Oxford which compared the cognition and behaviour of British and German green consumers. Research was conducted on an 'interdisciplinary' level, from management and social studies to psychology and anthropology.

Environmentally oriented consumer behaviour provided the opportunity to study cognition in daily life: how environmentally friendly products were evaluated and chosen by consumers; what information was paid attention to and what was ignored; what learning processes could explain how consumers created 'green meaning' regarding a certain product; and how skilful and intelligent was the green shopping problem solved by consumers.

Since antiquity, philosophers have discussed the question of how we develop knowledge, create meaning and apply this to problem solving and decision making. Over the past century, a philosophical discussion of cognition has been rivalled, and some might argue it has even been replaced, by the scientific investigation of cognition in the field of psychology, and especially in the sub-discipline of cognitive psychology. Despite the long history of cognitive research, scientific insights and scholarly studies into how the human mind works *in real life* have been extremely rare. An understanding of human cognition in everyday life has remained dismally low as leading figures in cognitive psychology regularly remind conference audiences in keynote speeches. But little has actually been changing over the past decades.

The basic reason for this unsatisfactory state of affairs in cognitive research is the attempt of the cognitive psychologist to copy the research approach of the natural sciences. Psychology has succeeded in applying the *empirical* research method of the natural sciences to its problems, namely laboratory experiments, but this has come at the price of the relevance, the analytical power and the theoretical fruitfulness of research at a *conceptual* level:

- When it comes to human cognition, the 'whole' nearly always tends to be more than just the sum of its parts, but traditionally cognitive research problems have been formulated on a highly focused basis: different aspects of cognition are rigorously isolated and reduced to potentially nonsensical units of research which are then objectively measured, through laboratory experiments.

- Research problems that concern atoms or the reaction of chemical elements may fundamentally differ from research problems that concern human behaviour. Human behaviour is of a highly historical and contextual nature. However, contextual and historical-experiential aspects of cognition have been widely neglected in cognitive psychological research.

Through the study of green consumer cognition, central issues are debated in this book regarding how to reorientate cognitive research. Some critical questions are asked:

- How should a cognitive research problem be formulated that can avoid the reduction of units of research to non-meaningful units?
- How can empirical research escape from the laboratory into a real-life context?
- Should the idea of causality as the underlying principle of cognitive research be given up, and if so, how could it be replaced by other principles?

This book does not arrive at final answers to these questions. For one thing, the discussion here may still be too much caught up by the language and the ideas of the 'old' to think clearly through what a 'new' approach to cognition means. But at least it seems rather clear what should *not* be done.

The study applied ideas from both cognitive psychology and cognitive anthropology to research on green consumers. From a cognitive psychological point of view, a research problem was formulated in a comprehensive way that had little in common with the normally reductionist approach in psychology. Rather, it was formulated in the tradition of the early cognitive psychological research of the 1930s, such as Frederic Bartlett's *Remembering: A Study in Experiential and Social Psychology* or Paul Lazarsfeld's psychological consumer study of *Shoe Buying in Zurich*. In this study, green consumer cognition has been examined at three levels: knowledge content; cognitive operations which are beneath a knowledge content level; and formatting features of cognition that are below an operational level. The applied framework was a synthesis of contemporary cognitive psychological thought, but it also connected to early cognitive studies. As a result of the research undertaken, the applied framework was extended and modified. For instance, a debate on the nature of schematic thinking was traced back from its contemporary position to its origins in the works of Immanuel Kant, and one outcome of this study was that recommendations for the further development of schema theory could be given.

In addition to a psychological perspective, the green consumer was approached from the point of view of the cognitive anthropologist. In order to gain an understanding of how cognition works in daily life, ideas from Claude Lévi-Strauss and his study of *The Savage Mind* were drawn upon. Problem solving behaviour was explained in relation to the context in which it occurs. It was pointed out that psychological IQ tests are incapable of capturing intelligence shown during contextually oriented problem solving.

The empirical research conducted was qualitatively oriented, although certain aspects of green consumer cognition were successfully quantified ('triangulated') and then subjected to a correlational analysis and a cluster analysis. The study was quite rigorous and systematic when it came to data processing and the 'measurement' of knowledge. This should help to pre-empt and refute criticism that qualitative research is unscientific (although one need not accept for good qualitative research the same kind of quality standards that are proposed for good quantitative research).

At the heart of the argument of this study lies the contention that human cognition cannot be understood unless its contextual and experiential nature is paid attention to. Once this is acknowledged by a cognitive research programme, fundamental insights into the working of the human mind and what constitutes human intelligence can be gained.

1

A COGNITIVE STUDY INTO ENVIRONMENTALLY ORIENTED CONSUMPTION

THE GREEN CONSUMER

In recent years, environmental issues have received much attention, reflecting rising public concern and awareness of environmental problems. Pressure groups have been campaigning vigorously for the environment; media reporting on environmental issues has increased dramatically; the environment has moved up on the agenda in political decision making; numerous regulations and laws for the protection of the environment have been passed; and through the Earth Summit in Rio de Janeiro in 1992 and its follow-up summits in Berlin in 1995 and in New York in 1997, targets have been set for international co-operation and action (Keating 1993).

There is considerable evidence that most western markets have been affected by green consumer behaviour, that means by behaviour that reflects concern about the effects of manufacturing and consumption on the natural environment. Besides legal changes, over the past decade many companies began to feel the impact of market forces, such as changing buying habits of environmentally oriented consumers and boycotting behaviour that resulted from media reporting and pressure group activity. It has been suggested that up to 70 per cent of consumers have occasionally considered environmental issues in their shopping behaviour. Surveys of environmentally oriented consumer behaviour indicate that the number of consumers who include environmentally oriented considerations in their buying decisions has been comparatively stable (Worcester 1996: 7–9, Wong *et al.* 1995: 2, 8–12, 16, Peattie 1995: 5, Upsall and Worcester 1995: 9, Billig 1994: 9, 101–2, Sloan 1993: 72, Simon 1992: 272). A hard core of about 10 per cent of British consumers is said to have integrated environmental issues very consistently in their buying behaviours. In other markets like the USA, Canada, Germany, the Netherlands or the Scandinavian countries, such a market segment of highly committed green consumers may be somewhat bigger.

Whether there has been a reversal over the years regarding the occurrence of green consumer behaviour is hotly debated. Green product options have stayed on the shelves of many retailers, which indicates that green consumers have

1

remained at least a niche market that is worth catering for. But in general, the British green consumer can still be considered a 'sleeping giant' (Worcester 1995: 1; also Strong 1995: 104–5) who only awakes from time to time to flex his muscles, for instance at the time of Shell's *Brent Spar* experience in 1995.

Green consumer behaviour raises a host of intriguing questions that cover a wide range of issues and that cut across many social science disciplines:

- What drives the green consumer? What are the values, motives, desires and needs behind green consumer behaviour? What emotions and feelings are connected with green shopping?
- Does green consumer behaviour carry an ethical, religious and/or spiritual dimension?
- What knowledge and understanding of environmental issues is held by green consumers? How does learning occur regarding green consumption?
- Does the green consumer have a distinctive socio-demographic profile? Is the occurrence of green consumer behaviour related to age, gender, income, political views, etc.?
- What influence is exerted by peer groups and social networks to make a person behave in an environmentally friendly way?
- Is green consumer behaviour an expression of a specific life-style choice?
- What impacts do media reports and pressure group campaigns have on 'public opinion' and on the occurrence of green consumer behaviour? Is the impact temporary or lasting?
- How far is green consumer behaviour shaped by the cultural climate in which it takes place? How far is green consumer behaviour developing a cultural impact of its own?
- Is green consumer behaviour part of a counter-culture that attracts only individuals who have disengaged from society at large? Does green consumer behaviour reflect consumer alienation with conventional social practices?

These questions touch upon issues examined by different academic disciplines such as psychology, economics, sociology, anthropology, moral philosophy, theology, etc. No single study can hope to answer all of these questions (and many others that might be raised in relation to green consumer behaviour). This study focused on knowledge and learning related to green consumer behaviour. It approached the green consumer from a *cognitive* perspective which is traditionally associated with psychological research. Cognition refers to *knowledge and intelligence*, to *understanding and learning*. It reflects processes of self-communication at the level of the mind of the individual.

Cognition was researched in this study from the subjective standpoint of the consumer: behaviour was approached from the point of view that '[a] situation has meaning only through people's interpretations and definitions. Their actions, in turn, stem from this meaning' (Bogdan and Taylor 1975: 14). How consumers solved the *green shopping problem* was examined: how the environmental friendliness of a product was assessed, what information was paid attention to when a buying decision was being made, and how experience affected the build-up of knowledge over time.

Consumers apparently find it difficult to assess the environmental friendliness of a product. Consumer confusion and scepticism about the greenness of products is reported to be widespread. This is thought to present an important (cognitive) barrier to the adoption of green products, which, in turn, prevents the market mechanism from developing an ethical impact on companies.

The findings made by this study on green consumer cognition are of practical relevance. They can be related to normative questions as they are addressed in management studies or public policy studies. A cognitive understanding of green consumer behaviour is highly relevant for a number of corporate activities, ranging from product development and market segmentation to branding strategies and communications management (Nelissen and Scheepers 1992: 21, Frost and Mensik 1991: 71, Vandermerve and Oliff 1990: 15). For instance, it has been pointed out that market segmentation should focus on 'abstract' product benefits rather than 'objective' product attributes (Johnson and Fornell 1987: 215, Haley 1968) – and environmental friendliness can provide for such an abstract product benefit. Similarly, research findings on consumer cognition can contribute to the structuring of communications management. Questions can be addressed like how green marketing communications should be organized or how consumer education should be structured through public policy bodies. When companies first encountered green consumer behaviour in the late 1980s and early 1990s, a communication problem quickly developed. Some companies put forward slogans and claims regarding the environmental friendliness of a product without backing them up by the actual greening of manufacturing processes. Such a superficial and sometimes even deceptive approach led to public perceptions of companies as jumping on to a 'green bandwagon'. Accusations of 'green hype' followed swiftly (Eden 1994–5: 1–5, Simon 1992: 280, MacKenzie 1991: 74, Mintel 1991: 9, CA 1990: 10–12, CA 1989: 433). But 'green bandwagon' accusations also seemed to affect companies which had put a substantial effort into making their products and production processes less environmentally damaging. In the end, they were not rewarded in the marketplace (Wong *et al.* 1995: 2–3, 8–14).

The failure of much green communication, both corporate and non-corporate, has been related to a lack of understanding of green consumer behaviour at a cognitive level: 'As far as the requirement to "be understood" is concerned, far too much communication has assumed detailed consumer knowledge . . . across a whole range of environmental issues' (Clifton and Buss 1992: 248; also Wong *et al.* 1995: 13–15, Keating 1993: 6–7, Simon 1992: 276). This highlights the need for cognitive research into green consumer behaviour.

Issues of how to apply cognitive research findings on green consumer behaviour to practical tasks, such as communications management, are not assessed in detail here. They have been examined in depth elsewhere (Wagner

1996a: 245–92, Wagner 1996b, Wagner 1997, Wagner forthcoming/a). What is outlined in this study are findings on green consumer cognition. ✒

This study has contributed to a better understanding of green consumption, which is a contemporary phenomenon in many western societies. In terms of its theoretical contribution, the study provided insights into certain aspects of cognition. The methodological approach taken was distinctively different from traditional psychological research both with regard to its conceptual approach, which aimed for theory exploration and generation, and, related to it, its qualitatively oriented empirical research design, which approached research in a 'real-life' context. Certain ideas from cognitive anthropology were drawn upon for theory generation and for the conducting of empirical research.

This discussion addressed some central issues in social science research, namely *how* to conduct research into human behaviour (here: consumer cognition). For some time, stern criticism has been voiced regarding the way cognitive psychology and consumer behaviour research have tried to generate scientific knowledge. Accusations of irrelevance and triviality are widespread (see this chapter and also chapters 2 and 3). Such criticism has been taken seriously here. The study has demonstrated that cognitive research can be both insightful and relevant.

A RESEARCH PROGRAMME FOR CONSUMER BEHAVIOUR

Traditionally, scientific research into consumer cognition, and into cognition in general, has been conducted within a psychological framework. Since such an approach was extended in this study to include anthropological ideas, it appears worthwhile to clarify some of the general principles and recommendations that are given by a philosophy of science debate on how to conduct 'interdisciplinary' scientific research. The notion of 'interdisciplinary' research is applied somewhat hesitantly in this context since it may bias the discussion of how to structure scientific research from its outset (as will be explained subsequently).

Disciplines and research programmes

In the following, principles for the structuring of (positive)[1] interdisciplinary scientific research draw upon Karl Popper's and Imre Lakatos's suggestions on how to organize scientific research.

In a broad sense, science as such can be understood as 'one big' research programme that is ruled and organized by certain principles, which are discussed and developed in a philosophy of science debate. In this sense, all scientific disciplines, e.g. physics, chemistry, biology, psychology, economics, etc., can be considered as part of a single research programme – the scientific enterprise as such. However, in the following a more discriminatory understanding of 'research programme' is applied.

4

The idea of a *discipline* reflects how the investigation and discovery of knowledge has historically been institutionalized at universities in the form of faculties or departments, e.g. psychology, sociology, anthropology, physics, chemistry, biology, etc. While a discipline orientation is in one way or another unavoidable and possibly even desirable for all scientific research, it also carries a certain methodological baggage which the enlightened scientist should be aware of: first, through a purely discipline-oriented perception of research problems, the researcher may be 'blinded' and remain unaware of interesting 'interdisciplinary' problems. Second, in discipline-oriented research, underlying assumptions and maxims on how to conduct research are rarely questioned and made explicit. Through the concept of a research programme, the 'hidden' methodological baggage of disciplinary research can be dragged into the open.

The idea of a *research programme* partly coincides with, partly diverts from the concept of a discipline. In general, the idea of a discipline is narrower than that of a research programme. The idea of a discipline can always be subsumed under the concept of a research programme while the reverse may not be the case. Hence, a discussion of principles for structuring a research programme applies equally to discipline-oriented and interdisciplinary research. They are governed by the same methodological principles. Subsequently, principles for the structuring of a research programme are discussed (a) with regard to the specific subject matter under investigation (Popper's principles of problem dependence); and (b) with regard to how the solving of a research problem is to be organized (Lakatos's principle of the heuristic nature of research). On the basis of this discussion, implications for the structuring of a research programme for consumer behaviour research are outlined.

Problem dependence

Scientific disciplines can be understood as *general* research programmes within which only certain problems are investigated that differ from discipline to discipline. As indicated, the idea of a research programme encompasses both disciplinary and interdisciplinary research. A discipline is always classified as a research programme whereas the reverse need not necessarily be the case.

General research programmes, e.g. in the form of a discipline such as psychology, further developed over time into *special* research programmes either at sub-discipline level, e.g. cognitive psychology, or at interdisciplinary level, e.g. a cognitive research programme which would not define itself by a discipline but rather by the problem under investigation.

Every research programme (and every discipline) is narrowly focused in terms of the subject matter that is investigated. 'Reality' as such is *not* researched. Rather, what drives the structuring of scientific research is problem dependence. A research programme is essentially built in reference to a certain 'problem-situation', to use a term from Popper:

> every *rational* theory, no matter whether scientific or philosophical, is
> rational in so far as it tries to *solve certain problems*. A theory is compre-
> hensible and reasonable only in its relation to a given *problem-situation*,
> and it can be rationally discussed only by discussing this relation. . . . The
> conscious task before the scientist is always the solution of a problem
> through the construction of a theory which solves the problem.
>
> (Popper 1978: 199, 222)

Research within the boundaries of a discipline can be interpreted as a special case of problem-driven research. Every discipline has a certain, very narrow focus for investigating only some problems of 'all' interesting problems. An answer to the question of what problems a scientist should investigate as far as subject matter is concerned is not possible. The choice of a research problem carries an arbitrary element which cannot be resolved by a philosophy of science debate.

Popper stresses that a research problem, but not necessarily a discipline, should instigate the logic for the organization of scientific research. He points out that a discipline orientation is unimportant for the structuring of scientific research: 'We are not students of some subject matter but students of problems. And problems may cut right across the borders of any subject matter or discipline' (Popper 1978: 67; see also Fuller 1993: 33–8, Becker 1976: 4–5) – or they might not, one could add here. This implies that subject matter as such is comparatively unimportant for the structuring of scientific research.

The principle of problem dependence highlights the fact that the researcher has considerable degrees of freedom in framing and choosing a research problem. Degrees of freedom exist in terms of whether a disciplinary or an inter-disciplinary problem is researched. This distinction is only worth mentioning because of the discipline-oriented way scientific research developed historically. Scientists today cannot ignore this process: each discipline has developed a certain problem focus as well as a certain way of solving problems. This makes the job of the scientific researcher less difficult when it comes to the structuring of research.

Degrees of freedom also exist in terms of the type of theories and empirical research methods that are applied to an investigation. Depending on the research problem, an appropriate approach for 'theorizing' or 'conceptual research' and, related to it, an appropriate approach for empirical research, has to be chosen. As Friedman put it: 'Everything depends on the problem' (Friedman 1966: 36; also Homann 1994: 11–12, Suchaneck 1992: 39–44, Lévi-Strauss 1985: 6–7, 25).

With regard to the specific nature of a research problem, trade-offs on a theoretical plane between disciplinary and interdisciplinary research as well as trade-offs on an empirical plane between quantitative and qualitative research methods have to be decided upon. The issue at stake is not to decide between less systematic or more systematic research: disciplinary research is neither superior nor inferior to interdisciplinary research *per se*, and neither is quantitative research better or worse than qualitative research as such. Rather, different systematic strengths and weaknesses have to be negotiated and traded off when a specific research problem is framed (chapters 2 and 3 illustrate this framing process for research on green consumer cognition).

As has been pointed out, certain degrees of freedom exist regarding the choice and framing of a research problem, but this does not imply that anything goes (and for that reason the notion of 'degrees of freedom' has been applied here). Trade-off decisions in framing a research problem relate strongly to the way a research programme is organized *heuristically*: what restrains the scientist's freedom in choosing and framing a research problem is the heuristic nature of research. Also, Popper stressed that subject matter as such is quite unimportant for structuring a research problem, but interestingly, he went on to acknowledge that most problems '"belong" in some sense to one or another of the traditional disciplines' (Popper 1978: 67). This 'belonging' of research problems to certain disciplines reflects the process whereby the investigation of problems has historically been institutionalized at universities (in the form of departments, faculties, etc.) – and this leads directly back to issues relating to the heuristic nature of research.

The heuristic nature of research

A discipline reflects certain long-established traditions, not only in terms of subject matter regarding what problems are investigated, but also in terms of preferred methods of problem solving: regarding how some subject matter is to be theoretically rationalized and empirically investigated. Discipline-oriented research frames a research problem through its particular approach, which is not questioned from within a discipline. Over time, problem dependence has been very narrowly institutionalized by the scientific disciplines – with great success. Historically, every discipline has rationalized 'its' problems in a powerful way: every discipline has its own models and instruments to research, to conceptualize and to explain certain problems.

At first glance, it may seem that the way in which problems are investigated and rationalized within a discipline just reflects some 'arbitrary traditions' (Dahrendorf 1973: 70; similarly Kuhn 1996: 13, 34, 96), which might imply that 'anything goes' (Feyerabend 1993: 14, 151–8, 230–1). However, a certain structure to how such 'arbitrary traditions' were established and institutionalized within a discipline can be made out. Interestingly, the underlying structural principle applies to both disciplinary and interdisciplinary research: the structural logic that drives and organises scientific research is shared by all research programmes, both disciplinary and interdisciplinary ones. The principle that organises 'arbitrary traditions' can be referred to in short as the *heuristic nature of research*.

Lakatos points out that a research programme is structured around 'a conventionally accepted (and thus by provisional decision "irrefutable") *hard core*' which encapsulates the general conceptual research strategy followed by a scientist. The hard core is put into action through a

> *heuristic* which defines problems, foresees anomalies and turns them victoriously into examples according to a preconceived plan [the hard core]. . . . It is primarily the . . . heuristic which dictates the [researcher's] choice of his problems. . . . A research programme should successfully predict novel facts, but also . . . the protective belt of its auxiliary hypotheses should be largely built according to a preconceived unifying idea, laid down in advance in the . . . heuristic of the research programme.
>
> (Lakatos 1978: 148)

A heuristic can be understood as a pre-empirical (re-)search instruction that guides the researcher in the attempt to solve a certain problem. The heuristic represents a problem solving apparatus which gives autonomy to a research programme in a quasi-tautological way. It specifies the 'irrefutable' research strategy – the hard core – of a research programme (Lakatos 1978: 4, 47–52, Lakatos 1970: 132–7; see also Suchaneck 1992: 56–7, Homann 1988: 88, Lakatos 1976: 144, 153, D'Amour 1976: 87–8, Friedman 1966: 37, Lindsay 1934: xv–xvii, Wagner forthcoming/b). Or, as Wittgenstein put it for the formulation and answering of philosophical problems, of which scientific problems can be considered a sub-group: 'The meaning of a question is the method of answering it. . . . A question denotes a method of searching' (Wittgenstein 1975: 66, 77; see also Meyer 1995: 39, Becker 1976: 5).

Research traditions are less arbitrary than they might appear: Lakatos stressed that problem dependence has to be handled systematically (or 'rationally', to use Popper's terminology) through heuristics. On the basis of Lakatos's idea of the heuristic nature of research, Popper's recommendations regarding the problem dependence of research become truly fruitful. Popper emphasized the importance of problem dependence, but he did not say much about *how* a research problem is to be solved through theoretical and empirical research.

Heuristics are central to the organization of a research programme. Through research heuristics, the complexity of a real-life phenomenon is reduced and boundaries for research are erected, thus ultimately enabling problem-dependent research. 'Real life' is extremely, possibly infinitely complex (Popper 1978: 129). Hence, scientific research (like all other thinking) is always in need of reduction in complexity. Popper related this to the problem dependence of research. While Popper gave advice on problem formulation, Lakatos concentrates on problem solving: a research heuristic is a problem solving apparatus. Without heuristics, scientific research problems could not be solved. The heuristic achieves complexity reduction by instructing the researcher to focus very narrowly on how to explain conceptually ('theoretically') a certain problem. And related to this, the heuristic also instructs the researcher how to investigate empirically a certain problem situation (see Figure 1.1). Heuristics are equipped with assumptions and definitions when it comes to the *specification* of a research problem. For

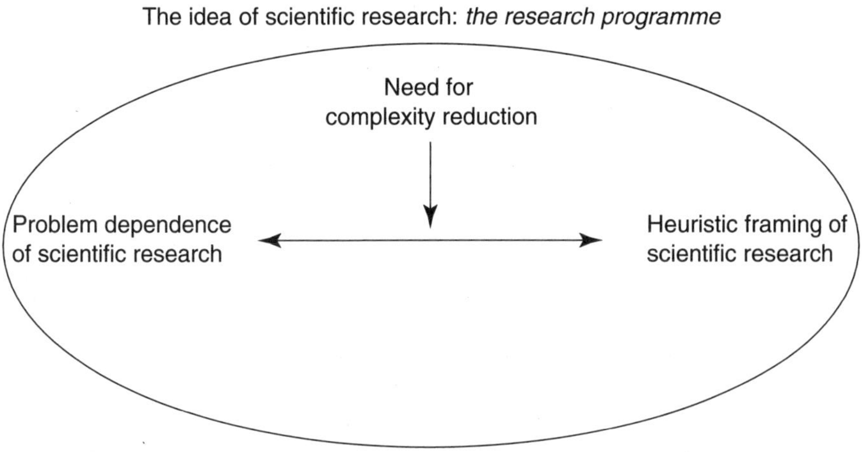

The idea of scientific research: *the research programme*

Figure 1.1 Research programme

instance, a scientific investigation of cognition can be conducted within psychology, where it is likely to take place within the sub-discipline of cognitive psychology.

All scientific disciplines apply their own 'hard core' conventions and pre-empirical heuristics. In social science, each of the social science disciplines is grounded on a simple heuristic model of man: for instance, the *Homo sociologicus* in sociology, the *Homo psychologicus* in psychology, the *Homo economicus* in economics, or *cultural man* in anthropology. These heuristic models are intentionally unrealistic constructs. They are quasi-tautologies which are necessary images to enable *rational* scientific theorizing in the Popperian sense.

The key criteria in framing a research problem heuristically are explanatory and predictive power, theoretical fruitfulness, and analytical relevance but not descriptive and empirical accuracy (Suchaneck 1992: 97–9, Lakatos 1978: 52, Dahrendorf 1973: 76, Friedman 1966: 33–7; see also Laudan *et al.* 1992: 14–17). Criticism of heuristic models as 'unrealistic' is misdirected and can be classified as 'naive empiricism' (Pies 1992) since heuristics are not meant to be 'empirically correct' in the first place (see also chapter 7: 'A Note on Rationality'). This carries implications regarding what can constitute an 'interesting' research problem for the researcher to choose. It was pointed out above that the researcher enjoys certain degrees of freedom when framing a research problem. This freedom of choice is limited by the heuristic power a research programme can develop (in terms of explanatory and predictive power, theoretical fruitfulness, and analytical relevance).

The principle of the heuristic nature of research is a pervasive one. At its most basic level, the scientific enterprise as such is heuristically grounded. The 'classic', most general heuristic of science is the principle of causality discussed by Immanuel Kant in his *Critique of Pure Reason*. This heuristic

9

principle underlies – *empirically untested* – 'all our theorizing *and* experiment' (Lindsay 1934: xvi, emphasis added). Science can only discover causality in the form of 'A causes B' because it assumed the existence of causality in the first place. By doing so, the potentially highly complex relationship between A and B is heuristically reduced to a causal one.[2] For the natural sciences, like physics, chemistry, etc., the heuristic principle of causality has apparently worked rather well (except for certain issues in quantum physics where the limits of the causality principle are reached). For the social sciences, it appears to be generally advisable to question the heuristic principle of causality before it is applied or replaced by other principles, since problems in social science research may be quite different from those in the natural sciences (see also Grandy 1992: 229–30).

All social science research draws on the ideas (a) that human behaviour is non-random, (b) that human behaviour follows certain rules, and (c) that these rules are – as is human behaviour in general – of a historical nature (Dahrendorf 1973: v). Different social science disciplines investigate different problems of non-random, historical human behaviour by applying different problem solving apparatuses in the form of heuristic models of man. A critical question for social science research is whether non-random, rule-bound human behaviour and its historic nature is best researched on the basis of the causality principle, or whether alternative principles may be more suitable, e.g. a principle such as 'historical non-randomness'.

Summing up

Scientific research is governed by problem dependence and by the heuristic framing of research problems. A discipline orientation is not a requirement for scientific research, although through a discipline orientation, research problems can be easily 'discovered' and heuristics for solving a certain research problem are readily at hand. Historically, disciplines have developed powerful heuristics for solving certain problems and it is not advisable for any research programme to ignore the outcome of this historic process. As Popper noted, all problems seem to belong in a sense to certain established disciplines, although the idea of the problem dependence of research *per se* is independent of a discipline-orientation.

A research problem can be framed in an 'interdisciplinary' way, but interdisciplinary research comes at the price of increased complexity in theoretical and empirical research, and whether and how a proper research heuristic can be developed and applied has to be examined. Scientific research today appears to be in a somewhat better position than before to cope with higher complexity in a research problem since more basic questions have been investigated and 'answered' by previous research (within disciplines) (Horgan 1996). In addition, the availability of sophisticated information technology for word processing, the statistical analysis of data, the graphical presentation of data, etc., enable the researcher today, to an extent, to increase the a priori complexity of a research problem.

Problem dependence and the heuristic nature of research are two fundamental principles that structure scientific research. As a matter of enlightened research, scientists should be aware of these principles. Criticism that a research programme is 'under-achieving' (or praise that it is highly successful) is likely to relate to these issues of problem dependence and heuristic framing. For cognitive consumer research, how successfully it researches problems of consumer behaviour, with reference to these principles, will be examined further in this study.

How to research consumer behaviour

Consumer behaviour research, like any other type of research, has to examine critically what kind of problems it is interested in and what research heuristics it is applying for theorizing and empirical research. Traditionally, the psychological heuristic has been widely applied in consumer behaviour research (Mittelstaedt 1990: 303–8, Sheth and Gross 1988: 11, 16–18, 21). Stern criticism within psychology and within consumer studies, as voiced consistently over the past decades (Shimp 1994: 1–3, Wells 1993: 490, Herrmann and Gruneberg 1993: 553–6, Eysenck 1986: 364, Bhaskar 1979: 203, Neisser 1978: 12–13, Harre 1974: 248–9; chapters 2 and 3 go into details), should encourage consumer researchers to review and examine their problem focus and the kind of research heuristics they use.

Through the choice of a research heuristic, a scientist puts on glasses that make him or her see the world in a certain, very particular way. Not wearing such blinkers is not an option to the scientist, not even for interdisciplinary research: as has been pointed out, without heuristics the scientist would be lost in a blurred, too complex world. Heuristics are like fog lamps which allow the researcher to see in an otherwise too foggy 'reality'. In this study, the question of how to frame consumer research heuristically is examined. This discussion can also be considered a test case for social science research in general that tries to reach beyond traditional (discipline-oriented) research approaches. For consumer behaviour research, a reorientation has long been called for. Such calls are taken up here. The traditional approaches to consumer research are extended from their psychological, 'quantitative' orientation towards an anthropological, 'qualitative' focus. And interestingly, such an approach seems to lead back to the very beginnings of consumer behaviour research, which was qualitatively oriented (Fullerton 1990: 319–21, 327, referring to Paul Lazarsfeld's study of *Shoe Buying in Zurich* in 1933).

Consumer behaviour has been defined as 'the acquisition, consumption, and disposition of goods, services, time and ideas by decision-making units' (Jacoby 1976b: 332, similarly Foxall 1993: 46, Holbrook 1987: 129–30). Most works in consumer behaviour research subscribe to such a general view that incorporates ideas of an information-processing and decision-making paradigm. What is *not* assumed by this conventional view of consumer behaviour is a (motivationally) highly involved consumer who engages in complex, sophisticated information search and decision making. The basic assumption is that consumer behaviour is a purposeful, meaningful process but not a random or stochastic one. This assumption is applied by the overwhelming majority of works on consumer behaviour (Alba *et al.* 1991: 4, Hoyer 1986: 32–3, Antil 1984: 207, Hastie 1981: 44, Jacoby 1976b: 334; see also CA 1995: 31). It can be understood as what Lakatos described as the 'irrefutable' hard core of a research programme – and, as such, it is not questioned here. What is examined in this study is how alternatives to the psychological heuristic can be related to this 'hard core' assumption on consumer behaviour.

The history of consumer behaviour research goes back some thirty years. Initially, consumer behaviour research was expected to develop an 'interdisciplinary and pioneering field of study and practice' (Monroe 1993: n.p.; similarly Wells 1993: 489, 500, Grafton-Small 1987: 66), but it never did so. Traditionally, consumer behaviour research has been conducted in a discipline-oriented way, predominantly in the footsteps of psychological research. This warrants a closer look at the way psychology developed and applied its research heuristic.

Causality principle With regard to its conceptual and empirical research approach, psychology modelled itself very closely on the research tradition of the natural sciences: in its founding days, psychology imported rather uncritically the heuristic principle of causality into its research programme. For the investigation of human behaviour, this may be generally problematic. Kant, for instance, strongly doubted that psychology could ever establish itself as a scientific discipline that is heuristically grounded in the causality principle.

Theoretical fragmentation Psychology has a tendency to fragment a phenomenon under investigation into small, isolated units of research. As has been pointed out, there is a need for complexity reduction in all scientific research, but the critical issue is how far complexity reduction can go before scientific research loses its relevance. When it comes to phenomena of human behaviour, the 'whole' nearly always tends to be more than just the sum of its parts. This points towards the need for a more comprehensive conceptual approach.

Laboratory empiricism Related to a preference of the psychologist to isolate strongly theoretical research units, the traditional psychological approach favours a quantitative laboratory approach for empirical research. Investigations are conducted context-free – in an artificial research environment that has not much in common with everyday, 'real' life.

Not surprisingly, psychological research and, similarly, consumer behaviour research, which copied the psychological approach, have come under severe criticism from within their fields and from the outside with regard to their conceptual and empirical research approach. Most consumer behaviour research has been accused of generating uninteresting theoretical insights that are of no practical relevance (this will be discussed in the subsequent chapters of this study). It can be suggested that issues of problem dependence and how to handle them heuristically have been wrongly approached in psychological research.

In general, the formulation and heuristic framing of a research problem is probably the most demanding part of the whole research process. It can be argued that a research programme for consumer behaviour is probably best developed by questioning some of the traditional ways in which psychologically oriented consumer research has been structured.

Practical problems In order to ensure relevance, a practical (normative) problem from fields like management studies, public policy studies, or educational studies should be chosen at the outset. Only subsequently should a theoretical research problem be formulated. A problem for positive scientific research should be formulated in a way that is ultimately capable of contributing to the solution of a practical problem.

Conceptual comprehensiveness A theoretical research problem should be formulated so as to contribute to the solving of the initial practical problem. The theoretical approach taken can be a disciplinary or an interdisciplinary one. Accordingly, research heuristics used for addressing the theoretical research problem should be carefully chosen and examined. In particular, theoretical reductionism should be avoided.

Real-life research Empirical research should be conducted outside the laboratory in its real-life context. What constitutes a 'proper' sampling population that exhibits behaviours as they occur in real life has to be examined critically.

Negotiating trade-offs Trade-off decisions in the conducting of research have to be made: it has to be decided which principles for the conducting of good (positive) scientific research are adhered to and which ones are not. A single social science theory cannot be equally strong on construct validity, simplicity (or 'parsimony' as it is referred to by Popper), and internal validity. Related to trade-offs in theorizing, further trade-off decisions have to be taken regarding empirical research. Trade-offs between the precision (statistical significance), the external validity, and the reliability of empirical research have to be negotiated. Questions on how to generate theory and how to conduct empirical research are interdependent; for instance, the decision to conduct theoretical research in the form of testing a certain hypothesis through a statistical significance test is likely to require a quantitative empirical research approach.

Questioning causality An uncritical application of the causality principle for explaining human behaviour should be avoided. Alternative principles may have to be considered.

These issues are elaborated on in the following sections of this chapter and in more detail in chapters 2 and 3 with regard to the specific subject matter of this study – environmentally oriented consumer behaviour. How the methodological issues raised above were resolved by this study, e.g. how trade-off decisions in the organization of theoretical and empirical research were taken, is examined.

RESEARCHING GREEN CONSUMER BEHAVIOUR

The research problem of this study is a cognitive one. The study investigates how consumers understand the green product, what information they pay attention to, and how learning affects product choice over time. For researching these questions, ideas from cognitive psychology and from cognitive anthropology were drawn upon. Practical considerations, such as how to communicate successfully with the green consumer in the context of corporate marketing or public policy communications, presented the starting point for looking into issues of green consumer cognition, but they are not elaborated further here (see Wagner 1996a: 2–6, 19–21, 240–92, Wagner 1996b, Wagner 1997, Wagner forthcoming/a).

Green consumer behaviour raises a host of interesting questions, as briefly discussed above. It is a highly complex phenomenon and no single scientific research programme can hope to rationalize this phenomenon in its entirety. As a basic requirement of any scientific investigation, only a specific problem of limited complexity can be researched. Different approaches to consumer behaviour can be distinguished with regard to the major determinants of consumer behaviour that are focused on by a research programme, e.g. motivation, cognition, socio-demographics, social aspects, life-style, etc. (Cohen and Chakravarti 1990: 244, Engel *et al.* 1990: 505). What has been excluded here from green consumer research is psychological issues of motivation; sociological issues of peer group influence, social status, etc.; or socio-demographic and life-style issues, although certain observations were made on these issues as a by-product of the cognitive research conducted.

Intersections amongst life-style research, socio-demographic research, motivational research, and cognitive research can be observed. These research approaches are highly complementary since they address different problems related to consumer behaviour. Motivational variables are likely to influence cognitive processes in various ways, as may socio-demographic and life-style variables. Socio-demographic findings can provide clues regarding the motivation of environmentally oriented consumption. For instance, the observation that mothers with young children showed a high concern for environmental issues (Hawes and Murphy 1989: 70) may indicate an offspring-related 'altruistic' motivation for green behaviour.

In the following, the cognitive research problem of this study is introduced in more detail. Subsequently, it also indicates what the research problem of this study was *not* by examining briefly alternative research approaches to green consumer behaviour, namely motivational, sociological, socio-demographic and life-style research.

The cognitive heuristic

↑Cognition refers to understanding and learning. The cognitive approach examines information processing and decision making behaviour. It addresses the question of how understanding occurs, and how in turn understanding affects behaviour. The 'cognitive how' of product evaluation and choice is investigated.

In general, a scarcity of scientific research into cognitive aspects of green consumer behaviour has been observed (Thorgesen 1994: 154, 156–7, Coddington 1993: 98, Smith 1992: 2, 4, Petkus 1992: 861, Olney and Bryce 1991: 693, MacKenzie 1991: 75, Cope and Winward 1991: 83, 86, Hawes and Murphy 1989: 73, O'Riordan 1981: 209, 217). As early as the mid-1970s, operational and empirically based measures for assessing green consumer behaviour were called for (Webster 1976: 128–9). With regard to socio-demographic and life-style issues, such measures have been provided to some extent. Regarding the cognition of the green consumer, the void has remained unfilled.

In cognitive consumer research, a product is heuristically understood as a bundle of tangible and intangible product attributes: it is viewed as a 'bundle of information cues (e.g. price, package, brand name, etc.) which the consumer selectively attends to and uses in arriving at product evaluations and a purchase decision' (Jacoby 1976b: 336; also Johnson and Fornell 1987: 214, Friedman and Lessig 1986: 338, 340, Levitt 1980: 84–5, Levitt 1981: 96). This study examined which product attributes were paid attention to by the green consumer, and how this could be explained. A cognitive conceptualization of a product tends to 'begin' where a motivational conceptualization of a product would 'end': in motivational research, a product is conceptualized as the promise of a bundle of value expectations from which the customer derives need and value satisfaction when he buys. As has been indicated, motivational issues relating to green consumer behaviour were basically excluded from this study.

Product attributes may be thought of as 'objectively given'. For instance, a product may be thought of as having a certain colour, brand name, size, weight, image, etc. (Zeithaml 1991: 30) and, in line with such an approach, 'environmental friendliness' could be viewed as just another objective quality of a product. However, the way consumers interpret 'objectively given' product characteristics and the way they derive meaning from them is likely to be of a highly subjective nature. All 'objectively given' product characteristics and product qualities are subjectively discovered and experienced or not. Cognitive consumer research tries to understand these subjective processes of discovery. The need for a cognitive understanding of consumer behaviour has long been pointed out: Thorstein Veblen stressed that consumer behaviour should be understood not just in economic and utilitarian terms: 'the ultimate problem in understanding industrial societies is not how goods come to be made but how they take on meaning' (Diggins 1978: 100; also Leigh and Gabel 1992: 27–8, Campbell 1989: 49, Hirschman 1986, Mead 1934). Cognitive research conceptualizes this very process of how meaning is subjectively created by a person. Different branches of cognitive research, such as cognitive psychology and cognitive anthropology, conceptualize this creative process differently: they apply different heuristics to explaining 'meaning'.

The cognitive psychological approach

In cognitive psychology, cognition is understood as conscious information acquisition, retrieval, and application as well as subconscious processes that underlie information processing. Neisser (1967: 4) defined cognition as 'all the processes by which the sensory input is transformed, reduced, stored, recovered, and used. . . . *Information* is what is transformed, and the structured pattern of its transformation is what we want to understand.' Similarly, Wagenknecht and Borel (1982: 177) defined cognition as 'every process by which a living creature obtains knowledge of some objects or becomes aware of its environment (perception, discovery, recognition, imaging, judging, memorizing, learning, thinking)'. The core question of the cognitive psychological research programme is the following:

> As cognitive psychologists, we are interested in a wide domain of inquiry: how people perceive, represent, remember, and use knowledge. . . . Cognitive psychology deals with how we gain information of the world, how such information is represented and transformed as knowledge, how it is stored and how that knowledge is used to direct our attention to behaviour.
>
> (Solso 1988: 1–2)

The cognitive psychological heuristic is framed, like any research heuristic, by 'axiomatic beliefs' shared by cognitive psychologists (Gardner 1987: 6, Eysenck 1986: 5). These beliefs can be understood – in Lakatos's words – as the 'hard core of ideas' that guides the researcher when developing a theory (see above, pp. 7–8).

A central methodological belief held by the cognitive psychological researcher is that empirical research has to be conducted under controlled laboratory conditions. Related to this, the empirical research tradition of cognitive psychology is strongly quantitatively oriented (Eysenck 1986: 5). Issues related to it will be assessed in more detail in chapter 3, when the empirical research design of this study is outlined.

The research heuristic of cognitive psychology focuses solely on cognition. Motivation and cognition are treated as 'independent' entities. The model depicted by Figure 1.2 draws on the Fishbein model and suggestions by

16

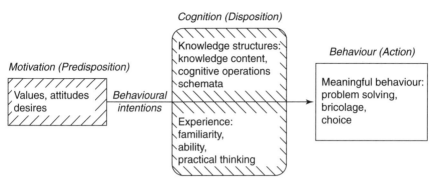

Figure 1.2 Explanation of behaviour

Thorgesen (1994: 155–9). Feedback loops from behaviour to motivation and cognition, and from cognition to motivation were not included. The cognitive psychological research programme ignores other psychological variables for the explanation of behaviour (Gardner 1987: 6, Eysenck 1986: 5, Neisser 1967: 4–5). Interdisciplinary research has been suggested as desirable for cognitive psychology (Medin and Ross 1992: 30, Gardner 1987: 6–7, Bryce 1985: 83), but, as briefly outlined above, interdisciplinary research comes at the price of increased complexity in the phenomenon under investigation. Only in relation to particular research problems can it be decided whether interdisciplinary research should be conducted or not.

In this study, knowledge structure theory was drawn upon as a specific variant of the cognitive psychological paradigm. The concept of knowledge structures forms the theoretical basis for the psychological investigation of green consumer cognition. Knowledge structures reflect more or less consciously accessible knowledge content and the underlying, largely subconscious information processing that has led to the creation of knowledge content. Knowledge content reflects what kind of product attributes a consumer has attended to and what information has been used for the assessment of the environmental friendliness of a product. Chapter 2 outlines the concept of knowledge structures in detail. Through the examination of knowledge content, the ways in which consumers have derived subjectively psychological 'meaning' from the consumption of green products can be studied.

The cognitive anthropological approach

In general, anthropology examines comparatively 'large' units of behaviour, namely variables relating to the phenomenon 'culture'.[3] Traditionally, anthropology has studied tribal behaviour. A (stereo-)typical image of the anthropological researcher would be that of an explorer who studies in exotic and far-away places the behaviour of the natives. Although this still constitutes a major area of research within anthropology, anthropological research has turned its attention to the problems of industrialized society. Consumption phenomena like supermarket shopping or TV advertising have been increasingly researched in terms of their cultural significance and relevance. Anthropological consumer research has examined, for instance, the symbolic value of certain products in youth cultures: what is perceived as 'cool' among teenagers, e.g. wearing Reebok trainers or an Adidas shirt; or cultural semiotic aspects of advertising (Gordon and Valentine 1996: 36–9). Consumption phenomena can be treated in the same way as traditional anthropological issues, such as tribal behaviour, e.g. the way a certain tribe dresses or uses 'make-up' in order to establish a cultural identity. Despite the potentially high cultural significance of many consumption issues, anthropology has had comparatively little impact on mainstream consumer behaviour research.

Cognitive anthropology approaches research into cognition from a different angle from that of cognitive psychology. While cognitive psychology researches cognition from an information processing perspective, focusing rather narrowly on structured patterns of information usage and transformation, cognitive anthropology conceptualizes cognition as problem solving behaviour, trying to understand how people develop and use knowledge purposefully in their daily life. The cognitive psychological approach can be understood as a 'micro-approach' to cognition, whereas cognitive anthropology would be classified as a 'macro-approach' that examines cognition in a context-related way.

An important methodological belief held by the cognitive anthropologist is that empirical research has to be conducted in the context of everyday life. In cognitive anthropology, empirical research is typically conducted through the case study approach.

A landmark study in cognitive anthropology was Claude Lévi-Strauss's study of *The Savage Mind* (1966), which investigated the thinking, knowledge development and problem solving behaviour of indigenous peoples. Lévi-Strauss investigated how patterns of knowledge structures were developed by different tribes, e.g. how plants were hierarchically ordered into certain categories and sub-categories. In order to understand such patterns of knowledge structures, Lévi-Strauss stressed the purposeful nature of the uses to which knowledge was put in daily problem solving.

In this study, the cognitive anthropological approach was applied to examine how the consumer defined and solved the green shopping problem in daily life. The impact of familiarity and intelligence on green consumer behaviour was assessed. Certain ideas from Lévi-Strauss, such as the concepts of practical thinking and bricolage (explained in chapter 2), were employed to shed light on green consumer cognition.

This study drew upon both cognitive psychology and cognitive anthropology for the analysis of different but related aspects of green consumer thinking: through the cognitive psychological approach, a 'micro level' of cognition, namely the knowledge structures of green consumers, was explored. Through the cognitive anthropological approach, a 'macro level' of cognition, namely problem solving behaviour and learning in the context of daily life was investigated. Particulars of the research heuristics of cognitive psychology and cognitive anthropology are outlined in chapter 2. The two approaches are complementary: how green consumers solve green shopping problems is reflected in the kind of knowledge they hold about green consumption. For understanding green consumer cognition, such an 'interdisciplinary' approach appears highly promising.

Alternative approaches to consumer research

In the following, the research problem of this study is demarcated negatively: it indicates what aspects of green consumer behaviour were not researched – namely issues of motivational research, sociological research, socio-demographic research, and life-style research. The discussion outlines the 'negative heuristics' of the study – to use Lakatos's term. It also puts the cognitive research conducted into perspective with regard to the wider context and complexity of green consumer behaviour.

Motivational research

Motivation refers to a very basic level of the psychological make-up of human beings: it refers to the 'why' of human behaviour. A motivational approach investigates predispositional and aspirational aspects of consumer behaviour, such as needs, wants, desires, values, involvement, etc. Motivation has been defined as the driving force within an individual that impels him or her to action (Schiffman and Kanuk 1987: 67, Maslow 1970: 38). This driving force can be produced (a) by a subjectively, and not necessarily consciously, experienced state of tension which is due to experiences of scarcity – unfilled needs, desires or motives – or (b) by values and attitudes (Schiffman and Kanuk 1987: 70, Schwartz and Bilsky 1987, Rothschild 1984: 217, Maslow 1970: 28–33).[4]

Awareness and concern about the effects of the industrial society on the natural environment have existed since the early days of industrialization:

> In New Hampshire five hundred men and women petitioned the Amoskeag Manufacturing Company's proprietors in 1853 not to cut down an elm tree to allow room for an additional mill: 'It was a beautiful and goodly tree' and belonged to a time 'when the yell of the red man and the scream of the red eagle were alone heard on the banks of the Merrimack, instead of two giant edifices filled with the buzz of busy and well-remunerated industry.'
>
> (Gutman 1976: 29)

Such concern about environmental destruction can be located at the level of human motivation. On a motivational level, a sound environment, or living in harmony with one's environment, may be desired. Such a desire probably exists in all cultures, although the importance and definition of a 'good environment' may vary considerably from one culture to another. Spiritual and philosophical concepts of western culture, e.g. the Judaeo-Christian tradition, tend to view the environment as being there to be taken possession of. Other cultures, for instance the American Indian one, aspire to a less possessive, more harmonious relationship with the natural environment. Also, over time, the importance and definition of 'good environment' may change as a result of the cultural evolution of a society.

An increasing awareness of environmental problems and the deepening of attitudes towards the environment have been observed in many western societies over the past decades. Surveys reported that large segments of the population were concerned or highly concerned about the state of the environment (Sloan 1993: 72, MacKenzie 1991: 70, Young 1991: 114, 119, Parker 1989: 20). What puzzled some researchers, however, was that deep concern about the state of the environment did not match actual behaviours. The individual was found not to relate his or her own behaviour to the deterioration of the environment. This caused some researchers to diagnose a so-called 'attitude–behaviour gap' or 'words–deeds inconsistency' (Wong *et al.* 1995: 2, 3, 14, Peattie 1995: 5, Meffert 1993: 51, Grunert 1992: 11–12, McIntosh 1991: 207, O'Riordan 1990: 24, O'Riordan 1981: 208–10, O'Riordan 1976: 7, 22).[5] Such a diagnosis may be problematic: it has been pointed out that attitudes or concern can only be considered a reliable variable for the prediction and explanation of behaviour if, and only if, attitudes are *issue-specific* (Ajzen and Fishbein 1980, Fishbein and Ajzen 1976, Fishbein and Ajzen 1975).[6] The commonly identified 'words–deeds inconsistencies' would not be considered as inconsistencies on the basis of the explanations and predictions offered by the Fishbein model: a general concern about the state of the environment does not classify as an issue-specific attitude, and consequently, such general concern about the state of the environment would not be expected to lead to actual behaviour. Only attitudes towards certain, specific, environmentally oriented behaviours, e.g. an attitude towards green consumption or an attitude towards green investment, are classed as issue-specific, and only based on such issue-specific attitudes could actual behaviour be explained or predicted. In view of this, it may be difficult to speak of an 'attitude–behaviour gap' or a 'words–deeds inconsistency', since consistency was not to be expected in the first place.

It is likely that strong motivation regarding environmental issues is a necessary factor for the occurrence of issue-specific, environmentally oriented behaviours (consumption, investment, campaigning, etc.), but general concern, even if it is strong, about environmental problems appears not to be sufficient to lead to actual behaviours. It seems that, as an intermediary motivational development, a general concern about a topic, such as environmental destruction (or nuclear armament, women's rights, etc.), has to develop into specific attitudes towards certain behaviours before such behaviours would actually occur. Such a link can be expected to develop in numerous ways: first, it might develop on the motivational level itself ('motivational route'); second, it might develop through cognition ('cognitive route'); or third, such a linkage might develop through actual behaviour ('behavioural route'). Perhaps it is most likely that it is an intricate combination of all three factors. The question of what comes first – assuming this is a sensible question at all – motivation, cognition or behaviour, appears to be an open one.

A gap between motivation and behaviour may be considered a quite 'natural' phenomenon in so far as both motivation and cognition are likely to be necessary for the occurrence of behaviour. Ludwig von Wittgenstein noted: 'There is a gulf between an order and its execution. It has to be filled by the *act of understanding*' (Wittgenstein 1967: 128, emphasis added). A similar gulf can be expected to exist between motivation and actual behaviour. Between an order and its execution, a reasoning process can be expected to occur. The question of where an order came from, how it came into being in the first place, could be said to be a motivational issue. Motivational issues pose a number of interesting questions with regard to green consumer behaviour. In this study, however, motivation has been excluded from the heuristic framing of the research problem. In this study, only cognition has been researched. The research problem of this study 'begins' where motivational research tends to 'end'. Motivational research would focus on the explanation of the initial how and why an 'order' came into existence, whereas here the act of under-standing – 'the bridging of the gulf between an order and its execution' to use Wittgenstein's phrase – was examined.

Sociological research

Sociology examines human behaviour in the context of social structures and social institutions. Individual behaviour is explained through the concepts of *social roles* or *social positions* as they are defined and redefined by a group of people, e.g. an organisation, or a society at large (Worsley 1991a: 1, Worsley 1991b: 9, Dahrendorf 1973: 12, 19). The heuristic model of man applied by sociology is the *Homo sociologicus*. It reduces the complexity of human behaviour to rational sociological terms. The *Homo sociologicus* is as much an intentionally unrealistic construct (Dahrendorf 1973: 7, 76–7) as the related models of man in other social science disciplines, such as the *Homo economicus*, *Homo psychologicus*, etc.

How the individual behaves within a group and how the group influences individual behaviour is at the centre of sociological research. Of key interest to the sociological researcher are the social 'mechanisms' through which group influence works, such as peer group pressure, opinion leadership, social acceptance, social reassurance, social compliance, social status, etc. While the traditional image of the sociological researcher is defined by the kind of problems he or she looks into, it is also heavily shaped by the kind of methods that are traditionally applied in sociology, namely survey research on the basis of statistical sampling (Worsley 1991a: 1).

Sociological consumer research examines group influences that shape consumer behaviour. The influence of family members, friends, colleagues, neighbours or other peer groups is discussed in order to explain individual buying behaviour. Related to this, sociological consumer research would interpret a product as an expression of social status, social reassurance, social compliance, etc.

Within sociology, a branch of research exists that examines consumption issues in detail, for instance Campbell (1989), but up to date little connection has been made between such sociological consumer research and traditional 'consumer behaviour research'. Out of the more than 100 articles that make up the annual publication of *Advances in Consumer Research*, at best a handful qualify as sociological research. The vast majority of papers discuss psychological aspects of consumer behaviour, such as motivational and cognitive ones. An example of green consumer behaviour research that touched upon sociological issues is Myburgh-Louw and O'Shaughnessy's (1993–4) research of consumer perceptions of green advertising claims. They related the buying of green products to issues such as social reassurance and compliance.

Socio-demographic research

A socio-demographic approach to green consumer behaviour addresses the question of *who* the green consumer is in terms of age, marital status, number of children, socio-economic status, educational background, etc. The 'socio-demographic who' is focused on in this branch of research. Socio-demographic research plays an important role both in positive and in normative research. Often in psychological or sociological research, socio-demographic variables present independent variables through which dependent ones – certain psychological or sociological phenomena – are explained. Also, for addressing normative questions, e.g. for the purpose of marketing management, socio-demographic variables can provide a guide for action; for instance, a concept for market segmentation may draw on certain socio-demographic features of a population.

In terms of socio-demographics, the green consumer has been characterized as tending to be affluent, to be a member of the higher socio-economic groups A, B and C1, to be more highly educated, and to have politically liberal views (Worcester 1995: 9, Upsall and Worcester 1995: 10, Witherspoon and Martin 1992: 10, 16, Jacobs and Worcester 1991: 87, Young 1991: 130, Schwartz and Miller 1991: 29–32, Adams 1990: 83, Hawes and Murphy 1989: 70, Belck 1979: 78, Kinnear *et al.* 1972: 34, 40). A critical question regarding such socio-demographic profiling of the green consumer is whether the green consumer has a distinctive socio-demographic profile at all. It has yet to be examined whether certain socio-demographic tendencies are indicative of green consumer behaviour. For instance, that the green consumer tends to be a member of the higher socio-economic groups A, B or C1 rather than C2, D or E is a rather broad generalization, but even such a broad income-related tendency has been questioned by other studies (Worcester 1994a: 2, Skretny 1993: 343–3, SM 1992: 12). Similarly, a gender tendency of green consumerism towards the female that has been discovered might not be particularly indicative of green consumer behaviour if one considers that, in general, shopping for groceries tends to have a gender bias towards the female. Other surveys could not confirm a strong gender tendency in green consumption either (Worcester 1995: 9–10, Upsall and Worcester 1995: 10, 19, Skretny 1993: 342–3).

The question of whether environmentally oriented consumer behaviour can be depicted in distinctive socio-demographic terms is an important one. Socio-demographic attempts to profile the green consumer have not always yielded strongly indicative results, and the results produced by one study have been repeatedly contradicted by another. This might indicate that it might be better to focus on other variables, possibly motivational or cognitive ones. Schultz *et al.* (1992: xi) claim that a socio-demographic approach to consumer research, e.g. the aggregation of consumers by demographics for purposes of market segmentation, has survived only because of the absence of more appropriate frameworks.

Life-style research

In life-style research, consumer profiles are developed on a fairly comprehensive basis. Life-style profiles are based on a number of variables such as socio-demographic, psychological (e.g. motivational and cognitive) and sociological. The comprehensive approach of life-style research makes it difficult to handle at a positive theoretical level because of its great complexity. But it appears that such a comprehensive focus is particularly valuable when it comes to the practical, normative application of research findings, e.g. for the purpose of marketing or consumer education.

Life-style characterizations of the green consumer that were based upon a VALS typology (Kotler 1988: 184) divided green consumers into categories such as 'true-blue greens', 'greenback greens' and 'sprouts' (Schwartz and Miller 1991: 29–32, Simon 1992: 275). Other life-style categorizations distinguished 'premium greens', 'red, white and greens', 'no-cost ecologists' and 'convenient greens' (Simon 1992: 275, also SRI 1992: 10, Winkler and Voller n.d.).

What previous life-style categorizations missed out to a degree was a rather small segment of philosophically, spiritually or politically-ideologically committed green 'consumers'. The term 'consumer' may be inappropriate here since this group resents consumption in general, and supermarket shopping in particular (although members of this group have continued to shop sporadically or even regularly at supermarkets for convenience reasons). To a certain extent, this group has disengaged from society at large (Wagner 1996a: 257–8).

These green utopian 'consumers' may not be of central interest to consumer behaviour or marketing research. The segment may be quite small; it is probably much below a fraction of 1 per cent of the total population. However, since it represents an extreme category at one end of the spectrum of environmentally oriented behaviour, it may offer interesting anthropological, sociological and life-style insights into certain aspects of consumer behaviour.

What is correct green consumer behaviour?

A study of green consumer cognition sooner or later arrives at the question of how to assess the quality of knowledge and behaviours: whether and, if so, how a standard for 'proper' green consumer behaviour can be defined.

In general, faith in science and technology appears to be a widespread attitude in western societies. Consumers, pressure groups, politicians, managers, etc. might turn for guidance to the scientist when it comes to the question of what constitutes 'proper' environmentally friendly behaviour (Worcester 1996: 1, Milstein 1979: 46). It has been argued that, ideally, a green consumer should assess the environmental friendliness of a product on the basis of a 'cradle-to-grave' analysis with regard to the energy and the type and quantity of materials consumed for (a) the production of a product and its packaging,[7] (b) transportation activities related to the sourcing and the distribution of a product, (c) the actual consumption process, and (d) the disposal process. Such an evaluation of all the value chain activities of a product is generally referred to as impact analysis or life-cycle analysis (LCA) (Gloria *et al.* 1995, Kirkpatrick 1994, Weitz *et al.* 1994).

LCA is highly complex. An illustration of the complexities of LCA is provided by the 'The Phosphate Report', a more than 250-page-long report of the life-cycle analysis of the alternative detergent ingredients 'phosphate' and 'zeolite A-PCA' (LERC 1994). Sixteen scientists from various British universities were involved in conducting this study of one, single ingredient of the product 'detergent'. The study ranged in geographical terms from European countries to Africa, North America and Australia.

In general, a comprehensive LCA that comprises all product ingredients and all value chain activities from sourcing to production, distribution and the final consumption of a product is not feasible:

- There are too many factors to be considered.
- Certain environmental impacts may yet be unknown or difficult to measure.
- System boundaries of an LCA are difficult to draw; if pushed to its extreme, an LCA has to be conducted on a global, industry-wide basis because of interlinking sourcing and production processes.

- There is no common denominator or 'currency' for assessing and comparing different environmental impacts.
- There are likely to be trade-offs between different environmental impacts within an LCA; for instance, a reduction of resource depletion may lead to an increase in waste generation.

Even a partial LCA that focused only on certain aspects of value chain processes, e.g. energy consumption, or that examined only certain ingredients of a product tends to end with rather subjective assessments then being made by a scientist. Notwithstanding the enormous practical problems of collecting information for LCA, there is limited scientific consensus on how to structure LCA conceptually. Scientists and experienced practitioners are not consistent in making environmental judgements (Wagner 1996a: 11–12, Troge 1993: 14–16, Olney and Bryce 1991: 693, Gray 1990: 86).[8] Similarly, experts normally fail to agree what product attributes should be included and how product attributes should be weighed in order to characterize an objectively 'good' product (Zeithaml 1991: 30).

On a theoretical plane, the LCA concept can set out what the proper and correct environmentally oriented behaviour of consumers or companies should look like. However, such theoretical advice is of only limited value because of the complexity and information provision problems that are encountered when an attempt is made to implement the LCA concept in practice. For practical applications, the complexity of LCA has to be reduced by certain shortcuts and through the use of certain assumptions. A degree of subjectivity appears to be unavoidable – and even necessary – in order to make this concept work.

Although LCA provides the 'correct' theoretical yardstick for assessing green behaviour, for an assessment of actual behaviour in daily life this yardstick cannot be applied in any straightforward way. In this study, the quality of green consumer behaviour was assessed by drawing on anthropological concepts in the first place: successful green consumer behaviour was not examined in terms of LCA criteria, but with regard to the contextual nature of skilled behaviour in everyday life. The heuristic idea was drawn upon that for problem solving in daily life the consumer behaves as a bricoleur. Lévi-Strauss (1966: 13–17) defined the bricoleur as a handyman who thinks practically and who uses simple and ingenious means to solve a problem. This concept has been used to assess green consumers' intelligence. On the basis of such a cognitive anthropological understanding of green consumer behaviour, the question of whether and how LCA issues were actually considered by consumers in everyday life was then examined.

Research questions and further course of study

The question has been raised as to how the term 'environmentally friendly product' is to be interpreted: 'What does this all too common term really mean anyway?' (Prothero 1990: 97). As has just been discussed, one could try to settle this question in a normative and theoretically abstract fashion through LCA. In contrast, the cognitive approach followed by this study addresses this question from a different angle: the subjective reasoning processes underlying green consumer behaviour are examined from the standpoint of the actual consumer by applying cognitive psychological and cognitive anthropological ideas.

So far the notions 'green' and 'environmentally friendly' have been freely and synonymously applied without their meaning being clarified in much detail. To an extent, such a clarification is not necessary here since it is the main objective of this study to find out how consumers subjectively interpret the idea of green consumption. The above discussion of the concept of LCA, however, provided an opportunity for touching upon the kind of wider issues that mark the boundaries of this study: what is excluded here from the concept of 'green' or 'environmentally friendly' is animal rights issues and fair trade issues as well as other ethical or political-ideological issues. The natural environment only is related to the notion of 'green' or 'environmentally friendly'.

In brief, the research questions of this study can be summarized as follows: *first, what understanding in terms of knowledge structures is held by the green consumer?* This question is examined through a cognitive psychological approach, albeit one that deviates considerably from the traditional cognitive psychological framework. And second, *how does the green consumer solve the green shopping problem?* This question is investigated from a cognitive anthropological point of view. Empirical research was conducted within a qualitatively oriented research design, although, in the interest of 'triangulation', certain quantitative techniques were applied.

Regarding the chosen product focus of the study, the research project was generic rather than product-specific or shopping place-specific. Environmentally oriented consumer behaviour was examined with regard to products consumed on a daily basis. Products such as foods, cleaning products, and toiletries – groceries or typical 'supermarket'[9] products – were at the centre of the study. For an investigation of consumer cognition under real-life conditions such a generic focus appears to be essential.

In the following, chapter 2 introduces the cognitive psychological and cognitive anthropological concepts that make up the framework for the investigation of green consumer behaviour. Chapter 3 discusses the empirical research approach of the study. A qualitatively oriented approach is outlined for the examination of consumer cognition. Chapter 4 presents the results of a cluster analysis of data on knowledge structure variables. So-called 'cognitive categories' of green consumers are distinguished. Chapter 5 interprets consumer cognition from a largely psychological point of view. A cognitive taxonomy of green consumers is developed. Chapter 6 extends the interpretation of consumer cognition to anthropological aspects. The influence of experience on knowledge development and intelligent problem-solving behaviour is assessed. Chapter 7 concludes the study. The main findings are summarized, suggestions for the future development of cognitive consumer research are made, and limitations of the research conducted are outlined.

2

COGNITIVE CONSUMER RESEARCH

UNDERSTANDING 'UNDERSTANDING'

A cognitive research programme tries to provide a scientific explanation of how understanding occurs and works in everyday life. In general, 'meaning' is viewed as the critical explanatory research unit that distinguishes the social sciences from the natural sciences (Silverman 1985: 43, Bhaskar 1979: 203). Knowledge and understanding, or *cognition*, is one critical variable in behaviour. The outcomes of reasoning are understood in cognitive research as knowledge, as the subjective product of making sense or *meaning*.

Scientists studying consumer behaviour have increasingly paid attention to how consumers deal with information related to buying decisions and how they create 'meaning' during such information processing. The need for integrating a consumer's subjective perception of a product into consumer behaviour and marketing models has been pointed out, and further research into consumer cognition has been called for (MacInnis *et al.* 1992: 260, Payne *et al.* 1992: 89–91, Park *et al.* 1992: 197–8, Alba *et al.* 1991: 1–3, 36–7, Bettman *et al.* 1991: 76, Zeithaml 1991: 45, Hoch and Deighton 1989: 1, 16).

In the following, the way in which cognitive consumer research should be heuristically organised is discussed first. The traditional cognitive psychological approach is criticized as too narrowly framed. For research into cognition in everyday life, (a) a reframing of the cognitive psychological heuristic is suggested, and (b) ideas from the cognitive anthropological approach are recommended. Subsequently, how this study approached the research of green consumer cognition is examined.

How to organize 'theorizing' about cognition

As pointed out in chapter 1, scientific investigations are heuristically framed: a research programme is equipped with a certain problem solving apparatus – its heuristic – that guides research at both a conceptual and an empirical level. In general, the complexity of any 'real-life' phenomenon has to be reduced before it can be subjected to scientific research. The critical question is how to frame a research problem heuristically, in particular how to achieve complexity reduction so that the fruitfulness and relevance of research for explaining a particular phenomenon is guaranteed.

Each social science discipline approaches the explanation of 'meaning' and 'meaningful behaviour' from a certain narrow angle that reflects its heuristic model of man. A hard core convention in psychology is that meaningful behaviour is understood as *motivated and reasoned* behaviour. In the context of cognitive research, a heuristic instructs the researcher how to analyse and explain the way people think. 'Psychological meaning' can be defined as the subjective perception and understanding of a certain concept (Friedman and Lessig 1986: 339; also Day and Castleberry 1986: 94). This idea of meaning refers to *semantic* knowledge content (as discussed below) and it reflects consciousness (Tulving 1972: 386, Bartlett 1932: chapter 10). The idea of psychological meaning (and similarly the idea of anthropological meaning) has little to do with physiology or neurology (Bartlett 1932: 234).[1]

In anthropology, meaningful behaviour is related to the concept of *culture* – the way rituals and rationalities are developed and negotiated by a group of people. Cognitive anthropology tries to understand how knowledge is gained in everyday life; for instance, how the idea of a plant or an animal is understood and classified by indigenous peoples (Levy-Bruhl 1926, Lévi-Strauss 1966). In the context of consumption, the cognitive anthropologist conceptualizes products as 'systems of sensibility' through which the everyday world is interpreted as sensible by consumers (Grafton-Small 1987: 67–8, Douglas and Isherwood 1980).

Traditionally, cognitive psychological research has been conducted in a very fragmented way, especially research into 'psychological meaning', which has focused on highly specified units of research; likewise, empirical research has been conducted on a quantitative basis in highly controlled settings, normally the laboratory. It seems that for cognitive psychological research complexity reduction has gone too far. Often non-meaningful units of behaviour have been researched, taken out of their natural context and sharply isolated from other units (Bhaskar 1979: 203, Neisser 1978: 12–13, Harre 1974: 248–9). There is a clear trade-off between the narrow heuristic framing of a research problem and the potential of research to explain cognition as it occurs in real life: 'the more successful we are in examining part of the cognitive system in isolation, the less our data are likely to tell us about cognition in everyday life' (Eysenck 1986: 364). Frederic Bartlett had already pointed out in the 1930s that for explaining 'any genuine psychological problem we are bound to accept certain complex activities, or functions, as our starting points' (Bartlett 1932: 187; also Jenkins 1977: 427). However, Bartlett's call has been widely ignored. As a result of a reductionist approach in psychology, only 'trivial problems that have no potential social relevance' have been tackled, for instance problems like 'Can canaries fly?' (Eysenck 1986: 375). It appears that much psychological research has been phenomenon-driven rather than problem-driven (Eysenck 1986: 360).

A reductionist approach to psychology raises serious questions of relevance not only for explaining cognition in everyday life, but also for the application of research findings to practical tasks (Herrmann and Gruneberg 1993: 553–6, 562). Since the early 1980s, there have been some cautious developments in cognitive psychology, especially in the field of applied cognitive psychology, towards approaching research differently (Eysenck 1986: 373–5), but, in general, psychological research has remained distinctively reductionist on a conceptual level when it comes to its heuristic for 'theorizing'.

How to structure scientific research on both a conceptual and an empirical level is closely interconnected through the heuristic framing of a research programme. The reduction of psychological research at a conceptual level appears to be at least partly motivated by a desire for laboratory empiricism and a desire to copy the research approach of the natural sciences (see also chapter 3). In a sense, the cart has been put before the horse: a preference for quantitative empirical research methods rather than problem-oriented research at a conceptual level has guided the structuring of much psychological research (Eysenck 1986: 359–64). A reorientation of cognitive psychological research has long been demanded both with regard to its conceptual aspect – to approach problems on a broader, less reductionist basis – and with regard to its empirical research aspect – to escape from the laboratory and to examine cognition under real-life conditions:

> What we want to know, I think, is how people use their own past experience in meeting the present and the future. We would like to understand how this happens under natural conditions: the circumstances in which it occurs, the forms it takes, the variables on which it depends, the differences in individuals in their uses of the past. 'Natural conditions' does not mean in the jungle or in the desert, unless that happens to be where our subjects live. It means at school and at home, on the job and in the course of thought, as carefree children and as reflective old men and women.
>
> (Neisser 1978: 13–14)

Neisser's call for a reorientation of psychological research touches upon both conceptual and empirical research issues. The traditional heuristic for cognitive psychological research is fundamentally questioned and certain anthropological undertones can be detected in his call. Regarding theorizing, a broader, experience-based approach for the research of everyday cognition is called for and, related to that, for empirical research, a 'naturalistic' approach is recommended.

Since consumer behaviour research modelled itself very closely on the psychological research programme, it has been criticized in the same way as psychological research. Initially, in the early 1970s, consumer behaviour research was expected to examine problems from everyday life, generating relevant advice for the solving of 'real' problems. However, a general accusation of irrelevance of most consumer behaviour research has been upheld over the past decades: 'As we know now . . . [c]onsumer research has not "achieved better" than the other social sciences with respect to "richness of thinking, comprehensiveness of theorizing, and testing of theories in naturalistic and realistic settings"' (Wells 1993: 490 who quotes here from Sheth 1972: 572, similarly Shimp 1994: 1–3, Sheth 1992: 348).

Despite three decades of intensive consumer research, the understanding of consumer cognition in everyday life, which can be considered a genuine psychological problem in Bartlett's sense, has been assessed as 'dismally low' (Alba *et al.* 1991: 36; also Wells 1993: 497–8). Not surprisingly, a reorientation of consumer behaviour research in general (Shimp 1994, Wells 1993), and of cognitive consumer research in particular (Bettman *et al.* 1991: 76, Alba *et al.* 1991: 36, Bettman and Park 1980: 245), has been called for.

What this study intends to demonstrate is that cognitive research can tackle interesting and non-trivial problems that are of a social and practical relevance. For the study of consumer cognition, a conceptual framework is developed in this chapter that aims at the analysis and explanation of thinking and problem solving behaviour in a day-to-day context. Both cognitive psychological and cognitive anthropological ideas were drawn upon to develop this framework. The advice of Bartlett and Neisser has been heeded. In the first place, this discussion aims at an audience that is interested in consumer behaviour, but researchers from psychology and other social science disciplines may also gain inspiration and encouragement from what is said here about traditional methodological beliefs on how to structure 'theorizing' about cognition. Issues concerning how to frame a cognitive research problem at its conceptual level are considered in this chapter, while issues of empirical research methods are only considered in detail in chapter 3.

Researching green consumer cognition

The basic research problem of this study is to gain an understanding of green consumer thinking. In general, cognitive research is based on the information processing paradigm: a person is viewed as an information processor who takes in information from the environment, processes it, and stores certain outcomes of information processing in memory (for an overview, see Massaro and Cowan 1993). The information processing paradigm provides a hard core – to use Lakatos's term – of the research heuristic of a cognitive research programme. For tackling a certain, specific cognitive research problem, the idea of information processing should be further specified regarding its scope and the particular theoretical concepts that are applied.

The model of the consumer as an information processor is not questioned by this study. Rather, it is adapted, as called for, for instance, by Foxall (1993: 46). Such an adaptation of the information processing model is achieved by approaching psychological research from a more comprehensive theoretical basis and by drawing on certain cognitive anthropological ideas in addition to psychological ones (and also by conducting empirical research outside the laboratory, as discussed in chapter 3).

Two different variants of the information processing paradigm can be distinguished as research heuristics for cognitive consumer research: the *choice model* and the *judgement model.* This distinction is a crude one, but it is helpful for illustrating how the research problem of this study was framed and how it was *not* framed. The choice model approaches the information processing and decision making of consumers from a comprehensive problem solving perspective, while the judgement model approaches consumer behaviour from a narrow decision making perspective which focuses on certain aspects of information evaluation ('judgement') only.

The choice model

The choice model views the consumer as an information processor who subjectively collects and evaluates information in order to solve a shopping problem. Consumers are expected to devote attention to information *that is perceived* to be relevant for the attainment of certain ends.[2] A single piece of information is not thought to have an 'objective' meaning. Personal experience is likely to influence such processes of interpretation over time. Consumer behaviour is understood as an ongoing process of learning that consists of the phases product acquisition, consumption and disposal (Tybout and Artz 1994: 141–4, Alba *et al.* 1991: 24–37, Friedman and Lessig 1986: 340, Hoyer 1986: 32, Hoch 1984: 478, Bettman *et al.* 1984: 466, Bettman 1979b: 6, 25). The acquisition process can be conceptually broken down into a number of sub-processes such as information search, information evaluation (comparison of alternatives), and making a purchase decision (applying a decision rule).

The choice model distinguishes two types of information search processes – internal and external information search. Their relationship can be complementary or substitutive (Brucks 1986: 62, Bettman 1979a: 38–9, Bettman 1979b: 105–11). Internal search processes are concerned with the collection of information from memory. External information search is directed at the collection of information from sources other than memory. External information search can be actively pursued, by selecting external information sources, e.g. a book, a newspaper, etc., or it can take the form of a passive process whereby information provision 'happens' to an individual, e.g. through advertising spots on TV, or reading a newspaper and stumbling over an interesting piece of information (Alba *et al.* 1991: 3–5, Hoch 1984: 478). When it comes to a shopping problem, internally or externally collected information is interpreted by a consumer with regard to product attributes that are considered by him or her as salient. Through the application of a choice rule, a decision between buying alternatives is made (Wright 1975: 60, Bettman 1979b: 179–84, Cohen and Chakravarti 1990: 249, Chaiken 1980: 752).

An understanding of the consumer as a decision maker who moves sequentially through various stages – from information search to information evaluation and then to a final choice – is a commonly applied perspective in consumer research. However, most researchers make qualifications arising from the fact that these processes are likely to be interrelated, that certain processes might occur simultaneously or that they might not occur at all (Jacoby 1976b: 340, also Schultz *et al.* 1992: 23, Petty and Cacioppo 1984: 668, Bettman *et al.* 1984: 466). In choice situations that are perceived to be difficult to handle, the information search process and the choice process can be tied together very closely. Information search and information evaluation are likely to take place alternately and nearly simultaneously (Bettman 1979b: 22–4, 32).

The judgement model

An alternative research heuristic for cognitive consumer research is provided by the judgement model. The judgement model fragments and reduces the conceptualization of consumer cognition (and, related to it, its empirical investigation) greatly: a judgement process is investigated as an *evaluative process* in which given multiple product alternatives are assessed on the basis of given multiple product attributes (Johnson and Russo 1984: 543–5, also Alba *et al.* 1991: 24–37). How consumers evaluate products is investigated: the researcher provides the number and type of product attributes and the number and type of products that are to be considered by the consumer. Certain pieces of information on given product attributes are missing: the research objective is then to examine whether a missing piece of information is deduced by a person either through the evaluation of information provided on the other attributes of same products ('same-brand strategy') or through the evaluation of information provided on attributes of other products ('other-brand strategy') (Ross and Creyer 1992, Sirdeshmukh and Unnava 1992, Ford and Smith 1987, Wright 1975).

The judgment model has a different and much narrower scope than the choice model. With regard to its conceptual focus, judgement research concentrates on certain aspects of the product acquisition phase only. It does not attempt to examine cognition from a comprehensive problem solving perspective: through providing product alternatives and certain information on them, the researcher solves on behalf of the consumer considerable parts of a shopping problem. Judgement research leaves little room for either subjectivity or sensibility. Its reductionism is characteristic of mainstream psychological research. Subjects are given little chance to develop meaning on their own. Not surprisingly, the relevance of judgement research for understanding consumer behaviour in everyday life cannot be ascertained yet (see also chapter 3, where the contrast between the choice model and the judgement model is examined with regard to empirical research issues).

Choice or judgement research?

Depending on the research problem, methodological decisions on how to structure research heuristically have to be made. For addressing a cognitive research problem in the context of management studies or public policy studies, with their pragmatic, practice-oriented focus, the heuristic framing of cognitive consumer research through the choice model appears to be generally advisable. The research problem of this study is to gain an understanding of green consumer cognition in everyday life – and the choice model seems to be the appropriate model for researching such a problem.

The choice model provides – as a variant of the information processing paradigm – the general research heuristic of this study. The consumer is understood as a choice-maker who operates in 'real life': collecting information in daily life, evaluating it from his or her subjective point of view, and finally making a buying decision.

The choice model is still a rather general research heuristic. In this study it is made more specific, first through the cognitive psychological concept of *knowledge structures*. Knowledge structures reflect what kind of understanding a person holds. The concept of knowledge structures is closely intertwined with the information processing paradigm: knowledge is developed and applied through information processing.

Subsequently, the heuristic reduction of cognition to a purely psychological level and the screening off of experiential and contextual factors is given up. The influence of experience, of familiarity and ability, on cognitive development is examined. Certain ideas from cognitive anthropology are drawn upon. The concepts of *practical thinking* and *bricolage* are applied to investigate the problem solving behaviour of consumers in everyday life.

In consumer studies, anthropological ideas have rarely been related to consumer behaviour. At the outset one might be sceptical regarding the extent and nature of the problem solving behaviour of green consumers. Apparently, science is not capable of setting out and measuring what constitutes the environmentally friendly product (see the discussion of LCA in chapter 1). Hence, one might be tempted to ask critically how a consumer could ever hope in an everyday situation to assess the greenness of a product. Such scepticism may be misplaced: cognitive anthropologists have found that mastery of some of the great arts of civilization has taken place in the absence of scientific knowledge, driven by imagination and intuition (Lévi-Strauss 1966: 13–15; see also below). Similarly, consumer intelligence can be explained as a creative and intuitive performance of a task rather than a scientific one.

The choice model is comprehensive enough to accommodate both research on 'genuine psychological problems', as called for by Bartlett and Neisser, and cognitive anthropological research. Through the choice model, this study interrelates cognitive psychological and cognitive anthropological ideas, thus generating a broader and better understanding of consumer thinking (see also Figure 1.2).

KNOWLEDGE STRUCTURES

The concept of knowledge structures is the key heuristic concept through which psychological aspects of consumer thinking are explored in this study. The concept of knowledge structures is a comprehensive one. It has been pointed out that 'before a phenomenon can be measured one must clearly define what it is and what it is not. . . . [S]uch conceptual definitions ought to precede and determine one's operationalization [for empirical research] rather than vice versa' (Jacoby and Kyner 1973: 1). In order to make the concept of knowledge structures a useful heuristic device, its various dimensions have to be spelled out. Conceptualizations of knowledge structures that do not distinguish different dimensions of knowledge, such as knowledge content and operational modes that underlie the 'use' of knowledge content, and that do not distinguish different types and structural properties of both knowledge content and cognitive operations, can be characterized as simplistic and inappropriate for conceptualizing cognition (Alba and Marmorstein 1986: 446; also Abelson and Black 1986: 4, 18, Tulving 1985: 386, Tulving 1983: 8–9, 28, 35, Tulving 1972: 383–6).

A framework for knowledge structure research is outlined in the following. Knowledge structures relate to more or less consciously accessible knowledge content (a 'data files' level, to use a computer analogy), to underlying, largely subconscious cognitive operations (an 'applications software' level), and to schematic knowledge features (a 'systems software' level). The 'hardware' level – neurological and physiological issues related to cognition – is not examined in this study (see Figure 2.1).

While knowledge content relates to conscious cognition, cognitive operations reflect subconscious processes that organize the 'use' of knowledge content. Different processes and modes of cognitive operations can be distinguished. The question of whether and what kind of structural patterns possibly underwire knowledge content and cognitive operations relates to a formatting level of cognition.

The content dimension of knowledge structures

Knowledge structures 'contain' stored information – knowledge content or *meaning*. In order to solve a choice problem, a consumer attends to information, processes and evaluates it, and subsequently stores it in his or her memory. In contrast to other dimensions of knowledge structures, the knowledge content dimension is of a largely conscious nature (Tulving 1985: 88). This explains why knowledge content has been focused on for empirical research.

Declarative and procedural knowledge

Knowledge content can be of a *declarative* or of a *procedural* nature. Declarative knowledge refers to knowledge about objects and ideas, while procedural

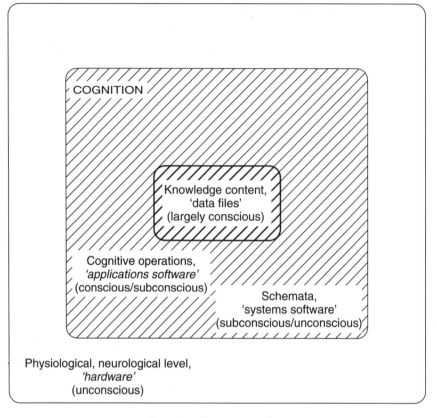

Figure 2.1 Computer analogy

knowledge refers to knowledge of rules for taking action (Cohen 1989: 176, Brucks 1986: 58–60, Anderson 1976).[3]

Declarative knowledge content mirrors a plan of what an object or idea looks like. Nearly synonymous terms like 'expectations', 'hypotheses', 'stereotypes', 'images' or 'beliefs', amongst others, have been used for this notion (Brown 1992: 793, Raaij 1991: 401–3, Gregory 1990: 312, Sujan and Bettman 1989: 455, Alba and Hutchinson 1987: 414, 422–3, Reynolds and Jamieson 1985: 115–16, Crocker 1984: 472, Venkatraman and Villarreal 1984: 355, Gregory 1980: 181). Declarative knowledge can be understood as a 'naive theory', as 'hypotheses' held by a person regarding a certain knowledge domain.

While declarative knowledge refers to a mental plan of an object or idea, procedural knowledge content refers to knowledge about the execution of a plan. Procedural knowledge is knowledge of how to solve a problem. In the context of consumer behaviour, it refers to knowledge about how to conduct an information search, how to evaluate information and how to make a final buying decision (Schurr 1986: 498, Smith and Houston 1986: 504, Brucks

1986: 58, Venkatraman and Villarreal 1984: 355, Alba and Hasher 1983: 203–5, Neisser 1976: 54). Particularly in a real-life context, knowing what a problem looks like, as reflected by declarative knowledge content, and solving the problem, as reflected by procedural knowledge content, can be nearly equated. If the defining features of a problem are known (in terms of variables such as objects or ideas), the problem is basically solved: 'understanding the problem and solving it is nearly the same thing' (Rumelhart 1984: 185; see also Maturana and Varela 1992: 244–8, Scribner 1986: 21–2, Brucks 1986: 59).

Procedural aspects of knowledge that relate to problem solving have been examined in this study in more detail when consumer cognition was approached from an anthropological perspective, in particular when the relationship of experience and knowledge structure development was assessed (see below). For the purpose of psychological knowledge structure research, declarative knowledge content was focused on. Such a 'division of work' between cognitive psychology and cognitive anthropology for the interpretation of consumer cognition reflects the respective strengths of these different approaches.

Episodic and semantic knowledge

A further typological distinction of knowledge content refers to the *episodic* or *semantic* character of knowledge (Tulving 1983: 35–40, Tulving 1972). Episodic knowledge is of a highly concrete nature: it is knowledge about temporally dated events, e.g. a holiday trip to France last summer. It is only slightly abstract and highly autobiographical, and it can be comparatively comprehensive. Semantic knowledge is factual or conceptual knowledge, such as that characterizing a certain object or idea, e.g. general reflections on what makes a 'good' holiday (see Figure 2.2).

In the further course of this study, episodic knowledge is touched upon now and then, but the main focus of research is on semantic knowledge, and hence mainly on declarative knowledge content. How the consumer understood the green product semantically has been examined.

Hierarchical nature of knowledge structures

Knowledge content is commonly conceptualized as domain-related knowledge that is structured hierarchically (Alba *et al.* 1991: 7, Mick 1988: 6, Smith and Houston 1986: 504, Crocker 1984: 472–4, Hastie 1981: 43). The idea that knowledge is organized in domains, not randomly, appears to be a fairly conservative and conventional assumption about knowledge structures. A domain is characterized by its variables, such as objects and ideas. With regard to declarative consumer knowledge, one can think of objects as 'products', such as milk, bread, butter, etc.; and ideas would relate to 'product quality considerations', such as environmental friendliness, performance, convenience, taste, etc. The generic notion 'product' can also be considered to be an idea,

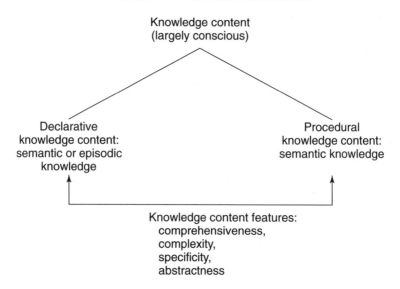

Figure 2.2 Knowledge content

whereas specific examples of a product such as bread, milk and butter, or brands of these products would count as objects (see Figure 2.3).[4] Hierarchical knowledge content structures reflect how idea and object variables relate to each other, and variable attributes are created as categories and sub-categories (Crocker 1984: 472–3; see also Alba and Hutchinson 1987: 417, Smith and Houston 1986: 504).

A hierarchical organization of knowledge raises the question of what the 'organizing' units of a knowledge hierarchy are. In the context of consumer research, it can be suggested that products rather than product attributes represent the organizing units of a knowledge hierarchy. Consumers seem to think of shopping in terms of products, e.g. 'I need bread, butter and milk', rather than product attributes. (This assumption is reflected in the way the empirical research method, in particular the interview procedure, has been structured – namely in a product-oriented way.)

As indicated, knowledge develops with regard to certain domains. In this study, the notions of 'domain', 'objects' and 'ideas' have been interpreted as follows:

- 'Green consumption' represents the knowledge domain this study is interested in.
- Domain-related objects are classified as 'products', e.g. milk, bread, butter, etc. Only products consumed on a daily basis have been researched.
- Domain-related ideas are thought of as 'product attributes', e.g. for the product 'floor cleaner', a consumer may consider product attributes such as environmental friendliness, performance, convenience of use, smell, price,

etc. Declarative knowledge content reflects how a consumer subjectively defines a product in terms of product attributes, of what is perceived as an indication of a desired product quality. The product attribute that was examined in detail in this study was the 'environmental friendliness' or 'greenness' of a product.

• A product attribute can be broken down into a number of sub-categories, e.g. for the product 'floor cleaner', the attribute 'environmental friendliness' might be broken down into sub-categories such as product ingredients, packaging material, packaging images, etc.

The question of how the consumer understands the idea of the environmentally friendly product was researched by drawing on this operationalisation of knowledge content.

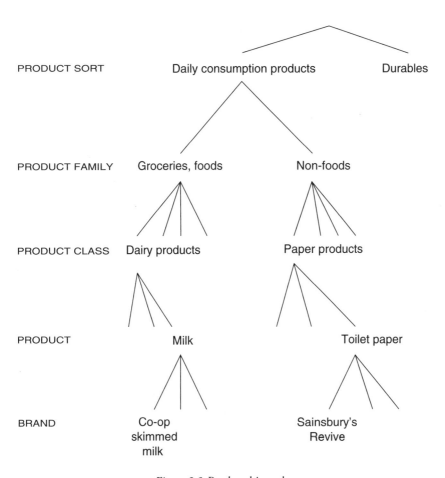

Figure 2.3 Product hierarchy

Features of knowledge content

The nature of knowledge content is characterized by the structural properties it exhibits. Different *knowledge content characteristics* can be distinguished. For the purpose of a knowledge-based categorization of green consumers, the conceptualization of these properties is very important. It provides the basis for empirical research into green consumer knowledge. Three properties of knowledge content are generally distinguished: comprehensiveness, complexity and abstractness. Additionally, a further characteristic of knowledge content – knowledge specificity – was distinguished by this study:

- Knowledge *comprehensiveness* refers to the amount of domain-related information held in a knowledge structure.
- Knowledge *complexity* refers to the number of hierarchical levels, the number of knowledge content features at each level as well as the interdependence of knowledge features. Knowledge structure complexity can vary considerably. Some objects may be broken down into only a few categories and sub-categories while others may be thought about in sophisticated ways. The number of interrelations between categories and sub-categories of the same object and between categories and sub-categories of different objects contributes to knowledge structure complexity (Alba and Hutchinson 1987: 415–17, Selnes and Gronhaug 1986: 68, Johnson and Fornell 1987: 215–17).
- Knowledge *abstractness* relates to how technical the knowledge is. Abstractness has been defined as 'the inverse of how directly an attribute denotes particular objects or events' (Johnson and Fornell 1987: 214; also Johnson *et al.* 1992: 131–2, Smith and Houston 1986: 506, Brucks 1986: 58–9).
- Knowledge *specificity* refers to how concrete the knowledge is. Frequently knowledge specificity has been distinguished as a particular value of the variable 'knowledge abstractness' rather than as a variable itself. In chapter 3, when the measurement of knowledge content is discussed, why and how knowledge specificity was distinguished by this study as a variable on its own is explained.

These properties of knowledge content are not expected to be independent of each other. Rather, they are likely to relate strongly to each other: for instance, a high positive correlation has been observed between knowledge complexity and abstractness (Johnson *et al.* 1992: 132, Alba and Hutchinson 1987: 415–16, Johnson and Fornell 1987: 216–17, 225).

The operational dimension of knowledge structures

Cognitive operations are of a largely subconscious nature (Tulving 1985: 387–8, Markus and Zajonc 1985: 174). They determine the development, organization and application of knowledge content. The idea of cognitive operations can be traced back to John Locke:

We have hitherto considered those ideas in the reception whereof the mind is only passive, which are those simple ones received from sensation and reflection. . . . But when it has got once these simple ideas it is not confined barely to observation and what offers itself from without: it can, by its *own power*, put together those ideas it has and make new complex ones, which it never received so united. . . . [S]o that those even large and abstract ideas are derived from sensation and reflection, being no other than what the mind, by the ordinary *use of its own faculties*, employed about ideas received from objects of sense or from the operations it observes in itself about them, may and does attain unto.

(Locke 1991: 76–9, 2.12.1, 2.12.2, 2.12.8, emphasis added)

Cognitive operations provide a grammar for reasoning. They may be compared – to use a simple metaphor – to the applications software of a computer. This analogy, however, falls short of the nature of the relationship between cognitive operations and knowledge content. The traditional computer model conceptualizes data files and applications software (and similarly systems software) as closed, independent entities, but this is not the case for the 'software' of the mind.

Cognitive operations and knowledge content closely reflect each other. It has been suggested that the view that 'cognition is reflected by mental representations' should be balanced against the view that 'talk of mental representations turns out in the end to be talk of cognitive activities' (Goodman 1990: 363, 358). In a sense, the content dimension and the operational dimension reflect different sides of the same coin.

Processes of cognitive operations

Different processes of cognitive operations can be distinguished such as selection, abstraction, interpretation and integration (Alba and Hasher 1983: 203–12; also Schurr 1986: 498, Costley 1986: 18–19, Bettman 1979a: 38–9, Craik and Lockhart 1972: 676). In line with the introduction of the distinction of knowledge specificity as a further characteristic of knowledge content (in addition to comprehensiveness, complexity and abstractness), a further operational process – specification – was distinguished in the course of the study (see Figure 2.4):

- *Selection* is a process that filters and selects only some of the total incoming information for cognitive representation in the form of knowledge content.
- *Specification* is a process that leads to the naming of objects and ideas.
- *Abstraction* is a process that stores the technical meaning of a piece of information without reference to its original syntactic and lexical content.
- *Interpretation* is a process by which relevant knowledge is generated to aid comprehension.
- *Integration* is a process by which holistic knowledge structures[5] are formed from the outcomes of the previous processes.

41

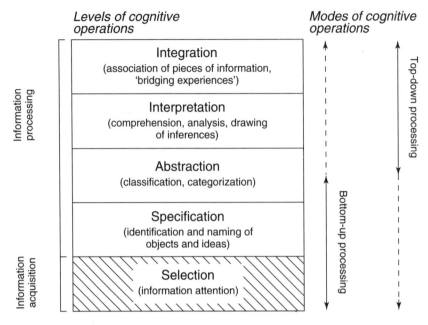

Figure 2.4 Cognitive operations

As already mentioned, cognitive operations and knowledge content are strongly related to each other. Through cognitive processes, knowledge content is built up. In turn, knowledge content features are reflected by cognitive operations; for instance, advancing processes of interpretation and integration are thought to relate to knowledge content that shows high degrees of abstractness and complexity.

Modes of cognitive operations

Cognitive operations can be conceptualized as *modes* as well as processes. Simplistically, one could think of cognitive processes as different levels of a cognitive ladder, while operational modes could be compared to different types of movements across the levels (see Figure 2.4). Two extreme types of operational modes have been discussed (Wenben Lai 1994: 489–90, Solso 1988: 133, Rumelhart 1984: 170, Craik and Lockhart 1972: 679):[6]

- A low-level processing mode that is largely restricted to the levels of selection, specification and abstraction only. It tends to focus on perceptual information and the amount of information provided.
- A high-level processing mode that largely concentrates on cognitive operations at the levels of interpretation and integration.

Different terms have been applied nearly synonymously to refer to these two

Table 2.1 Notational references to modes of cognitive operations

Notational reference	Applied by
Bottom-up processing vs. top-down processing	Wenben Lai (1994: 489–90), Gregory (1990: 315), Gardner (1987: 124), Nakamoto (1987: 12–13, 24), Abelson and Black (1986: 4), Costley (1986: 20)
Accommodation vs. assimilation	Sujan and Bettman (1989: 455–6), Costley (1986: 20), Hoch (1984: 479)
Data-driven processing vs. concept-driven processing	Hoch and Deighton (1989: 7), Friedmann and Lessig (1986: 340), Rumelhart (1984: 170); similarly Wenben Lai (1994: 489–90), Tybout and Artz (1994: 136–7), Gregory (1990: 315, 329)
Non-analytic processing vs. analytic processing	Alba and Hutchinson (1987: 418–23); similarly Alba *et al.* (1991: 7–8, 17–19)
Molar processing vs. modular processing	Gardner (1987: 124, 132–5); similarly (Nakamoto 1987: 24)
Passivist processing vs. activist processing	Gregory (1990: 311–15)
Peripheral route processing vs. central route processing	Cacioppo and Petty (1984: 673–4), Petty and Cacioppo (1984: 668)

extreme types of operational modes of thinking (see Table 2.1). In the further course of this study, the notions 'bottom-up processing' and 'top-down processing' are used to discuss these different types of cognitive operational modes.

Bottom-up processing can also extend to higher levels of cognitive operations, such as interpretation and integration. When bottom-up processing extends to interpretation and integration, such processing appears to be overall evaluation-based (related to 'halo effects'), similarity-based, or correlational, i.e., causally or logically irrelevant information for solving a problem is processed. In contrast, top-down processing draws to a greater extent than bottom-up information processing on abstract and complex knowledge structures. Information is more likely to be interpreted and weighted according to its relevance. Irrelevant information is expected to have less of an impact here.

In contrast to knowledge content, cognitive operations are of a largely subconscious nature. This has implications for empirical research. While knowledge content can be 'measured' comparatively easily because of its largely conscious nature, cognitive operations have to be inferred from the observation of knowledge content (Solso 1988: 387, Berry and Irvine 1986: 274, 280, Tulving 1985: 387–8, Tulving 1972: 394).

The formatting dimension of knowledge structures

In the previous section 'applications software' was discussed; this section turns to the 'systems software' of the mind that guides the categorizing activities of the mind. Categorizing appears to be a universal principle of human reasoning that is independent of cultural context (Solso 1988: 389, 445, Gardner 1987: 129–30, 224, 257, Rosch *et al.* 1976: 382–3, 428–34, Lévi-Strauss 1966: chapter 2; see also Cazeneuve 1972 who refers to Levy-Bruhl 1926). A categorizing activity of the mind is reflected both by the hierarchical organization of knowledge content and by the way cognitive operations function, in particular during processes of knowledge integration (see Figure 2.4). A critical question is whether a categorizing activity of the mind relates to a 'systems software' level of the mind at all, and, if so, what such systems software could look like.

The schema concept

Schema theory explains the categorizing activity of the mind by formatting principles that underwire thinking, guiding it. In modern cognitive psychology, the concept of schema has played a prominent role, but also a controversial one. The schema notion was first applied in a philosophical discussion of reason by Immanuel Kant. Kant (1990: 23) refers to schemata as pure mental representations 'wherein nothing is met with that belongs to sensation':

> The schema is . . . always a mere product of the imagination. But . . . the schema is clearly distinguishable from the image. . . . This formal and pure condition of sensibility, to which the conception of the understanding is restricted in its employment, we shall name the *schema* of the conception of the understanding. . . . The *image* is a product of the empirical faculty of the productive imagination – the *schema* of sensuous conceptions . . . is a product . . . of the pure imagination *a priori*.
>
> (Kant 1990: 61–2)

The idea of 'image', as Kant is using it here, can be understood as what is referred to in this study as knowledge content. Kant (1990: 14–15) urged that the possibility, the principles and the extent of human knowledge 'a priori' be examined. He suggested that the mind could be very active in the formation of mental representations (knowledge structures). He extended the approach of empiricists like Locke who stressed the passivity of the mind. Kant's view of thinking was not meant to replace earlier concepts of reasoning but to supplement them. Locke distinguished primary sensual (empirical) perceptions, which he called 'sensations', from the organizing and compounding of these sensations into 'complex ideas'. He introduced the conceptual differentiation of empirical sensations and reflections on sensations from non-sensual cognition. The build-up of non-sensual cognition, however, was in the empiricist tradition still closely linked to empirical, sensual cognition.[7] Kant introduced the idea of a non-empirical level of knowledge structures only later, through the schema concept.

The idea of schematic cognition entered psychological thought through the works of Frederic Bartlett and Jean Piaget (Piaget 1959: 228–36, Bartlett 1932: 199–201, 204, Head 1920: 605–6; see also Wadsworth 1996: 14–20). Bartlett discussed a schema as an organizing principle that results from experience, is of a subconscious nature and actively guides cognition. This study has approached schemata as *categorizing, formatting principles* that guide cognitive operations and that are responsible for the organization of knowledge content.

A schema is an '... abstract or generic knowledge structure, stored in memory, that specifies the *defining features* and *relevant attributes* of some *stimulus domain* and the interrelations among those attributes' (Crocker 1984: 472, emphasis added; see also Stayman *et al.* 1992: 240, Brucks 1986: 58, Alba and Hasher 1983: 203, Hastie 1981: 42). The idea of a schema refers to a *mobile frame*, an information processing format of a largely subconscious, higher order system. A schema is a data structure, but not knowledge content itself (Abelson and Black 1986: 18, Markus and Zajonc 1985: 151–63, Rumelhart 1984: 163–4, Wickelgren 1979: 297–300, Neisser 1967: 286–7; see also Mick 1988: 8, Schurr 1986: 498, Venkatraman and Villarreal 1984: 355, Alba and Hasher 1983: 203–4).

There has been some controversy over whether the schema notion refers to both knowledge content and cognitive operations or solely to cognitive operations (Markus and Zajonc 1985: 164; also Abelson and Black 1986: 1–5). The idea of a 'knowledge content schema' can be followed in so far as it is meant to refer only to a *frame* or *format* for knowledge content, but not to knowledge content itself.

The notions of 'feature' and 'attribute', as understood in the above definition of schema, do not refer to concrete values of variables, e.g. a certain brand name; rather they refer to variables as such, e.g. product attributes, and how those are related to each other. As indicated above, knowledge content is researched in this study regarding the 'domain' of green consumption (daily consumption products). 'Products' and 'green product attributes' have been examined as variables. Values of variables would be, for instance, for the variable 'packaging material': plastic, tetrapack, glass bottle, paper wrapping, etc.

A controversial issue in schema theory relates to the question of what variables and the values of variables are; and, related to this, what a generic or abstract knowledge feature is relative to a non-generic or non-abstract one. Because of the explorative focus of this study, such questions need not be answered at the outset. Research focused on knowledge content in the first place, and schematic knowledge features were only subsequently interpreted on the basis of the observation of knowledge content and cognitive operations, e.g. patterns of knowledge complexity and the way knowledge integration worked. For an identification of schematic knowledge characteristics, the question was examined of whether and, if so, how consumers' descriptions of green products showed patterns in terms of configurations of green product attributes.

Assessments of schemata are tricky, not only because they are located on a subconscious level of cognition, but also because they reflect some of the most basic principles of self-organization and self-transformation of the human brain. Principles of self-organization are difficult to observe because of their very nature. In a self-organizing ('autopoietic') system, such as the human brain, components are highly and dynamically interrelated: the system can produce its own components, thus transforming itself (Maturana and Varela 1992: 44, 244, Varela *et al.* 1991: 85, 151, Maturana 1979).

For the self-organizing system the 'human brain', basically four components can be distinguished (see also Figure 2.1):[8]

- a neurological, physiological component (unconscious),
- a 'systems software' component, e.g. innate cognitive abilities, schemata, etc. (unconscious/subconscious),
- cognitive operations (subconscious/conscious),
- and knowledge content (largely conscious).

It is generally agreed that schemata are of a subconscious nature. There have been suggestions that they may even border on an unconscious, physiological level of the mind, reflecting genetically determined, innate cognitive abilities. There appears to be growing evidence that the human brain is to a certain extent physiologically, neurologically 'pre-wired' (McClelland and Plunkett 1995: 193, Gardner 1987: 129, 324 – who refers to the works of Roger Shepard). Such pre-wiring at a neurological level can be expected to impact on cognition and the way it organizes itself. It is in this subconscious 'area' between unconscious neurologically 'pre-wired' structures and subconscious cognition that the idea of schema is located. As a result of the cognitive research conducted by this study certain suggestions about the nature of these principles, e.g. whether they are of an innate nature or not, have been made.

Suggestions of schema theory

In this study, green consumer cognition was explored with respect to suggestions of schema theory, namely suggestions on what the schematic 'systems software' of the mind looks like. The main suggestions are:

- Schemata are connected to other schemata through a *hierarchical network of associations*. Such networks may consist of sub-ordinate and super-ordinate schemata, e.g. a schema for 'tree' may be linked to a schema for 'plants' which may be linked to a schema for 'living beings' (Cohen 1989: 71, Mick 1988: 6, Gardner 1987: 347, Brucks 1986: 58, Smith and Houston 1986: 504, Markus and Zajonc 1985: 163, Crocker 1984: 472–4, Taylor and Crocker 1981: 92, Hastie 1981: 43, Rumelhart and Ortony 1977: 101, 106–9).

- At the centre of hierarchical networks of schemata, so-called *prototypes* are expected. The prototype concept is a specific variant of the schema concept.

A prototype defines what an ideal member of a certain domain looks like. The prototype is a data structure exemplifying good variables and variable attributes. It can be thought of as a data structure nucleus around which other defining features cluster (Medin and Ross 1992: 368–9, Ratneshwar and Shocker 1988: 380, Gardner 1987: 346–8, 354, Markus and Zajonc 1985: 147, Brucks 1986: 58, Rumelhart 1984: 163, 167, Wickelgren 1979: 297, Rosch *et al.* 1976: 433–4). The prototype concept, like the schema concept, does not refer to values of variables; rather, it refers to variables as such, and how they are configured.

- Schemata can be found for all processes and for all modes of cognitive operations (Abelson and Black 1986: 5, Rumelhart 1984: 162, 169, Brewer and Treyens 1981: 216, Piaget 1959: 230–1, Bartlett 1932: 31–3, 201–4). Similarly, all knowledge content can exhibit 'schematic characteristics'. Even rather concrete, only slightly abstract knowledge content and, associated with it, bottom-up information processing may be schematic.[9]

- Schemata have a *central information processing function* for cognition. They affect the interpretation of information, its storage in memory, and the retrieval of stored information (Gardner 1987: 114–30, 354–55, Schurr 1986: 498, Markus and Zajonc 1985: 151–63, Rumelhart 1984: 166–7, 185, Venkatraman and Villarreal 1984: 355, Alba and Hasher 1983: 203–4, Wickelgren 1979: 300, Markus 1977: 64, Bartlett 1932: 14, 25–7, 31–3). The importance of schemata for problem solving is acknowledged.

- Schemata provide *information filters* in the form of formats for product attribute perceptions related to a certain domain. Schemata are thought to be important for framing pre-purchase information search behaviour (determining the type and extent of internal and external search activities) and for information processing related to the evaluation and selection of products. Schemata determine what information is actively attended to, how much importance is attached to it, and how it is interpreted (Schurr 1986: 498–9, Venkatraman and Villarreal 1984: 355).

- *Schema development* can occur through the creation of a new schema, the transfer of an existing schema to a new domain, or the association of incoming information with existing schemata and their subsequent modification (Cohen 1989: 175, Hull *et al.* 1988: 518, Smith and Houston 1986: 505, Costley 1986: 18, Venkatraman and Villarreal 1984: 356, Crocker 1984: 474, Rumelhart 1984: 180–2). It can be expected that only a few schemata are maintained for reasoning related to a certain domain (Nakamoto 1987: 16, Bartlett 1932: 197–201, 205).

- The availability of schemata leads to *efficiency gains* in cognition since they reduce the amount of cognitive elaboration and external information search (Nakamoto 1987: 18, Rosch *et al.* 1976: 384, 428–9; also Craik and Lockhart 1972: 676).

- Schemata exert *self-reinforcing tendencies* regarding the search for and processing of information that is congruent with existing schemata. Information that is incongruent with a schema is more rarely attended to and processed. This tendency to discount disconfirming information has been described with the phrase that 'people tend to see what they expect to see' (Elliot and Roach 1991: 6, 10, Alba *et al.* 1991: 22, Cohen 1989: 71, Hoch and Deighton 1989: 3, Alba and Hutchinson 1987: 412–14, Hoch 1984: 479–82, Bettman *et al.* 1984: 467, Bettman 1979b: 208, Neisser 1967: 289).[10] In Gestalt psychology, this tendency to perceive objects in terms of familiarity has been extensively investigated (Solso 1988: 425). Besides an information search bias, a related evaluative bias has been observed that favours confirmation rather than disconfirmation of evaluated purchase alternatives. Schemata close gaps in perception through providing images of completeness where there is objectively none (Elliot and Roach 1991: 6–7, Spiggle and Sanders 1984: 337, Bettman *et al.* 1984: 467, Hoch 1984: 479–80; also Alba and Hutchinson 1987: 421–3).

As indicated, the schema concept was applied in this study for the exploration of the categorization patterns of the green consumer. Whether and, if so, how schemata and prototypes play a 'systems software' role in human reasoning was also examined in this way. It has been suggested that a qualitatively oriented approach, as followed by this study, may be particularly well suited for research on schematic knowledge structures (Cohen 1989: 71, Nakamoto 1987: 25, Abelson and Black 1986: 3; also Wickelgren 1979: 297). While qualitative research into schematic knowledge has been called for, there have not been many investigations of this type.

A parallel can be suggested between the idea of a schema and the idea of a scientific research heuristic. A research heuristic frames a research programme: it can be understood as a 'methodic schema' that is applied by the scientist. Heuristics, like schemata, underwire and guide reasoning. They focus attention in a selective and exclusive way. And, also like schemata, heuristics are often applied in an implicit manner, on a basis that is not openly negotiated (see chapter 1). As Maturana and Varela (1992: 242) note: 'We do not see what we do not see, and what we do not see does not exist.' In science this may happen as a matter of tradition, convention and convenience as it has historically developed within disciplines. In a philosophy of science debate, such issues that relate to the 'schematic' format of the scientific method are scrutinized and made explicit.

EXPERIENCE, KNOWLEDGE STRUCTURE DEVELOPMENT AND INTELLIGENCE

The concept of knowledge structures focuses on structural properties of cognition. It is a typically psychological concept of cognition that sidelines procedural issues of how knowledge structures developed in line with problem solving behaviour and the build-up of experience.

Experience reflects past reasoning. It can be understood as *existing* domain-specific knowledge: as knowledge content that accumulated over time, and cognitive operations and formatting processes that developed in relation to it (Alba and Hasher 1983: 205; also Gregory 1990: 311–16, 329–30, Mick 1988: 6, Gregory 1980: 196). Over time, the nature of reasoning changes because of the accumulation of knowledge – knowledge structures develop and experience builds up. Once knowledge structures have developed, and hence experience 'exists', information search may largely consist of the recall of knowledge. In relation to the build-up of knowledge, a consumer's subjective perceptions of a choice task and its characteristics are likely to change. But also, knowledge structures tend to 'stabilize' over time and develop some resistance to change, as reflected by behavioural habits.

The conceptualization of 'degrees of prior knowledge' (Bettman and Park 1980: 245) has been called for in order to explain consumer behaviour. At the heart of research into knowledge structure development lies the question of how to conceptualize experience, in particular, whether there are certain experiential factors that influence cognitive development. Basically, two types of influences on knowledge structure development are distinguished (McClelland and Plunkett 1995: 193):

- experience that arises from a person's interactions with the 'environment' (context);
- innate abilities, e.g. schemata.

The question is whether one of these two factors determines knowledge structure development on its own (if so, which one) or whether it is a 'combination' of these two factors (if so, what can be said about the nature of their relationship).

In daily life, experience builds up through *problem solving behaviour in a particular context*. The contextual nature of consumer cognition is characterized by a choice task that is subjectively perceived by a consumer when he or she tries to solve a shopping problem (Warlop and Ratneshwar 1993: 377, 380–1; see also Gordon and Valentine 1996: 35–7). Cognitive anthropological ideas have been applied in this study to examine this experiential nature of cognition. Consumer cognition was approached as 'lived human experience' (Maturana and Varela 1992: 244–8). This project departed from the mainstream approach to psychological consumer behaviour and its non-experiential treatment of knowledge (see Figure 2.5 and also Figure 1.2 in chapter 1).

The contextual nature of consumer behaviour has long been acknowledged. But in actual research into consumer behaviour, context was often ignored or treated as a 'black box', or research projects that opened the black box 'context' tended to view it as an independent variable that could be 'manipulated' for explaining cognition (Warlop and Ratneshwar 1993, also Maturana and Varela 1992, Varela *et al.* 1991, Neisser 1978, Jenkins 1977, Bransford *et al.* 1977). In general, relationships among context, experience and knowledge structure

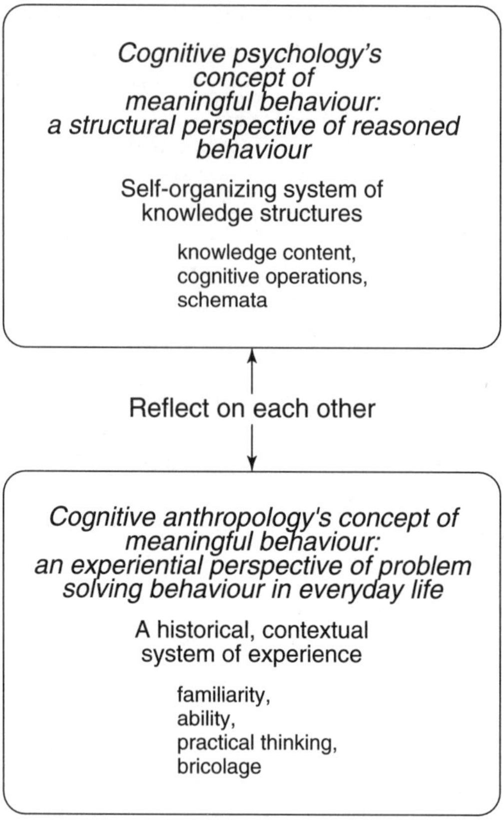

Cognitive psychology's
concept of
meaningful behaviour:
a structural perspective of reasoned
behaviour

Self-organizing system of
knowledge structures

knowledge content,
cognitive operations,
schemata

Reflect on each other

Cognitive anthropology's concept of
meaningful behaviour:
an experiential perspective of problem
solving behaviour in everyday life

A historical, contextual
system of experience

familiarity,
ability,
practical thinking,
bricolage

Figure 2.5 Cognitive research heuristics

development have been approached on the basis of the causality principle, distinguishing dependent and independent variables. Experience has been treated either as an independent variable for explaining certain aspects of consumer cognition (Engel *et al.* 1990: 381, 384, 504–7, Jacoby *et al.* 1986: 469, Kaas 1984: 585, Petty and Cacioppo 1984: 668, Bettman 1979b: 41, 175, 186), or as a dependent variable that was explained through the independent variable 'knowledge structures' (e.g. Alba and Hutchinson 1987). Such a causality-based approach was not followed in this study. Research was conducted with the aim of exploring and explaining the contextual and experiential nature of knowledge structure development and the kind of interdependences that might exist between reasoning and actual behaviour. In the following, first, different aspects of experience – familiarity and ability – are outlined. Subsequently, the cognitive anthropological concepts of practical thinking and bricolage are drawn upon. They suggest a concept of experience that actively draws on the context in which problem solving behaviour occurs.

Familiarity

Two dimensions of experience, *familiarity* and *ability* (or expertise), are generally distinguished (Alba and Hutchinson 1987: 411–12, Crocker 1984: 474, Taylor and Crocker 1981: 127). Both shed light on experience and knowledge structure development but from different angles. While familiarity carries a quantitative connotation, ability carries a qualitative one.

In the context of consumer behaviour, familiarity has been defined as the number of product-related experiences accumulated over time (Alba and Hutchinson 1987: 411). The learning route that leads to familiarity-type experience is a 'learning-by-doing' or 'trial-and-error' route. When familiarity has built up, the need for external information search decreases, and information search may largely consist of internal information search, i.e., the 'use' of existing knowledge. Skilled behaviour may be generally thought of as habitual or 'automatic' behaviour (Alba *et al.* 1991: 2–10, Tulving 1983: 9).

Familiarity effects can be expected to play at least some role in daily shopping. The buying of products for daily consumption, as it was examined in this study, is classified as repeat purchase behaviour. The interval between purchases of the same product is usually small, ranging from a single day to some days or some weeks at the most. Through past product-related experiences, familiarity builds up and habit formation takes place. A process of habituation is characteristic for repeat purchase situations in which information search and processing is nearly automatically and effortlessly performed. Choice behaviour is routinized and simplified in this way (Alba and Hutchinson 1987: 412–14, also Engel *et al.* 1990: 485, Bettman 1979b: 254, 280).

There has been some debate as to what the relationship between increasing familiarity and the extent of cognition may be. Two competing curves have been discussed to conceptualize such a relationship: an inverted U-shaped curve, and a positively climbing curve (Johnson and Russo 1984, also Kardes and Strahle 1986). The question was raised as to which of the two curves depicts better the relationship between familiarity and the extent of information processing (Johnson and Russo 1984: 542–3). To a degree, this discussion suffered from a lack of conceptual distinction between internal and external information search. Once such a conceptual distinction is introduced, the two curves appear highly complementary. Wilkie and Dickson (1991: 2, 15) have pointed out the general importance of distinguishing internal information search from external (similarly Selnes and Gronhaug 1986: 67). It appears plausible that the inverted U-shaped curve depicts a relationship between familiarity and external information search, while a positively climbing curve depicts the relationship between familiarity and internal information search. In line with increasing familiarity, external information search is likely to become less important while internal information search and processing is likely to increase.

Ability

Besides familiarity, experience and the development of knowledge structures are reflected by ability. Ability refers to successful problem solving and task performance (Alba and Hutchinson 1987: 411; also Park *et al.* 1992: 193, Selnes and Gronhaug 1986: 67, Jacoby *et al.* 1986: 469, Price and Feick 1984: 251). Ability is reflected by the development of more comprehensive, more complex and more abstract knowledge structures (Alba and Hutchinson 1987: 415–16, also Zeithaml 1991: 33). While familiarity results from an instance-related learning route, ability is often associated with a learning route that might be labelled as a 'learning-by-being-taught' route (Crocker 1984: 474, Payne *et al.* 1992: 89).[11]

Ability relates to the concept of *intelligence*. Intelligence can be defined as the ability to classify information, to discover rules and principles from specific instances, and to see patterns in problem solving (Solso 1988: 445–6). Intelligence is a key concept in cognitive psychology and there has been much debate on how to measure it (Gardner 1987: chapter 13). Traditionally, ability has been related to scientific, rational thought. And psychology has traditionally measured intelligence through so-called IQ tests: through numerical or graphical ordering exercises (Medin and Ross 1992: 490, Park *et al.* 1992: 193, Alba and Hutchinson 1987: 411–20, 427–8; see also Thorgesen 1994: 154, Payne *et al.* 1992: 90, Zeithaml 1991: 30, Milstein 1979: 46).

A critical question for intelligence and ability assessments is what constitutes 'successful' problem solving and how to measure it. It appears that the psychological concept of ability sidelines potential qualitative aspects of familiarity: 'Knowing is doing' (Maturana and Varela 1992: 244–8).[12] Learning-by-doing seems to be a very fundamental and ancient form of human learning. Successful learning often relates to familiarizing, learning-by-doing experiences, e.g. learning to ride a bike, or even learning to play chess (Wittgenstein 1967: 15–16). In an experiment in which people were asked to wire conventional and unconventional plugs it was found that 'even in the case of unfamiliar tasks people seem to prefer to act rather than to reflect' (Hull *et al.* 1988: 518). Rather than interpreting such behaviour as unreasonable or irrational, as the cognitive psychologist might be inclined to do, the cognitive anthropologist would try to explain such behaviour as sensible on the basis of familiarity effects and a contextual view of cognition.

There might be some substance to the objection of psychologists that through increased familiarity alone a premature sense of successful task handling is acquired (Park *et al.* 1992: 193, 197, Wilkie and Dickson 1991: 18–19, Hoch and Deighton 1989: 3, Alba and Hutchinson 1987: 414, 422, Jacoby *et al.* 1986: 469, Selnes and Gronhaug 1986: 67, Bettman *et al.* 1984: 467). But familiarity – 'mere doing' – appears to be at least a necessary factor, possibly even a sufficient one in certain circumstances, for successful problem solving. Hence, it cannot be completely separated from a concept of ability.

Besides sidelining qualitative aspects of familiarity, a psychological concept of ability tends to define successful task performance very narrowly in terms of factual, 'scientific' correctness. Psychology has a very narrow idea of what constitutes intelligence and how to measure it. It is fairly safe to say that at best certain aspects of intelligence can be captured by the traditional psychological approach to measuring intelligence. For assessing the ability of the green consumer, life-cycle analysis (LCA) may be thought of as a proper scientific concept through which the factual correctness of green consumer behaviour could be measured. However, because of the enormous theoretical complexity of this approach and unresolved conceptual issues, LCA is difficult to apply in practice, in daily life: neither the green consumer nor some observer or adviser of the green consumer is likely to be capable of measuring the success of green shopping through LCA (see chapter 1).

Practical thinking

A different concept of ability altogether, which departs from the concept of 'scientific' ability, is referred to as 'science of the concrete' or 'practical thinking' (Gardner 1987: 238–41, Berry and Irvine 1986: 271–2, Scribner 1986: 13–15, Lévi-Strauss 1966: 16, 269). The concept of practical thinking relates to an 'intellectual, theoretical plane' of behaviour, whereas the subsequently discussed concept of bricolage reflects a 'technical, practical plane' of behaviour (Lévi-Strauss 1966: 17, 30).

Practical thinking refers to an application-oriented, contextual concept of ability as it has been discussed in cognitive anthropology.

> Certainly the properties to which the savage mind has access [through practical thinking] are not the same as those which have commanded the attention of scientists. The physical world is approached from opposite ends in the two cases: one is supremely concrete, the other supremely abstract; one proceeds from the angle of sensible [empirical] qualities and the other from that of formal properties.
>
> (Lévi-Strauss 1966: 269)

The concept of practical thinking suggests that in daily life problem solving is approached purposefully through the very context of a task that is to be performed. In practical thinking, task and task context are treated as inseparable. A problem is solved in relation to its context. In general, context-dependent know-how is considered the very essence of cognition and a central reflection of human existence (Varela *et al.* 1991: 148, 206–7). It has also been pointed out that cognitive skills are difficult to understand independent of the context in which they were developed and applied (Nakamoto 1987: 22, Berry and Irvine 1986: 290, 294, Scribner 1986: 15, 23–4, Bryce 1985: 78–83).

While so-called 'savages' tend to fail psychological IQ tests, cognitive anthropologists found that their logical thinking and practical know-how for problem solving in the context of daily life was rather high:

These studies . . . clearly indicate that logical thinking is available to non-literate and nonschooled people . . . but that its use depends on context. . . . Under day-to-day conditions of living, logical thinking is purposefully linked to the solution of practical problems . . . as it is for most folk in Western industrial societies.

(Berry and Irvine 1986: 290; see also ibid. 286, 298,
Gardner 1987: 376–8)

Cognitive psychology treats context-dependent knowledge as a residual artefact (Varela *et al.* 1991: 148, Jenkins 1977: 426, Bransford *et al.* 1977: 441, 463; see also Ericsson and Oliver 1995: 45), which is likely to be related to psychology's empirical research preference for context-free experimental (laboratory) research (see chapter 3). Early calls in psychology to 'conceive a system of concepts appropriate to the analysis of an individual psychology of rule-following' (Harre 1974: 255, also 254) have basically been ignored. It could be argued that such a project is probably most easily achieved by a cognitive anthropological approach.

Practical thinking yields efficiency gains since time and mental effort spent on internal and external information search processes is reduced. 'Efficiency' refers here to simplicity and economy but not to an engineering-like under-standing of efficiency (Scribner 1986: 25). Practical thinking may even have effectiveness gains as compared with scientific ability (Medin and Ross 1992: 407–8, Gardner 1987: 376, Nakamoto 1987: 18–19, Harre 1974: 254, Craik and Lockhart 1972: 677). Hence, practical thinking should not be regarded as some kind of inferior version of scientific thinking. Rather, practical and scientific thinking should be viewed as two different modes for acquiring knowledge: '[They] both . . . require the same sort of mental operations and they differ not so much in kind as in the different types of phenomena to which they are applied' (Lévi-Strauss 1966: 13).

Practical thinking has a much longer history than scientific thinking and it has yielded some of the great technological advances of mankind:

It was in neolithic times that man's mastery of the great arts of civilization – of pottery, weaving, agriculture and the domestication of animals – became firmly established. No one today would any longer think of attributing these enormous advances to the fortuitous accumulation of a series of chance discoveries or believe them to have been revealed by the passive perception of certain natural phenomena. Each of these techniques assumes centuries of active methodical observation, of bold hypotheses tested by means of endlessly repeated experiments.

(Lévi-Strauss 1966: 13–14)

Cognition that led to these advances was 'quasi-scientific' in that it was system-atic, but it was also driven by perception, imagination and sensible intuition, which are normally removed from scientific enquiry (Lévi-Strauss 1966: 15).

'Theorizing' and 'hypothesis testing' were apparently conducted in everyday life long before they were codified and regulated as scientific thought.

Scientific thinking can be viewed as a special case of practical thinking, representing a stringently formalized and abstracted version of practical thinking. Through formalization and abstraction, pure 'scientific' knowledge is gained (and a philosophy of science debate provides recommendations on how such formalization and abstraction should be organized). However, in the course of formalizing and abstracting thinking into 'scientific thinking', often the practical relevance of knowledge is lost, yielding the commonly found 'theory–practice' gap, and the resulting need to transform positive scientific knowledge into normative knowledge that can be applied to practical tasks (see also chapter 7 for some concluding remarks on this important issue).

Bricolage

Related to the cognitive anthropological concept of practical thinking, behavioural aspects of task performance or problem solving in daily life can be conceptualized as bricolage: as 'work of an odd-job sort' where simple and easily available means are flexibly applied to frame and solve a problem (Berry and Irvine 1986: 271, Lévi-Strauss 1966: 16–18). Lévi-Strauss (1966: 17, 30) speaks of a 'technical, practical plane' on which bricolage is located and contrasts it with the 'intellectual, theoretical plane' on which practical thinking dwells. Practical thinking finds its behavioural expression in bricolage. The concept of bricolage explains how problem solving is purposefully linked through behaviour to a task context in daily life.

> The 'bricoleur' is adept at performing a large number of diverse tasks; but, unlike the engineer,[13] he does not subordinate each of them to the availability of raw materials and tools conceived and produced for the purpose of the project. His universe of instruments is closed and the rules of his game are always to make do with 'whatever is at hand'. . . . The set of the 'bricoleur's' means cannot therefore be defined in terms of a project.
>
> (Lévi-Strauss 1966: 17)

Problem solving is cut short by the bricoleur through the perception of what problem solving tools are available in a certain task context. A problem is framed – and solved – through task characteristics and task constraints as they are subjectively perceived and imposed by the bricoleur. The perception of 'what is at hand' is of a highly subjective and personal-historical nature that varies from bricoleur to bricoleur.

Practical thinking and bricolage relate to a concept of intelligence and ability (Berry and Irvine 1986: 300, 303). They draw, however, on a concept of logical thinking that incorporates the context: successful task performance is not assessed on the basis of 'scientific', factual, objective correctness, but with regard

to how skilfully a problem was framed through (perceived) choice task characteristics and constraints. In general, contextual problem solving, of which
bricolage is one form, can be viewed as a necessity for solving problems in 'real
life'. Often, a 'scientific' approach is not a practical option in everyday life (as
in the case of LCA).

> He [the engineer] is no more able than the 'bricoleur' to do whatever he
> wishes when he is presented with a given task. He too has to begin by
> making a catalogue of a previously determined set consisting of theoretical
> and practical knowledge, of technical means, which restrict the possible
> solutions. The difference is therefore less absolute than it might appear. It
> remains a real one, however, in that the engineer is always trying to make
> his way out of and go beyond constraints imposed by a particular state of
> civilization while the 'bricoleur' by inclination or necessity always remains
> within them.
>
> (Lévi-Strauss 1966: 19)

Problem framing and solving occurs through the subjective perception of
problem characteristics and the subjective imposition of task constraints
for problem solving. Depending on how a problem was framed and constrained,
a solution is arrived at. The engineer may more readily question how problem
constraints were imposed and whether they could possibly be relaxed. But
in problem situations where constraints cannot be relaxed, e.g. a severe time
constraint is active, scientific problem solving quickly turns into bricolage, being
then determined by the knowledge and means that are instantly available.

An example of scientific thinking turning into practical thinking and
bricolage is provided by man's first landing on the moon (BBC2 1994). In 1969,
when the Apollo space capsule with Neil Armstrong and Edwin Aldrin on board
detached from the mother spaceship and started its descent to the lunar surface,
this was closely monitored by ground control in Houston, Texas. Prior to the
space mission, elaborate computer programs had been developed that allowed
the ground control scientists to monitor the space mission of Apollo 11 closely.
Brilliant computer and astrophysical scientists had been recruited for that
task. Much 'theoretical science' had been put into monitoring programs. An
elaborate system of alarms had been established to warn of any danger to the
mission and the astronauts' lives. Many variables had been covered in these
programs and manuals had been compiled to provide explanatory information
on these variables and alarm messages.

When Armstrong and Aldrin were approaching the lunar surface, a couple
of minutes before touchdown, one of the monitors in their capsule suddenly
emitted an alarm warning: 'Alarm 1201'. Immediate contact was made with
ground control in Houston to check whether the mission should be aborted or
not. In Houston, neither the guidance officer in charge, a young computer
scientist, nor any of his colleagues knew immediately what 'Alarm 1201' stood
for, and there was no time to consult the manuals that had been compiled.

A decision that would possibly affect the lives of the astronauts and the success of the mission had to be taken instantly. Later the guidance officer recalled: 'I glanced at the screen, looked at the speed at which they descended, and a few other things, and that all seemed to be O.K., so I shouted "Go".' Only the values of a very few variables that were on-screen at the time could be checked. Many other variables were ignored since there was no time to check on them. One or two minutes later another alarm was reported and, again, it was dealt with in the same way.

This incident demonstrates that even scientists who find themselves in environments that are biased towards proper scientific thinking (here: the ground control centre of NASA) can and must behave as bricoleurs, drawing just on perception and sensible intuition and cutting out theoretical science (here: alarm warnings, off-screen variables, computer manuals, etc.) if task characteristics and task constraints demand this.

The concepts of practical thinking and bricolage put psychological concepts of intelligence and the psychologist's favoured approach to measuring intelligence through IQ tests into perspective. Undoubtedly, certain aspects of intelligence can be measured by IQ tests, but they are anything but an answer to what constitutes human intelligence and how to assess and measure it. Certain types of intelligence probably cannot be captured by IQ tests at all: in general, intelligence in the form of practical thinking, because of its contextual and experiential nature, tends to evade the IQ test. The IQ test appears to be ill equipped to measure context-dependent cognitive skills as they are required for problem solving in everyday life. Also, as Lévi-Strauss pointed out, the IQ test strongly favours those who have been brought up in the western tradition of rational thought, as it is passed on at schools and universities in western societies. African or Asian immigrants, for example, might command a different type of intelligence which IQ tests cannot capture. Similarly, innate aspects of intelligence, as they are shown by very young children, are beyond the reach of the IQ test. Berne (1974: 104) pointed out that any two-year-old has a vastly more comprehensive knowledge of human affect, emotion and motivation than a grown-up psychologist could ever hope to accumulate. Likewise, mentally handicapped people, for instance those suffering from Down's syndrome, may fail to be classified as intelligent because their behaviour just cannot be assessed and measured through traditional IQ tests. These potential shortcomings of the IQ test should at least be recognized before it is applied.

The consumer as bricoleur

Problem formulation appears to be an integral and important element in successful task performance under real-life conditions. Cognitive anthropological ideas appear to be especially valuable for explaining it. The concepts of practical thinking and bricolage have rarely been related to consumer behaviour research (an exception is Grafton-Small 1993: 42; see also Gordon and Valentine

1996: 35–7). In this study, through the concepts of practical thinking and bricolage, green consumer cognition has been examined as a practical problem of task performance in daily life.

The question has been raised of how consumers frame and interpret a shopping task and its requirements (Nakamoto 1987: 25). It has been pointed out that the consumer subjectively frames a choice problem through the perception of the choice task:

> it is the task – the decisions problem as interpreted by a consumer – that instigates the logic of organization and control in decision, and which molds the evolution of mental representations. Rather than a sensorimotor computational device, the consumer becomes an active, if less precise, interpreter of his environment.
>
> (Nakamoto 1987: 24–5; see also Gardner 1987: 376)

Choice task characteristics to which consumers are sensitive may be irrelevant from a normative scientific perspective (Payne et al. 1992: 90, Fletcher 1988: 59, Nakamoto 1987: 24–5). Choice task constraints apparently work as subjective perceptions. In order to understand and explain the development of knowledge structures, the question of how problem solving and the application of practical know-how occur in a certain context must be examined. In daily life, many problems may have some shape but no precise definition (Solso 1988: 424, Scribner 1986: 21–2). Problem formulation and problem solving are thought to be essentially linked to context dependence. Through anthropological ideas, such as bricolage and practical thinking, consumer behaviour can be examined as context-dependent problem solving behaviour: knowledge is viewed as a rational reflection of contextual experience. How the clever consumer 'muddles through' (Schultz et al. 1992: 23) a shopping problem and how systematically this is achieved[14] can be studied.

The task of choosing supermarket products has been characterized as a simple problem (Burnkrant 1978: 724–5). Traditional buying considerations associated with buying products for daily consumption may be viewed as only slightly complex and easily comprehensible, e.g. taste, smell, price, etc. However, 'information problems' quickly arise even for the buying of supermarket products when further buying considerations such as nutrition, health, environmental friendliness, animal rights, fair trade, etc. are considered. If shopping as such is not yet thought of as an odd job for which practical thinking and bricolage have to be conducted, at least through including ideas like 'environmental friendliness' in one's shopping considerations, the shopping problem becomes odd-shaped.

The psychological literature on consumer decision making is rich with references on the impact on cognition of choice task characteristics, such as task difficulty (Cohen and Chakravarti 1990: 268, Alba and Hutchinson 1987: 411, 413, 420, Leigh and Gabel 1992: 32, Engel et al. 1990: 504, Payne et al. 1992: 90, Olson 1977: 283, Venkatraman and Villarreal 1984: 356, Bettman and Park

1980: 235). For instance, the perception of task difficulty is related to information availability, information processability (information technicality), or information relevance.[15] However, what has been underrated in traditional consumer behaviour research is the subjective nature of how choice task characteristics and constraints are perceived by a person in daily life. Varela *et al.* (1991) criticize strongly a 'representationist', objectivist approach to cognition and argue for a phenomenological, subjective approach. Neither a product nor a choice task situation has certain given, 'objective' characteristics: choice task characteristics and choice task constraints are only very subjectively developed and perceived by the consumer. The way consumers perceive and constrain a choice situation depends upon their experience, e.g. their ability in practical thinking and in bricolage – or the lack of it.

Issues of task difficulty were approached in this study not solely from a psychological perspective, e.g. looking into how consumers perceived information availability, information processability, information relevance, etc. Rather, such constructs were interpreted from a cognitive anthropological perspective. Green consumer cognition was investigated in terms of how the green shopping problem was formulated: how it was subjectively framed, constrained and subsequently solved. Green consumers were researched in terms of how they engaged in practical thinking and bricolage; in particular, the means and methods they invented and applied were examined. The success of green problem solving was assessed in relation to the context. On a comparative basis, assessments of the quality of practical thinking can be made: how inventively, flexibly and skilfully the bricolage of the green shopping problem was conducted – how a problem was formulated and solved in relation to the subjective perception of a choice task (Scribner 1986: 22–8, Berry and Irvine 1986: 298–300).

Green problem solving behaviour was studied from the point of view of the cognitive anthropologist. Such an approach built on the cognitive psychological approach, especially the concept of knowledge structures, but it also extended it considerably. It appeared that these research programmes are highly complementary: it can be expected that the logic of problem solving as developed by a consumer in everyday life is reflected by the kind of knowledge structures held (Nakamoto 1987: 24–5, Gardner 1987: 376, Lévi-Strauss 1966: 15–22). And in turn, it might be very difficult to understand knowledge structure development of 'real' people (in contrast to laboratory subjects) without the ideas of cognitive anthropology.

RESEARCH QUESTIONS ON GREEN CONSUMER COGNITION

In the previous sections of this chapter, a number of psychological and anthropological constructs were introduced for the purpose of cognitive consumer research:

- Along a knowledge content dimension, knowledge characteristics (comprehensiveness, complexity, abstractness and specificity) were distinguished.
- Along a cognitive operational dimension, five cognitive operational processes (selection, specification, abstraction, interpretation and integration) and two cognitive operational modes (bottom-up processing and top-down processing) were elaborated on.
- Along a formatting dimension of cognition, organizing principles of knowledge structures, such as schemata and prototypes, were identified.
- For an assessment of knowledge structure development and consumer intelligence, experience constructs, such as familiarity, ability, practical thinking and bricolage, were drawn upon.

Through these constructs, the research questions of this study, as initially put forward in chapter 1, can now be specified in a sharper way:

1 What and how do green consumers know?

- *What knowledge content or 'psychological meaning' is held regarding the green product?*
  Knowledge content of green consumers was examined regarding the structural properties it exhibited, namely comprehensiveness, complexity, abstractness and specificity. Since knowledge content is of a largely conscious nature, it can be empirically researched: the 'knowledge domain' that was researched is green consumption; researched 'objects' were products (those for daily consumption), and for them it was assessed how consumers understood the idea 'green' in terms of product attributes.

- *Do patterns exist at the operational level of cognition?*
  Cognitive operations reflect an 'applications software' level of cognition. In contrast to knowledge content, cognitive operations are of a subconscious nature. They can only be inferred on the basis of observed knowledge content features. On such an inferential basis, processes of cognitive operations, e.g. specification, abstraction, integration, etc., and modes of cognitive operations, e.g. bottom-up processing and top-down processing were investigated.

- *Do patterns exist at the formatting level of cognition?*
  Schematic knowledge features refer to a 'systems software' level of cognition, which is, like cognitive operations, of a subconscious nature (bordering even upon an unconscious level of the human mind). The 'measurement' of schemata depends upon the quantification of structural knowledge content features at a knowledge content and at a cognitive operational level (Smith and Houston 1986: 504). Whether and, if so, how schemata and prototypes underwired the thinking of the green consumer had to be inferred on the basis of observed features of knowledge content and cognitive operations.

2 How do consumers solve the green shopping problem?

- *How is familiarity reflected by knowledge structure development?*
  The green consumer who is actually behaving has obviously solved the green shopping problem in some way. How far familiarity affects cognitive development was examined. Experience in the form of familiarity could be comparatively easily assessed because of its rather 'quantitative' nature.

- *How intelligent is the green consumer?*
  An assessment of ability is of a 'qualitative' nature. It is necessary to set out what is to be understood by successful green consumer behaviour. The cognitive anthropological concepts of practical thinking and bricolage were drawn upon to examine how green consumers formulated and solved their shopping problems. A contextual orientation of problem solving was focused on. Ability was assessed on a comparative basis regarding the practical know-how shown by consumers.

- *Can green shopping be approached with scientific precision?*
  Green shopping behaviour can be compared against a scientific yardstick, for instance as set out by the concept of life-cycle analysis (LCA). How far science could possibly help the green consumer to put green shopping intentions into actual behaviour was discussed in this way.

CONCLUSIONS

A cognitive framework has been outlined in this chapter. It provided the conceptual basis for researching green consumer behaviour. The framework distinguished three psychological 'levels' of cognition: knowledge content, cognitive operations, and schemata. In terms of a computer analogy, the knowledge content level was (simplistically) compared to data files, cognitive operations to applications software, and schemata to systems software.

Knowledge content is, in contrast to cognitive operations and schemata, of a largely conscious nature. For that reason, empirical research focused on the investigation of knowledge content. An examination of cognitive operations and schematic knowledge characteristics then built on the findings made regarding knowledge content.

Through the concept 'experience' (knowledge accumulated in the past), knowledge structure development and how this reflects on the successful problem solving behaviour of the green consumer was assessed. Two different aspects of experience were discussed – familiarity and ability. For an ability assessment of successful green task performance, the cognitive anthropological concepts of practical thinking and bricolage were drawn upon. They reflect that successful problem solving is highly subjective and contextual in nature.

The knowledge structure framework outlined has reached a degree of complexity. In that respect, it differs from a traditional psychological approach that isolates and focuses strongly on a single 'unit of research' or a few units. Bartlett early on pointed out that for explaining 'any genuine psychological problem we are bound to accept certain complex activities, or functions, as our starting point' (Bartlett 1932: 187). The research problem of this study – examining consumer cognition in a real-life context – can be considered a genuine psychological problem in Bartlett's sense. For researching such a problem, certain complexities have to be accepted at the outset.

This study was not designed for the empirical testing of psychological hypotheses, e.g. those suggested by schema theory. Rather, an interpretative approach was taken that aimed at the exploration and generation of insights into consumer cognition. This project contributed to a better understanding of cognition under real-life conditions, besides contributing to a better understanding of green consumer cognition, which represents a contemporary consumption phenomenon in many western markets. For application-oriented research in management studies or public policy studies, such a 'real-life' approach appears generally advisable.

The next chapter addresses methodological questions regarding empirical research into green consumer cognition. Amongst other questions, that of how knowledge structures of green consumers can be empirically researched and 'measured' is examined, thus showing how the framework outlined in this chapter can be put into effect.

3

EMPIRICAL RESEARCH INTO GREEN CONSUMER BEHAVIOUR

QUALITATIVE VERSUS QUANTITATIVE COGNITIVE RESEARCH

In a broad sense, methodology can be defined as 'the process, principles, and procedures by which we approach problems and seek answers' (Bogdan and Taylor 1975: 1). In this sense the research questions of this study are 'methodological questions' in so far as green consumers are investigated as 'theorists' with regard to the 'methodology' they apply for developing 'hypotheses' on environmentally oriented shopping. As Lévi-Strauss pointed out, systematic 'theoretical' thinking existed long before it was formalized as 'scientific thinking' (see chapter 2).

In science, methodology refers to the way a conceptual or empirical investigation is structured in order to advance the growth of (scientific) knowledge. Methodological principles guide such an investigation. The *conceptual* approach taken by this study and methodological principles related to it have been outlined in the previous chapters. Methodology decisions on how to structure *empirical* research are closely intertwined with the conceptual approach taken for tackling a certain research problem. They are discussed in more detail below.

Strengths and weaknesses of qualitative and quantitative research

In the social sciences, the two main empirical research traditions are the *quantitative* approach that draws on techniques such as experiments, surveys, histories, analysis of archival information, etc., and the *qualitative* one that utilizes techniques such as case studies, participant observation, open interviews, etc. (Frankfort-Nachmias and Nachmias 1996: 281–6, 304–9, Creswell 1994: 10–12, Patton 1990: 14, 36–9, 162–6, Yin 1989: 8, 17–22, Day and Castleberry 1986: 94–5, Vinehall 1979: 108–15, Bogdan and Taylor 1975: 3–7, LaPiere 1934: 237). The labels 'quantitative' and 'qualitative' research are interchangeable with notions like 'objective' and 'subjective' research (Burrell and Morgan 1979: 1–8).[1] The quantitative approach tends to be related to logical positivism, the traditional empirical research paradigm of the natural sciences, while the idea of qualitative research relates to a phenomenological, hermeneutic research tradition that originated in the social sciences. The phenomenological approach can be traced back to the sociologists Max Weber and George Herbert Mead and the philosophers Edmund Husserl and Ludwig von Wittgenstein.

Both the quantitative and the qualitative approaches have strengths and weaknesses. Their respective strengths and weaknesses can be discussed along three dimensions: external validity, reliability and precision. *External validity* (or 'ecological validity') refers to the possibility of generalizing findings on a researched population to other populations, ideally to populations as they can be found in the 'real world'. External validity touches upon issues related to the relevance of research (Coolican 1990: 36, Yin 1989: 41–4). *Reliability* refers to the possibility that a study can be repeated by another researcher and yield the same results (Silverman 1993: 145, Coolican 1990: 34, Yin 1989: 41, 45).[2] *Precision* refers to the numerical accuracy that can be attributed to research findings. It relates to the *quantitative significance* of empirical research (Yin 1989: 40–3, Weick 1979: 35–6, Thorngate 1976: 406).

Quantitative and qualitative research acknowledge different trade-offs regarding external validity, reliability and precision (Stoecker 1991: 92–3, Coolican 1990: 34–8, Patton 1990: 14, Bruner 1979: 2–3, Weick 1979: 35–6, Thorngate 1976: 406, LaPiere 1934: 237). As LaPiere pointed out in the 1930s:

> Quantitative measurements are quantitatively accurate; qualitative evaluations are always subject to the errors of human judgement. Yet it would seem far more worth while to make a shrewd guess regarding that which is essential than to accurately measure that which is likely to prove quite irrelevant.
>
> (LaPiere 1934: 237)

Quantitative methods, through their strict control and manipulation of their research environment, e.g. a laboratory, tend to have an edge over qualitative methods with regard to precision and reliability. The possibly lower precision of qualitative methods is due to their information richness (Stoecker 1991: 91, Cohen 1989: 13, Bartlett 1932: 12). For instance, in qualitative research precision cannot be expressed through numerically calculated significance levels.

A quantitative approach may have weaknesses with respect to external validity. The rigidity of control and the artificiality of the research environment – normally the laboratory – pose threats to external validity. Irrelevance, triviality and a weak record regarding external validity are evident in much quantitative research in cognitive psychology. Such stern criticism comes both from within the field (Varela *et al.* 1991: xvi, Coolican 1990: 36, Gardner 1987: 134, Tulving 1985: 395, Bryce 1985: 79, Bruner 1979: 28, Neisser 1978: 3, 11–12, Bartlett 1932: 2–9; see also chapter 2), and from a qualitatively committed research community (Silverman 1985: 43, Harre 1981: 4, 15–17, Gross 1974: 42, Rowan 1974: 86–7, 96, Husserl 1954: 201–12).

In short, the results of a hundred years of the psychological study of memory are somewhat discouraging. We have established firm empirical generalizations, but most of them are so obvious that every ten-year-old knows them anyway. . . . We have an intellectually impressive group of theories, but history offers little confidence that they will provide any meaningful insight into natural behaviour.

(Neisser 1978: 12–13)

Similar accusations have been voiced for consumer behaviour research (Shimp 1994: 1–4, Wells 1993: 490–3, Foxall 1993: 46) and for applied cognitive psychological research (Herrmann and Gruneberg 1993: 553–6, 562). Methodological pluralism has been called for in consumer behaviour research to amend that situation (Foxall 1993: 46) but little has been achieved in that respect so far. The accusation that most consumer behaviour research has been motivated by 'the availability of easy-to-use measuring instruments . . . and/or the almost toy-like nature of sophisticated quantitative techniques' (Jacoby 1976a: 2) has been upheld over the past two decades since first voiced in the mid-1970s (Shimp 1994: 5, Wells 1993: 490; see also Jacoby 1976b, LaPiere 1934: 237). When it came to the structuring of scientific research, apparently, empirical research has driven conceptual research rather than the other way round.

The main reason for the lack of external validity in quantitative research is the artificiality of the laboratory environment which requires the researcher to isolate and reduce 'units of research' in order to make them quantifiable and controllable. Often 'non-meaningful units of behaviour' – taken out of their natural context, and sharply isolated from other units – are researched. Bruner (1979: 28) notes: 'The more rigorously isolated from context and the more tightly controlled the conditions of experiments, the more precise and the more modest have results been.' In addition, convenience sampling that is based on untypical populations, such as undergraduates, is frequently relied upon in quantitative psychological research,[3] which poses a further external validity problem. In general, an external validity problem is not an insignificant problem since 'laboratory research is not meant to be generalized only to other laboratories' (Kidder 1981b: 252, also Wells 1993: 492).

External validity is likely to be higher in qualitative research since the context and the phenomenon under investigation are not artificially separated (Coolican 1990: 237, Cohen 1989: 13, LaPiere 1934: 236–7). Meaningful units of research are approached on a more comprehensive basis as they are likely to occur in 'real life'. There has been a strong call for so-called real-life studies of psychological phenomena from within the field of psychology (Alba et al. 1991: 36, Gardner 1987: 135, 258, 298, Neisser 1978: 11–14, Thorngate 1976: 406–7, Neisser 1967: 305, Bartlett 1932: 12). Qualitative research, despite being rare, has a long tradition in psychology and it has yielded valuable contributions in cognitive and in social psychology, for instance Sacks (1991), Luria (1987), Sacks (1986), Janis (1983) and Bartlett (1932) who also refers to

Cassel (1895); and also Lazarsfeld's studies in consumer psychology in the 1930s (Fullerton 1990, Neurath 1988). However, as indicated, real-life studies come at a methodological cost regarding precision and reliability. Certain techniques may be applied to increase the precision and the reliability of qualitative approaches, but even then a quantitative approach is likely to be superior in that respect.

A qualitative or a quantitative approach to the green consumer?

The decision between whether to adopt a quantitative or a qualitative empirical research method depends most importantly upon the potential contribution of either method to solving the chosen research problem (Wells 1993: 493, 497–8, Cohen 1989: 4–6, Grunert 1988: 176, Day and Castleberry 1986: 94–6, Reynolds and Jamieson 1985: 118, 121, Gutman and Alden 1985: 102; see also Wittgenstein 1967: 20, 109). In the previous chapters, a conceptual research problem for cognitive consumer research was outlined and framed as a problem of choice behaviour. A combined cognitive psychological–cognitive anthropological approach was suggested in order to provide an understanding of how green consumers approach problem-solving behaviour in a day-to-day context. A qualitative, real-life research approach is likely to be the appropriate empirical research method for the type of investigation of choice behaviour that tries to capture the subjective standpoint of the consumer. Actual contact with 'real' consumers has to be made. As Gestalt psychologists have stressed:

> A theory of human behaviour that fails to make contact with man's conceptions of *his world and his way of knowing*, that sets these aside as epiphenomena – this will neither be an adequate theory of human behaviour nor will it prevail in common sense.
> (Bruner 1979: 43, emphasis added; see also Wells 1993: 492, 497–8,
> Friedman and Lessig 1986: 338, Bruner 1979: 29)

Consequently, an open and only semi-structured empirical research technique was applied in this study to investigate consumer cognition.

A qualitative research programme for consumer choice behaviour contrasts strongly with the quantitative approach that is taken by so-called consumer judgement research. Judgement research has modelled itself very closely on the traditional approach of psychology with regard to both its conceptual and its empirical research methodology. As pointed out in chapter 2, judgement research focuses at the conceptual level very narrowly on certain aspects of decision making processes. Regarding its empirical approach, judgement research separates the phenomenon of consumer behaviour from its real-life context; empirical research is conducted in a laboratory setting in which the research context can be tightly controlled (Ross and Creyer 1992, Sirdeshmukh and Unnava 1992, Ford and Smith 1987, Wright 1975).

Some contradictory research results have been observed between findings from qualitative field research and quantitative findings from laboratory research. For instance, in consumer judgement research it was found that the presentation and the control of product attributes can be sufficient to prompt an interviewee to make inferences which would not have occurred in a real-life choice context (Tybout and Artz 1994: 144, Sirdeshmukh and Unnava 1992: 284, 289, Ford and Smith 1987: 370, Johnson and Russo 1984: 549, Wright 1975: 66; see also Alba *et al.* 1991: 29). Through the control and manipulation of the research environment, in particular through the provision of product alternatives and their attributes, a well-defined structure is imposed by a researcher on what in 'real life' is likely to be perceived by a consumer as an ill-structured, 'odd' problem (Brucks 1991: 56, Lynch and Srull 1991: 103). The researcher solves in advance the kind of problem that the 'bricoleur' consumer has to solve in an everyday context on his or her own.

In the following, the qualitative empirical approach that was taken by this study is outlined. Methodological issues relating to how and from whom data were collected are examined first. Subsequently, methodological issues are discussed that relate to the analysis of the data.

DATA COLLECTION

The empirical research design of this study is a qualitatively oriented one. In this section, the selection of a data collection technique, its application to research on consumer cognition, and the sampling of interviewees is assessed. How data were collected through open interviews and how certain interview biases were controlled for is discussed. Subsequently, the interview procedure and the sampling procedure are outlined.

Data collection through open, semi-structured interviews

Systematic interviewing is a principal data collection technique in qualitative and applied research (Mantwill *et al.* 1995: 68–9, Robson 1993: 228–31, Ackroyd and Hughes 1992: 100–4, Strauss and Corbin 1990: 18, Patton 1990: 10, Yin 1989: 19, Sampson 1986: 32–3, Merton and Kendall 1945–6). Utilizing the language of the consumer is an essential requirement of empirical research that investigates a cognitive research problem such as that raised by this study: semi-structured, open interviews were conducted with individual consumers.

Research into intended behaviour versus actual behaviour

Consumer cognition can be approached through interviews that enquire either about intended, future behaviour or about actual, past behaviour:[4] the latter approach, which is favoured by this study, draws on *retrospective recall*, which means that interviewees have to search their memories for recollections, while the former approach draws on *hypothetical reasoning*.

Research into intended, future behaviour may be biased because of its hypothetical and/or prospective character. When asked, consumers might readily say that they would shop in an environmentally friendly way in future. The cognitive complexities and practical difficulties of 'going green' and overcoming them might be underestimated or wrongly judged because of the lack of actual experience. A gap between intended and actual behaviour could result, and an interview technique based on hypothetical reasoning has not much to offer to deal with such a gap.

Intention research into green behaviour may also elicit responses from consumers on the basis of a heightened *general* environmental awareness only, e.g. a heightened concern about topical environmental problems such as global warming. Such a general awareness can normally not be expected to lead (directly, imminently or unavoidably) to *specific* behaviours, such as green consumption or green investment. An observed 'words–deeds inconsistency' between intended behaviour and actual behaviour can be partly attributed to misguided attempts to deduce specific behaviours from a general awareness (see chapter 1). The Fishbein model clearly states that only attitudes and intentions regarding a specific issue but not a general one determine actual behaviour (Ajzen and Fishbein 1980, Fishbein and Ajzen 1976, Fishbein and Ajzen 1975; see also chapter 1). In addition, an intention–behaviour gap may partly be due to a social desirability bias. Voicing non-green buying intentions during an interview might be experienced as socially embarrassing (Mintel 1992: 2, MacKenzie 1991: 71, Wimmer 1988: 76).

Actual behaviour appears to play an important role when it comes to knowledge development and the build-up of experience: 'Knowing is doing' (Maturana and Varela 1992: 244–8; see also LaPiere 1934: 236–7). Research on past behaviour that draws on retrospective recall has been successfully applied to consumer behaviour research in general, and to cognitive research of repeat purchase decisions in particular. This technique can be used when prior knowledge – experience – exists (MacInnis *et al.* 1992, Zeithaml 1991, Eisenhardt 1989a, Brucks 1986, Hoyer 1986, Smith and Houston 1986, Reynolds and Jamieson 1985, Duncan and Olshavsky 1982, Bettman 1979b, Markus 1977). Major market researchers, such as MORI or Mintel, have also researched green consumer behaviour with regard to past behaviours rather than intended ones (Worcester 1995: 7–9, Upsall and Worcester 1995: 8–10, Worcester 1993a: 318, Worcester 1993b, MORI 1992, Jacobs and Worcester 1991, Mintel 1991).

Interview biases

The kind of biases from which intention research tends to suffer present less of a problem for research of actual behaviour through retrospective recall. A general advantage of a research procedure that draws on retrospective recall lies in the fact that it does not interfere with the cognition and behaviour that occurred in its real-life context in the past. However, other biases have to be checked for. Retrospective recall may be affected by bias because of inferences in recall – a so-called 'theorizing' or 'rationalizing' bias – and a cognitive retrieval bias related to the phenomenon of forgetting.

Ideally, verbal statements of interviewees should reflect past cognition and behaviour. Any question asked by an interviewer presents an interviewee with information that is meant to stimulate a verbal response. Inferences in recall refer to the change in knowledge structures as 'new reasoning patterns' are applied to 'old behaviours' at the point of questioning, e.g. a change in the abstractness of cognitive processing might occur (Johnson and Fornell 1987: 219, Brucks 1986: 60, Bettman 1979b: 196). The creation of new knowledge that is due to inferences in recall is undesirable. Through the structuring of an interview, in particular through the way in which retrieval of knowledge is organized and questions are sequenced, an inferences in recall bias can be minimized. One advantage of open interviews over open mail questionnaires is that the sequencing of questions is likely to be more effective. In the case of an open mail questionnaire, people can skim through before answering it, and thus sequencing effects that might help to restrain inferences in recall are eliminated. This issue will be returned to when the interview procedure is outlined.

Some cognitive research projects have deliberately structured interviews to force 'the consumer up the ladder of abstraction' (Zeithaml 1991: 28, also Gutman and Alden 1985: 103–4, Reynolds and Jamieson 1985: 121–2) in order to gain an understanding of his or her cognitive operations. Such an approach deliberately attempts to utilize inferences in recall. Its highly manipulative and hypothetical nature makes it inappropriate for capturing the actual standpoint of the green consumer, which is attempted in this study. However, a similarly hypothetical approach was applied by this study to a comparison group of so-called 'non-green' consumers (subsequent sections give more details on how non-green consumers were researched).

Besides inferences in recall, the phenomenon of forgetting can present a problem for any empirical research technique that enquires about past cognition and behaviour (Lynch and Srull 1991: 104). With regard to the product focus chosen by the study, this problem may be comparatively trivial. It has been found that recall is enhanced by the recency of behaviour, by its frequency, and by the involvement of the customer (Engel *et al.* 1990: 509, Alba and Hutchinson 1987: 434). For the buying of everyday products, such as groceries, recency and frequency are common characteristics. High involvement is normally not associated with the buying of products for daily consumption, but for green shopping some sort of involvement is likely to exist.[5]

The problem of forgetting may be reduced by prompting consumers, i.e. by asking highly specific questions that draw on so-called part listings, e.g. lists of certain products. A disadvantage of part listings is that they restrain recall and lead to a prompting bias since they focus recall narrowly. Through part listings, the nature of a recall task is changed from a free recall task, where there is no prompting, to a recognition task (Lynch and Srull 1991: 107, 113–14, Alba *et al.* 1991: 6, 19, Nickerson 1984: 531–2). Hence, the positive effects of part listings that help to reduce the problem of forgetting have to be balanced against their negative effects in restraining and focusing recall. Such a trade-off has to be kept in mind when the interview structure is designed.

Outline of interview structure

The main purpose of a cognitive research interview is to discover the knowledge content of a person's mind. The interview itself should attempt not to change existing knowledge but only to retrieve it. Inferences in recall should be kept to a minimum. At the same time the problem of forgetting has to be dealt with; and here, the positive and negative effects of part listings have to be traded off. As a consequence of these considerations, some structure has to be imposed on the interview procedure (Patton 1990: 43, 283, 288, 376, Cohen 1989: 6–7, Sampson 1986: 33, Merton and Kendall 1945–6: 545–7).

This study applied a question guide that divided the interview into four parts (see Appendix 3.1): in the first part of the interview, only open questions were asked and no part listings were used; in the second and third parts of the interview, part listings were used; the fourth and final part concluded the interview with a self-rating task and offered interviewees the opportunity to comment on further issues they wished to raise.

The first part of the interview contained only open questions drawing on free retrospective recall. No specific items, either products or product attributes, were singled out for an interviewee to comment on. No part listings were used. Thus, the recall restraining effect of part listings was avoided, but the problem of forgetting was not dealt with. The retrieval of knowledge content on green shopping was organized around products rather than product attributes. For supermarket products, product-related cognitive processing rather than attribute-related processing has been found to be dominant; examples of products can be expected to be easily recalled by an interviewee (Park *et al.* 1994: 79, Alba *et al.* 1991: 7–10, 21–5, Lynch and Srull 1991: 111, 122, Rothschild 1987: 569).[6] Hence, as a first step, green product examples were collected from an interviewee without the interviewer probing more deeply as to why and how an interviewee had come to view a product as green (in terms of product attributes). These examples of green products were then discussed with the interviewee who was asked about his or her subjective understanding of greenness. That kind of phased approach, starting with the recall of product examples that then provide the basis for the interviewee to discuss how he/she perceived green product attributes, appears to restrain inferences in recall best (Alba and Hutchinson 1987: 433, Smith and Houston 1986: 505, Markus 1977: 65).

In the second part of the interview, a part listing of products was used. Problems related to forgetting were reduced by this. The purpose of a part listing

70

is to provide retrieval cues. Part 2 (and also part 3) of the interview required the interviewee to perform a recognition task rather than a free recall task. Comprehensive product part listings are likely to contain more than forty product categories (see Figure 3.1). Both for reasons relating to the efficient collection and analysis of data and for reasons relating to the span of attention an interviewee is able and prepared to offer for the purpose of an interview – the interview was expected to last about 30 minutes – no all-out testing of product categories was possible. Only those product categories were included in the part listing that had frequently been mentioned as examples of green products in the pilot studies or in the literature on environmentally oriented consumption (Worcester 1994a: 5, Mintel 1992: 2, CA 1989: 433). In the

Food products

Dairy products:
milk
yoghurt
cream
cheese
butter
etc.

Plant products:
vegetables, fruit
pulses, grains: rice, lentils
coffee, tea
etc.

Meats:
meat, sausages
etc.

Drinks:
drinks: mineral water, beer, wine, soft
  drinks, orange juice
etc.

Bakery products:
bread
biscuits: cakes
flour
etc.

Others:
sweets
spreads: jam, margarine
eggs
baby food
ready made food
etc.

Non-food products

Toiletries:
hair spray, deodorant: sprays
shampoo, shower gel
cosmetics: cream, lotions, cleansers
soap, hand cleaner
toothpaste
etc.

Cleaning products/detergents:
washing powder/laundry detergent
fabric softener
washing-up liquid
cleaners: floor cleaner, toilet
  cleaner/bleach, window cleaner,
  surface cleaner polish
etc.

Paper products:
toilet paper
tissues: handkerchiefs
kitchen paper
nappies
women's sanitary products
etc.

Others:
bin bags
etc.

Figure 3.1 Products consumed on a daily basis

end, the part listing comprised eleven products. Such selective lists of product categories are commonly applied in consumer behaviour research (Hoyer 1986: 33–5). The part listing was applied by default, i.e. there was prompting for only those products of the part listing that had not already been discussed in the first part of the interview. Once an interviewee had responded positively to a product from the prompting list, a follow-up questioning comparable to that in part 1 was conducted.

In part 3 of the interview, a part listing was applied that comprised different types of information cues a consumer might have drawn upon to assess the greenness of a product. The part listing was constructed on the basis of the findings of the pilot studies and a literature review on consumer behaviour (Billig 1994: 161–9, 180–4). That kind of enquiry was put at the end of the interview because of its higher potential to cause inferences in recall. A general discussion of information related to the perceived greenness of a product is more prone to lead to inferences in recall.

In a final, fourth part, the interview was concluded with a self-rating task. The interviewee was asked for an overall self-assessment regarding the greenness of his or her shopping. On a scale ranging from zero to 100, interviewees had to rank themselves with regard to actual green consumption behaviour (see Figure 3.2). They were then given the opportunity to comment on any further issue they wanted to raise in relation to environmentally friendly consumption.

In addition to green consumers, a group of 'non-green' consumers was interviewed. Basically, the same interview procedure was applied, but with the omission of parts 1 and 4. Part 1 of the interview procedure, the free recall of green products and the discussion of them, had necessarily to be left out, as had a self-rating task regarding the greenness of the consumers' shopping. Parts 2 and 3 of the interview procedure used the same part listings, but (in a hypothetical fashion) with regard to intended behaviour. There were different start-ups to the interview with non-green consumers depending on how they had been recruited, either on the doorstep or through recommendations by previous interviewees.

The interviewer tried to minimize an inferences in recall bias by structuring the interview in a fairly concrete fashion with the focus of enquiry on product examples. If inferences in recall occurred despite these attempts to minimize them, the interviewer should be able to recognize them. For the recognition of inferences in recall that transcend mere constructive recall, a number of criteria have been suggested, such as long periods of silence, the absence of slang, or the

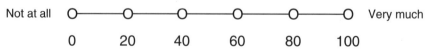

Figure 3.2 Self-rating scale

72

absence of redundancy, none of which is common in ordinary speech (Bettman 1979b: 232; also Markus 1977: 65). The researcher's impressions with regard to these issues provided the basis for assessing whether inferences in recall had actually occurred. Also, interviews with non-green interviewees on intended green shopping behaviour provided *post hoc* an idea of what extreme 'green' rationalizing and hypothesizing looked like. Since the non-green interviewees had very low levels of actual green shopping experience, they had to make shrewd guesses, i.e. invent hypotheses and rationalizations, on what makes a product green. (Chapter 5 returns to this issue of identifying 'rationalizing' when findings on the non-green interviewees are compared to the findings on green interviewees; see especially the section on schematic knowledge, where stereotyping by non-green interviewees is discussed.) In general, it appeared that inferences in recall presented an insignificant problem for the research conducted.

Sampling of interviewees

In quantitative research, sampling aims at the statistical control of internal validity; for statistical generalizations, randomized sampling is obligatory. This contrasts with sampling in qualitative research which is non-probabilistic: here, interviewees are not chosen for statistical reasons, but they are selected purposively. 'Theoretical sampling' is conducted: only particular instances of a certain phenomenon – here: green consumption – are investigated. Theoretical sampling in the form of variation sampling is meant to yield a sample of a diverse composition. It has little in common with probabilistic sampling in quantitative research (Patton 1990: 171–2, Eisenhardt 1989a: 537, Sampson 1986: 29, Kidder 1981b: 230, McClintock *et al.* 1979: 613, 619, Glaser and Strauss 1967: 30; also Stoecker 1991: 92).

In this study, theoretical sampling aimed at sampling consumers with varying levels of green consumption experience. The variable that was 'controlled' during the theoretical sampling process was the actual experience level of green consumption an interviewee had. Other variables, in particular socio-demographic ones, had to be left uncontrolled. Such a sampling approach strongly contrasts with a quantitative socio-demographic one that tries to profile the green consumer in terms of age, gender, income, education, etc. and which requires a statistically representative sample. For descriptive purposes, information on socio-demographic variables was collected by this study. However, even when the under- or over-representation of certain socio-demographic variables in the samples is known, the cognitive patterns found should not be projected to a larger, *socio-demographically profiled* population. Since the original samples were not statistically representative in socio-demographic terms, inferences of this kind cannot and should not be made.

All interviews were conducted by the author of this study. During the interview, the interviewer took on the role of a sympathetic listener rather than the role of an antagonizing educator or ethical inquisitor (Patton 1990: 139, Sampson 1986: 43, Merton and Kendall 1945–6: 547). Each interview was tape recorded and transcribed verbatim within twenty-four hours if possible (Robson and Hedges 1993: 31, Patton 1990: 379, Yin 1989: 91, 99, Eisenhardt 1989b: 574, Sampson 1986: 45). Each interviewee was also asked to complete a data sheet on socio-demographic variables after the interview. Furthermore, a recruitment protocol was compiled that gave information on how an interviewee had been recruited.

Sampling of green consumers

One of the main objectives of sampling was to collect a sample with a high diversity in actual green shopping experience. An ideal sample would be distributed equally throughout the range of green experience levels, from subjects with no green experience to subjects with extremely high levels of green experience. However, such an ideal sample is difficult to achieve, and it is not absolutely necessary: for the purpose of theoretical sampling, it is necessary only to sample subjects with different experience levels in sufficient numbers but not in equal numbers. A sufficient representation of different experience levels already allows for the diagnosis of certain patterns.

It was hoped that interviewees at the higher end of green experience levels would be discovered through members of environmental pressure groups. The medium and low levels were largely discovered by searching for interviewees on a house-by-house basis, or drawing on social contacts of former interviewees (see Table 3.1). In the end, some apparently very green consumers were also discovered through doorstep searches, while some of the interviewees who were members of green pressure groups fell into lower experience categories.

In theoretical sampling a recruitment interview plays an important role. It allows interviewees to be screened. A recruitment interview should be brief and collect information only on a few important criteria that enable the researcher to determine quickly whether a person exhibits the phenomenon under investigation. The recruitment interview should conceal the exact objective of the research interview in order to prevent the interviewee from preparing for the interview, thus leading possibly to an inferences in recall problem (Vinehall 1979: 118). The main criterion for the selection of interviewees was whether

Table 3.1 Recruitment of interviewees

	Pressure group contact	Doorstep	Social reference
British sample (n = 55)	27 (49%)	9 (16%)	19 (35%)
German sample (n = 36)	11 (31%)	3 (8%)	22 (61%)
Non-green sample (n = 10)	–	8 (80%)	2 (20%)

they had experience with green shopping. In addition to experience with green shopping, the recruitment interviewer always checked, both for green and for non-green interviewees, whether a person frequently and regularly shopped for products for daily consumption. Only those who regularly did so were interviewed. Interviewees were sampled in the Oxford area except for five persons who were interviewed in Colchester and who belonged to an environmentalist local exchange and trading system.

The number of interviewees sampled was chosen to be at the higher end of rule of thumb recommendations for theoretical sampling in qualitative research: in general, six to ten cases (here interviewees) have been found sufficient for analytic generalizations regarding an identified pattern (Yin 1989: 53, Sampson 1986: 51–3; see also Patton 1990: 186, Glaser and Strauss 1967: 30). The theoretical criterion underlying such rule-of-thumb estimates is that of 'theoretical' saturation (Eisenhardt 1989a: 545, Glaser and Strauss 1967: 61–2). One problem here was that the number of patterns was not known a priori. In the end, the British sample of green consumers comprised fifty-five persons. Such a sample size was at the very upper end of conservative suggestions for sample sizes.

Sampling of groups for comparison

Theoretical sampling across groups tends to increase external validity (Kidder 1981b: 249, Glaser and Strauss 1967: 55–8; also Coolican 1990: 32, Eisenhardt 1989a: 537, Vinehall 1979: 117). In general, external validity can be expected to be higher in qualitative research than in quantitative research since research is conducted in a natural context as opposed to a laboratory. In this study, an attempt was made to increase external validity by using two groups for comparison: a group of German green consumers – later referred to as the 'German sample' – and a group of non-green British consumers – later just referred to as the 'non-green sample'.

Through the group of German green consumers, an additional sample was gained from a different population which could be subjected to the same analytical routine as the sample of British green consumers. A cross-cultural focus provided here for an external validity check of explanations of knowledge structures and the problem solving behaviour of green consumers.

German green consumers were sampled in the Ingolstadt area in Germany, except for five interviewees who were sampled in the Munich region. Again, these exceptions related to these interviewees being supposedly highly active members of environmental pressure groups. The German sample comprised thirty-six persons.

Both sampling regions, Oxford and Ingolstadt, were selected for reasons of convenience. In infrastructure terms, Oxford and Ingolstadt are similar. They are both small cities of a little more than 100,000 inhabitants; their industrial structure is heavily dominated by car manufacturing; and both cities are similarly close to metropolitan areas, London and Munich respectively. Major infrastructure differences relate to the service sector. Oxford has a large research and student community, and tourism plays a significant role there.

A second group used for comparison comprised non-green consumers. A group of non-green consumers complemented the theoretical sampling strategy of variation sampling. In the beginning of the sampling process, nearly anybody could be invited to become an interviewee. If no 'green' experience was indicated during the recruitment interview, the interviewer attempted to recruit him or her as a 'non-green' interviewee. A consumer was assessed as non-green if it was found during the recruitment interview or if it became clear from the beginning of the interview that he or she did not consider environmental issues in daily shopping. However, it proved difficult to find interviewees with absolutely no experience whatsoever regarding green shopping. It might not even be desirable to think of the ideal non-green interviewee as someone who had not had any exposure to environmentally oriented shopping. Besides being difficult to find, someone with no green shopping experience at all is likely to be difficult to interview, even on a hypothetical basis, since any idea of what is meant by 'environmentally oriented behaviour' is lacking.

For the purpose in hand, interviewees with low green consumption experience were considered ideal 'non-green' interviewees for a hypothetical reasoning task. Low green consumption experience could mean: having seen green advertising spots on TV, having noticed green products on a supermarket shelf, having done some green shopping for a neighbour or friend, having recycled glass bottles, or having unsuccessfully tried green products. Media reports, advertising or on-package promotion of green causes may have been seen by very many consumers; for instance, 90 per cent of detergents are said to make some environmental claims as part of their packaging information (Myburgh-Louw and O'Shaughnessy 1993–4: 8–9).

There is no clear-cut borderline between non-green consumers and those who might be classified as weakly active green consumers. Experience levels are likely to vary along a continuum. Were it not for the different interview approaches that were applied to green and non-green consumers, the problem of an a priori identification of green and non-green consumers would not be worth discussing. In the end, there were consumers in the sample of green consumers who could also have been approached as non-green consumers and there were interviewees in the group of non-green consumers who at least at first glance seemed to compare to a certain type of weakly active green consumer. In that respect it was later interesting to see how the reasoning patterns of these green and non-green consumers differed. Such differences could then be related to differences in the research method used rather than to significant cognitive differences exhibited by interviewees, thus shedding light on the phenomenon of 'rationalizing'.

In all, ten non-green interviewees were sampled, also in the Oxford area. This number might appear low, but this group of interviewees was only meant to complement variation sampling rather than to launch a separate investigation.

Self-rating task

To make sure that the final sample covered a wide variety of green experience levels sufficiently, the level of green experience of interviewees was monitored and registered during the sampling process. The results of the self-rating task were used as indicators of the extent of green experience (see Figure 3.2 above).

In the self-rating task, interviewees had to rank themselves on a scale ranging from zero to 100. An accompanying statement was worded with respect to actual green shopping behaviour (as opposed to intended green behaviour, or a general attitude statement related to environmental causes). Quite a number of interviewees marked ranges rather than a single point on the self-rating scale, e.g. the range 60–80 was circled. In such cases and for the purpose of a distributional analysis, the centre of marked ranges was used as self-rating score. Since in most cases a brief comment by the interviewee accompanied the self-rating task, the transcribed interview data could also be drawn upon when there was doubt about values of scores because of unclear markings. Subsequently, the self-rating data were grouped and a distributional analysis was conducted (see Appendix 3.2).

The distribution of self-rating scores indicated that quite a variation in levels of green consumption experience had been achieved for the British and the German sample: the distribution of self-rating scores did not resemble an equal distribution, but the steady growth of the distribution function indicated that a considerable range of green experience levels had been sufficiently covered.

Self-rating tasks are of a subjective nature. There are likely to be a number of biases that may distort self-rating scores: a social desirability bias may occur at the lower end of the scale, and a 'modesty' bias, a feeling of not being perfect, may work at the other end of the scale. In addition, personality traits might affect a self-rating task, some people being generally cautious in assessing themselves while others might be less so. Since each interviewee went through the same interview procedure, the same 'standard' had implicitly been set for each interviewee in the self-rating task at the end of the interview. In particular, the extent of prompting in parts 2 and 3 of the interview, and the extent of positive and negative responses given there, can be expected to have been registered by an interviewee in some way, thus leading to some standard setting for a later self-assessment. Despite their high subjectivity, results from the self-rating tasks showed that interviewees were able to analyse their behaviours. Over- or under-rating apparently occurred, but this seemed to be a matter of degree rather than dramatic distortion.

Besides the self-rating data, the distributional analysis of knowledge structure variables also supported *post hoc* the view that a wide variation of green experience across the samples had been achieved (see below, when knowledge content is discussed). For these distributions, the parameters mean and median had similar values, which reflects the well-centred and symmetrical nature of the distributions. Since these distributions also covered a substantial range of values, as reflected by parameters such as minimum and maximum and by the way the distribution function grew (see Appendixes 3.3 and 3.7), it can be stated with some confidence that the objective of a wide variation in green shopping experience within the green samples was reached.

Socio-demographic structure of the samples

Theoretical sampling was conducted in order to achieve a wide variation in green consumption experience across a sample. As a consequence, socio-demographic variables, like age, gender, marital status, etc., were left uncontrolled. Indirectly, they possibly related to the variables that were deliberately focused on during the sampling process, in particular the variable 'membership in an environmental group'.

Socio-demographic information was collected at the conclusion of an interview, when the interviewee was asked to fill in a demographic data sheet.[7] Since the filling in of the data sheet was administered by the interviewer, explanatory information could be given to the interviewee; for instance, regarding the variable 'number of years in formal education', it was explained that this should include all years in formal education from primary school onwards. There were a few instances where information on certain variables was not volunteered or was forgotten; for instance, a couple of interviewees did not want to tell their ages. In such cases estimates were made. An assessment of the socio-economic status of an interviewee was derived from the interviewee's (and his or her partner's) occupation (Jacobs and Worcester 1991: 169). Since most interviews were conducted at the home of the interviewee, an assessment of an interviewee's socio-economic status could be supplemented by interviewer observations, in particular observations on the residential situation, e.g. the area the interviewee lived in, and the type of residence occupied.

Additional socio-demographic information was extracted *post hoc* from the transcribed interviews. During the sampling process it became apparent that there was a substantial number of vegetarians in the British sample. This life-style variable was originally not included in the demographic data sheet. However, since the product 'meat' was included in the prompting list for products, it caused little problem to collect information on the variable 'vegetarianism' from the actual interview data.

Table 3.2 summarizes the socio-demographic characteristics of the British, the German and the non-green samples.

As a by-product of theoretical sampling, certain values of socio-demographic variables seemed to be over- or under-represented as compared with the British and German populations as a whole:[8]

- Membership in an environmental group was high for both the British and the German sample. This variable was actively focused on during the theoretical sampling process to cover consumers with high experience levels.

Table 3.2 Socio-demographic data

	British green (n = 55)	*German green* (n = 36)	*Non-green* (n = 10)
Distribution of age ranges	[22, 29]: 9 (16%) [30, 39]: 26 (47%) [40, 49]: 15 (27%) [50, 59]: 3 (5%) [60, 65]: 2 (4%)	[19]: 1 (3%) [24, 29]: 6 (17%) [30, 39]: 15 (42%) [40, 49]: 7 (19%) [50, 59]: 6 (17%) [61]: 1 (3%)	[29, 41]: 9 (90%) [72]: 1 (10%)
Average age	37	39	38
Gender	F: 39 (71%) M: 16 (29%)	F: 27 (75%) M: 9 (25%)	F: 7 (70%) M: 3 (30%)
Marital status	Single: 16 (29%) Divorced: 1 (2%) Widowed: 2 (4%) Married: 21 (38%) L.w.p.: 15 (27%)	Single: 9 (25%) Divorced: 3 (8%) Widowed: — Married: 20 (56%) L.w.p.: 4 (11%)	Single: 4 (40%) Divorced: 1 (10%) Widowed: — Married: 3 (30%) L.w.p.: 2 (20%)
Number of children	[0]: 33 (60%) [1]: 7 (13%) [2]: 9 (16%) [3]: 5 (9%) [4]: 1 (2%) average.: 0.8	[0]: 15 (42%) [1]: 3 (8%) [2]: 14 (39%) [3]: 2 (6%) [4]: 2 (6%) average: 1.25	[0]: 7 (70%) [1]: 1 (10%) [2]: 1 (10%) [3]: 1 (10%) [4]: — average: 0.6
Average number of years in education	17	16	17
Univ. degree	Yes: 49 (89%) No: 6 (11%)	Yes: 22 (61%) No: 14 (39%)	Yes: 8 (80%) No: 2 (20%)
Socio-economic status	[A]: 4 (7%) [B]: 28 (51%) [C1]: 13 (24%) [C2]: 2 (4%) [D]: 4 (7%) [E]: 4 (7%)	[A]: 4 (11%) [B]: 18 (50%) [C1]: 11 (31%) [C2]: — [D]: 1 (3%) [E]: 2 (6%)	[A]: — [B]: 5 (50%) [C1]: 5 (50%) [C2]: — [D]: — [E]: —
Member of a political party	Green: 7 (13%) Conserv.: 2 (4%) Labour: 1 (2%) None: 45 (82%)	Green: — CSU: — SPD: 5 (14%) None: 31 (86%)	Green: — Conserv.: — Labour: — None: 10 (100%)
Member of an environmental group	No: 20 (36%) Yes: 35 (64%) of which activists: 18 (33%) sympathizers: 17 (31%) *(If Green party included: No: 17 (31%) Yes: 38 (69%)*	No: 17 (47%) Yes: 19 (53%) of which activists: 11 (31%) sympathizers: 8 (22%)	No: 9 (90%) Yes: 1 (10%) of which activists: — sympathizers: 1 (10%)

Table 3.2 cont.

	British green (n = 55)	*German green* (n = 36)	*Non-green* (n = 10)
	of which activists: 21 *(38%)* *sympathizers:* 17 *(31%))*		
Driving licence:	Yes: 43 (78%) No: 12 (22%)	Yes: 35 (97%) No: 1 (3%)	Yes: 7 (70%) No: 3 (30%)
Car owner:	Yes: 37 (67%) No: 18 (33%)	Yes: 28 (78%) No: 8 (22%)	Yes: 7 (70%) No: 3 (30%)
Gardening:	Yes: 43 (78%) No: 12 (22%)	Yes: 25 (69%) No: 11 (31%)	Yes: 3 (30%) No: 7 (70%)
Residence	Urban: 42 (76%) Rural: 13 (24%)	Urban: 22 (61%) Rural: 14 (39%)	Urban: 10 (100%) Rural: —
Vegetarian	Yes: 19 (35%) No: 36 (65%)	Yes: 1.5 (4%) No: 34.5 (96%)	Yes: 1 (10%) No: 9 (90%)

About two-thirds of the British sample and about half of the German sample belonged to one or more environmental groups. Those who belonged to an environmental group were distinguished as activists or sympathizers. Activists were defined as persons who had been actively involved in campaigning activities for environmental issues. Classification as sympathizers was based largely on regular donations of money to environmental causes. Nearly 40 per cent of the British sample were classified as activists and about 30 per cent as sympathizers; in the German sample, about 30 per cent counted as activists, and about 20 per cent as sympathizers. Environmental groups mentioned covered a wide range. For the British sample, it included Friends of the Earth, Greenpeace, Women's Environmental Network, permaculture and organic gardening groups, the Royal Society for the Protection of Birds, the Royal Society of Nature Conservation, World Wide Fund for Nature, Earth First!, Earth Watch, Transport 2000, SURVIVAL, Alarm UK, the Soil Association, Green Christians, local recycling groups, and the Oxford Business and Environment Forum (other pressure groups that have no clear-cut environmental orientation were not included here, e.g. the Royal Society for the Protection of Rural England). Environmental groups mentioned by the German sample included Bund Naturschutz, Greenpeace, Landesbund für Vogelschutz, World Wide Fund for Nature, and local Umweltgruppen. Of the non-green sample, one person was classified as a sympathizer of an environmental group.

• Regarding membership of a political party, some over-representation existed for the British and the German sample: 13 per cent of the British interviewees were members of the Green Party, and 14 per cent of the German inter-viewees were members of the Social Democratic Party (SPD).

• In terms of educational background, those with higher education appeared to be over-represented in all three samples.

• Regarding socio-economic status, the high income groups A and B were over-represented in the British and the German samples. Socio-economic statuses A and B accounted together for about 60 per cent of both the British and the German samples. For the total British population, about 40 per cent count as middle class, i.e. socio-economic groups A, B and C1 (CSO 1993: 261, SB 1992: 115, Jacobs and Worcester 1991: 166).

• Regarding vegetarianism, there was a strong over-representation in the British sample, where about one-third were vegetarians. Vegetarians are estimated to account for about 4 to 7 per cent of the total British population (Jacobs and Worcester 1991: 85).

A tendency towards a kind of life-style extremism in political and in socio-economic terms was prevalent. Considering the sampling strategy followed, this is not unexpected. For the British sample a tendency towards life-style extremism appeared to be somewhat stronger than for the German sample.

Because of the small sample sizes, no statistically significant or probable link between the 'uncontrolled variables', such as age, gender, vegetarianism, educational background, socio-economic status, etc., and the manipulated socio-demographic variables, such as membership of an environmental group, could or should be established. Similarly, it should not be attempted on the basis of the research conducted to establish a statistical link between knowledge structure variables and socio-demographic ones. However, there might be some room for tentative speculations; for instance, regarding vegetarianism, which was highly represented in the British sample. The purpose of such speculations could only be to provide some propositional input for studies that are interested in profiling the green consumer in socio-demographic and life-style terms.

DATA ANALYSIS

A clear separation of data description and data interpretation is recommended for qualitatively oriented research (Robson and Hedges 1993: 32, Coolican 1990: 233–7, Patton 1990: 374–5, Eisenhardt 1989a: 540–1, Yin 1989: 106–8, Harris 1986: 53–66). In a descriptive phase, the usually enormous amount of data collected is summarized. Such data handling is then followed by data interpretation. In general, it is difficult to draw an exact line between data description and data interpretation. The notion of 'description' connotes an objective activity. Because of the open format of data collection in this study, data had to be condensed and extracted from primary data sources – the open, semi-structured interviews. Such an extraction of data requires an analytical framework. The development and application of such a framework, however, is not a purely descriptive activity. It is intertwined with the condensing and extraction of data.

The following outlines what data analysis techniques were applied to handle and condense the collected interview data, and the results of this process are presented. Calls for a quantification of qualitative research ('triangulation') could be partly adhered to (Frankfort-Nachmias and Nachmias 1996: 204–6, Creswell 1994: 173–6, Stoecker 1991: 92, Crano 1981: 320–3, McClintock *et al.* 1979: 612–13, 622–3, Jick 1979: 602–9; see also Tybout and Artz 1994: 157): certain aspects of knowledge content characteristics, such as knowledge comprehensiveness, knowledge complexity, knowledge specificity and knowledge abstractness, were quantified. Data themselves are not interpreted in the following with regard to consumer cognition; this is only done in chapters 5 and 6.

Reporting and handling of data

Information richness can be a problem in qualitative research. In this section, a framework is outlined for ordering and compounding the interview data. The reduction of data is a prerequisite for a later interpretation of the knowledge structures of green consumers. The primary data source consisted of the verbatim transcribed interviews. First, an analytical framework was developed through which the interview data could be taken apart. Subsequently, how this framework was applied to the interview data, and what kind of derivative, compounded data sources were generated, is outlined.

Bracketing framework

Edmund Husserl's idea of 'bracketing' data in qualitative research into small units was followed (Husserl 1952: 131–7; see also Spiggle 1994: 492–6, Crabtree and Miller 1992: 93–109, Patton 1990: 407–8, Husserl 1954: 288–93, Husserl 1950: 56, 71–2). The structure of a bracketing framework is already implicitly reflected by the structure of the interview guide (Patton 1990: 376). The bracketing framework was structured around three 'axes'. The three axes were: first, the interviewees; second, products or product groups; and third, product attributes that related to the greenness of a product as perceived by the interviewee.

Naturally, the first axis of an analytical framework for ordering the interview data is the interviewees. The British interviewees were chronologically allocated the 'names' B01, B02, . . . B55; the German interviewees were named G01, G02, . . . G36; and the non-green interviewees were named N01, N02, . . . N10.

The second axis of a bracketing framework is also rather obvious: the products that were discussed during the interview. Some categorizing of products had to be undertaken, otherwise the number of products that had to be dealt with by the framework would have got out of hand. For food products, six *product classes* were distinguished: dairy products (unprocessed), plant products, meats, drinks, bakery products, and 'other food products'. For non-food products, four product classes were distinguished: toiletries, washing and cleaning products, paper products, and 'other non-food products'. Each such product class comprised a number of individual products or *product groups*, e.g. the class 'plant products' comprised four product groups: vegetables and fruit, pulses and grains, tea and coffee, and 'other plant products'. All in all thirty-nine products or product groups were distinguished (see Figure 3.1).

The third structural axis of a bracketing framework is represented by product attributes – more precisely by sub-categories of the product attribute 'green'. The demarcation of such product attributes is less 'obvious' than a demarcation of the structural axes 'interviewees' and 'products'. In the end, twenty-nine green product attributes were distinguished on the basis of the findings of the pilot studies, a literature review, and the analysis of the interview data.

Green product attributes can be grouped. Such a grouping of green product attributes is not very important at the data handling stage since the breaking up of the interview data worked at the level of the individual twenty-nine product attributes that were distinguished. But there was a certain structure behind the framework. Basically six groups of green product attributes were distinguished:

- *Product issues:* This group comprised the product attributes 'product ingredients', 'organic', 'seasonal', 'smell', 'taste' and 'home-made'.
- *Packaging issues:* This group comprised two product attributes – 'amount of packaging' and 'packaging material'.
- *Product and packaging issues:* This group covered ten product attributes – 'reusable', 'biodegradable', 'recycled', 'recyclable', 'packaging images', 'names', 'ecolabels', 'colour', 'texture' and 'size'. These product attributes could refer both to the generic product and to a product's packaging. For certain product attributes a clear classification as either a 'product issue' or a 'packaging issue' was difficult. For instance, an interviewee may have referred to the issue 'recycled' for the product toilet paper both with regard to its ingredients – consisting of recycled paper – and with regard to its packaging – e.g. consisting of recycled plastic. Other product attributes that could not be classified unambiguously as either a 'product issue' or a 'packaging issue' were also put into the 'product and packaging group', e.g. product attributes such as 'packaging images', 'names' or 'ecolabels'.
- *LCA issues:* This group comprised five product attributes – 'sourcing', 'production process', 'locally produced/retailed', 'disposal' and 'energy saving'.
- *Communication issues:* This group comprised the five attributes 'word of mouth', 'pressure groups', 'advertising', 'radio, TV, newspapers' and 'literature'.
- *Other issues:* This back-up group covered green product characteristics that did not fall into any of the previously discussed groups.

The bracketing framework provided the structural device for the reduction and ordering of the interview data. It was applied to green product examples and to non-green product examples as they were discussed by an interviewee. All the matrices, charts, protocols, etc. that are subsequently referred to were compiled separately for green and non-green product examples.

In order to facilitate the retrieval of information from the transcribed interviews (through the bracketing framework), certain pieces of information were marked in the interview text: product examples given by an interviewee were underlined; and information that was related by an interviewee to the greenness of a product was highlighted in bold. Information that was related by an interviewee to other ethical issues, such as animal welfare, fair trade issues, etc., was not marked. As indicated earlier, such issues have been excluded here from a discussion of green consumer behaviour. Similarly other issues, e.g. health issues, that were mentioned by an interviewee, were not earmarked. In the case that a piece of information was related both to green issues and to other ethical issues, e.g. it was pointed out that a certain fair traded coffee was also organically produced, or information was related both to green issues and to health issues, e.g. organic vegetables were viewed as 'good for the soil and good for my body', such information was marked and subsequently included in the analysis of data.

The information that was marked in the transcribed interviews was compiled into matrices (Creswell 1994: 153–7). Three types of matrices were derived, reflecting the three axes of the bracketing framework – interviewees, products, and green product attributes:

- 'products–product attributes' matrix, in short the 'PA matrix' (the Glossary has explanations of all the acronyms and variable names used). The PA matrix was compiled for each of the 101 interviewees. The PA matrix lists all products, as discussed by an interviewee, in the order of their occurrence during the interview. For each product discussed, product attributes that were referred to by an interviewee were listed in the PA matrix in the order of their occurrence during the interview.

- 'interviewees–product attributes' matrix, abbreviated as 'IA matrix'. This matrix was created for each of the thirty-nine products or product groups that were distinguished. The IA matrix lists (for a certain product or product group) interviewees in chronological order. For each interviewee, product attributes that were related by an interviewee to a certain product were listed in the IA matrix in the order of their occurrence during the interview.

- 'interviewees–products' matrix, abbreviated as 'IP matrix'. The IP matrix was created for each of the twenty-nine green product attributes that were distinguished by the bracketing framework. The IP matrix lists (for a certain product attribute) interviewees in chronological order. For each interviewee, products that were discussed by an interviewee regarding a certain product attribute were listed in the IP matrix in the order of their occurrence during the interview.

The matrices were created separately for each of the British, the German and the non-green samples, and all the matrices contained the language extracts that were marked in the interview data. Punctuation is important for an efficient collection of marked information into matrices. In the matrices, member categories, e.g. product attributes in the PA matrix, were separated by a semi-colon followed by a space unit. Information that characterized a certain member was attached to that member after a slash ('/'), e.g. language extracts from the interview that related to a certain product attribute. Different pieces of information that related to the same member were separated behind the slash only by a colon but no space unit (for an example, see Table 5.1 in chapter 5).

Analysis of interviewer influence (XYZ code)

For each interview, the interviewer influence was examined. For that purpose, a code called the XYZ code was devised for assessing the extent of interviewer influence that preceded the recall of a product by an interviewee:

- An *X code* was allocated to a product that was *freely recalled* by an interviewee in response to an open question. X coded products refer to products where no interviewer influence was exerted. The X code was further specified: an X1 code marks products that were mentioned by an interviewee as a direct response to an open question, while an X2 code refers to products that were freely recalled during a follow-up discussion of X1 products.
- A *Y code* was allocated to products that were recalled during a follow-up discussion of a product whereby the interviewer *probed* the interviewee. Probing was conducted with regard to a green product attribute that was previously freely recalled by an interviewee. For instance, if an interviewee had freely recalled 'recycled toilet paper', he or she may have been probed along the product attribute 'recycled', e.g. 'Do you buy other recycled products?' Product examples that resulted from such probing were marked with the Y code.
- A *Z code* refers to products that were prompted by the part listings (as discussed above). A Z1 code refers to products that were recalled as a direct result of prompting, while a Z2 code refers to products that were recalled by an interviewee during a follow-up discussion of Z1 products.

In general, X products and Y products could be expected to be found only in part 1 of the interview when the interviewee was asked open questions. Z products were only to be found in parts 2 and 3 of the interview when the interviewee was prompted by part listings of products and product attributes.

The main purpose of the XYZ coding of products was to distinguish freely recalled products (X products) from products where either a little or considerable interviewer influence was exerted (Y products and Z products). The subsequent assessment of knowledge characteristics largely draws only on freely recalled products (X products).

Analysis of actual buying frequencies (HMN code)

Interviews were always conducted with a focus on actual shopping experience: interviewees were asked about their past shopping behaviour. But this could mean rather different things in terms of actual buying frequencies: a certain green product may have been regularly bought; or it may have been only occasionally bought; or there may have been past trial behaviour that was referred to in the interview but that had actually not led to the adoption of a green product. Therefore, products as they were recalled by an interviewee were examined for actual buying frequencies. The purpose of this examination was to find out the extent to which a product which was recalled by an interviewee was actually bought or not bought. The 'actual buying frequencies' reflect the extent to which green products were bought and used in the past. On the basis of these frequency codes, the effects of certain experiences on knowledge structure development could be examined. Three frequency codes (HMN code) were used:

- The *H code* refers to the frequent buying of a certain product. Frequency codes were allocated on the basis of verbal indications an interviewee made regarding how often and regularly a certain product was bought. The high frequency code 'H' was allocated when verbal references were made such as 'always', 'only', 'generally', 'regularly', 'usually', 'frequently', 'often' or 'I buy . . . '.
- When an interviewee made a strong reservation regarding the frequency of buying a certain product, the *M code* was allocated. Verbal indicators here were 'sometimes', 'occasionally', 'I try and buy . . . ', 'I tend to buy . . . ', 'I started buying . . . '.
- The *N code* was allocated to a certain product if it was not bought or had not been bought recently, e.g. an 'N' was given when there had been an unsuccessful trial of a green product in the past. The N code refers to products that were not bought, but known by an interviewee. Verbal indicators here were 'not', 'never', 'I have tried but stopped buying . . . '.

It might have been desirable to discriminate these frequency codes more strongly, but such discriminatory information was difficult to retrieve from the interview data (see also Wright *et al.* 1994: 492–4). The broad classifications and discriminations applied in this study appeared to be sufficient for the purpose in hand of gaining some understanding of how much actual shopping experience existed in relation to a certain product. Subsequently the distribution of X, Y and Z products was adjusted for actual buying frequencies by substituting: $N = 0$, $M = 0.5$, and $H = 1$. Thus, the distributional analysis of the number of X-, Y- and Z-coded products was crudely refined.

An adjustment for actual buying frequencies revealed that there was a difference between the number of green products freely remembered by an interviewee and the number of green products that were regularly bought. An adjustment of the number of freely recalled products for actual buying frequencies yielded the following results (for the 'non-green' sample, a qualification for actual buying frequencies was not possible because of the hypothetical character of the interview procedure):

- For the British sample, the mean number of freely recalled products (X products) dropped because of an adjustment for actual buying from 6.6 to 5.5 (–17%). The median dropped from 6 to 5. The distributional range for freely recalled products changed from [2, 15] to [0.5, 14.5].
- For the German sample, the mean number of freely recalled products (X products) fell from 8.5 to 7.6 (–11%) owing to an adjustment for actual buying frequencies. The median dropped from 8 to 7. The distributional range of freely recalled products changed from [4, 16] to [1.5, 14].

A similar picture emerged for the total number of products when they were adjusted for actual buying frequencies.

The positional relation between the parameters mean and median changed as a result of an adjustment for actual buying frequencies. This was particularly clear for the German sample where, after adjusting for actual buying frequencies, the median was higher than the mean (total number of products); for unadjusted product frequencies the reverse had been the case. This seemed to indicate that distributions 'lost' more at their bottom ends than at their top ends because of the adjustment for actual buying frequencies. The same was basically indicated by the way minima and maxima of distributions changed because of the adjustments. An examination of quartiles of the respective distributions was conducted to clarify whether actual buying frequencies were proportionally higher at the top end of the distribution than at its lower end. If this were the case, it would mean that those interviewees who knew many green products also actually bought them with a relatively higher frequency than interviewees who knew fewer green products and who bought these fewer examples relatively less frequently. Such a relatively higher actual buying frequency of interviewees at the top end of the distribution could be interpreted as a kind of higher 'behavioural consistency' and would have implications for a later assessment of experience effects, in particular in relation to familiarity effects.

For clarification, the distribution of freely recalled products (and also the distribution of the total number of products) was divided into quartiles. Quartile means were calculated for the unadjusted distributions and for the distributions that had been adjusted for actual buying frequencies: for each quartile, the mean number of products discussed and the mean number of products actually bought was calculated. The relative drop of a quartile's mean that was caused by an adjustment for actual buying frequencies was calculated in this way (see Appendix 3.4). The relative drop caused by the adjustment was from the first (bottom) quartile through to the fourth (top) quartile:

- for the British sample: –33%, –20%, –13%, –11%
- for the German sample: –24%, –12%, –8%, –7%

For both samples a similar trend emerged. Apparently, interviewees at the bottom end of the distribution – those who remembered only a few green product examples – actually bought these few products relatively less frequently than the interviewees at the top end of the distribution who had recalled many green products and who had actually bought these many products with proportionally higher frequencies.[9] This trend basically held up for the distribution of the total number of products, although it was watered down to a small extent.

Analysis of order of occurrence of freely recalled products (PPO analysis)

Information about products and product attributes was retrieved into matrices in their *actual order of occurrence* during the interview. For products, the order of their occurrence during the interview was further analysed through what is known as *products' position of occurrence analysis* (PPO analysis). The PPO analysis played an important role when certain structural features of knowledge were interpreted. An analysis of the sequential order of recall reflects what knowledge was most easily accessible to a person, thus hinting at certain cognitive features, such as knowledge integration, and schematic, prototypical knowledge characteristics.

The PPO analysis could only be conducted for freely recalled products (the so-called X products) where the order of recall was solely determined by the interviewee. Three PPO parameters were calculated: median, mean and mode. Of these, mode and median can be considered to be particularly indicative of typical PPOs, whereas the parameter mean is particularly sensitive to PPO outliers. On the basis of these PPO parameters, product rankings were compiled (see Table 3.3).

For the British sample, the best PPO parameters had detergent, washing-up liquid, and vegetables + fruit. Detergent had the lowest – the 'best' – PPO parameters: it had a median of 2, a mean of 2.4 and a mode of 1. Regarding its mode, 42 per cent of those who recalled detergent recalled it as the first product in the sequence of freely recalled products. Washing-up liquid and vegetables + fruit followed in ranks 2 and 3. Washing-up liquid had a PPO median of 2, the same as detergent, a mean PPO of 3.5 and a mode of 2. Very similar values could be observed for vegetables + fruit: they had a PPO median of 3, a mean of 3.2 and a mode of 1. For the German sample, milk, bread, and vegetables + fruit had the best PPO parameters. Milk had the lowest PPO median, mean and mode; its PPO median was 2, its mean 2.8 and its mode 1. Again, for the mode, it could be found that a very high proportion, 48 per cent, of those who had discussed milk as an X product recalled it as first product. In the PPO rankings, milk was followed by bread, vegetables + fruit, yoghurt and drinks.

For the British sample, washing + cleaning products had the best PPO parameters: three washing + cleaning products were in the top four, and there were only five food products in the top eleven PPO ranks. This contrasted with the

Table 3.3 Products' position of occurrence (PPO)[1]

British sample

freely recalled products (X product)	r[x][2]	PPO parameters				PPO-mode[3]	
		PPO-median	Rank	PPO-mean	Rank		
detergent	0.91	2	1	2.4	1	1	0.42
wash. up liq.	0.60	2	1	3.5	3	2	0.30
veg. & fruit	0.76	3	3	3.2	2	1	0.29
cleaners	0.51	3	3	4.2	4	3	0.36
toilet paper	0.60	5	7	4.9	7	5	0.30
bread	0.27	4	6	4.1	5		
pulses, grains	0.18	3.5	5	4.5	6		
meat	0.25	5.5	8	5.4	8		
drinks	0.20	5.5	8	7.4	10		
cosmetics	0.16	7	10	6.2	9		
shampoo	0.20	9	11	7.6	11		

Left-margin group labels (British): rows 1–5: r[x] ≥ 0.50; rows 6–9: 0.15 ≤ r[x] ≤ 0.50; rows 10–11: 0.50 > r[x]

German sample

freely recalled products (X product)	r[x][2]	PPO parameters				PPO-mode[3]	
		PPO-median	Rank	PPO-mean	Rank		
milk	0.86	2	1	2.8	1	1	0.48
bread	0.61	3	2	4.3	3	3	0.32
veg. & fruit	0.92	4	3	3.5	2	4	0.33
						1	0.16[4]
meat	0.53	4	3	5.4	5	4	0.16
yoghurt	0.58	4	3	5.7	7	2	0.19
						2	0.21[4]
drinks	0.53	5	7	5.4	5	5	0.21
detergent	0.61	6	9	5.7	7	6	0.27
cleaners	0.67	6	9	6.0	9	7	0.29
cheese	0.28	4	3	4.5	4		
cream	0.28	5.5	8	6.3	10		
cosmetics	0.22	6	9	7.0	11		
wash.up liq.	0.19	8	12	8.1	12		
shampoo	0.19	8	12	8.4	13		
dairy etc.	0.22	9	14	9.0	15		
butter	0.22	10	15	8.9	14		

Left-margin group labels (German): rows 1–9: r[x] ≥ 0.50; rows 10–16: 0.15 = r[x] ≤ 0.50; 0.50 > r[x]

Notes:
1 PPO = products' position of occurrence in the (recall) sequence of freely recalled products
2 r[x] = relative frequency with which a certain product showed up in the British or German sample
3 = relative frequency of mode as share of r[x]
4 = multiple modes

German samples. Here, dairy products were prominently represented in the top PPO rankings: three dairy products were in the top six, and six in the top fifteen; in a top ten list of products, there were only two washing + cleaning products (detergent and cleaners) and their PPO ranks placed them at the end of the ranking. Good examples of green products were not the same for British and German consumers. While washing + cleaning products featured prominently for the British sample, dairy products ranked generally high in terms of PPOs for the German sample.

Product class-related patterns in the sequence of recall allowed for certain conclusions regarding knowledge integration and knowledge prototypicality (see chapter 5). The calculated PPO parameters provided a yardstick for assessing the extent of knowledge of good examples. Through the PPO analysis, it also became apparent that the relative frequency of a product (for the total sample) was strongly related to a product's PPO parameters: the higher a product's relative frequency was, the 'better' its PPO parameters tended to be. This suggests that a product's relative frequency, as calculated for a sample, could be used – as a matter of convenience – as a proxy variable in a PPO analysis.

Analysis drawing on the consumer interview index (CI analysis)

Besides marking interview data in bold or by underlining (see above), a marking index was used to examine the interview data. The *consumer interview index* (CI index) covered a variety of topics: 'knowledge characteristics', 'task considerations', 'buying frequency', 'errors', 'other product quality considerations' and 'non-cognitive issues' (see Appendix 3.5). Acronyms referring to the various topics were placed in black, blue or red ink on either the left-hand or the right-hand side of the transcribed interview text. Subsequently, these markings and a brief description of what they referred to were collected for each interviewee into a summary chart.

The following findings were made through the CI analysis:

- Certain knowledge characteristics were checked through the CI analysis. For the British and the German samples, issues like product group or product class references ('group'-variable), a knowledge of terminology ('tec'-variable) and dimensionally framed knowledge ('dim'-variable) were similarly frequent. Regarding episodic knowledge ('epi'-variable) and argumentative knowledge ('arg'-variable), the figures for the German sample were about 50 per cent higher than those of the British sample. For the non-green sample, only for the issue of argumentative knowledge some CI markings were found.

- Task considerations featured prominently in the CI markings of the interview data. For each sample, they accounted for about one-quarter of all CI markings. For the British and the German samples, task considerations were distributed quite similarly: availability of choice ('choice'-variable) was the most prominent issue. Trust issues, as covered by the variables 'credibility' ('trust'-variable) and 'distrust/naivety' ('cyn'-variable) also scored prominently for both samples, accounting together for more than 20 per cent of all task considerations. For the issues task difficulty ('diff'-variable) and availability of time ('time'-variable), some differences could be observed between the German and the British samples. For task difficulty, the British sample had nearly twice as many markings as the German sample, while for the issue availability of time the German sample had about 50 per cent more markings than the British one. For the non-green sample, task difficulty ('diff'-variable) and trust ('trust'-variable and 'cyn'-variable) accounted for about 40 per cent of all task considerations, which is about twice as high as for the green samples.

- In general, not many errors ('err'-variable) were found since only 'obvious' errors were marked, such as product property errors, errors relating to the availability of goods, or errors reflecting an incomplete or wrong recall of names. Errors were found to a similar degree in both green samples. Issues relating to LCA considerations were excluded from an assessment of errors.

- Under the heading of 'buying frequency', issues like the trial of green products, consumption reduction issues, or experience references were examined. For both the German and the British samples, issues related to buying frequencies accounted for about 10 per cent of all CI issues. Trial buying behaviour ('trial'-variable) was found to a very similar extent in both samples. Consumption reduction issues ('red'-variable) were about 50 per cent higher in the German sample while experience or habit references ('exp'-variable) were about a third higher for the British sample. For the non-green sample, buying frequency issues accounted for only about 5 per cent of all task considerations; of the issues discussed, unsuccessful trial buying was the most frequent one. This contrasted with the green samples, where trial buying references were the least prominent among buying frequency references.

- Product characteristics other than 'greenness' were excluded from the research focus of this study. However, as a by-product of the open, semi-structured approach to interviewing, interviewees touched now and then upon product features other than the greenness of a product. On a *post hoc* basis, such issues were analysed by means of the CI analysis. The product characteristic 'price' ('price'-variable) was the most frequently mentioned one for the British and the German samples. For the British sample it accounted for a third of the 'other quality considerations', and for the German sample it was even more prominent both in absolute and in proportional terms, accounting here for nearly 50 per cent of all 'other quality considerations'. Performance issues ('perf'-variable) were considered to a similarly high degree by the British and the German samples. Health issues ('health'-variable) were also prominent in both samples; here the German sample had about a 50 per cent higher score than the British one. For the non-green sample, health issues and performance issues were the most frequent ones.

A major difference between the British and the German samples related to ethical considerations ('eth'-variable), such as fair trade or animal rights issues. They were the second most prominent issue for the British sample, accounting for about a third of all 'other quality considerations'. For the German sample, ethical considerations made up less than 10 per cent of the 'other quality considerations'. The contrast became even stronger if political considerations ('pol'-variable) were included which are close to ethical considerations, e.g. issues of ownership.

- Non-cognitive issues, as covered by the CI index, related to affective ('aff'-variable), motivational ('mot'-variable) and life-style issues ('cul'-variable). They accounted for about 10 per cent of all CI markings for the British and the German samples. Affective issues accounted for about half of the non-cognitive CI markings for both samples. Regarding motivational and life-style issues, some differences between the British and German samples were observed. Motivational and life-style issues accounted each for about a quarter of non-cognitive issues discussed by the German sample. For the British sample, motivational issues made up 6 per cent of the non-cognitive issues, while more than 50 per cent were accounted for by life-style issues. The prominence of vegetarianism in the British sample is reflected by this high score for the life-style variable. For the non-green sample, the absolute number of non-cognitive CI markings was much lower than those for the British and the German sample. Affective issues were least frequent, accounting for about 10 per cent of non-cognitive issues; about equally prominent were motivational issues and cultural issues.

Through the CI analysis, additional information on an interviewee's knowledge was derived that had eluded the matrices that were discussed above. Also, certain issues relating to experience effects and task constraints were covered by the CI analysis. Results from the CI analysis were drawn upon for a number of supplementary assessments of knowledge structures. For each sample, a CI matrix was compiled that contained information on the CI markings of each interviewee.

Measurement of knowledge content

The study achieved, to a certain extent, a quantitative measurement of knowledge content characteristics. In the following, how the measurement of knowledge comprehensiveness, complexity, and abstractness was operationalized, and why and how a further knowledge characteristic – knowledge specificity – was distinguished, will be discussed.

Measurement of knowledge comprehensiveness

Knowledge comprehensiveness relates to the amount of knowledge a consumer had about environmentally oriented shopping. A quantification of knowledge comprehensiveness was achieved. Some ideas from content analysis, which is a technique for the numerical analysis of written documents, were applied (Holsti 1968: 597, 600–4, 647). The main measure for knowledge comprehensiveness was word counts.

Words were counted for interview extracts of green product-related knowledge as they had been retrieved into the PA matrix (product–product attributes matrix). The counting rule specified that only nouns, verbs, adjectives and adverbs were counted but not articles, conjunctions and negatives. Names consisting of more than one word, e.g. 'Neal's Yard', were counted as one word unit. The counting procedure was independently applied to both the PA matrix and the IA matrix (interviewees–product attributes matrix). Through comparisons of the respective counting results, a consistent application of the counting rule was controlled for. The word counts were summarized in a one-page condensed version of the PA matrix (for an example, see Appendix 3.6). Similarly, a condensed version of the IA matrix was developed.

Other word count measures for knowledge comprehensiveness drew on the actual interview data: the entire interview or parts thereof. These word counts were conducted with the counting facilities provided by word processing software. As a matter of convenience, the interviewer's speech during the interview was not eliminated from these counts. This has a slight and undesirable levelling effect on these word count measures which has to be kept in mind when they are interpreted.

For interview extracts, as contained in the PA matrix, the word count variables W1 and W2, and with regard to the actual interview data, the variables W3 and W4 were introduced (see Appendix 3.7).

There are certain differences in the syntactic pattern of word formation between the English and the German languages. Such differences exert a disturbing influence when word counts for the German sample are compared with those for the British sample. The German language has a certain tendency to combine words into single new words, whereas in English such a tendency is less prevalent. For instance, the German language equivalents of the English expressions 'environmentally friendly', 'glass bottle' and 'packaging material' are 'umweltfreundlich', 'Glasflasche' and 'Verpackungsmaterial'. For that reason, word counts for the German interviewees cannot be directly compared with those of the British green and non-green interviewees. Some adjustment for this syntactic language difference has to be made. An adjustment factor is not easy to quantify. In order to gain a rough estimate for an adjustment factor, 10,000 words of English and German actual interview data were edited: the edited text comprised interviews of varied length, long ones, short ones and ones of medium length in order to achieve a certain spread. The edited text comprised only the speech of interviewees. Text was edited in a continuous fashion, i.e. there were no paragraphs, and text was edited in the same format (same font, same page size, etc.).

The British text edition of 10,000 words stretched over 548 lines comprising 43,306 characters; the German text of 10,000 words made up 634 lines or 50,140 characters. This yielded an adjustment factor of 1.16, which represents a cautious estimate – a lower bound – for an adjustment factor. If one argued that articles, conjunctions, etc. only present some kind of 'noise' for the measurement of knowledge comprehensiveness, a more discriminatory adjustment factor could be developed by editing only nouns, adjectives, etc. On the basis of caution and convenience, the 1.16 adjustment factor was applied to adjust word counts of the German sample.

Results of the word count analysis for the variables W1, W2, W3 and W4 are reported in the appendices (see Appendices 3.7 and 3.8).

Measurement of knowledge complexity

Knowledge complexity refers (a) to the number of knowledge content features – here 'products' and 'green product attributes' – and (b) to how extensively knowledge content features were interrelated horizontally and vertically.

Horizontal complexity refers to interrelations of knowledge at the product level. The main measure for horizontal complexity drew on the number of green product attributes, as found in the PA matrix: first, the number of green product attributes per product was squared, and then these square numbers were summed over all products of the PA matrix (see Appendix 3.6). A compounded quantitative indicator of horizontal complexity was thus derived from the PA matrix. The number of product attributes per product was squared before they were summed in order to isolate horizontal complexity from vertical complexity.

Vertical complexity refers to interrelations of knowledge at the product attribute level. As the main indicator of vertical complexity, the number of products per green product attribute was drawn upon. An aggregate quantitative measure of vertical complexity was derived by squaring the total number of products per product attribute before summing them.

For measuring horizontal complexity, the variables C1 and C2 were introduced, as were the variables C3, C4 and C5 for the measurement of vertical complexity (see Appendices 3.7 and 3.9).

Besides quantitative indicators of knowledge complexity, further non-quantitative ones were derived through the CI analysis (see above).

Measurement of knowledge abstractness and knowledge specificity

An assessment of knowledge abstractness and knowledge specificity draws on the interpretation of language. It refers to the substance of knowledge that is held by a person. A couple of indicators of knowledge abstractness are referred to in the literature:

- *Indicator A:* It has been suggested that highly abstract knowledge is indicated by a knowledge of technical terminology (Brucks 1986: 58–9, Selnes and Gronhaug 1986: 68).
- *Indicator B:* It has been suggested that highly abstract knowledge is indicated by non-literal, semantic, hypothetical knowledge rather than by literal, episodic, concrete knowledge (Solso 1988: 140–1, Johnson and Fornell 1987: 214, Smith and Houston 1986: 506, Tulving 1972: 385–6).

However, these abstractness indicators produce, to some extent, contradictory results. An example illustrates the problem. One might try to rank the following features in terms of their abstractness. The features relate to the product attribute 'amount of packaging' and they were taken from the actual interview data:

- 'no extra packaging'
- 'no foil'
- 'reduced packaging to absolute minimum'
- 'no outer plastic coating'

With regard to knowledge concreteness (indicator B), 'no extra packaging' is more abstract than 'no foil' and 'no outer plastic coating', the last ones being more concrete. On the other hand, 'no outer plastic coating' is a highly technical description (indicator A), and hence may be classified as rather abstract. Comparing the examples 'no extra packaging', 'reduced packaging to absolute minimum' and 'no outer plastic coating', it is likely that 'no extra packaging' counts as less abstract than 'reduced packaging to absolute minimum' in terms of technicality but where should 'no outer plastic coating' be placed in that sequence? On the one hand, it might be argued that 'no outer plastic coating' is similarly or even more technical (indicator A) than 'reduced packaging to absolute minimum', but on the other hand, it appears to be more concrete (indicator B) than 'no extra packaging'.

Similarly contradictory results can be found regarding the product attribute 'product ingredients', e.g. the terms 'natural based', 'vegetable based' and 'no hydrogen chloride'; or for the product attribute 'production process', e.g. the terms 'less processed', 'non-use of bleaches in the process' and 'production twists world trade and ecology'.

The ranking problem appears to be caused by the implicit subsuming of two different knowledge characteristics into the idea of knowledge abstractness. To resolve this problem, knowledge concreteness – or *knowledge specificity* – was separated out from knowledge abstractness as an additional knowledge content characteristic. A high degree of knowledge specificity is indicated by highly concrete, literal knowledge (indicator B). Likewise, a high degree of knowledge abstractness is indicated by highly technical knowledge (indicator A). For instance, episodic knowledge would count as weakly abstract but highly specific. Based on this distinction, knowledge substance was classified in a two-dimensional way.

With a 2×2 matrix, which distinguished low and high degrees of abstractness and low and high specificity, the above examples can be re-examined:

- 'no extra packaging' would be classified as both weakly abstract and weakly specific,
- 'no foil' as weakly abstract but highly specific,
- 'reduced packaging to absolute minimum' as highly abstract but weakly specific,
- and 'no outer plastic coating' as both highly abstract and highly specific.

In order to assess the abstractness and the specificity of the interview data, first, for each of the twenty-nine green product attributes distinguished in the bracketing framework, a 2×2 abstractness/specificity matrix was developed. Typical language examples were classified by examining the IP matrices (for examples, see Appendix 3.10). It became apparent that certain product attributes did not cover all fields of a 2×2 matrix. For instance, for the product attribute 'names', there were no examples that were highly abstract and weakly specific. This was not unexpected considering the nature of this product attribute covering names.

The 2×2 abstractness/specificity matrices provided the basis for assessing the type of language used by an interviewee. A *binary four-digit code* was used to collect the abstractness/specificity assessments into a condensed, one-page numerical format of the PA matrix: the first digit, '1000', was allocated to low abstractness and low specificity, the second, '0100', to low abstractness and high specificity, the third, '0010', to high abstractness and low specificity, and the fourth, '0001', to high abstractness and high specificity. On the basis of these binary codes, the language extracts that were contained in the PA matrix (and also those contained in the IA matrix) were classified. Multiple scoring was allowed; for instance, a '0101' code indicates that a certain product description given by an interviewee contained both weakly abstract and highly specific knowledge substance and also a highly abstract and highly specific one. For example, the product toilet paper may have been described by an interviewee, with regard to its ingredients, as 'consisting of old newspapers and being non-chlorine bleached': the first description, 'old newspapers', would count as weakly abstract and highly specific (0100) while the second, 'non-chlorine bleached', would count as highly abstract and highly specific (0001). Hence, this would yield for the product attribute 'ingredients' of the product 'toilet paper' an abstractness–specificity score of '0101' (see appendix 3.11).

An aggregate measure takes the form of a series of four numbers, reflecting the four-digit code, and indicating how abstract and how specific a consumer's green product knowledge was.

The variables AS1, AS2, AS3, AS4, AS5, AS6, AS7 and AS8 were introduced to deal with the measurement of knowledge abstractness and knowledge specificity (see Appendixes 3.7 and 3.12).

Supplementary measures for the assessment of knowledge abstractness and knowledge specificity were arrived at by drawing on the actual interview data. The CI index contained search categories that were important for an assessment of the knowledge of terminology and the extent of episodic knowledge (see CI analysis above).

Interpretation of patterns of knowledge structures

An interpretation of knowledge structures was not in this study geared towards the testing of hypotheses. Rather, on the basis of the cognitive framework outlined in chapter 2, the thinking patterns of green consumers were explored. Both for cognitive psychology and for consumer behaviour research it has been pointed out that the challenge will be to shift from quantitative research that aims at testing hypotheses for their own sake to a qualitative use of hypotheses for exploring reality and theory building. This study followed a qualitatively oriented approach to data interpretation, which was supported ('triangulated') by the partly achieved quantification of knowledge content characteristics. Qualitative research was 'triangulated' in the following way:

- Certain aspects of knowledge content characteristics were quantitatively measured as outlined above.
- The development of cognitive categories of green consumers was approached through cluster analysis. As a result of cluster analysis, cognitive categories of green consumers were distinguished and paradigmatic subjects of green consumers were retrieved from the samples. Cluster analysis is one of the few statistical tools that can be utilized in qualitative research. Questions relating to the conducting of a cluster analysis and what results it produced are discussed in the next chapter.
- The cluster analysis was supported by the analysis of scattergrams and by a correlational analysis of knowledge content variables (see also the next chapter).

The cognitive categories and the paradigmatic subjects of consumers that were demarcated and retrieved as a result of the cluster analysis were subsequently interpreted regarding their knowledge structures. Chapter 5 approached the interpretation of cognition from a psychological perspective: knowledge content characteristics, cognitive operations and schematic knowledge features are examined there. As indicated, the examination of knowledge content could be conducted, to a considerable extent, on a quantitative basis. In contrast, cognitive operations and schemata had to be inferred from findings on knowledge content.

In chapter 6 experience effects on knowledge structure development and the problem solving skills of green consumers are explored from a cognitive anthropological perspective. Ability is investigated through a bricolage-type concept of ability (see chapter 2). As scientists found in the field of LCA assessments, questions related to what constitutes factually correct green behaviour are difficult to answer (see chapter 1). In this study, little attempt was made to assess or measure the factual correctness of knowledge content. The concepts of practical thinking and bricolage were applied to assess how successful consumers were in solving their green shopping problems.

Berry and Irvine (1986: 303) refer to the challenge to measure bricolage-type ability: in this study, the quality of practical thinking was interpreted on a comparative basis; consumers of different cognitive categories were compared in terms of how they had solved the green shopping problem, e.g. how creative, inventive or flexible they had been in collecting green information. How far the problem solving behaviour of the green consumer complied with the logic of an LCA could subsequently be assessed in this way.

It could be claimed that qualitative interpretations are largely or solely exploratory (Spiggle and Sanders 1984: 338, Punj and Stewart 1983: 143, 146). However, qualitative data interpretation can also be conducted on an explanatory basis: the explanation of consumer cognition can be based on *analytic induction* (Frankfort-Nachmias and Nachmias 1996: 294–6, Stoecker 1991: 102–5, Yin 1989: 106–7, 113–15, Crano 1981: 326–8, Kidder 1981b: 227–9, 241, Glaser and Strauss 1967). Such explanation building in qualitative research draws on *replication logic*, an iterative process of pattern matching across subjects. In general, gross matches rather than highly subtle matches are to be aimed for. Internal validity of explanations can be achieved through the observation of recurring regularities (Stoecker 1991: 94, Patton 1990: 60, 403, Bryce 1985: 82).

Replication and internal validity can be claimed if a number of subjects exhibit characteristics that support the same proposition. For subjects who show highly similar patterns of knowledge structures, *literal replication* can be claimed. For subjects who show differences in knowledge structures, claims to *theoretical replication* can be made if differences can be conceptually explained (Patton 1990: 169, Yin 1989: 43–4, 53–5, 109–13, Kidder 1981b: 248, Glaser and Strauss 1967: 55–6; also Cook and Campbell 1979: 118–19).

Through the application of a replication logic, empirical data were analysed on a comparative basis, and an attempt was made to control certain methodological problems related to the internal validity of qualitative research by this method (Coolican 1990: 237, Patton 1990: 462, Eisenhardt 1989a: 542, Yin 1989: 109–11, Kidder 1981b: 248–9, Glaser and Strauss 1967).

CONCLUSIONS

In this chapter, methodological issues that related to empirical research on green consumer cognition were outlined.

A real-life setting was considered mandatory for research into green consumer cognition. Such an approach should give this study an external validity advantage in comparison to laboratory research. As indicated earlier, real-life research into cognition in general, and into consumer cognition in particular, has been called for. Also, for schema research, a qualitative approach has been recommended.

'Theoretical sampling' was conducted. Its aim was to achieve a wide variation in levels of green consumption experience across a sample of green consumers. A non-green sample of consumers was used to complement variation sampling at its lower end. Statistical representativeness (or randomness) did not play a role in this study. The analysis of self-rating scores, together with the analyses of distributions and distribution functions of knowledge content variables, indicated that theoretical sampling had achieved its aim of yielding samples of a diverse composition.

Certain steps were undertaken to assure and increase precision: interviews were product-oriented and conducted on a free recall basis, thus restraining inferences in recall; a German sample of green consumers was involved in order to have a group for comparison, which is important for substantiating replication claims (and which also contributed to increased external validity); and certain quantitative techniques ('triangulation') were applied.

Early data analysis (as presented in this chapter) indicated behavioural differences *within* the green samples: when the number of recalled products was compared with actual buying frequencies, it appeared that interviewees who knew more green products also actually bought the many products they recalled to a proportionally higher degree than interviewees at the bottom end of the distribution who knew fewer green products and who actually bought these fewer products proportionally less frequently. An examination of quartiles of the respective distributions supported such a view.

An analysis of the sequential order of freely recalled products (PPO analysis) revealed a certain structure to the order of recall. From the PPO analysis it emerged that products were not recalled randomly. Certain products appeared to be particularly good examples of green products. For the British sample, washing + cleaning products featured prominently in terms of their PPO parameters, as did dairy products for the German sample. These findings are of interest to an assessment of knowledge integration and schematic, prototypical knowledge features.

For most of the knowledge content variables discussed above, the German sample 'outscored' the British one. However, this does not allow for conclusions regarding the British and German populations as a whole. Similarly, no statistical link can be suggested between certain socio-demographic observances and knowledge structure variables. As outlined, sampling did not aim to be statistically representative. The aim of variation sampling was to cover different levels of green experience sufficiently to identify different patterns of cognition, but *not* to find out how frequently such different patterns occurred in a certain population. Differences in distributional parameters between the British and German samples can only be interpreted as an indication that the two samples contained interviewees with different knowledge structure characteristics in apparently different shares. There was apparently a different over- or under-representation of certain green experience levels in the British and the German samples.

The discussion in this chapter went into some detail regarding the methods applied for data collection and data analysis, but not every detail could be specified. Methodological details are further elaborated on alongside the analyses of data as they are presented in the following chapters. The next chapter outlines the procedure and the results of a cluster analysis that grouped interviewees on the basis of knowledge content characteristics (and the knowledge content variables as they were introduced in this chapter). In the subsequent chapters 5 and 6, green consumers' thinking patterns are interpreted through the cognitive framework developed in chapter 2.

4

CLASSIFICATION OF CONSUMERS

CLASSIFICATION AND CLUSTER ANALYSIS

Classification – pattern finding and pattern matching – is at the heart of all human knowledge, philosophical, scientific, or commonsense knowledge (Everitt 1993: 1, Kaufman and Rousseeuw 1990: 1, Spiggle and Sanders 1984: 337; also Lévi-Strauss 1966: chapter 2). Cluster analysis is a quantitative classification technique used for descriptive and explorative purposes. It is known as an *interdependence* method, where no variables are singled out as dependent or independent variables. As a result of a cluster analysis, a total sample of subjects is divided into groups or *clusters* of subjects. A cluster can be defined as 'a continuous region of a p-dimensional space (with p being the number of variables included) containing a relatively high density of points, separated from other such regions by regions containing a relatively low density of points' (Everitt 1974: 44).

A cluster analysis is not the application of one single technique; rather it is a series of steps through which a structure that is inherent in empirical data can be systematically uncovered (Arabie and Hubert 1996: 8, Gordon 1996: 65, Mitchell 1993: 12, Everitt 1993: 10, 141, 149, Kaufman and Rousseeuw 1990: 37, Hair *et al.* 1987: 6–7, Punj and Stewart 1983: 134–6). Cluster analysis is one of the few statistical tools that can be applied in qualitative research (Everitt 1993: preface, McClintock *et al.* 1979: 623).

In this study, consumers were grouped or *clustered* into what are termed 'cognitive categories' on the basis of knowledge content variables. The software package SPSS for Windows, release 6.1, was used. The cognitive categories reflect the fact that people think differently about green consumption. Paradigmatic subjects of green consumers were selected from the cognitive categories. The paradigmatic subjects and the cognitive categories were subsequently focused on when the knowledge structures and the choice behaviour of green consumers were interpreted.

Problems in cluster analysis

There are a number of critically debated questions in cluster analysis:

1 Which cluster algorithm should be applied?
Hierarchical and non-hierarchical cluster methods are available. A *hierarchical* cluster algorithm constructs a tree-like hierarchy through which subjects are allocated to different branches or 'clusters'. A disadvantage of hierarchical cluster methods is that subjects who have once been joined in a cluster cannot be separated again at a later stage, which means that 'errors' at an early stage cannot be corrected later (Everitt 1993: 55–6, Kaufman and Rousseeuw 1990: 44–5, Hair *et al.* 1987: 293–4).[1]

A *non-hierarchical* cluster algorithm allocates subjects to a pre-determined number of clusters through an iterative process. Through initial starting points, which can be randomly or non-randomly selected, subjects are allocated and reallocated to clusters. The number of clusters has to be determined in advance. With each step of the clustering process, new cluster centres are calculated and reallocations of subjects between clusters take place. This process of reallocating subjects between clusters stops when the difference between a previously and presently calculated cluster centre becomes minimal, e.g. it falls below the arbitrarily chosen margin 0.000001 (Hair *et al.* 1987: 294, Punj and Stewart 1983: 13).

Of the hierarchical cluster methods, the group average method and Ward's method (minimum variance method) have been generally found to yield good results, as has the K-means method (also a minimum variance method) for non-hierarchical clustering (see literature as quoted above).

2 Which and how many variables should be used for generating a cluster solution?
A critical issue in cluster analysis, as in multivariate data analysis in general, is the choice of variables. There are no statistical guidelines for resolving this issue. Rather, conceptual and methodological reasons are referred to for selecting variable sets (Everitt 1993: 37, Spiggle and Sanders 1984: 338, Punj and Stewart 1983: 134, 143, 146, Everitt 1974: 48).

3 How should the number of clusters be determined?
Cluster algorithms divide a sample into groups of subjects, but they do not determine the number of clusters. The theoretical criterion for the best number of clusters is the 'maximum internal cohesion' of each cluster and 'maximum external isolation' among clusters. Ideally, clusters of subjects should be separated from each other by 'empty space'. Rules of thumb have been suggested for deciding the number of clusters, but the task remains an interpretative one (Everitt 1993: 6, 55, 73–4, 89; also Mitchell 1993: 14, Kaufman and Rousseeuw 1990: 1, 38, Hair *et al.* 1987: 293–5, 306, Punj and Stewart 1983: 134–7): in the case of a non-hierarchical cluster analysis, the number of clusters has to be decided by the researcher in advance. In the case of a hierarchical cluster analysis, it has to be decided what constitutes a significant distance – enough

'empty space' – between clusters as they are generated during the partitioning process. The partitioning process starts with the total sample (one cluster), and it comes to a conclusion at the level of individual subjects (each subject is then considered a 'cluster'). Between these two extremes, subjects are grouped together in different combinations.

4 How significant are clusters generated by a cluster algorithm?
An important issue is whether a cluster algorithm has discovered a 'real' structure in the data or whether the algorithm merely imposed an artificial structure on the data. Any cluster algorithm will produce a cluster solution. The question is whether the structure uncovered relates to distinctive groups that exist in the data (Everitt 1993: 69, 88, 141; also Arabie and Hubert 1996: 17, Mitchell 1993: 15, Kaufman and Rousseeuw 1990: 39).

Recommendations for conducting a cluster analysis

Some advice can be given regarding the questions raised. In general, a visual start-up of cluster analysis is recommended, for instance through the pairwise plotting of variables in *scattergrams*. Scattergrams can hint at structural patterns in the data, whether there are clusters at all, and if so, how many clusters show up and for which variables (Everitt 1993: 6, 11–12, 141, Kaufman and Rousseeuw 1990: 4).[2] Like an examination of scattergrams, a correlation analysis can also check for potential relationships between variables. This should help to select variables and decide the number of clusters.

Regarding how many clusters should be distinguished, rules of thumb and graphic tools, such as dendrograms in the case of hierarchical methods, can be drawn upon (in addition to the analysis of scattergrams). A *dendrogram* is a diagram, organized in a tree-like structure, that reflects how the partitioning process in hierarchical clustering branched out; it contains numerical information on the distance between clusters. A dendrogram represents a numerically 'valued tree' (Gordon 1996: 67–8, Everitt 1993: 73–4, 89, 143, Mitchell 1993: 14, Kaufman and Rousseeuw 1990: 38).

For theoretical and methodological reasons, the use of different variable sets is recommended, to conduct a sensitivity analysis and test the robustness of a cluster solution. This advice relates especially to the choice of variables and to the examination of the significance of a cluster solution. A good cluster solution should be insensitive to the deletion or the addition of one or two cluster variables, and it should be sensitive to fuzzy variable sets. In this study nine variable sets, as discussed below, were subjected to a cluster analysis.

A sensitivity analysis can be extended by subjecting the sample data to different cluster algorithms (Everitt 1993: 141–2, Kaufman and Rousseeuw 1990: 37, Punj and Stewart 1983: 134, 145). This study applied two hierarchical cluster methods (the group average algorithm and Ward's method) and one non-hierarchical cluster algorithm (the K-means method) to the sample data.

Also, through the manipulation of sample data, e.g. the random division of sample data into two halves, the robustness of an original cluster solution can be checked (Everitt 1993: 143, Mitchell 1993: 15). Different data set manipulations were carried out for that purpose: first, the British and the German sample data were halved; second, the British and German sample data were combined into one data set; and third, the non-green data were integrated with the already combined data set of the British and German samples. Each of these 'new' data sets was then subjected to a cluster analysis.

In the following section, the scattergrams and correlations are first discussed. Such an examination has implications both for the generation of variable sets and for the decision on the number of clusters. A hierarchical cluster analysis is conducted for the British, the German and the non-green samples, whereby the group-average method and Ward's method are applied. Subsequently, sensitivity analyses of cluster solutions are conducted by subjecting data to the non-hierarchical K-means method and by manipulating the sample data. In a final step, 'cognitive categories' of green consumers are demarcated and 'paradigmatic subjects' of green consumers chosen from the sample data.

ANALYSES OF SCATTERGRAMS AND CORRELATION MATRICES

It is generally recommended that a cluster analysis should be started with an analysis of scattergrams and a correlational analysis. A scattergram is a two-dimensional plot of a pair of variables. On the basis of observed relationships between variables, scattergrams and correlation matrices hint at which variables are well suited for a cluster analysis. In addition, an analysis of scattergrams can provide suggestions on the best number of clusters.

Analysis of scattergrams

A scattergram itself can be interpreted as a visual cluster analysis for a pair of variables. Through inspection, suggestions can be made regarding relationships between pairs of variables and regarding the number of clusters visible from a scattergram. Scattergrams were compiled for the knowledge content variables that were distinguished earlier (see Appendix 3.7). They related to knowledge comprehensiveness, knowledge complexity, knowledge specificity and knowledge abstractness. Variable pairs were plotted separately for variables that related to freely recalled products (the X products), and for variables that related to the total number of products discussed by an interviewee. Also, plots were separately generated for the British, the German and the non-green samples (for examples, see Appendix 4.1).

In general, when scattergrams were compiled for variables other than X variables, results tended to become less indicative of clusters, and data became more evenly spread. From the scattergrams it also became quickly apparent that there was, as expected, a positive correlation between variable pairs. The structure of plotted data resembled in most scattergrams a stretched cloud along a positively climbing axis. It was apparent that interviewees were quite static across different scattergrams. Those at the 'right-hand, top end' of one scattergram were likely to be there in other scattergrams as well. Such 'static behaviour' could be observed for interviewees in all locations of scattergrams. The clusters discernible for different pairs of variables contained basically the same interviewees.

For some scattergrams some distinct clusters could be made out, but in general, empty space between areas of higher density and lower density was not vast. For the British sample, scattergrams for which comparatively distinct clusters could be found related to the variable pairs C1–C3, C1–AS2 and to a lesser degree also to W1–C1, W1–C3 and W1–AS2 (for examples, see Appendix 4.1; see also Appendix 3.7). In these scattergrams, three to four groups could be distinguished and a number of outliers existed. For scattergrams which involved the variables AS1, AS3 or AS4 distinct groups were more difficult to make out. Particularly for AS1, scattergrams were more widely and evenly distributed and revealed less of a group-related structure; for the variable AS4, scattergrams suffered from the low range of values of this variable, which rendered the analysis of scattergrams difficult.

For the German sample, a number of scattergrams indicated distinctive clusters. This was the case for the variable pairs W1–C1, W1–AS2, C1–C3, C1–AS1, C1–AS2, C3–AS2 and to a lesser degree also for W1–C3. In some of these scattergrams two groups were very clearly distinguishable, in others up to four groups could be made out. Probably the most interesting scattergram was the one for the variable pair W1–C1: in a narrow band along a positively climbing axis, four clusters could be distinguished. The same pattern of four groups – each containing basically the same interviewees – could be found for variable pairs W1–AS2 and C1–AS2, but there the pattern was not as distinctive as for W1–C1.

For the non-green sample, despite a rather low number of interviewees, two clusters and two outliers could be identified. These patterns were discernible for a number of variable pairs, such as W2–C2, W2–C4, C2–C4, W2–AS6, C2–AS6 and AS6–AS7.

From the analysis of the scattergrams, it appeared that four variables were especially promising for a cluster analysis of the green sample data: W1, C1, C3 and AS2. For them, distinctive group-related patterns were found in the scattergrams. W2, C2, C4 and AS6 similarly appeared particularly promising for the non-green sample. These variables received special attention when variable sets were generated for a cluster analysis (see below).

In general, it is the case that group-related patterns that are discovered for a lower dimensional order, e.g. in a two-dimensional scattergram, are also present at a higher dimensional order when further variables are added, e.g. a four-dimensional variable set is created. Lower-dimensional patterns cannot be lost by adding further dimensions. This means that the four variables W1, C1, C3 and AS2 remain 'good' cluster variables when used in larger variable sets.[3]

Correlational analysis

An analysis of correlation matrices can be helpful for finding relationships between variables. Because a correlation analysis is conducted for a total sample, it cannot uncover group-related structures on its own, but if applied together with other tools, such as scattergrams, it can substantiate insights into which variables may be particularly suited for a cluster analysis.

An analysis of correlation matrices confirmed that there was a strong positive correlation between most knowledge structure variables. Correlation coefficients were of similar values for the British and the German samples. Naturally, the variable pairs W1 and W2, C1 and C2, C3 and C4, C3 and C5, C4 and C5, AS1 and AS5, AS2 and AS6, AS3 and AS7, and AS4 and AS8 had very high positive correlation coefficients of about 0.85 to 0.95. This is not surprising since the first variable in these pairs is a sub-set of the latter variable, its 'parent' variable, e.g. W1 reflects knowledge comprehensiveness in relation to freely recalled products, while W2 reflects knowledge comprehensiveness in relation to all products discussed by an interviewee. Otherwise, the highest correlation coefficients between pairs of variables were found among the variables W1, C1, C3 and AS2 with coefficients between 0.70 and 0.90 for the British sample, and between 0.80 and 0.90 for the German sample. These are the same variables for which relatively distinct clusters were made out in scattergrams.

For the non-green sample, similarities to the green samples but also differences from them emerged from a correlation analysis. Similarly, as for the green samples, the knowledge comprehensiveness and knowledge complexity variables W2, C2 and C4 correlated strongly with each other with coefficients between 0.81 and 0.98. Major differences in comparison with the green samples, however, were found for the knowledge abstractness and knowledge specificity variables AS5, AS6, AS7 and AS8. For the green samples, the high specificity–low abstractness variable AS2 correlated most highly with W1, C1 and C3 (0.80 to 0.90), and the same was the case when AS6 was paired with W2, C2 or C4 (0.80 to 0.88). For the non-green sample, a different pattern emerged: here, the low specificity–high abstractness variable AS7 correlated most strongly with the variables W2, C2 and C4 (0.75 to 0.93); also, AS5 correlated strongly with these variables (0.50 to 0.61), whereas AS6 had comparatively low correlation coefficients (0.17 to 0.48). In that respect, correlation coefficients for the non-green sample did not compare well with those of the green samples. This difference is likely to be due to (a) the lack of actual green shopping experience of non-green interviewees, and (b) the hypothetical approach taken to interviewing non-green interviewees. Non-green interviewees appeared to be particularly poor on highly specific knowledge (AS6), which can be related to their lack of actual green shopping experience.

Main findings

The analyses of scattergrams and correlation matrices indicated that there were certain group-related structures in the data.

- Interviewees were quite static across scattergrams: clusters discernible for different variable pairs contained basically the same interviewees.
- For a number of scattergrams two to four clusters could be clearly made out.
- For most variable pairs a strong positive correlation existed.
- The variables W1, C1, C3 and AS2 appeared to be particularly suited for cluster analysis. This suggestion was supported by the inspection of scattergrams and by a correlational analysis.

These findings, taken together, suggested I should move on to a full cluster analysis.

HIERARCHICAL CLUSTER ANALYSES

A hierarchical cluster analysis was conducted on a comprehensive basis, for both conceptual and methodological reasons. For the green samples, nine variable sets were each subjected to two hierarchical cluster algorithms, Ward's method and the group average method (subsequently, also, a non-hierarchical cluster algorithm, the K-means method, was applied in the context of a sensitivity analysis). For the non-green sample, variable sets had to be adapted for cluster analysis since certain variables, reflecting freely recalled products, were not available here.

Variable sets

Variable sets were generated on the basis of the analyses of scattergrams and correlation matrices as well as with regard to methodological considerations relating to a sensitivity analysis (see Table 4.1).

The first five variable sets contained in different combinations only X variables, i.e. variables that only reflected freely recalled knowledge: *variable set 1* contained the variables W1, C1 and C3, which related to knowledge comprehensiveness and knowledge complexity. These variables can be judged as structural variables in a narrow sense. Variable sets 2, 3 and 4 contained a mixture of structural and language-type variables. *Variable set 2* contained W1, C1, C3 and the high specificity–low abstractness variable AS2. *Variable set 3* contained W1, C1, C3 and the low specificity variables AS1 and AS3. *Variable set 4* contained 'all' variables that related to freely recalled products (W1, C1, C3, AS1, AS2, AS3 and AS4). *Variable set 5* contained only the language-type variables, AS1, AS2, AS3 and AS4.

While the main purpose of variable sets 1 to 5 was to check for group-related patterns in the sample data, the main purpose of variable sets 6 to 9 was to examine the robustness and significance of cluster solutions, thus conducting a sensitivity analysis. (But also, the cluster solutions suggested for variable sets 1 to 4 could be compared with each other for the purpose of a sensitivity analysis.) Variable sets 6 and 7 were minor variations of variable set 5. *Variable set 6* substituted C5 for C3, and in *variable set 7*, W1 was replaced by W3. Variable sets 6 and 7 examined the robustness of the cluster solution that was suggested by variable set 4. At the outset, one would expect that a cluster solution for variable sets 6 and 7 would be similar to a solution derived for variable set 4 if the solution for variable set 4 had been a good one.

Variable set 8 represented a variation on variable set 4. It contained the 'parent' variables that related to the total number of products recalled by an interviewee rather than just the freely recalled products, as did variable set 4. Variable set 8 was also the only variable set for the green interviewees that compared directly to a variable set of the non-green sample (NSet 4). *Variable set 9* was of a relatively fuzzy nature. It contained W3, C1, C3 and NX, the latter variable referring to the number of positive product examples recalled by an interviewee. For such a variable set, some mix-up in comparison with previous cluster solutions could be expected at the outset, if previous cluster solutions were 'good' ones.

For the non-green samples, variable sets had to be adapted since no variables reflecting freely recalled products were available here; eight variable sets were generated which were referred to as NSet 1 to NSet 8 (see Table 4.1).

Table 4.1 Variable sets

Variable sets for green samples

Set 1	W1, C1, C3
Set 2	W1, C1, C3, AS2
Set 3	W1, C1, C3, AS1, AS3
Set 4	W1, C1, C3, AS1, AS2, AS3, AS4
Set 5	AS1, AS2, AS3, AS4
Set 6	W1, C1, C5, AS1, AS2, AS3, AS4
Set 7	W3, C1, C3, AS1, AS2, AS3, AS4
Set 8	W2, C2, C4, AS5, AS6, AS7, AS8
Set 9	W3, C1, C3, NX

Variable sets of the non-green sample

NSet 1	W2, C2, C4
NSet 2	W2, C2, C4, AS6
NSet 3	W2, C2, C4, AS5, AS7
NSet 4	W2, C2, C4, AS5, AS6, AS7, AS8 (= Set 8 of the green samples)
NSet 5	AS5, AS6, AS7, AS8
NSet 6	W2, C2, C5, AS5, AS6, AS7, AS8
NSet 7	W4, C2, C4, AS5, AS6, AS7, AS8
NSet 8	W4, C2, C4, NT

Procedure for hierarchical clustering

The knowledge content variables used in the cluster analysis were standardized and z-scores were compiled. In particular, when value ranges of variables differ considerably, which was the case here, a standardization of data is recommended (Mitchell 1993: 13, Hair *et al.* 1987). Dendrograms and the numerical information contained in them were relied upon to interpret cluster solutions. Dendrograms reflect the partitioning process – the way subjects are grouped as clusters or isolated as outliers (see Appendix 4.2). Distances between clusters (and between clusters and outliers) are rescaled by SPSS to a range from 0 to 25 distance units, and this numerical distance information is contained in the dendrograms. Supplementary information for an interpretation of dendrograms was provided by agglomeration schedules, proximity matrices and icicle graphs as they are generated by SPSS.

In this study, a distance of 3 units was chosen for identifying clusters and outliers:[4] a *cluster* was (technically) understood as a combination of three or more interviewees who were linked by the partitioning process *at a distance of 3 units*. Distances of less than 3 units were used to distinguish *sub-groups* within a cluster. Single subjects or pairs of subjects who had not yet joined a cluster at the distance of 3 units were identified as *outliers*.

Because of the high positive correlation between the cluster variables (the knowledge content variables) and because of the static nature of subjects across different variable pairs (as found through the analysis of scattergrams and the correlational analysis), *relationships of dominance* could be established amongst clusters, their sub-groups and outliers: clusters, their sub-groups and outliers could be ordered *sequentially*. *Cluster sequences* were generated (see Appendix 4.3). Within a cluster or sub-group, subjects were ordered by ascending subject numbers as they had been allocated to interviewees on a chronological basis (see chapter 3). In order to determine the sequential order of clusters, sub-groups and outliers, the previously compiled scattergrams and data matrices were consulted. Ambiguous clusters or outliers where no clear relationship of dominance with other clusters could be found were marked. The cluster sequences proved insightful for analysing group-related structures in the data.

Hierarchical clustering in the British sample

Hierarchical clustering was also conducted with Ward's method, which minimizes the average distance within each cluster on the basis of a distance variance measure, and with the group average method, which minimizes the average distance within each cluster on the basis of a distance average measure. For most variable sets, Ward's method identified four to six clusters, while the group average method tended to identify three to five. The group average method isolated more outliers than Ward's method, and particularly for variable sets 7 to 9, the group average method fragmented the sample rather strongly.

An examination of the cluster sequences revealed that interviewees remained rather static across cluster sequences for different cluster algorithms and for different variable sets. This was particularly true for the variable sets 1, 2, 4, 6, 7. For these variable sets a number of patterns emerged for the British sample:

- At the top end of a cluster sequence, subject B11 was regularly identified as an outlier. Subjects B06, 40, 50, 52 made up a first top cluster that was closely followed by a cluster comprising subjects B10, 28, 30, 33, 47. The group average method fragmented these two clusters into outliers at a distance of 3 units. However, at a slightly bigger cluster distance of about 4 to 5 distance units, basically the same pattern of clusters emerged in the dendrograms as observed for Ward's method at a distance of 3 units. Subject B02 was jockeying between the top two clusters.
- Subjects located between the top clusters and clusters of a middle section were B01, 03, 08, 32, 45.
- In a middle section of the cluster sequence, two groups existed, B07, 15, 17, 25, 41, 42, 43, 44, 46, 48, 51 followed by B20, 21, 35, 36, 38, 53, 54.
- Subjects B09, B13, B14 and B31 were jockeying between the middle clusters and the bottom clusters.
- At the bottom end of the cluster sequence, basically one cluster was identified that comprised two sub-groups. A first sub-group comprised B05, 16, 18, 19, 24, 26, 27, 29, 39, 55 and at the very end of the cluster sequence the sub-group B04, 12, 22, 23, 34, 37, 49 appeared. These sub-groups were repeatedly identified by both cluster algorithms, and there was little jockeying going on between them.

A comparison of the cluster sequences of different variable sets and of different cluster algorithms showed that jockeying between clusters was insubstantial at the very top and at the very bottom end of the respective cluster sequences. Jockeying happened to some extent in the middle section. Inspection confirmed that the clusters and outliers identified through the cluster analyses corresponded with the group-related structures that were apparent from the scattergrams.

A comparison of the cluster sequences of variable sets 1, 2, 4, 6 and 7 with those from variable sets 3 and 5, showed that subjects B45 and B47 moved up in the cluster sequence, and no relationships of dominance could be clearly established for them. For the cluster sequence of variable set 8, a certain levelling effect could be observed. Particularly clusters at the top end got mixed. This may be due to top interviewees gaining comparatively little from a prompting task in terms of scores of knowledge structure variables (variable set 8 contained variables that reflected knowledge on prompted products). For the fuzzy variable set 9, some bigger mixing up and splitting up of previously distinguished clusters happened, e.g. subjects B36, 54 moved up, and B14, 50, 52 moved down in the cluster sequence. These results can be positively judged with regard to a sensitivity analysis.

Hierarchical clustering in the German sample

As for the British sample, hierarchical clustering was conducted for the German sample with Ward's method and the group average method. For nearly all variable sets, Ward's method identified three to four clusters, while the group average method identified two to three. Again, the group average method identified more outliers than Ward's method. At the sub-group level, the two algorithms produced similar results in terms of the number of sub-groups identified.

As previously found for the British sample, an examination of the cluster sequences indicated that subjects remained rather static across cluster sequences of different cluster algorithms and different variable sets, in particular the variable sets 1, 2, 4, 6 and 7. A number of patterns were found for the German sample:

- At the top end of the cluster sequences, subjects G01, G28 and G36 were regularly isolated as outliers, followed by the cluster G09, 12, 29. Subjects G11, 16, 21, 22, 34, 35 were sometimes identified as a single cluster or linked as a sub-group to the top cluster G09, 12, 29.
- Subjects G10, G30 and G15 were jockeying between the two top clusters.
- The subjects G05, G13, G19, G23, G32 and G33 were jockeying in the middle section of the cluster sequence. Especially for G23 and G32 often no clear relationship of dominance with preceding or succeeding clusters could be established.
- At the bottom end of the cluster sequence, frequently only one cluster was identified. Within this cluster two rather static sub-groups were found – G02, 04, 08, 26, 32 followed by the sub-group G03, 06, 07, 14, 17, 18, 20, 24, 25, 27, 31.
- Regularly, the two subjects G14, 17 formed a sub-group at the very end of the cluster sequence, sometimes joined by G20 and G27.

The clusters identified corresponded well with group-related structures that were visible from the scattergrams.

Variable sets 3 and 5 focused strongly on some of the abstractness–specificity variables. Variable set 3 contained the low specificity variables AS1 and AS3, while variable set 5 contained all but the abstractness–specificity variables. Particularly subject G23 clustered here to a degree higher than before. For other subjects, only some minor variations could be observed which can be interpreted positively in the context of a sensitivity analysis.

Variable set 8 was a variant of variable set 4. It contained the 'parent' variables that related to all products discussed by an interviewee and not just freely recalled products. As for the British sample, a certain levelling effect was found. At the top end, the otherwise identified outlier G36 was absorbed into a subsequent cluster. There was some jockeying going on in the middle section of the cluster sequence which was beyond the previously observed degree of jockeying. At the lower end, previously identified outliers G14, 17 were absorbed into the bottom cluster. For the fuzzy variable set 9, some mixing of previously distinguished clusters could be found. Subject G22 was now identified as the top outlier, and some of the top clusters were realigned. These changes were stronger than previously observed ones, which again can be positively interpreted with regard to a sensitivity analysis.

Hierarchical clustering in the non-green sample

For the non-green sample, Ward's method identified two clusters and one to three outliers. The group average method, again, fragmented the sample more rigorously:

- At the top end of the cluster sequences, subject N01 was identified as an outlier.
- A top cluster comprised the subjects N02, 03, 04; a bottom cluster consisted of N06, 08, 09. Subject N07 was jockeying between these two clusters.
- Subjects N05 and N10 were frequently identified as outliers at the end of the cluster sequence.

These findings corresponded largely with the ones from the scattergrams.

For variable set NSet 5, the cluster sequence was disturbed, which indicated the strong sensitivity of the non-green sample to the abstractness–specificity variables (as was similarly indicated by the correlational analysis).

SENSITIVITY ANALYSES

For the purpose of a sensitivity analysis, first, the sample data were subjected to non-hierarchical clustering, and second, the sample data were manipulated, halving and integrating previous data sets, thus testing the significance of previous cluster solutions.

Non-hierarchical cluster analysis

As a non-hierarchical cluster algorithm, the *K-means method* was applied which, like Ward's method, minimizes the variance of distances within each cluster. K-means clustering was conducted with random starting points determined by SPSS. Only the variable sets 1 to 4 were subjected to a non-hierarchical cluster analysis. This appeared to be sufficient for the purpose of a sensitivity analysis.

Findings from a hierarchical cluster analysis can be used as informational input for non-hierarchical clustering, especially with regard to determining k – the number of clusters – which has to be decided a priori in non-hierarchical clustering (Everitt 1993: 141, Punj and Stewart 1983: 134, 145). K has to be big enough to accommodate both the number of clusters as well as the number of outliers as they may be identified by the cluster algorithm. For instance, if k = 4 is chosen, it may happen that just three outliers are isolated by the algorithm and the rest of the subjects are grouped into one big cluster.[5] The hierarchical cluster analysis conducted previously gave some idea about the number of clusters and outliers that could be expected in the sample data. Hence, the K-means algorithm was run for k, varying between 6 and 10 for the green samples. For the non-green sample, k was chosen as 3 and 4. As before, clusters and outliers identified by the cluster algorithm were sequentially ordered into cluster sequences.

The results produced by the K-means algorithm compared favourably with those from the hierarchical cluster analysis. For both green samples, the K-means method identified more clusters and outliers in the top half of the cluster sequence than in the bottom half. This was especially the case for the British sample. This stronger fragmentation of the top half of the sample was to a degree already apparent from the hierarchical analysis, but it became clearer on the basis of the non-hierarchical analysis. Apparently, theoretical sampling had yielded in the case of the British sample a higher number of interviewees with a medium or low level of green knowledge than interviewees with a deep green knowledge.

Non-hierarchical clustering also yielded certain insights regarding subjects for which no clear relationship of dominance *vis-à-vis* other subjects could have been established in hierarchical clustering. Such subjects were better isolated and clustered by the K-means method. For the British sample, clusters in the middle section were, to a degree, demarcated more clearly. For the German sample, it now became clearer that subjects G15, 16 and to a lesser degree also G11, 33, 34 fell between clusters in the top half of the cluster sequence, jockeying there; in the bottom half, subjects G02, 03, 23 and to a degree also G24 appeared to have certain knowledge features which made them jockey between clusters.

In general, the cluster sequences produced by the K-means algorithm compared well with those of the hierarchical cluster analysis in terms of the clusters and outliers identified and in terms of the position at which subjects showed up in the cluster sequences. Such high correspondence between cluster sequences of hierarchical and non-hierarchical cluster analysis was based on the inspection of the respective cluster sequences in terms of what clusters were identified, what outliers were identified, and which subjects they comprised. This analysis supported the view that there were different, robust groups of interviewees in the sample data which shared a similar type of knowledge.

Cluster analysis of combined and halved samples

In a further step towards assessing the robustness and significance of cluster solutions, the sample data were manipulated. 'Good' cluster solutions are expected to be insensitive to manipulations of sample data, e.g. the halving of data sets. Three types of data manipulations were undertaken: first, the British and the German green samples were halved by grouping subjects with odd and even subject numbers together; second, the two green samples were integrated into one combined green data set; and third, the non-green sample was integrated with the combined green data set, forming a 'total' data set. These 'new' data samples were then subjected to selected cluster algorithms for selected variable sets:

- For the halved data samples, Ward's method and the group average method were applied to variable sets 1 to 4.
- The combined British and German green data set was subjected to Ward's method and the K-means method, for variable sets 1 to 4. Also, variable set 8 was subjected to Ward's method since variable set 8 was the only variable set that could be compared to a variable set of the 'total' data sample (namely NSet 4). Also, for the combined British and German data set, scattergrams were generated for selected variable pairs.
- The 'total' British, German and non-green data set was subjected to Ward's method for the first four variable sets – here NSet 1 to NSet 4.

That kind of focused cluster analysis seemed to be sufficient for extending a sensitivity analysis.

Cluster analysis of halved British and German samples

A cluster analysis of halved data samples has been suggested as a test of the robustness of cluster solutions (Mitchell 1993: 15, Everitt 1993: 143, Hair *et al.* 1987: 316, Punj and Stewart 1983: 145–6). The British and the German data samples were each halved by grouping subjects 'randomly' together – on the basis of odd and even numbers as they had been allocated to subjects in a chronological order (see chapter 3). Each of the four sample halves was subjected to a cluster analysis with Ward's method and the group average method. The variable sets 1 to 4 were tested out.

The results of this sensitivity analysis were highly encouraging. Cluster sequences generated for halved data sets showed a high degree of correspondence with cluster sequences of the data sets that had not been manipulated. Again, correspondence was assessed by inspecting how subjects were identified as clusters and outliers:

- For cluster sequences derived by Ward's method, the degree of correspondence was extremely high. For instance, for the German data set with odd subject numbers, the degree of correspondence for variable set 2 was nearly total. For the group average method, correspondence was in general slightly lower than for Ward's method, but it was still quite high.
- Through halving the original samples on the basis of odd and even subject numbers, it happened that entire clusters which had been suggested by the previous cluster analysis were allocated to one of the halved data sets. For

instance, one of the top clusters of the British sample contained only subjects with even numbers – B02, 06, 40, 50, 52. When such entire clusters were subsumed completely in one of the halved data sets, cluster solutions remained robust: the allocation of B02, 06, 40, 50, 52 to the halved data set with even numbers did not affect cluster solutions of this data set negatively, and neither was the data set with odd subject numbers negatively affected where this top cluster was 'missing'. No significant realignment of clusters could be observed as compared with the original clustering of the British sample.

- Similarly, both odd- and even-numbered subjects showed up in the cluster sequences of the halved data sets fairly consistently, as they had done previously in the whole clusters.

The results of the cluster analysis of the halved British and German samples indicated a high significance for the previously generated cluster solutions. The cluster sequences of the halved samples compared very well with those of the original data.

Cluster analysis of combined British and German sample

The purpose of a cluster analysis of the combined British and German data sample was twofold: first, it extended a sensitivity analysis, and second, it examined how the two samples were distributed within the merged samples. From previous examinations of the distributions of the knowledge structure variables it was known that the German sample had somewhat higher values of distributional parameters than the British sample. The British sample seemed to contain more subjects with low levels of knowledge. At the outset one could expect that such a finding would be reflected in the way the British and German subjects were distributed within a single cluster sequence.

As a preparatory step towards a cluster analysis of the combined British and German sample, scattergrams were compiled. The scattergrams of the combined British and German sample indicated certain patterns in the data:

- Three to four areas of higher density could be distinguished quite clearly for the variable pairs W1–C1, W1–C3, C1–C3 and C1–AS2. Again, for the variable pair W1–C1 clusters and empty spaces between clusters were quite clearly discernible. For the variable pairs W1–AS2 and C3–AS2 some clustering of data could be observed, but patterns were not so easily identifiable.
- Some group-related structures were now, to a degree, better identifiable than for the corresponding scattergrams of the data that were not combined. The British sample seemed to contribute in particular to a better identification of bottom clusters. German subjects, such as G14, 17, who could have been regarded as outliers when the German sample was examined on its own, were now embedded in a fairly cohesive group of subjects. At the top end, the German data seemed to integrate British outliers into more cohesive

structures. At the outset, one might have expected that through an integration of the British and German samples group-related structures would get blurred and that as a result of the samples' integration just one big cloud of points would appear in a scattergram. Apparently, this did not happen, and to a degree, certain group-related structures became even clearer.

A cluster analysis confirmed the impressions gained from the scattergrams. Again, clusters and outliers were ordered in cluster sequences in the same way as outlined above:

- When the clusters of the combined British and German data set were examined for groups and sub-groups of British and German subjects respectively, it appeared that these groupings were highly similar to clusters as they were identified previously in the separately conducted cluster analyses of the British and the German samples.
- Jockeying between clusters and a realignment of clusters occurred only as a matter of degree, and, if it happened, it was restricted to minor movements within cluster sequences.
- The cluster sequence reflected the fact that the German sample was more strongly represented at the top end of the cluster sequence, while the British sample contributed more strongly to the bottom half of the combined data set. In the middle section of the cluster sequence, the two samples seemed to have similar shares of subjects in clusters.

The analysis of the combined British and German data set yielded some interesting results. First, it supported further claims to cluster robustness and significance. Second, it produced insights into how the British and the German samples were distributed within one single cluster sequence. Based on the previous analyses, it was not unexpected that British subjects were more strongly represented in the bottom half of the cluster sequence of the combined British and German sample, while German subjects had higher shares in the top half. And third, on the basis of the analysis of the combined British and German data sample, cautious replication claims could be made. Clusters and sub-groups that had been identified separately for the British and for the German sample data showed up in a highly similar fashion for the combined data sample: clusters and sub-group patterns found for the individual samples survived the integration of data. This indicates that similar and quite robust clusters existed in the British and the German samples, and that patterns of clustering – and potential patterns of knowledge structures that might be 'behind' such cluster patterns – were apparently independent of social and cultural differences which are likely to exist between Britain and Germany.

Cluster analysis of combined British, German and non-green samples

The integration of the non-green sample with the combined British and German sample yielded the so-called 'total' data set. This integration of data followed a similar purpose to the previous integration of the British and the German samples. Objectives were to test for cluster robustness and to find out how the respective samples were distributed in a single cluster sequence. Such a project was more complicated here since for the 'total' sample the variable sets that had to be used were different from those that were used for clustering the British and the German samples: variables reflecting freely recalled knowledge were not available for the non-green sample. Since variable sets 1 to 7 and variable set 9 contained such variables (X variables), these variable sets had to be excluded from the analysis here. Subsequently, only the 'non-green' variable sets, NSet 1 to 4, were subjected to a cluster analysis of the 'total' British, German and non-green data set. Since NSet 4 is identical with variable set 8 (of the green samples) some limited comparisons with previous analyses were possible (see Table 4.1).

When cluster solutions of the 'total' sample are being compared with previous results, it has also to be kept in mind that the approach to the non-green sample was methodologically different from that to the green samples. For the British and the German samples, a free recall method was applied that was only supplemented by prompting. In contrast, the non-green sample was involved in a hypothetical reasoning task based on prompting (see chapter 3). One might expect that a hypothetical approach would have given the non-green consumers a productive advantage in terms of the extent of 'knowledge' they could produce through rationalizing in comparison with the free recall exercise the green consumers went through.

The 'total' sample was clustered with Ward's method for variable sets NSet 1 to NSet 4. As it turned out, the non-green interviewees joined a cluster sequence of the 'total' sample at its bottom end. Only interviewee N01 managed to get classified in the middle of the cluster sequence. For variable set NSet 4, which was identical to the variable set 8, a high degree of correspondence to previously compiled cluster sequences could be found. The non-green interviewees joined the green interviewees at the very end of a cluster sequence, in the last and in the second to last cluster. That the non-green consumers joined a cluster sequence at its end was a reassuring result regarding the objective that the non-green sample was meant to complement variation sampling at its lower end. As indicated, due to the different variable sets used here, the contribution of a cluster analysis of the 'total' sample to a sensitivity analysis was limited.

PARADIGMATIC SUBJECTS AND COGNITIVE CATEGORIES

The cluster analyses indicated that there were significant and robust clusters in the sample data. Certain 'core parts' of clusters seemed to be quite stable and were little affected by jockeying when they were compared across different variable sets, different algorithms, and manipulated data sets. These static parts of cluster sequences were drawn upon to demarcate *cognitive categories* of green consumers. In the further course of the study, it was not possible to assess all interviewees of static core parts of clusters in detail. Instead, only a handful of *paradigmatic subjects* who were at the centre of clusters of cognitive categories were examined. Such a focused approach to data interpretation (as presented in the following chapters) was supplemented by quantitative and/or qualitative analyses of further subjects and of the demarcated cognitive categories where appropriate and possible.

Demarcation of cognitive categories and selection of paradigmatic subjects

Suggestions from the previous cluster analyses on how many clusters should be demarcated as cognitive categories were not entirely conclusive. The scatter-grams had indicated the existence of clusters, but their number varied from two to four for the British and German samples respectively. When scattergrams of the combined British and German sample were compiled, it appeared that up to five groups existed. Also, the cluster analyses did not yield unambiguous results regarding the number of clusters in the data. For both hierarchical clus-tering and non-hierarchical clustering, the number of clusters was in general between four and six for the British sample and between three and five for the German sample. An analysis of the combined British and German sample yielded mostly four to five clusters.

In the end, the issue of how many clusters should be demarcated was resolved pragmatically: five cognitive categories were distinguished. There were sufficient indications in the previous cluster analyses and the analysis of scattergrams that a demarcation of five cognitive categories could be justified. Also, it seemed to be advisable to be discriminative rather than too crude at this stage, keeping the interpretative purpose of the further analysis of knowledge structures in mind (Mitchell 1993: 14, Hair *et al.* 1987: 306).

From static core parts of the cluster sequences of the British and the German samples, five paradigmatic subjects were selected. The selection of subjects was accompanied by an examination of how they were located in the scattergrams *vis-à-vis* other subjects in the same clusters. Interviewees who were in the centres of clusters were looked for. Membership in the cognitive categories was deter-mined on the basis that a person had been very static across cluster sequences of different variable sets. Only those interviewees who had been associated with a certain cognitive category for *four out of four* variable sets tested (in K-means clustering with the paradigmatic subjects as non-random starting points, as discussed below) were included as members of one of the five cognitive categories demarcated. A more relaxed demarcation included interviewees as members of a certain cognitive category who had been associated with the same cluster centre for *three out of four* variable sets tested. If not otherwise indicated, the notion of 'cognitive categories' refers to the rigorous '4 out of 4' demarca-tion. If the 'enlarged cognitive categories' are referred to, which were generated

Table 4.2 Cognitive categories

British cognitive categories: '4 out of 4' demarcation
(in brackets: additional subjects due to '3 out of 4' demarcation)

    Cognitive category 1: B04, B12, B22, B23, B34, B37, B49
    Cognitive category 2: B05, B13, B18, B20, B24, B27, B55 (B16, B29, B39)
    Cognitive category 3: B03, B07, B17, B25, B42, B44, B48, B51, B54 (B21,
      B41, B43, B53)
    Cognitive category 4: B02, B10, B28, B30, B33, B45, B47 (B01, B08)
    Cognitive category 5: B11, B40

German cognitive categories: '4 out of 4' demarcation
(in brackets: additional subjects due to '3 out of 4' demarcation)

    Cognitive category 1: G14, G17
    Cognitive category 2: G20, G25, G27, G31
    Cognitive category 3: G02, G04, G23, G32 (G13, G26)
    Cognitive category 4: G10, G11, G21, G22, G30, G34, G35 (G12, G15, G16)
    Cognitive category 5: G28, G29, G36 (G09)

through the 'relaxed' demarcation, this is explicitly stated in subsequent chapters (see Table 4.2).

In the same way as paradigmatic subjects were retrieved from the British and the German samples, paradigmatic subjects were also retrieved from the non-green sample. From the analysis of the 'total' British, German and non-green sample, it had been apparent that the non-green sample aligned with the green samples at the bottom end of cluster sequences. From the non-green sample two paradigmatic subjects were retrieved.

The notational reference to paradigmatic subjects and cognitive categories in the further course of this study is outlined by Table 4.3. The notions 'cognitive category 1', 'B1' and 'G1' refer to interviewees with the *lowest* scores of knowledge content variables, while the notions 'cognitive category 5', 'B5' and 'G5' refer to interviewees with the *highest* scores.

The British paradigmatic subject B1 and the German paradigmatic subject G5 could be characterized as outliers at the top and bottom ends of their

Table 4.3 Notational reference to cognitive categories and paradigmatic subjects

Cognitive category	Paradigmatic subjects of the British sample	Paradigmatic subjects of the German sample	Paradigmatic subjects of the non-green sample
5	'B5' (B40)	'G5' (G29)	—
4	'B4' (B28)	'G4' (G21)	—
3	'B3' (B17)	'G3' (G04)	—
2	'B2' (B18)	'G2' (G27)	'N2' (N04)
1	'B1' (B22)	'G1' (G17)	'N1' (N08)

respective cluster sequences. But viewed on the more comprehensive basis of the combined British and German sample, these 'outliers' were embedded in groups of subjects. All the other paradigmatic subjects were already well embedded in groups of subjects at the level of their individual samples.

Checks of good typicality

Two checks were made in order to ensure that 'good' paradigmatic subjects had been retrieved. One control involved the application of the K-means algorithm with non-random starting point, whereby the paradigmatic subjects were used as non-random starting points. A second control was conducted by drawing on the results of the CI analysis.

For a first check, the sample data were subjected to the K-means algorithm with five non-random starting points (k = 5); variable sets 1 to 4 were tested. The five identified paradigmatic subjects were used as non-random starting points for K-means clustering. If the suggested subjects were good cluster centres, the cluster solution generated should compare favourably with the results of the previous cluster analyses of the British and the German samples. This application of the K-means method led to the rejection of those other subjects who had been considered as paradigmatic subjects. For instance, it appeared that G11 was inferior to G21 to mark a cluster centre of cognitive category 4, as G19 was inferior to G04 as a cluster centre of cognitive category 3. With the suggested paradigmatic subjects as starting points, cluster sequences could be reproduced that compared favourably with previously compiled ones:[6]

- Paradigmatic subjects were not allocated to the same clusters as a result of K-means clustering.
- Across variable sets 1 to 4, only locally restrained movements in the cluster sequences could be observed in comparison with previous cluster sequences. Since only five clusters (k = 5) were generated, some merging of previously distinguished clusters and outliers happened. Such merging occurred with a high degree of correspondence when compared with the original cluster sequences, in particular with regard to the cluster sequences of the combined British and German sample.

A second check of typicality of the suggested paradigmatic subjects was conducted on the basis of the CI analysis (see chapter 3). The CI analysis comprised a number of search categories, e.g. certain knowledge structure characteristics, for which the interview data had been marked:

- Scores on the CI analysis on certain aspects of knowledge structures suggested that each of the five paradigmatic subjects had a rather different extent of knowledge from that of the others, and such differences in CI scores between the paradigmatic subjects were in line with the rankings of the paradigmatic subjects.

- In general, scores from the CI analysis regarding knowledge structure characteristics corresponded with the findings from the cluster analyses. The highest and lowest scoring individuals in the CI analysis tended to be the ones who were found at the extremes of cluster sequences. This was generally reassuring regarding the results of the cluster analysis.
- Also, by comparing the results from the cluster analyses with the results from the CI analysis, some apparently 'exceptional' cases of consumer behaviour were found: for the British sample, B53 had a very high score in terms of argumentative knowledge which did not correspond to his/her position in the bottom half of the cluster sequence. Similarly, in the German sample, G14 had the highest score for argumentative knowledge, but ranked right at the end of the cluster sequence. A slightly less extreme finding was made for G24. These exceptional cases are returned to in more detail in the next chapters (especially in chapter 6).

The checks for the typicality of the suggested subjects indicated that the proposed subjects were well suited to represent cluster centres.

CONCLUSIONS

An analysis of scattergrams revealed that there was a strong positive correlation between the various knowledge content variables. Interviewees were distributed over quite a range, which confirmed earlier assessments that theoretical sampling had yielded diverse samples. Comparing scattergrams with each other showed that interviewees were fairly static regarding their locations in scattergrams. For a number of knowledge content variables (W1, C1, C3 and AS2) group-related structures were discernible, although, for other variables, areas of higher and lower density were not always separated by vast areas of empty space.

A correlation analysis indicated that, for the pairs of knowledge content variables for which group-related patterns had been discerned in the scattergrams, correlation coefficients were especially high. This made these variables particularly interesting for cluster analysis.

Regarding the correlation coefficients of the knowledge comprehensiveness variables with the knowledge complexity variables, there were no major differences between the green and the non-green samples. However, regarding correlation coefficients of the language-type variables with the other knowledge content variables (knowledge comprehensiveness and knowledge complexity variables), differences existed between the green samples and the non-green sample. This can be related to differences in actual green shopping experience between green and non-green interviewees and the different research methods applied.

Because of the high positive correlation between the knowledge content variables, clusters and outliers could be ordered sequentially into cluster sequences. There were only a few exceptions where no clear relationship of dominance could be established amongst clusters, sub-groups and outliers. By comparing cluster sequences of different variable sets and of different algorithms, fairly static parts of cluster sequences were identified.

In order to check the significance of the cluster solutions that had been generated, a comprehensive sensitivity analysis was conducted. The correspondence of cluster sequences was checked by inspection. On the basis of the application of different variable sets, different cluster algorithms, and different sample data sets, cluster sequences were replicated to a high degree. The robustness and significance of identified clusters seemed to be assured.

The cluster analyses of integrated samples, such as the combined British and German sample and the 'total' British, German and non-green sample, yielded interesting insights regarding how the samples aligned with each other. The British sample appeared to contain more interviewees with low knowledge than the German sample. Non-green interviewees aligned in cluster sequences with those interviewees of the green samples who had exhibited rather low knowledge levels.

On the basis of a cluster analysis of the combined British and German sample, certain replication claims were made regarding patterns of knowledge structures. Clusters of British subjects and clusters of German subjects, that were identified in separately conducted cluster analyses of the British and the German samples, 'survived' the integration of sample data. For the combined British and German sample, they joined to form new clusters without being split or realigned.

Based on the cluster analyses and the analysis of scattergrams, five categories of consumers were demarcated. They were labelled cognitive categories 1 to 5. Cluster centres of these cognitive categories are represented by 'paradigmatic subjects'. They formed the basis for the interpretation of the knowledge structures of green consumers.

5

INTERPRETATION OF KNOWLEDGE STRUCTURES

In the previous chapter, consumers were categorized by a cluster analysis with knowledge content variables. Five so-called 'cognitive categories' 1, 2, 3, 4 and 5 were distinguished and paradigmatic green consumers were selected for each of these categories. The main purpose of this chapter is to profile consumers of the respective cognitive categories psychologically in terms of how they think about green consumption. The knowledge structure framework outlined in chapter 2 is drawn upon. Three different levels of cognition were discussed there:

- a *knowledge content* level that reflects what people actually know;
- a *cognitive operational* level that reflects how knowledge is 'used' when thinking goes on;
- and a *formatting* level of cognition that reflects how the organization of knowledge content and cognitive operations is underwired.

In terms of the computer analogy, knowledge content was compared to data files, cognitive operations to applications software, and a formatting level to systems software. The knowledge content level is a largely conscious level of cognition, which means that people are to a considerable extent aware of what they know. Knowledge content can be recalled and verbalized. In contrast, an operational and a formatting level of cognition are not consciously accessible. They are of a largely subconscious nature. People are normally not aware of how their thinking is organized. Only in special enquiries, such as cognitive psychology, has there been any attempt to understand how thinking 'works'.

Along this distinction, knowledge structures of green consumers were interpreted in terms of differences and similarities across the cognitive categories. *What* green consumers know in terms of knowledge content, and *how* green consumers know in terms of cognitive operations and schematic knowledge features that are beneath a knowledge content level, have been examined. This discussion focused on the paradigmatic subjects. When quantitatively based assessments of knowledge content were made, the assessment of individual paradigmatic subjects was supplemented by average values for the cognitive categories they belonged to.

In general, interpretations were closely based on empirical evidence. In the following, empirical evidence is presented extensively when knowledge content is investigated. This was done at the risk of becoming tedious at times, but since empirical findings on knowledge content present the basis for the subsequent interpretation of cognitive operations and schematic knowledge features, it was thought wise to follow a 'data-driven' route.

KNOWLEDGE CONTENT

Four characteristics of knowledge content were investigated for the green consumer: knowledge comprehensiveness, knowledge complexity, knowledge specificity and knowledge abstractness. The appendices provide a general overview on the values of these knowledge structure variables (see Appendices 3.7, 5.1 and 5.2).

Knowledge comprehensiveness

Knowledge comprehensiveness is a rather 'quantitative' knowledge characteristic. It refers to how much a person knows about a certain domain, reflecting the amount of knowledge held. An assessment of knowledge comprehensiveness was based on two different word count indicators: first, words were counted for *interview extracts* that reflected knowledge about the green product; and second, words were counted for the *total interview*. The latter indicator is much cruder and less indicative of knowledge comprehensiveness; it includes all the words a person said during an interview independent of whether or how they related to green consumption or not. It was found that knowledge comprehensiveness increased strongly from the bottom cognitive category 1 to the top cognitive category 5.

Knowledge comprehensiveness in terms of interview extracts

One main indicator of knowledge comprehensiveness drew on word counts of interview extracts that reflected freely recalled knowledge of the green product (variable W1). W1 was compiled on the basis of the PA matrix (products–product attributes matrix). Values for the German consumers were adjusted by 1.16 to allow for syntactic language differences between the English and the German language (see chapter 3):

- The amount of freely recalled knowledge decreased from more than 100 words for the British and German paradigmatic subjects B5 and G5 to values in the tens for B1 and G1. Such a strong trend was confirmed by an analysis of W1 averages for cognitive categories 1, 2, 3, 4 and 5 (see Figure 5.1 and Appendix 5.3; see also Appendixes 5.1 and 5.2).
- Average values of W1 for the British and German cognitive categories matched very well, which supported replication claims. This also hinted that the cluster analysis had produced sound results.

124

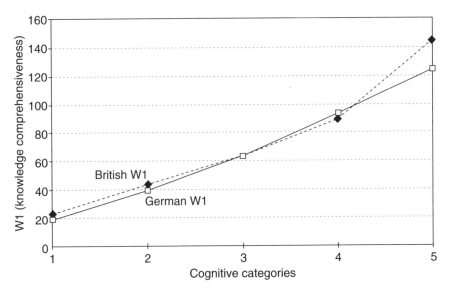

Figure 5.1 Knowledge comprehensiveness

The increase in knowledge comprehensiveness from cognitive category 1 to cognitive category 5 was of a slightly progressive nature, i.e. differences in the amount of knowledge tended to become bigger when comparing cognitive category 1 with cognitive category 2, 2 with 3, 3 with 4, and 4 with 5. This is an interesting result for a debate on how product familiarity relates to knowledge comprehensiveness (the amount of information recalled).[1] The findings made here supported the 'enrichment hypothesis', which suggests a progressive (and possibly an even exponential) relationship between product familiarity and the amount of information recalled (see chapter 2). A learning curve can be suggested where extended experience leads to not just marginally but progressively increasing benefits to the learner. It appeared that a knowledge advantage in terms of knowledge comprehensiveness became increasingly greater from cognitive category 1 to cognitive category 5.

A similar picture to that for freely recalled green product knowledge emerged when interview extracts were examined for all products, both freely recalled and prompted ones (W2 variable). Again, knowledge comprehensiveness increased strongly across the cognitive categories. Since prompting was conducted on a default basis, a certain levelling effect could be observed across the cognitive categories: the gap between the lower cognitive categories and the higher ones narrowed to some extent. This is also reflected by the ratio W1/W2, which expresses the amount of freely recalled knowledge as a share of the total amount of knowledge recalled by a person. For the top cognitive categories 4 and 5, the ratio was over 80 per cent for most members, while for cognitive category 1 it decreased to about 30 per cent (see Appendices 5.1 and 5.2).

The W2 values of the non-green interviewees were comparable with those of green consumers of cognitive categories 1 and 2.

Knowledge comprehensiveness in terms of total interview data

Besides an assessment of knowledge comprehensiveness based on word counts of interview extracts, knowledge comprehensiveness was also examined on the basis of word counts for the total of the interview (W4 variable). Similarly, words were also counted for part one of the interview (the open-question, free recall part) (W3 variable). A trend of decreasing values from the top to the bottom cognitive categories was still discernible, but it was less clear than for the W1 and W2 variables. This also seemed to be reflected by the comparatively low correlation coefficient between W3 and W1 and also between W4 and W1, which was around 0.5 in both cases.

In general, variables W1 and W2 can be considered to be the better indicators of knowledge comprehensiveness since they filtered for relevant knowledge, and, to a degree, also for personality traits like being of a bubbly and talkative nature. Some interviewees spoke a lot during an interview, but did not say much about the characteristics of green products and such an effect was not eliminated by W3 and W4.

Efficiency of recall

If one relates the W1 and W2 variables to the W3 and W4 variables respectively, conclusions regarding the 'efficiency' of recall can be drawn. For instance, the quotient W1/W3 assesses the amount of freely recalled, green product knowledge (W1) as a share of the amount of freely recalled, total knowledge (W3). Values of the quotient W1/W3 indicated that persons in the higher cognitive categories were more 'efficient' in recalling knowledge; the ratio was markedly smaller for persons from the lower cognitive categories. The same was reflected by the ratio W2/W4 (see Appendix 5.1). Apparently, members of the higher cognitive categories did not talk around the issues. They could express and formulate thoughts about the green product more precisely.

Knowledge complexity

Complexity refers to the number of elements a system contains and the way system elements interrelate. The 'system' discussed here was knowledge content; 'system elements' were the knowledge content features 'products' and 'product attributes' (more precisely: 'green product attributes'). Knowledge complexity refers to the number of knowledge content features and the extent and nature to which knowledge content features are interrelated. Hence, an examination of knowledge complexity deals, on the one hand, with a *frequency assessment* of knowledge content features and, on the other hand, with an assessment of *how* knowledge content features are interrelated. An examination of interrelations between knowledge content features reflects on the idea of a knowledge hierarchy: an assessment of knowledge complexity should shed light on the question of whether green consumer knowledge is organized in a hierarchical fashion and, if so, what role the knowledge content features 'products' and 'product attributes' play in the organization of knowledge.

A frequency assessment of knowledge content features is a fairly straightforward counting exercise, whereas an assessment of interrelations between knowledge features needs some further elaboration. Two types of interrelations amongst knowledge content features can be distinguished: *product class-related grouping* and *networking*. Both patterns were assessed in relation to the sequence of freely recalled products as it developed during the interview (in short: the 'recall sequence'). The notion 'recall sequence' is used in this technical sense in the following.

- 'Product class-related grouping' refers to product class-related patterns in recall, such as the recall of products of the same product class, e.g. dairy products, in sequence. An examination of product class-related grouping draws implicitly on the concept of a hierarchy of products, in particular the definition of a product class (see Figures 2.3 and 3.1).
- 'Networking' refers to interrelations between products and product attributes. Networking was diagnosed if products that were recalled in sequence were related by the interviewee consistently to the same product attributes (more precisely: to the same *sub-categories* of the product attribute 'greenness') as they had been distinguished by the bracketing framework.

An examination of knowledge complexity had to focus on freely recalled products only. In the case of prompting, the sequence of products discussed by an interviewee was determined by the researcher (through the prompting list), and consequently no 'recall sequence' existed. Hence, patterns of interrelations between knowledge content features for prompted products could not be investigated (this also means that an assessment of knowledge complexity for the non-green interviewees was difficult to conduct since they were only involved in a prompting task).

Product frequencies and product class-related grouping

In the following, first, frequencies of the knowledge content feature 'product' are assessed. Second, recall sequences are examined with regard to product class-related grouping.

Quite a large distributional range of the number of products recalled was found for the interviewees sampled. With regard to the cognitive categories, it appeared that the number of freely recalled products (NX variable) increased from the bottom towards the top cognitive categories: British and German consumers of the top cognitive category 5 freely recalled on average more than

13 products, while for cognitive category 1 this number decreased to below 5 products (see Appendix 6.1).

As indicated, product class-related grouping was diagnosed when products of the same product class, e.g. dairy products, were recalled in sequence: 'sequentially recalled' could refer either to products mentioned in sequence during the open recall phase of the interview (then marked as X1 products) or it could refer to products that emerged in the follow-up discussion of a previously mentioned X1 product (such products, recalled later, were classified as X2 products). The following patterns of product class-related grouping were found for the paradigmatic subjects (products other than freely recalled X products are explicitly marked, and where products of one product class had apparently 'entered' a recall sequence of another product class, this is indicated by putting apparent 'non-product class members' in brackets):

- *B5*: for the product class *washing + cleaning products*: 'detergent and washing-up liquid and cleaners (Y product)', and for *toiletries*: 'soap and cosmetics and shampoo (and milk)'.

- *G5*: for *dairy products*: 'yoghurt and kefir', and for *plant products*: 'grains and vegetables/fruit and coffee'.

- B4: for *washing + cleaning products*: 'washing-up liquid and detergent and (soap) and cleaners and (shower gel/shampoo)', and for *paper products*: 'kitchen rolls and toilet paper and cat litter and (bin liners)', and also for *plant products*: 'soya milk/soya yoghurt and muesli/dried fruit'.

- *G4*: for *dairy products*: 'milk and yoghurt and cream and (drinks)'.

- *B3*: for *washing + cleaning products*: 'washing-up liquid and detergent and cleaners'.

- *G3*: for *dairy products*: '(drinks) and milk and yoghurt', and for *paper products*: 'toilet paper and kitchen rolls'.

- *B2*: for *washing + cleaning products*: 'detergent and fabric conditioner'.
- *G2*: no patterns of product class-related grouping.

- *B1*: for *washing + cleaning products*: 'detergent and fabric conditioner'.
- *G1*: no patterns of product class-related grouping.

For the paradigmatic subjects of the higher cognitive categories more instances of product class-related grouping could be observed, and patterns of product class-related grouping were more extensive, i.e. more products of the same product class were recalled in sequence than for the lower categories. There also appeared to be certain relationships among product classes: certain product classes seemed to be closer together than others; for instance, for British interviewees the recall of toiletries products was prone to mix with the recall of washing + cleaning products; similarly, the recall of drinks products was mixed with that of dairy products for German interviewees. It appeared that those product classes especially tended to be mixed in recall sequences that were close together in terms of their locations in a product hierarchy (see Figure 2.3). These findings support the idea that knowledge is hierarchically organized, and that product class-related grouping plays an important role when it comes to understanding the complexity of consumer knowledge.

Also, the CI analysis had previously hinted at stronger patterns of product class-related grouping for the higher cognitive categories when it was found that product class terms, e.g. 'dairy products', 'toiletries', etc., were more frequently mentioned by members of the higher cognitive categories (see chapter 3).

Frequencies of product attributes

As a first step, the frequency of the knowledge feature 'product attributes' was assessed; the second step was to examine which product attributes were the most prominent ones for the paradigmatic subjects.

The bracketing framework for analysing and reducing the interview data contained twenty-nine sub-categories of the product attribute 'greenness'. Hence, an interviewee could touch at maximum upon twenty-nine different product attributes when describing green products. The highest numbers of green product attributes were found for the top cognitive categories (see Appendix 6.1). Persons from cognitive category 5 described green products by up to fourteen different green product attributes. This number decreased sharply from the top cognitive categories to the bottom ones. The average number of different product attributes used by cognitive category 1 was about five. Figures for the British cognitive categories were comparable to those for the German ones. A similar picture emerged when product attributes were counted for *each* product separately, and then summed up (thus allowing multiple counts of same product attributes). For cognitive category 5, on average forty-five product attributes were touched upon to characterize green products (X products). For cognitive category 1, this number was down to about eight.

In a subsequent step, frequencies of the most prominent product attributes were investigated (again, for freely recalled X products, if not otherwise indicated). The following lists the number of products the most popular product attributes showed up for:[2]

- *B5*: packaging material (5), home made (5), locally produced/retailed (5), ingredients (4), and reusable (4).
- *G5*: home made (7), reusable (6). If taken together, the packaging attributes 'amount of packaging' and 'packaging material' (5), and attributes relating to communication issues (5) as a whole had some prominence.

- *B4*: ingredients (4), packaging symbols (4), and recycled (4).
- *G4*: reusable (7), amount of packaging (5), locally produced/retailed (4), and communication issues (4) as a whole.

- *B3*: organic (3).
- *G3*: reusable (3), amount of packaging (3), and word of mouth (3).

- *B2*: packaging symbols (3), ingredients (3).
- *G2*: packaging material (3), locally produced/retailed (3).
- *N2* (only prompted products available): product ingredients (3), and product attributes relating to LCA issues (6) as a whole.

- *B1*: when prompted products were included, recyclable (3).
- *G1*: when prompted products were included, reusable (4) and packaging material (3).
- *N1* (only prompted products available): 'others' (3).

The top cognitive categories had a number of product attributes with high product frequencies; for the lower cognitive categories, product frequencies per product attribute decreased. Certain product attributes apparently played a more prominent role in the organization of knowledge than others. It also appeared that the higher cognitive categories covered different groups of product attributes, e.g. ingredients, packaging, communication, or LCA product attributes, more comprehensively than the lower categories. The lower cognitive categories seemed to focus more selectively on certain groups of product attributes only: the German lower cognitive categories focused strongly only on certain packaging-related product attributes, while the British lower cognitive categories focused on ingredients-related product attributes. This indicates that knowledge complexity built up around different areas of knowledge for British and German interviewees.

Some exceptional patterns could be observed for the non-green interviewees: they characterized green products very consistently along certain product attributes only, and they referred to product attributes which appeared 'atypical' in comparison with the ones of green interviewees (in particular, the product attribute 'others'). Such a pattern can be related to the hypothetical, prompting approach taken to interviewing non-green consumers. It will be interpreted in more detail in later sections when cognitive operations and schematic knowledge features are assessed in relation to the issue of rationalizing.

Networking of products and product attributes

The assessment of the knowledge content features 'products' and (green) 'product attributes' indicated a hierarchical organization of knowledge: product class-related grouping was apparent and the high prominence of a few product attributes in terms of product frequencies per product attribute was found. So far, not much could be said about interrelations among products and product attributes. This is now addressed when, first, 'horizontal' and 'vertical' complexity is examined and, second, the nature of how products and product attributes related to each other is discussed. Whether and how product attributes interrelated across products and product classes is outlined.

Certain aspects of how the knowledge content features 'products' and 'product attributes' interrelated were captured by the complexity variables. These

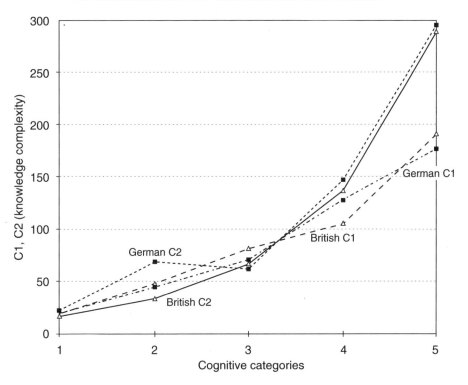

Figure 5.2 Knowledge complexity

variables were compiled for a quantitative assessment of the extent of horizontal and vertical complexity. The C1 variable assessed the horizontal complexity of knowledge: the degree to which product-related knowledge (of X products) was networked across product attributes. The C3 variable assessed vertical knowledge complexity: the degree to which product attribute-related knowledge was networked across products (X products) (see Figure 5.2, Appendices 3.7 and 5.4; see also chapter 3).

The quantitative analysis of the complexity variables revealed a strong trend towards falling values from cognitive category 5 to cognitive category 1 for both horizontal (C1 variable) and vertical (C3 variable) complexity. The analysis indicated that products and product attributes were considerably more strongly networked by persons in the higher cognitive categories. Only certain aspects of complexity are captured by these variables. In particular, they are oriented towards assessing the *extent* to which products and product attributes are networked. They do not distinguish for structural networking patterns, e.g. product class-related patterns of networking. Hence, they are only of limited value for assessing the *nature* of networking patterns.

The nature of networking between products and product attributes was investigated in terms of whether same product attributes related to sequentially recalled products: how product attributes were 'shared' by products along the recall sequence was examined, e.g. whether product class-related networking or networking across product classes occurred. The following networking patterns of the paradigmatic subjects were observed along the recall sequence:

- *B5* had the products 'soap and cosmetics and shampoo and milk' networked along the product attributes 'packaging material' and 'reusable'. The products 'detergent and washing-up liquid and vegetables/fruit' shared the product attributes 'ingredients' and 'locally produced/retailed'. For the food products 'vegetables/fruit and rice/pulses and meat and eggs' networking happened – not comprehensively, but to a high degree – along the attributes 'organic', 'home made' and to a lesser degree also for attributes relating to the LCA issues 'locally produced/retailed' and 'production process'. Besides these comparatively 'long' networking patterns, there were also a number of 'shorter' ones. In its structure, networking reflected strongly product class-related grouping, but networking also cut across different product classes: the products 'shampoo and milk' were recalled sequentially in one reasoning process along the product attributes 'reusable' and 'packaging material'; similarly, 'jam' was recalled in relation to the product attribute 'home made' after the product 'drinks' had been discussed regarding 'home made' issues.

- *G5* networked the products 'bread and grains and vegetables/fruits' along the product attributes 'organic' and 'home made'. The 'home made' attribute played a generally important role: the products 'bread and grains and vegetables/fruit and cleaners and yoghurt and kefir' were recalled in a strongly sequential fashion and all related to 'home made'. The actual recall sequence of these products was: 'bread and grains and vegetables/fruit and coffee and honey and cleaners and yoghurt and kefir', but for coffee and honey the product attribute 'home made' was not touched upon; in a kind of 'excursion' to the attribute 'locally produced/retailed', negative considerations were related to these two products and it was explained why they were not bought. After this 'excursion', further 'home made' products – cleaners, yoghurt and kefir – were recalled. Product class-related grouping played some role, but for G5 it was even more apparent than for B5 that networking cut across product classes; and this happened mainly along the product attributes 'home made' and 'reusable'. As indicated, products that were related to the attribute 'home made' showed a high diversity of product classes. With regard to the product attribute 'reusable', the product 'drinks' was recalled coming from the product 'milk' (referring to reusable glass bottles); and also the product 'cheese' was recalled along the attribute 'reusable' coming from the product 'bread' (referring to reusable packaging).

- *B4* networked the products 'washing-up liquid and detergent and soap and cleaners' strongly but not comprehensively along the two product attributes 'ingredients' and 'biodegradable'. For 'washing-up liquid and detergent', networking also happened along a third product attribute, 'packaging symbols'. The products 'toilet paper and kitchen rolls and cat litter and bin liners' were networked along the product attribute 'recycled'. To some extent, networking cut across different (non-food) product classes, but the networking of B4 had a relatively strong orientation towards product classes.

- *G4* had the products 'milk and yoghurt and cream and drinks (Y product)' networked along the two product attributes 'reusable' and 'locally produced/ retailed'. Milk and yoghurt were also networked along a third product attribute, 'amount of packaging'. The packaging-related product attributes, and here in particular 'reusable', were generally prominent.

- *B3* related the products 'vegetables/fruit and bread and drinks' to the product attribute 'organic'. In general, recall was product class-oriented. The products 'washing-up liquid and detergent and cleaners' were recalled in sequence, but little networking along product attributes existed for them.

- *G3* networked the products 'drinks and milk and yoghurt' along the product attribute 'reusable', and partly also along 'packaging material' and 'word of mouth'. The products 'fruit/vegetables and cheese and sausage' were networked along the product attribute 'amount of packaging'.

- *B2* recalled the products 'detergent and fabric conditioner and sprays' along the two product attributes 'ingredients' and 'packaging symbols'.

- *G2* networked knowledge partly for the products 'butter and bread and milk and fruit/vegetables' along the product attributes 'packaging material' and 'locally produced/retailed'. The latter product attribute, however, was ambiguously paired with shopping interests such as a local patriotic buying motive.

- *N2* (no free recall sequence existed): non-green product examples were given for the prompted products 'deodorant and detergent and toilet paper and shampoo and vegetables/fruit and cleaners'. They were all related to 'product ingredients'.

- *B1* developed no networking patterns for freely recalled products. However, during the prompting phase an interesting pattern of recall was developed along the product attribute 'recyclable' whereby the idea of 'recyclable' was obviously applied in a factually wrong way. Such patterns were otherwise only found for non-green interviewees.

- *G1* showed basically no patterns of networking.

- *N1* (no free recall sequence existed): non-green product examples were given for the prompted products 'vegetables/fruit and drinks and cleaners and meat and milk'. They were all related to the product attribute 'others' which reflected rather abstract reasoning that referred to issues like 'non-essential needs', 'over-production' and the 'balance of the ecosystem'.

The examination of interrelations between 'products' and 'product attributes' yielded some interesting results. For cognitive category 1, neither product class-related grouping was observed (and subsequently no networking in relation to product class-related grouping could be examined for), nor did networking that cut across product classes exist. For cognitive categories 2 and 3, some restrained product class-related grouping was previously observed, and in relation to that, some networking existed. But there were many instances of product class-related grouping for cognitive categories 2 and 3 where little or no networking had occurred. For the higher cognitive categories 4 and 5, the number and extent of instances of product class-related grouping increased, as did networking in relation to product class-related grouping: product class-related networking occurred not just along one product attribute but often along two or even more product attributes. For persons of cognitive category 5, extended networking existed regarding both product class-related grouping and networking that cut across different product classes; even products of product classes that were 'far apart' from each other in terms of their location in a product hierarchy, e.g. 'detergent and vegetables' or 'shampoo and milk', were networked along the same product attributes. When networking cut across different product classes for the middle cognitive categories, which was rarely the case anyway, this related to product classes which were comparatively 'close' together in a product hierarchy, e.g. 'shampoo and cleaners' or 'milk and drinks'.

The non-green interviewees showed some highly untypical networking patterns which were not comparable to findings in the lower cognitive categories 1 and 2. Apparently, through rationalizing, they networked on the spot the sequence of products they were presented with by the interviewer (through the prompting list of product examples). They returned very consistently to the same product attributes, and to a degree, they did so even more consistently than the higher cognitive categories.

In summary, it emerged that the higher cognitive categories had a vastly more complex knowledge than the lower ones:

- In terms of the number of freely recalled products and the number of product attributes a person used to characterize the greenness of a product, a strong increase from the bottom to the top cognitive categories could be observed.
- The complexity variables C1 and C3 indicated that the extent to which knowledge was networked 'horizontally' and 'vertically' across products and product attributes increased strongly from cognitive category 1 to cognitive category 5.
- Regarding the networking of knowledge, there were patterns of concentration that related both to certain products and to certain product attributes. Information was apparently not equally distributed across all the products that were recalled by a person, nor was more information recalled in relation to certain product attributes.
- An examination of the nature of complexity patterns revealed that 'product class-related grouping' and 'networking' occurred to a different extent and in a different way for the cognitive categories. Product class-related grouping

and networking were virtually absent for cognitive category 1. From cognitive category 2 onwards, product class-related grouping increased, and the networking of products intensified from the middle cognitive categories onwards. Networking developed first in relation to product class-related grouping, before it began to cut across product classes. To an extent, the top cognitive category 5 networked knowledge independent of product class-related grouping. Such a pattern could not be found for the other cognitive categories.

• Findings on the non-green interviewees provided some idea of how prompting distorts research on knowledge structures. Some strong, but rather untypical patterns of knowledge integration, as compared with the green interviewees, were found. This indicated a certain influence of rationalizing (naive theorizing) and stereotyping on thinking.

These findings reflected how the recall sequence of freely recalled products was 'interwoven' along product attributes. For cognitive category 5, one could 'travel' along product attributes through the recall sequence with very few or no interruptions; for cognitive category 4, the number of interruptions started to increase, which related to a stronger orientation of networking towards product classes; for the lower cognitive categories 1 and 2, when they were moving from one product to another in the recall sequence, interruptions along product attributes happened with nearly every move.

The findings made here on knowledge complexity are in line with propositions in the literature that differences in the organization of knowledge between 'experts' and 'novices' could be expected in terms of the size and the nature of knowledge structures (Tybout and Artz 1994: 136–7, Alba and Hutchinson 1987: 417–18). The findings made here on knowledge complexity not only supported strongly the idea that knowledge is hierarchically organized (Alba *et al.* 1991: 7–9, Smith and Houston 1986: 504), but they illuminated in detail what the hierarchical nature of knowledge complexity looks like. Such detailed insights into the complex nature of consumption knowledge were possible because of the open, free-recall focus of this study.

The different patterns of knowledge complexity that emerged for the various cognitive categories can be related to a process of knowledge structure development (learning), which will be returned to in the next chapter in more detail when experience effects are discussed.

Knowledge abstractness and specificity

An assessment of knowledge specificity and knowledge abstractness examines knowledge substance, i.e. the type of language used by a person. Knowledge abstractness refers to the technical degree of knowledge substance, while knowledge specificity refers to the literal degree of knowledge. Highly specific knowledge is, for instance, a knowledge of names, while highly abstract knowledge reflects conceptual knowledge, e.g. a knowledge of ideas such as 'recycled', 'organic', etc.

Knowledge abstractness and knowledge specificity were measured through the 2×2 abstractness–specificity matrices. These matrices were developed for the twenty-nine sub-categories of 'greenness' as contained in the bracketing framework (for examples, see Appendix 3.10). The abstractness–specificity variables AS1, AS2, AS3 and AS4 reflected for each interviewee the extent of highly and weakly abstract knowledge and of highly and weakly specific knowledge.

Knowledge abstractness

Knowledge abstractness refers to the technicality of language. Highly concrete, technical knowledge (AS4 variable) was comparatively rare for all cognitive categories. The following AS4-type notions were used by the paradigmatic subjects (for characterizing freely recalled X products):

- *B5*: 'totally organic, no chemical, artificial fertilizers, no pesticides, no herbicides, no fungicides' with reference to fruit and vegetables, and 'totally organic, no drugs and concentrates' for meat.
- *G5*: 'sortenreines aufteilen und verwerten, aluschmilzanlage' [category based separation and re-usage, aluminium melting plant] related to the disposal of the packaging of sweets, 'molkebasis' [whey-based] related to cleaners, and 'milchsäure' [milk acid] related to washing-up liquid.
- *B4*: 'weak solution of hydrogen chloride' related to cleaners, and '80 per cent or 100 per cent recycled paper, regurgitated paper' in relation to the products kitchen rolls, toilet paper and cat litter, and '80 per cent recycled plastic' for dustbin bags.
- *G4*: 'einwegflasche' [one-way bottle] related to milk.
- *B3*: no findings.
- *G3*: 'aus ökologischem anbau, ungspritztes getreide, ohne künstlichen dünger' [ecological cultivation, untreated grain, with artificial fertilizer] related to bread.
- *B2*: no findings.
- *G2*: 'mehrwegflasche' [bring-back bottle] related to milk.
- *N2*: 'no polystyrene container' in relation to the prompted product 'meat'.
- *B1*: no findings.
- *G1*: '100 per cent altpapier' [waste paper] related to toilet paper.
- *N1*: 'too many cows upset the ecosystem' in relation to the prompted product 'meat'.

It appeared that examples of highly technical language were rarer for the paradigmatic subjects of the lower cognitive categories than for the top ones. This was also reflected by the decrease in the average value of the AS4 variable from cognitive category 5 to cognitive category 1. Furthermore, values of the tec-variable of the CI analysis, which reflected technical knowledge, indicated a positive relationship between membership in the higher cognitive categories and the extent of technical knowledge (see chapter 3 and Appendix 5.2).

Certain technical notions, like 'pfandflasche' [deposit bottle] for the German sample or 'recycled' for the British sample, were quite common across all cognitive categories. Such notions can be characterized as comparatively abstract, but weakly concrete (AS3 variable). Similarly 'popular' were other AS3-type notions, like 'organic' for vegetables and 'biodegradable' for washing + cleaning products. These notions have made inroads into commonsense knowledge: they have been around for some time and they have become quite popular in everyday speech. Issues like 'recycled', 'organic' or 'biodegradable' have played a prominent role in a public discussion over the years in Britain (see Wild 1995: 49-54). Similarly, the packaging concept of reusable bottles reflects a rather traditional way of packaging drinks in Germany, e.g. for mineral water, beer, etc.[3] It also appeared that highly technical knowledge (AS4) that the lower cognitive categories of the German sample had related to some of those traditional concepts.

In a further examination, the actual interview was searched for a knowledge of maxims for green shopping. Such knowledge can be related to schemata for green shopping (as discussed below). Maxims for green shopping tended to pop up right at the beginning of the interview. This happened despite an interview approach that was geared towards the concrete, trying to retrieve product examples: an initial question which enquired about what green products a person bought was often answered in a comparatively abstract way that summarized in a few, short, maxim-like statements an interviewee's basic approach to green shopping.[4] In the following, such maxims are discussed. Where no abstract maxims were found – that were void of literal knowledge – next-best ones were listed which contained some sort of concrete, literal reference either to products or to values of product attributes:

- *B5*: 'think about things that get flushed down the system', 'think about things that get thrown out', 'no plastics', 'buy organic', 'tend to shop locally'.
- *G5*: 'abfallvermeidung' [waste avoidance], 'transport', 'geringe menge' [little quantity], 'wenig dosen' [few cans].
- *B4*: 'buy the ones called environmentally friendly', 'buy things from recycled paper', 'buy recycled things'.
- *G4*: 'geringe verpackung' [little packaging], 'verpackungsmäßig keinen abfall' [packaging-wise, no waste], 'verpackung vermeiden' [avoidance of packaging].
- *B3*: 'buy supermarket's own brand green products', 'minimize packaging', 'get old-fashioned things, avoid buying'.
- *G3*: 'pfandflaschen' [deposit bottles], 'verpackungsaspekt' [packaging aspect], 'minimale verpackung' [minimal packaging].
- *B2*: 'buy Eco-something', 'avoid things with CFC'.
- *G2*: 'von der verpackung her' [packaging-wise], 'keine eingeschweißten

lebensmittel' [no plastic-sealed groceries], 'unverpackte produkte' [unpackaged products].

- *N2*: (not available due to hypothetical interview approach.)

- *B1*: 'these global issues', 'consumerism in the supermarket'.

- *G1*: 'verpackungen' [packaging], 'vermeide Hollandsachen' [avoid Dutch things], 'abfall' [waste], 'biologisch abbaubare sachen' [biodegradable things].

- *N1*: (not available due to hypothetical interview approach.)

A distinction between weakly abstract and highly abstract notions, as made above, can be applied to a discussion of maxims, too. There was a tendency towards higher abstraction in the top cognitive categories. For the lower cognitive categories, examples of weakly abstract maxims were the only ones that could be found and they were frequently related to a concrete issue. Weakly abstract, concrete maxims could also be found for the higher cognitive categories, but there highly abstract maxims also existed. In the very bottom cognitive category, B1 knew some abstract notions, such as 'these global issues' and 'consumerism in the supermarket', but they were not maxims for green shopping; rather, they related to more general issues.

Knowledge specificity

Knowledge specificity refers to literal knowledge. Knowledge specificity is strongly reflected by a knowledge of names. The paradigmatic subjects had developed the product attribute 'names' to a varying degree. In general, the higher cognitive categories knew more names, and they knew more specialist names. Often, the lower cognitive categories referred to names on a weakly specific basis, such as 'supermarkets'. The higher categories specified frequently certain specialist shopping places, e.g. 'wholefood shops', either by their names or with reference to their locations, e.g. a street name (see Table 5.1). At one extreme, B4 recalled names such as 'Co-op, Body Shop, Sainsbury's, Green Care, Ecover, Down To Earth, Holland and Barrett, Traidcraft, Neal's Yard, Boots'; at the other extreme, B1 recalled only one name, 'Sainsbury's'. To a degree, the paradigmatic subject B5's knowledge of names compared to that of the middle cognitive categories; B5 referenced a number of products with regard to the product attribute 'home made', and consequently the product attribute 'names' was less developed than for the other members of the higher cognitive categories (who focused on the product attribute 'home made' less strongly).

Another indicator of knowledge specificity is the extent of episodic knowledge. Episodic knowledge refers to autobiographical knowledge of temporally dated events (see chapter 2). It is of a highly specific but weakly abstract nature. Such knowledge was not captured by the high specificity–low abstractness variable AS2 since this variable only reflected knowledge that related to product characteristics but not to experience events. Episodic knowledge basically reflects stories that relate to green consumption;[5] for instance, one interviewee explained

Table 5.1 Names recalled

British paradigmatic subjects (from the PA matrices)

B5: rice, pulses/wholefood shop in Hadley; meat/shot by a friend, butcher in a large
shop; washing powder/Co-op, Ecover; washing-up liquid/Ecover, wholefood shop;
cleaners/Ecover; toilet paper/wholefood shop; soap/Body Shop; cosmetics/Body
Shop; shampoo/Body Shop; milk/dairy at the back of Co-op, Hadley, local shops;
vegetables, fruit/shops around here, Co-op, wholefood shop in Hadley, Tesco

B4: vegetables, fruit/Caribbean, Sainsbury's, Traidcraft; washing-up liquid/Co-op,
Ecover, Down to Earth, Sainsbury's; soap/Co-op; shower gel, shampoo/Co-op, Body
Shop, Holland & Barrett, Neal's Yard, Boots; washing powder/Co-op, Sainsbury's,
Green Care, Ecover, Down to Earth; cleaner/Ecover, Down to Earth, Sainsbury's,
Co-op; kitchen rolls/Co-op, Sainsbury's, Green Care, Holland & Barrett, health
store; toilet paper/Sainsbury's, Green Care, Holland & Barrett, health store,
Traidcraft; soya milk, soya yoghurt/Holland & Barrett; muesli, dried fruit/Holland
& Barrett, Neal's Yard; cat litter/Sainsbury's; P^1:drinks/Holland & Barrett;
P:packaging material → peanut butter/Neal's Yard, Holland & Barrett

B3: washing-up liquid/supermarket's own brand green products, Sainsbury's, Green
Care, Ecover; washing powder/supermarket's own brand green products,
Sainsbury's, Green Care, Ecover; cleaners/supermarket's own brand green products,
Sainsbury's, Green Care; vegetables/scheme, farm, Sainsbury's; bread/Sainsbury's,
Neal's Yard; P:toilet paper/Green Care; P:shampoo/Body Shop; P:meat/one butcher

B2: washing detergent/eco, Eco-cover, eco-something, Sainsbury's, local health shop;
fabric conditioner/eco, Eco-cover, eco-something, Sainsbury's, Tesco's own brand;
vegetables/Sainsbury's; toilet paper/Traidcraft, local supplier, Sainsbury's, church
function; P:toilet paper → kitchen rolls/Traidcraft, local supplier, Sainsbury's,
church function; P:washing-up liquid/Sainsbury's; P:cleaners/Sainsbury's

B1: detergent/Sainsbury's, Novolon; fabric softener/Sainsbury's, eco-something; paper
towels/Sainsbury's; P:toilet paper/Sainsbury's make; P:milk/milkman; P:literature →
bleach/Sainsbury's own

German paradigmatic subjects (from the PA matrices)

G5: bread/bioladen; grains/biobauern, bioladen, Mailing, nächste in der umgebung;
vegetables, fruit/direkt vom bauernhof, biobauer; coffee/Dritte Welt-Laden;
honey/Dritte Welt-Laden; drinks/Ehekirchen, abfüllerei, genossenschaften; milk/
supermarkt; cleaners/bioladen, Frosch, Hara; sweet/bioladen; P:washing
powder/Skip, bioladen, besseren supermärkte; P:toilet paper/Danke;
P:shampoo/Sebamed, Body Shop, Weleda; P:washing-up liquid/Conley, München,
Frosch, Hacka

G4: milk/bauern, Am Platz; drinks/weingut, weingut in Ingolstadt, getränkemarkt;
meat/metzger; vegetables, fruit/supermarkt, wochenmarkt, stände; washing
powder/Hobbythek, geschäft, stadtmitte; yoghurt/Edcka, Delta, Nestlé, Landliebe;
cream/Weihenstephan, Goldmilch; P:toilet paper/Pro Natur, Hackle;
P:shampoo/friseur; P:washing up liquid/Frosch; P:washing-up liquid →
cleaners/Frosch

cont . . .

Table 5.1 cont.

G3: fruit, vegetables/obstgeschäfte, H & L-Markt, gemüseladen; drinks/getränkemarkt, H & L-Markt; bread/Hofpfisterei; toilet paper/umweltschutzpapier, H & L-Markt, Plus; kitchen towels/umweltschutzpapier; P:washing powder/spezialläden

G2: bread/bäckerei; milk/bauern, Goldmilch; fruit, vegetables/Edeka-laden, bauern; drinks/getränkefahrer; P:washing powder/umweltwaschmittel; P:toilet paper/ umweltpapier, Blümia, Edeka-laden; P:shampoo/Hackawerke; P:washing-up liquid/Hacka; P:yoghurt/Ehrmann; P:organic → meat/bauern

G1: vegetables, fruit/reformkostläden, Spanien, Italien, markt; cleaners/bio-Abflußfrei, Froschmarke, supermarkt, drogeriemarkt; P:washing powder/Ariel, Rei; P:toilet paper/Natur; P:washing-up liquid/Froschmarke; P:yoghurt/Landliebe, Weihenstephaner

---

Note: 1 P: = prompted

that she had started buying cat litter half a year earlier because at that time her cat had suffered an injury which prevented it from leaving the house; subsequently, this interviewee discussed certain environmental product characteristics for the product cat litter (and only this latter discussion was captured by the abstractness–specificity variables).

Both an examination of the actual interview data of the paradigmatic subjects and the CI analysis (through the epi-variable which reflected the number of instances of episodic knowledge an interviewee had) indicated a comparatively even spread of episodic knowledge across all cognitive categories. Top scoring interviewees in terms of the number of episodes recalled were in the higher cognitive categories 5, 4 and 3, but trends were not very clear. That trends remained unclear may reflect on the kind of interview method used in this study. The research interview collected episodic knowledge only as a by-product. It was not geared towards retrieving and measuring episodic knowledge in the first place (rather it attempted to observe product-related knowledge). Lacking patterns in the distribution of the number of episodes across the cognitive categories may reflect this decision concerning method.

Interrelations between knowledge specificity and knowledge abstractness

The correlation analysis in chapter 4 indicated certain differences in knowledge abstractness and specificity between the green samples and the non-green sample: highly abstract knowledge played quite a prominent role for the green samples, while for the non-green sample weakly specific knowledge played a more important role. These analyses, however, could not reveal whether there were significant differences regarding knowledge abstractness and specificity *within* the green samples. An examination of this has only begun in this chapter.

An assessment of knowledge abstractness and knowledge specificity indicated that there was a strong quantitative difference in terms of the distribution of highly specific and/or highly abstract knowledge among the cognitive categories, i.e. within the samples. It also hinted at certain qualitative differences regarding the nature of specific and abstract knowledge that was found for the different cognitive categories: highly technical knowledge (AS4) was particularly prominent for the higher cognitive categories, whereas certain types of other abstract knowledge were fairly common across all cognitive categories (AS3). A highly specific knowledge of names (AS2) was also held by the top cognitive categories, whereas the lower cognitive categories relied more on 'general' names, e.g. category headings like 'supermarket' (AS1).

Patterns in the relationship between knowledge abstractness and knowledge specificity are now examined in more detail. The abstractness–specificity variables AS1, AS2, AS3 and AS4 capture the extent to which an interviewee held highly and weakly abstract and also highly and weakly specific knowledge. A distributional analysis of these variables, especially how they were distributed in relation to each other, provided insights into the knowledge substance characteristics of the cognitive categories. For each of the abstractness–specificity variables, the average per cognitive category was calculated (see Appendixes 5.1 and 5.2).[6] The series of *absolute average values* for AS1, AS2, AS3 and AS4, followed by the series of *their percentage split*, is shown in Table 5.2.

In terms of absolute numbers, there was quite a strong decrease in values for each of the abstractness–specificity variables from the top cognitive category 5 to the bottom cognitive category 1. In proportional terms, the distribution of the four abstractness–specificity variables showed certain similarities for all five cognitive categories: the high specificity–low abstractness variable AS2 always

Table 5.2 Abstractness/specificity values of British and German samples

	Absolute[1]	*Relative*[1]
British sample		
Cognitive category 5	11-32-13-4	0.18 - 0.53 - 0.22 - 0.07
Cognitive category 4	5-19-8-2	0.15 - 0.56 - 0.24 - 0.06
Cognitive category 3	7-11-7-1	0.27 - 0.42 - 0.27 - 0.04
Cognitive category 2	5-7-3-0	0.33 - 0.47 - 0.20 - 0.00
Cognitive category 1	2-5-2-1	0.20 - 0.50 - 0.20 - 0.10
German sample		
Cognitive category 5	15-28-11-5	0.25 - 0.47 - 0.19 - 0.08
Cognitive category 4	10-21-7-1	0.26 - 0.54 - 0.18 - 0.03
Cognitive category 3	5-11-7-2	0.20 - 0.44 - 0.28 - 0.08
Cognitive category 2	7-10-2-1	0.35 - 0.50 - 0.10 - 0.05
Cognitive category 1	5-4-3-0	0.42 - 0.33 - 0.25 - 0.00

Note: 1 Series of AS1, AS2, AS3, AS4.

had the biggest share (except for cognitive category 1 in the German sample which had only two members, thus making it particularly sensitive to outlier effects). And the high specificity–high abstractness variable AS4 always had the lowest share.

Besides these similarities, there were differences in the way the abstractness–specificity variables were distributed in each cognitive category: it appeared that the high specificity–low abstractness variable AS2 had a marginally bigger share in the top cognitive categories. For the high abstractness–low specificity variable AS3, cognitive category 3 had a proportionally bigger share than the other cognitive categories. Cognitive categories 1 and 2 were, again in proportional terms, particularly strong for the low specificity–low abstractness variable AS1. For the German cognitive category 1, a distributional pattern of the abstractness–specificity variables emerged that compared to the one for the non-green sample (see Appendix 3.12).

These shifts in the distributional patterns of the abstractness–specificity variables across the cognitive categories were ones of degree. Before they were further interpreted, whether their significance could or could not be substantiated by additional analyses was examined.

The cognitive categories had a comparatively low numerical basis which made them prone to be affected by outlier effects. Hence, their distributions may have reflected spurious trends, or 'real' trends may have been blurred. A larger numerical basis was thought to be desirable for further analyses. In order to get a bigger numerical basis, the British and German samples were integrated, and for the combined British and German sample distributional patterns were re-examined (this also provided another test for the robustness and significance of the findings). For the cognitive categories of the combined British and German sample, the series of absolute average values of the abstractness–specificity variables and their percentage splits is presented in Table 5.3.

As before, in absolute terms there were quite dramatic decreases for all of the four abstractness–specificity variables from the top cognitive categories to the bottom ones. As a result of the integration of samples, the distributional shifts across the cognitive categories that had been found earlier appeared to become clearer. An increased numerical basis seemed to reduce outlier effects:

Table 5.3 Abstractness/specificity values of combined British and German sample

	Absolute[1]	*Relative*[1]
Cognitive category 5	14-29-12-4	0.24 - 0.49 - 0.20 - 0.07
Cognitive category 4	7-20-8-2	0.19 - 0.54 - 0.22 - 0.05
Cognitive category 3	6-11-7-1	0.24 - 0.44 - 0.28 - 0.04
Cognitive category 2	6-8-3-0	0.35 - 0.47 - 0.18 - 0.00
Cognitive category 1	2-4-1-0	0.29 - 0.57 - 0.14 - 0.00

Note: 1 Series of AS1, AS2, AS3, AS4.

- The high specificity–low abstractness variable AS2 again had the highest share in each cognitive category.
- The bottom cognitive categories 1 and 2 had a higher proportional share when it came to weakly abstract–weakly specific knowledge (AS1). Its share increased towards the lower categories.
- The middle category 3 had a comparatively strong focus on weakly specific–highly abstract knowledge (AS3). The AS3 variable appeared to have an inverted U-shaped distribution across the cognitive categories, with a peak share for cognitive category 3.
- For the high specificity–high abstractness variable AS4, shares increased from the lower to the higher cognitive categories.
- Cognitive categories 4 and 5 had an edge over the other cognitive categories with regard to knowledge specificity, particularly regarding highly specific–highly abstract knowledge (AS4), but to a degree also for highly specific–weakly abstract knowledge (AS2).
- With regard to the AS1 variable, the picture remained a more ambiguous one.

In a further analysis of these trends, the 'dimensions' of the previous distributional analysis were swapped. How the language of each of the cognitive categories was distributed for language types AS1, AS2, AS3 and AS4 has been examined above. The following examines how a certain type of language is distributed across the five cognitive categories 1, 2, 3, 4 and 5, again for the combined British and German sample (see Table 5.4). Figure 5.3 depicts how the absolute numbers of the language-type variables were distributed for the cognitive categories.

Table 5.4 can be interpreted 'horizontally' for each of the four language types as reflected by the variables AS1, AS2, AS3 and AS4 (horizontally, the relative frequencies add up to 1), and it can be interpreted 'vertically' for each of the five cognitive categories. The horizontal distributions reflect each cognitive category's share of a certain type of language as it was found for the total sample (the combined British and German sample); for instance, of all the weakly specific and weakly abstract knowledge (AS1) found, cognitive category 5 had a share of 40 per cent, cognitive category 4 had 20 per cent, cognitive category 3 17 per cent, cognitive category 2 17 per cent, and cognitive category 1 had a mere 6 per cent.

Vertically, each column reflects what shares a cognitive category had of the four different types of language found in the total sample; for instance, cognitive category 5 had the biggest shares of each type of language: 40 per cent of AS1 (weakly specific–weakly abstract knowledge), 40 per cent of AS2 (highly specific–weakly abstract knowledge), 39 per cent of AS3 (weakly specific–highly abstract knowledge), and 57 per cent of AS4 (highly specific–highly abstract knowledge). The table reflects impressively how differently concentrated knowledge was across the cognitive categories.

AS1, AS2
AS3, AS4

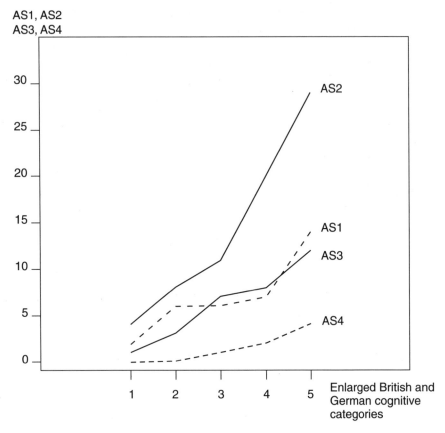

Figure 5.3 Knowledge abstractness and specificity

Table 5.4 Shares of cognitive categories

Variables	Cognitive category 5	Cognitive category 4	Cognitive category 3	Cognitive category 2	Cognitive category 1
AS1	0.40	0.20	0.17	0.17	0.06
AS2	0.40	0.28	0.15	0.11	0.06
AS3	0.39	0.26	0.23	0.10	0.03
AS4	0.57	0.29	0.14	0.00	0.00

For a 'horizontal' interpretation, 'plateaux' and 'jumps' between neighbouring cognitive categories were defined in order to gain a yardstick for a *comparative* assessment. As a matter of convention, a 'jump' was diagnosed if the lower category's value deviated by more than a third from the higher category's value. Otherwise a 'plateau' was diagnosed. Comparing each cognitive category with its neighbouring category, the following plateaux and jumps were found:

144

- *Category 5 compared with category 4:* For all four language-type variables jumps could be diagnosed.
- *Category 4 compared with category 3:* For AS1 and for AS3 plateaux could be found, and for AS2 and for AS4 jumps could be identified. High specificity, as reflected by AS2 and AS4, seemed to differentiate cognitive category 4 from cognitive category 3.
- *Category 3 compared with category 2:* For AS1 and, to a degree, also for AS2, plateaux existed; for AS3 and for AS4 jumps could be diagnosed. High abstractness, as reflected by AS3 and AS4, apparently distinguished cognitive categories 3 and 2.
- *Category 2 compared with category 1:* Except for AS4, jumps could be diagnosed for the other language-type variables. Cognitive category 1 appeared to be, like cognitive category 5 at the other end of the spectrum, a 'class apart' from the middle cognitive categories.

Table 5.4 can also be examined vertically. Each column can be interpreted to show how big each cognitive category's share of a certain type of language was (for the combined British and German sample). Again, a very strong relationship of dominance was apparent amongst the cognitive categories: each cognitive category dominated its neighbouring category, i.e. for all four language-type variables AS1, AS2, AS3 and AS4, cognitive category 5 had the highest shares, cognitive category 4 had the second highest shares, cognitive category 3 the third highest ones, and so on. To find out what type of language was comparatively strongly focused on by each cognitive category, which language-type variable had the peak share per cognitive category was examined:

- For *cognitive category 5*, highly abstract–highly specific knowledge (AS4) had the biggest share (0.57).
- For *cognitive category 4*, no distinctive top share could be made out: AS2, AS3 and AS4 were about equally high (0.28, 0.26, 0.29).
- For *cognitive category 3*, highly abstract–weakly specific knowledge (AS3), which strongly reflected commonsense knowledge of 'traditional' green concepts such as 'recycled', had the highest share (0.23).
- For *cognitive category 2*, weakly abstract–weakly specific knowledge (AS1) had the biggest share (0.17).
- For *cognitive category 1*, weakly abstract knowledge (AS1 and AS2) had the biggest share (0.06 respectively).

These findings are in line with the previous ones. In general, it appeared that the subtle shifts in the distribution of the specificity–abstractness variables across the cognitive categories, as they are demonstrated above for the British and German samples individually, could be substantiated by further analyses.[7] The analyses revealed a clear differentiation between the cognitive categories: an assessment of distributional shares of the language-type variables per cognitive category indicated that cognitive category 5 was particularly strong on highly specific–highly abstract knowledge (AS4); that cognitive category 3 had a comparatively strong emphasis on highly abstract–weakly specific knowledge (AS3); and that cognitive category 2 and, to a degree, also cognitive category 1 focused comparatively strongly on weakly specific–weakly abstract knowledge (AS1). These findings on knowledge abstractness and knowledge specificity subsequently provided the basis for the assessment of the cognitive operational processes of specification and abstraction, and they provided certain clues regarding how learning occurred in terms of the build-up of increasingly abstract and increasingly specific knowledge.

Conclusions

For each of the knowledge content characteristics discussed, a strong relationship of dominance existed between the cognitive categories: the comprehensiveness, complexity, specificity and abstractness of knowledge increased rapidly from the bottom cognitive categories to the top ones.

Knowledge comprehensiveness increased slightly progressively from the lower cognitive categories towards the top cognitive categories,[8] supporting the so-called 'enrichment hypothesis' regarding familiarity-effects on the amount of information recalled.

The higher cognitive categories recalled knowledge more 'efficiently' than the lower ones. Green knowledge extracts, expressed as a share of all words spoken during an interview (reflected by the ratios W1/W3 and W2/W4), doubled from the bottom towards the top cognitive categories. Such a difference probably had to be related to differences in knowledge content characteristics as well as underlying operational and schematic knowledge features, which are interpreted below.

Regarding knowledge complexity, substantial differences among the cognitive categories were identified. 'Product class-related grouping' and 'networking' occurred to a different extent and in a different way: they were basically absent for cognitive category 1; from cognitive category 2 onwards, product class-related grouping increased; from the middle cognitive categories onwards, the networking of products intensified in relation to product class-related grouping; the top cognitive category 5 had, to an extent, knowledge networked independent of product class-related grouping. The build-up of knowledge complexity seemed to work first in a product class-related way, before a networking of knowledge began to cut across product classes.

Regarding the degree of the specificity and abstractness of knowledge, shifts in the distribution of high and low abstractness and high and low specificity of knowledge were found across the cognitive categories. The lower cognitive categories 1 and 2 appeared to be relatively strong on weakly abstract and weakly specific knowledge. Cognitive category 3 had a comparatively strong focus on weakly specific and highly abstract knowledge, reflecting abstract knowledge of 'traditional' ideas, e.g. 'recycled', 'biodegradable', 'organic', etc. The top category

146

5 had in proportional terms the biggest advantage over the other cognitive categories regarding highly specific and highly abstract knowledge.

COGNITIVE OPERATIONS

This section discusses how differences in knowledge content characteristics of green consumers reflected on their cognitive operations. Knowledge content is a relatively static concept that relates to a consciously accessible level of cognition. In terms of the computer analogy, the knowledge content level compares to 'data files', whereas a cognitive operational level compares to 'applications software'. In contrast to knowledge content, cognitive operations are of a subconscious nature. They cannot be 'observed' and 'measured' as knowledge content can. The nature of cognitive operations has to be deduced from findings on knowledge content.

In the preceding assessment of knowledge content, cognitive operations were touched upon; for instance, knowledge complexity readily reflects on cognitive operational processes of knowledge integration, and similarly reflects an assessment of knowledge specificity and abstractness on cognitive operations such as abstraction and specification. The operational dynamics of how knowledge content is 'used' are discussed in the following in more detail. First, different *processes* of cognitive operations are assessed, as they were distinguished in chapter 2 as selection, specification, abstraction, interpretation and integration. Complementary to the distinctions between processes of cognitive operations, two different types of operational *modes* are assessed, top-down processing and bottom-up processing.

Processes of cognitive operations

Cognitive operations provide a grammar for the development, organization and application of knowledge content. Five processes of cognitive operations were distinguished earlier: selection, specification, abstraction, interpretation and integration (see chapter 2 and Figure 2.4). While selection is *perceptually* oriented – it refers to information attention and acquisition – the other cognitive operational processes refer to information processing and to the storage of meaning, i.e. they are *conceptually* oriented. In the following, the conceptual processes of cognitive operations are first dealt with, before perceptual processes of selection are commented on.

Specification

Specification refers to the development of concrete, literal knowledge content. Through specification, a knowledge of names or name substitutes, e.g. category headings such as 'supermarket', is developed. From the previous analysis of knowledge specificity it was apparent that the specificity of names increased from the bottom to the top cognitive categories. For the lower cognitive categories, a knowledge of names consisted of comparatively general terms, e.g. 'supermarkets' own green products'. In contrast, those in the higher cognitive categories knew specific names, e.g. 'Neal's Yard', for a considerable range of products. In the following, I shall examine whether names of products, retailers or manufacturers were volunteered during the interview or had to be enquired about by the interviewer. Such a discussion reflects on the role specification plays in the build-up of knowledge (learning).

Names played a different role across the cognitive categories in the recall of green product-related knowledge. The free recall part of the interview (part 1) basically consisted of two phases: an initial, start-up phase when product examples were freely recalled, and a subsequent part which comprised a follow-up discussion of these examples. For the British paradigmatic subjects, it was found that, in the start-up phase of the interview, B5 and B4 of the top cognitive categories referred to issues like ingredients or packaging; names played a comparatively insignificant role in characterizing the green product. Product or retailer names had to be enquired about in more detail in the follow-up discussion. In contrast, the paradigmatic subjects B3 and B2 volunteered names like 'supermarkets' own green brands' in the start-up phase of the interview. While B5 and B4 quickly related the initial recall of product examples to certain product attributes like ingredients or packaging, the paradigmatic subjects B3 and B2 focused strongly on names for an initial characterization of the green products. For B1, neither names nor product attributes played a significant role in the start-up phase since recall of product examples was minimal.

Similar findings were made for the German paradigmatic subjects. All of them touched upon the packaging issue in some way during the start-up phase of the interview. Packaging was, in general, a dominant issue. After an initial reference to packaging, this issue was, however, differently followed up. The paradigmatic subjects in the higher cognitive categories G5 and G4, and to an extent also G3, began to dwell further on the packaging issue, relating it to product attributes such as 'packaging material', 'amount of packaging' or 'reusable'. Still in the initial start-up phase and following a brief discussion of packaging issues, other product attributes like LCA considerations were also related to green product examples. The paradigmatic subjects in the lower cognitive categories, G2 and G1, had also initially related the recall of green product examples to 'packaging', but then rather quickly made a connection to the product attribute 'names', e.g. references to certain shopping places. To a degree, G3 also started on such a line of reasoning but at a later point in time than G2 and G1. For G1, recall was strongly oriented towards names in a way similar to that of the paradigmatic subjects of the lower cognitive categories of the British sample.

The analysis of when names were referred to by interviewees showed that, for both British and German consumers, the higher cognitive categories did not draw strongly on names during the start-up phase of the interview: rather than characterizing recalled products in terms of their brand or retailer names, green product examples were characterized in terms of certain green product attributes. In contrast, for the lower cognitive categories, names played a prominent role in the start-up phase of the interview: names were quickly volunteered to characterize green product examples.

As it turned out during the follow-up discussion of product examples, the higher cognitive categories had a quantitative as well as a qualitative advantage regarding a knowledge of names: once they were asked about names, it became clear that they knew more names and they knew more specific names than those in the lower cognitive categories did.

These differences in the organization of the recall of names supported the idea that specification precedes abstraction: the higher cognitive categories had apparently gone through deeper and more extended processes of specification; but names as such were not (or no longer) 'viewed' as overridingly important for characterizing the green product; rather they focused on 'issues' describing the green product in terms of certain attributes. In contrast, the lower cognitive categories tended to describe the green product with a strong focus on names. They had only some vague idea of what buying a green product meant in terms of green product characteristics other than names.

Regarding the nature of knowledge structures, these findings can be related to the idea that consumption knowledge develops hierarchically and, related to that, that knowledge development goes through different phases.[9] Specification or 'naming' processes regarding a product seemed to be a prerequisite for thinking about a product 'more deeply' – along product attributes other than names. A naming of knowledge content features, such as 'products' or 'product attributes', appeared to be essential for the development of an understanding of concepts, such as a product and its characteristics. This highlights the importance of names promotion and names rehearsal for a communication policy that is directed at consumers in the lower cognitive categories (and much TV advertising seems to be quite poor in that respect, mentioning product names just in the last fraction of a second of a TV spot).

Abstraction

Abstraction refers to the generation of technical meaning. Certain 'traditional' abstract concepts, like 'recycled', were known by members of all cognitive categories, except for cognitive category 1, where even a 'commonsense' abstraction of green concepts seemed to have been only very rudimentary. This was also indicated by the extent of classification errors in this category. For instance, the idea of 'recyclable' was related by B1 to products such as toilet paper or kitchen towels (similar classification errors could be observed for the non-green interviewees who sometimes characterized green products in an erroneous way that was untypical of the green interviewees). Cognitive category 3 already had levels of abstract knowledge similar to those of cognitive category 4 in terms of 'traditional' abstract concepts. For the higher cognitive categories, abstract ideas, such as 'recycled', were further elaborated on in a highly technical manner, e.g. '100 per cent recycled from waste paper but not from factory off-cuts'. Highly technical ideas and highly abstract shopping maxims were most common for the top cognitive categories. Such highly technical knowledge was of a different nature from knowing 'traditional', commonsense abstract concepts. Also, regarding the extent of such highly abstract knowledge, gaps between the cognitive categories were markedly bigger: for cognitive categories 1 and 2, values for highly technical knowledge (AS4 variable) were very low; only from cognitive category 3 on, levels of highly abstract and highly specific knowledge started to increase step by step, and the top cognitive category 5 distinguished itself especially with regard to highly technical knowledge from the other cognitive categories (see above, pp. 140–6).

These findings on knowledge abstractness can be related to different types of abstraction processes. Apparently, the build-up of increasingly abstract knowledge occurred in steps. Processes of abstraction appeared to start in cognitive category 2 regarding 'traditional' abstract shopping concepts, such as 'reusable' for drinks products in Germany or 'recycled' for paper products in Britain. In contrast, highly abstract, technical knowledge was only present among the higher cognitive categories. Two different abstraction processes can be suggested, one that resulted in highly technical knowledge (AS4 variable), and one that led to 'commonsense' technical knowledge (AS3 variable); and such 'commonsense' abstraction seemed to precede that yielding highly technical knowledge.

The following offers a brief assessment of how specification and abstraction were interrelated regarding knowledge structure development (learning), re-examining the distributional patterns previously found between knowledge specificity and knowledge abstractness. An examination of the abstractness–specificity variables had revealed that the lower cognitive categories 1 and 2 focused comparatively strongly on weakly specific and weakly abstract knowledge (AS1 variable), and cognitive category 3 focused on weakly specific and highly abstract knowledge (AS3 variable), while cognitive category 5 had an extended knowledge of highly specific and highly abstract knowledge concepts (AS4 variable) (see Tables 5.2, 5.3 and 5.4). It also appeared that the higher cognitive categories had some advantage with regard to highly specific and weakly abstract knowledge (AS2 variable), but values for the AS2 variable were relatively high across all cognitive categories. These findings on knowledge specificity and abstractness indicated certain relationships between the processes of specification and abstraction:

- Before abstraction started (from cognitive category 2 onwards), only some rather general terms-thinking (AS1 variable) appeared to occur. The bottom cognitive category 1 was especially strong regarding the AS1 variable.
- 'Commonsense' abstraction, as reflected by increasing values of the AS3 variable for cognitive category 3, seemed to precede the further development

of a knowledge of names (as reflected by the AS2 variable). The higher cognitive categories knew more names and they knew more specific names.

- Extended specification (AS2 variable), in turn, appeared to precede the development of highly specific and highly abstract knowledge (as reflected by the AS4 variable).

A 'low-level' learning process, as reflected by a learning sequence such as 'AS1 → AS3', seemed to lead to an initial build-up of some abstract commonsense knowledge. It characterized the learning of the lower cognitive categories which led in its advanced stages to membership in cognitive category 3. There were indications that extensive specification, leading to a comprehensive build-up of AS2-type knowledge, and abstraction, leading to AS4-type knowledge, reflected learning at a later stage. A learning process can be suggested for the higher cognitive categories such as 'AS2 → AS4' and 'AS3 → AS4', depicting 'high-level' learning.

Assessing specification *vis-à-vis* abstraction, it appeared that specification processes that yielded highly specific knowledge (AS2 and AS4) 'alternated' to a degree with abstraction processes that yielded highly abstract knowledge (AS3 and AS4). Tentatively, a process of knowledge structure development can be suggested that resembles a staircase relation (see Figure 5.4). The 'staircase' relation indicates a high interdependence and a change in the relative importance of abstraction and specification when it comes to the question of knowledge structure development (learning). Changing slopes of the abstraction–specification relation seemed to indicate an alternation in the importance of specification and abstraction during knowledge structure development: 'between' the lower cognitive categories 3 and 4, specification seemed to play a slightly more important role than abstraction, while 'between' cognitive categories 4 and 5 abstraction took on such a role. The slopes of the specification–abstraction relation 'between' the higher cognitive categories 1 and 2, and 'between' 2 and 3, reflected that increasing abstraction followed a phase of intensive specification. Extending specification could be observed 'between' the higher cognitive categories 1, 2 and 3, whereby specification happened to a proportionally larger degree than for the lower cognitive categories.

Interpretation

The cognitive operational process of interpretation refers to argumentative and inferential processes through which comprehension is aided. Processes of interpretation were assessed in terms of the degree of 'sophistication' of reasoning patterns: (a) the extent of argumentative and counter-argumentative knowledge that was held by an interviewee; (b) dimensionally framed knowledge; and (c) errors made regarding the naming of products and product attributes. A more detailed discussion of what is meant by these different aspects of 'sophistication' is given in the course of the following discussion.

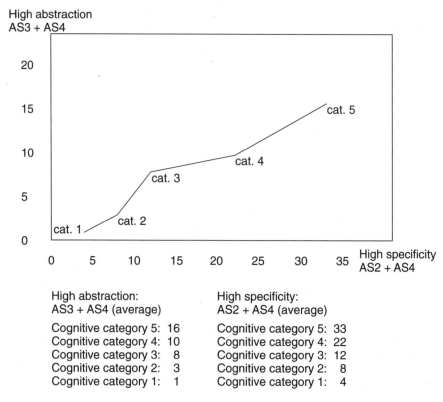

Figure 5.4 Staircase relation

Argumentative knowledge was briefly touched upon in the CI analysis when instances of arguments were marked in the interview data (see chapter 3). The availability of arguments and similarly of counter-arguments as opposed to simple information cues is viewed as an indication of sophisticated reasoning (Friedman and Lessig 1986: 340, Costley 1986: 1, Brucks 1986: 59, Schurr 1986: 502). It appeared that those interviewees who had comparatively high scores of argumentative knowledge tended to be members of the higher cognitive categories, such as cognitive categories 4 or 5. But not necessarily all members of the top cognitive categories had high CI scores for argumentative knowledge. The following reasoning patterns that showed argumentative and in particular LCA-type knowledge were found for the paradigmatic subjects:

• *B5* showed some depth of LCA-related knowledge. The idea of the green product was comparatively widely approached, including the disposal of a product as part of the consumption process. Regarding the reuse of milk bottles and the recycling of tins, there was some quite detailed knowledge on recycling locations and processes.

- *G5* showed in general a balanced and deep understanding of environmental issues, particularly on LCA-related issues. Some extensive knowledge on 'home made' issues and on waste separation existed. Also, for a number of prompted products fairly extensive reasoning was shown. Information search and processing reflected the reading of literature that referred to LCA.

- *B4* had sophisticated knowledge concerning the recycling of certain products. An understanding of production processes of certain products was also shown, e.g. on growth conditions of bananas. For cleaners, a detailed argument about environmental friendliness was developed. Packaging symbols were quite heavily but not exclusively relied upon to choose a product.

- *G4* classified herself as a 'layman' rather than as a 'scientist' when it came to green shopping. Instead of getting involved in 'scientific' decision making, e.g. deciding which plastics are better or worse for the environment, she explained that she avoided plastic products altogether. A sophisticated understanding of issues, such as the recycling, reuse and avoidance of certain packaging materials, was shown and this was partly integrated with matters reflecting the LCA consideration 'locally produced/retailed'. In general, considerations reflecting concern for 'locally produced/retailed' were quite prominent for a number of products. Also, for cleaners, a deep understanding of ingredients-related issues was shown.

- *B3* knew about the use of natural or simple household products, e.g. using beeswax instead of highly processed, 'chemical' cleaners. Expert friends were referred to for decision making on green cleaners. Some confusion was voiced regarding glass recycling. Disposal and production processes were touched upon.

- *G3* had some knowledge about certain scientific aspects of green shopping which were related to her own professional background in chemistry. Regarding packaging and organic products, a comparatively deep under-standing was shown. Organic products were considered a health issue rather than an environmental one (which reflected a different motivational drive). Other products were discussed as environmentally friendly by reference to visual product attributes, e.g. the colour grey for toilet paper.

- *B2* discussed cleaning products only with regard to their names and advertising. For food products, additives and health issues, such as allergies, were raised.

- *G2* showed some understanding of LCA issues, but repeatedly paired the LCA consideration 'locally produced/retailed' with loyalty to local shops. Similarly, country of origin issues were intertwined with health issues. The packaging of drinks was elaborated on in some detail.

- *N2* discussed non-food and food products in terms of rather non-specific references to product ingredients. A few general LCA references were made.

- *B1* had little knowledge of environmental issues. Inferences made, e.g. 'Green consumers don't flush the toilet', were of a partly naive, partly cynical nature.

- *G1* had some knowledge of green cleaning products related to the unsuccessful trial of such products. When prompted, some knowledge regarding toilet paper and detergent was revealed.
- *N1* related nearly all products discussed to 'other' issues. A few general LCA references were made.

It appeared that the higher cognitive categories had achieved a more balanced view on what makes a product a green one. The extent and also the quality of argumentative knowledge, especially LCA-type knowledge, increased from the bottom towards the top cognitive categories. LCA-type knowledge can be thought of as highly indicative of sophisticated reasoning due to its rather technical nature – and the higher cognitive categories apparently engaged more frequently in such LCA-type reasoning. When members of the lower cognitive categories took account of LCA considerations, they partly interrelated and mixed up LCA issues with other buying considerations, e.g. a patriotic buying motive or health issues. Such mix-ups were not observed in the higher cognitive categories.

The interpretation processes of the non-green interviewees reflected rationalizing. This was basically due to the hypothetical approach taken to interviewing them. Different products were rather consistently characterized along the same product attributes and argumentative knowledge showed low degrees of sophistication.

Counter-argumentative knowledge, like argumentative knowledge, reflects complex inferential processes. In general, a search through the actual interview data for counter-argumentative knowledge yielded few examples. The examples found were given by the members of the higher cognitive categories:

- *G5* produced a sophisticated argument for, and then also a counter-argument against, the recycling of certain packaging materials, such as aluminium, when packaging for sweets products was discussed.[10]
- B3 suggested for the product 'drinks', when prompted, a counter-argument related to the glass recycling of drinks packaging. Some confusion about what is the best packaging for drinks was voiced.
- Besides these two examples of counter-argumentative knowledge, some further counter-arguments were found but they did not relate (entirely) to green issues; for instance, B5 developed a counter-argument in relation to animal welfare issues, and G4 suggested a counter-argument related to transportation considerations and the price of a product when discussing the product 'cream'.
- For the interviewees B4, G3, B2, G2, N2, B1, G1 and N1 no counter-arguments were found.

Instances of counter-argumentative knowledge were generally rare. The few instances of counter-argumentative knowledge found came from interviewees in the higher categories. Also, the quality of counter-arguments seemed to be higher for the top cognitive categories. This view was also supported by findings from the CI analysis ('arg'-variable; see chapter 3).

A further stage was the examination of the sophistication of knowledge with regard to so-called *dimensionally framed* knowledge. Dimensionally framed knowledge was identified on the basis that an interviewee discussed a certain product attribute on a *graded* basis, i.e., different green options were ranked in comparison with a non-green option (Johnson *et al.* 1992: 132–3, Johnson and Fornell 1987: 214, 216, 225). As with counter-argumentative knowledge, examples of dimensionally framed knowledge were generally rare. Again, the few examples of dimensionally framed knowledge that were found were given by the paradigmatic subjects in the higher cognitive categories:

- B5 had, for the products 'vegetables and fruit', dimensionally framed knowledge related to the product attribute 'organic'. Values of the variable 'organic' were distinguished: 'non-organic', 'not 100 per cent organic', and 'totally organic, conservation grade organic'.
- G4 had dimensionally framed knowledge for the packaging of milk. Three different types of milk packaging were ranked for the product attribute 'reusable': values were 'throw-away bottle', 'returnable bottle from a dairy firm', and 'refillable can that is carried to a local farm'.

Again, it appeared that there was some relationship between membership in the higher cognitive categories and the extent of dimensionally framed knowledge. This view was also supported by findings from the CI analysis (dim-variable).

An assessment of the interpretation processes of green consumers was concluded with the examination of certain types of errors made by the interviewees. An assessment of errors reflects on how processes of interpretation went 'wrong'. As indicated earlier, an assessment of errors relating to LCA was not attempted here. Only so-called 'classification errors' were identified as errors. A handful of classification errors could be found:

- B2 recalled a couple of names wrongly or incompletely, e.g. 'Ecocover' instead of 'Ecover'.
- B1 classified a number of paper-based products, such as kitchen towels and toilet paper, wrongly as 'recyclable' instead of 'recycled'.

Such classification errors, which also reflected on processes of specification and abstraction, appeared to be more frequent for the lower than for the higher cognitive categories. Also, for non-green interviewees, similar classification errors could be observed, e.g. for N07 and N09 (who were members of cognitive category 1).

As a result of the various analyses of knowledge sophistication, certain suggestions regarding cognitive operational processes of interpretation emerged. There seemed to be some variation in interpretive processes across the cognitive categories: an examination of arguments, counter-arguments and dimensionally framed knowledge indicated that knowledge interpretation was greater among the higher cognitive categories, but less developed in the lower cognitive categories. Also, errors relating to the naming of knowledge content features appeared to be more common for the lower cognitive categories.[11]

Integration

Integration refers to cognitive operational processes through which pieces of information are associated and interrelated with each other, and 'bridging experiences' are developed. Integrative processes determine the way in which knowledge content features – 'products' and 'product attributes' – structurally relate with each other and the extent of that relationship. The outcome of knowledge integration is reflected by how complex a person's knowledge is.

Knowledge complexity was examined earlier in terms of frequencies of the knowledge content features 'products' and 'product attributes' and in terms of the type of structural relations that could be observed between them, such as 'product class-related grouping' and 'networking'. It was found that the frequencies with which products and product attributes were mentioned increased strongly from the lower cognitive categories to the higher ones. Also, product class-related grouping and networking occurred to a different extent and in a different way for the cognitive categories. Product class-related grouping occurred only from cognitive category 2 onwards, and networking began, first in relation to product class-related grouping, only from the cognitive category 3 onwards. For the top cognitive categories, in particular cognitive category 5, knowledge was networked, to a degree, independently of product classes. The build-up of knowledge complexity seemed to work first in a product class-related way, before there was any networking of knowledge along product attributes.

An examination of counter-arguments and dimensionally framed knowledge, as conducted above, also shed light on processes of knowledge integration. Counter-arguments reflect the fact that knowledge is related to different product attributes. Similarly, dimensionally framed knowledge reflects a comparatively complex structural organization of a product attribute. It was found that the higher cognitive categories knew more counter-arguments and had a better developed dimensionally framed knowledge than the lower ones.

These observed differences in knowledge complexity indicate that the integration of knowledge differed amongst the cognitive categories. In the following, an examination of the integration of knowledge is extended regarding the way knowledge complexity built up. In particular, the role of *good examples* of products and product attributes in the integration of knowledge is examined.

As a first step, whether the extent of the knowledge of good product examples related to membership in the cognitive categories was examined. The products' position of occurrence analysis (PPO analysis) was drawn upon (see chapter 3). An examination of PPOs produced a yardstick of what were good examples of green products. The British interviewees recalled most easily products such as detergent or washing-up liquid, while for the German interviewees products like milk or bread had the best PPO scores (see Table 3.3). Findings on PPOs hold clues regarding the way knowledge integration works: they hint at the role good examples play in the build-up of knowledge complexity.

For examining the role of good product examples in knowledge integration, the first two products recalled by an interviewee were compared with PPO parameters as compiled for the British and German samples.[12] As a result of this analysis, it became clear (a) that products were *not* recalled randomly: there was a structure to the sequence of freely recalled products, and (b) that the lower cognitive categories knew as many good examples of green products as the higher cognitive categories (see Appendix 5.5). Products with good PPO parameters were recalled sooner rather than later by *all* interviewees, i.e., independent of membership in cognitive categories. It seemed that good examples were known by everybody. Such a result may appear surprising in view of the knowledge structure differences that were previously observed among the cognitive categories. But if we regard the way knowledge integration occurs, such a result makes sense. It indicated that the build-up of knowledge complexity is organized around good examples from an early stage of knowledge structure development. Good examples seem to be instrumental for the integration of knowledge structures, which explains their prominence across all cognitive categories.

This finding was further examined in relation to the previously identified patterns of knowledge complexity – product class-related grouping and networking. For the lower cognitive categories, product class-related grouping occurred to only a limited extent; persons of the bottom cognitive category 1 even recalled products independent of product class. But the product examples recalled by them were, when compared with PPO parameters, as good examples of green products as those recalled by the higher cognitive categories. For the higher cognitive categories, it appeared that product class-related grouping developed around good examples. Patterns of product class-related grouping were regularly 'initiated' (along the recall sequence) by products that had ranked very high in terms of their PPOs. Further products of the same product class were then recalled either immediately following the recall of a particularly good example or cropped up later during the follow-up discussion (and were then classified as X2 products).

A typical recall pattern that reflected product class-related grouping being initiated by a good example was for the British sample a sequence such as 'toilet paper – kitchen towels – (paper) handkerchiefs'; or for the German sample, 'milk – yoghurt – cream – butter'. Products of the same product class were apparently not randomly recalled. Rather, good examples initiated the recall of further product examples of the same product class. For instance, for the German sample, the product 'yoghurt' had a PPO mode of 2, a PPO median of 4, and a PPO mean of 7. This reflected a certain structural pattern in the recall of the product 'yoghurt' and its relationship to the product 'milk'. Frequently, milk and yoghurt were recalled together in the initial start-up phase of the interview, where the recall of milk regularly preceded the recall of yoghurt. Such a recall pattern was reflected by the PPO modes of milk and yoghurt, which were 1 and 2 respectively. But it also occurred in quite a number of cases that the product 'yoghurt' was only recalled later during the follow-up discussion of previously recalled products, and then particularly when the product 'milk' was discussed (yoghurt was classified often as an X2 product rather than as an X1 product, as milk was, and such later recall of yoghurt is reflected by the lower values of the PPO parameters median and mean). These findings indicated that good examples play a fundamental role in initiating and guiding knowledge integration.

An increase in networking has previously been observed for the higher cognitive categories (see above, pp. 131–5). The integration of products along product attributes seemed to relate to particular product attributes: for the German sample, integration seemed to happen particularly with regard to product attributes related to packaging issues, while for the British sample, ingredients-related product attributes played a prominent role. There were indications of good examples of product attributes.[13] This raises the question of whether knowledge integration also related to good examples of product attributes.

An assessment of good examples of product attributes was harder to conduct than for good examples of products. The interview procedure was geared towards the retrieval of product examples. Only after the recall of product examples were product attributes discussed, which made the sequential recall of product attributes more difficult to assess. In the same way as for products, good examples of product attributes were assessed regarding the first two product attributes that were mentioned by an interviewee: it was found that the packaging issue was highly prominent for the German sample, and product ingredients-related issues for the British sample. Packaging issues and related product attributes such as 'packaging material', 'amount of packaging' and 'reusable' had a comparatively strong prominence across all cognitive categories in the German sample, as had product attributes such as 'recycled', 'organic' or 'biodegradable' for the British sample (see Appendix 5.5).[14] It also appeared that good examples of certain products were framed in terms of certain product attributes only. For the German sample, the product 'milk' was commonly related to the product attribute 'reusable', as was the product 'drinks' (regarding their packaging); and for the British sample, the product 'washing-up liquid' was commonly related to 'biodegradable', as was 'toilet paper' to 'recycled'. Apparently, certain product attributes played a more prominent role in the organization of knowledge than others and there were indications that the build-up of knowledge worked along combinations of good product examples and good product attributes. As pointed out, such patterns are likely to require further investigations, possibly with a stronger research focus on product attributes rather than products.

It could be speculated that an integrative mechanism at a formatting level of cognition facilitated the integration of knowledge, for instance with regard to the recall initiating function of good examples. Good examples played a generally prominent role across all cognitive categories in the organization of knowledge. This can be related to knowledge prototypicality. Such schematic aspects of knowledge structures are assessed in more detail below.

Selection

As a matter of completeness, cognitive operational processes of selection are briefly reviewed in the following. Selection refers to information attention. Processes of selection can be thought of as an 'interface' level of internal and external information search. Selection differs from the other operational processes of specification, abstraction, interpretation and integration in so far as it is a perceptual rather than a conceptual cognitive process. Since the empirical research approach of this study focused on the investigation of conceptual processes rather than perceptual ones, suggestions on processes of selection have to be induced from previous findings on the other cognitive operational processes.

In general, existing knowledge content reflects the way selection has occurred, particularly regarding how internal information search has taken place (Alba and Hasher 1983: 205, 212–13; also Bettman 1979a: 37–8). All 'existing' knowledge relates to processes of selection in one way or another.

Patterns of knowledge complexity reflect on selection. The higher cognitive categories knew more product examples and more product attributes. They had their attention apparently more 'widely' focused. Besides such a quantitative difference, there also appeared to be a qualitative deepening in terms of the range of different types of product attributes that were attended to. The top cognitive categories had a stronger focus on LCA issues and communication issues as compared with the lower categories (this was checked not only for the paradigmatic subjects, but also for the total samples). Communication issues in the German sample, as reflected by references to 'pressure groups' and 'literature', were much more prominent for the top cognitive categories 5 and 4; for other communication issues, e.g. 'TV, radio, newspapers', this was less the case. For the British sample, references to communication were, to a degree, more evenly spread across all cognitive categories.[15]

Advancing specification is likely to feed back into selection processes, guiding and facilitating information filtering processes. 'External memory', which can be defined as 'information [that] is available without needing to be stored in the consumer's memory' (Bettman 1979b: 153, Bettman 1979a: 38), e.g. on-package information, shopping guides, etc., apparently played a significant role in all cognitive categories. The cognitive categories seemed to rely strongly on an external memory system that was geared towards information stimuli provided by a product, e.g. a product name like 'Green Choice' or a packaging symbol like a little tree. Once a detailed knowledge of names has developed, information attention at the point of shopping can be expected to be brand-oriented. For the higher cognitive categories, the use of external memory was accompanied by a strong reliance on internal memory. This was particularly the case for product attributes that reflected LCA issues and communications issues. The higher cognitive categories applied certain conceptual ideas from internal memory in conjunction with perceptual information from external memory.

Patterns of knowledge integration are also likely to affect selection. A knowledge of good examples can be expected to impact on information attention and information filtering. For the higher cognitive categories, where knowledge integration was more extensive, good examples seemed to have further influenced information attention regarding what type of green products were bought – 'product class-related grouping' effects were here observed – and also regarding what type of product attributes were attended to, thus reflecting on the networking of product attributes across products.

In general, there appeared to be differences in how selection had occurred for the higher cognitive categories in comparison with the lower ones.

Modes of cognitive operations

Differences in the cognitive operational levels of specification, abstraction, interpretation, integration and selection reflect the fact that the cognitive categories differed in their operational dynamics regarding the development, organization and application of knowledge content. Observed differences among the cognitive categories seemed to change on a comparatively gradual basis. These differences can be related to different modes of cognitive operations: *bottom-up processing* and *top-down processing* (see chapter 2 and Figure 2.4).

The top-down processing mode is characterized by a focus on the higher levels of cognitive operations, such as interpretation and integration. It draws to a greater extent on complex and abstract knowledge than bottom-up processing. From the knowledge content analysis and the analysis of cognitive operations some distinctive differences between the members of the higher and the lower cognitive categories were apparent. Findings on the higher cognitive categories matched the description of a top-down processing mode:

- Specification and abstraction appeared to go considerably deeper for the higher cognitive categories. They had an extensive knowledge of names, and they were particularly strong on highly abstract and highly specific knowledge.
- The higher cognitive categories interpreted green consumption more deeply. More often product attributes, such as the ones relating to LCA or 'specialist' communication issues, e.g. 'literature' or 'pressure groups', played a role; and a high degree of knowledge sophistication was apparent.
- Knowledge integration in the higher cognitive categories was more strongly integrated along product attributes, even cutting across product classes in some cases. They could apparently access and apply knowledge in a fashion that reflected a considerable degree of networking. Their knowledge structures were not solely organized around product classes. To a degree, they were able to access and use knowledge along both knowledge content features – 'products' and 'product attributes'.

In bottom-up processing a lower degree of knowledge interpretation and integration is expected. Bottom-up processing is also said to utilize to a greater extent irrelevant information when it comes to interpretation. Previously, the knowledge content analysis had yielded substantially lower scores for knowledge structure variables in the bottom cognitive categories. There also appeared to be differences in the way the cognitive operational processes of selection, specification, abstraction, interpretation and integration worked. These findings corresponded with a description of a bottom-up processing mode:

- An examination of specification and abstraction processes indicated a different type of reasoning. A knowledge of names was less developed. As far as abstraction occurred, this appeared to be related to 'traditional' concepts but less so to LCA-type knowledge.
- Regarding knowledge integration, no networking happened for the lower cognitive categories, and product class-related grouping occurred to a limited extent.
- Processes of interpretation in the form of correlational processing, which is based on unclear distinctions between product attributes, is said to indicate bottom-up processing (see chapter 2). Instances of correlational processing were found for the lower cognitive categories. For instance, G17, a member of cognitive category 2, had some LCA-related knowledge, but LCA considerations were interrelated with other issues such as loyalty in buying locally produced goods: this was intertwined with such considerations as 'Cows in our region produce such nice butter.' Similarly, B2 discussed organic meat with regard to sighting cows in fields and finding them in an apparently happy state: 'They look so happy.' Such a correlational approach contrasted with the reasoning shown by the members of the top cognitive category 5.
- The reasoning of the lower cognitive categories was to a degree more strongly influenced by classification errors. For instance, the idea of 'recyclable' was repeatedly related by B1 to products such as kitchen towels or toilet paper (a similar finding was made for non-green interviewees). For the lower cognitive categories, product attributes were more vaguely established and fewer product attributes were known.

Interviewees across all cognitive categories seemed to utilize the entire range of processes of cognitive operations. But besides such a general similarity, qualitative differences regarding modes of cognitive operations could be found. There were clear indications of different processing modes for the members of the lower and the higher cognitive categories: the processing mode of the higher cognitive categories compared to top-down processing, while the processing mode of the lower cognitive categories matched a description of bottom-up processing. The identification of top-down processing for the higher cognitive categories and bottom-up processing for the lower ones is in line with suggestions in the literature on how knowledge structure differences, such as knowledge content differences and differences in cognitive operational processes, are reflected by differences in cognitive operational modes.

Conclusions

A number of findings were made on how cognitive operational processes worked for the green consumer. Specification extended from the bottom to the top cognitive categories, reflecting previous findings on knowledge specificity. Naming processes seemed to play an important role in the build-up of knowledge.

Abstraction processes changed in their degree and nature from the bottom to the top cognitive categories. In the lower cognitive categories, comparatively high levels of fairly general knowledge were found. A kind of 'commonsense' abstraction was observed from cognitive category 2, relating to 'traditional' abstract concepts. Abstraction seemed to develop first in relation to concepts like 'recycled' (in Britain) or 'reusable' (in Germany). A more technical abstraction process was only found in the higher cognitive categories.

Certain observations regarding the interaction of specification and abstraction were made. In the higher cognitive categories, an extended specification of knowledge seemed to precede the build-up of highly technical knowledge. Tentatively, a staircase relation was suggested regarding the changing relative importance of specification and abstraction in the build-up of knowledge.

The higher cognitive categories showed more sophisticated processes of interpretation. They had a more deeply argumentative, counter-argumentative and dimensionally framed knowledge than the lower cognitive categories. Classification errors were more frequent for the lower cognitive categories.

Consumers of all cognitive categories had a wide knowledge of good examples of green products. Patterns of knowledge integration, such as product class-related grouping and networking, were organized around good examples. This indicated the fundamental role of good examples in knowledge integration. Also, good examples of green product attributes seemed to contribute to knowledge integration.

Differences in cognitive operations between the higher and the lower cognitive categories matched descriptions of different processing modes. A top-down processing mode was identified for the higher cognitive categories, while bottom-up processing could be identified for the lower cognitive categories.

SCHEMATIC NATURE OF KNOWLEDGE

Schemata can be understood as a body of formatting and organizing principles that structure a grammar for knowledge. In terms of the computer analogy, a schematic level of knowledge structures is comparable to 'systems software'. Schemata are 'guiding' principles that underwire the organization of knowledge content and cognitive operations. They are located at a subconscious level of cognition, which means that they cannot be directly 'observed' and 'measured'. Only as a matter of interpretation of knowledge content and cognitive operations can schemata be assessed (see chapter 2).

In the previous sections, schematic features of cognition were touched upon; for instance, a knowledge of highly abstract shopping maxims can be related to a general ('super-ordinate') schema for green shopping, just as a knowledge of good examples can be related to prototypical knowledge structures. Such formatting features of knowledge structures are examined in more detail in the following.

A critical question for an assessment of schematic knowledge features is what should be relied upon as a significant indication of schematic knowledge – of organizing principles that guide the structuring of knowledge. On the one hand, knowledge could be safely identified as non-schematic if no distinctive structural relations among knowledge content features were apparent. On the other hand, it may not be wise to infer schemata solely on the basis that some kind of structural organization was observed; otherwise, basically any categorizing activity of the mind, as reflected by findings on knowledge complexity and cognitive operational processes of knowledge integration, would qualify as 'schematic'. A strong case for schematic knowledge can be made, if patterns in a categorizing activity of the mind can be identified that exhibit distinctive *schematic* features.

The prototype concept makes specific suggestions as to what schematic knowledge looks like: it suggests that the organization of knowledge content and of cognitive operations is underwired by what are known as *prototypes*. A prototype is understood as a data structure which reflects that the build-up of knowledge occurred around an ideal member of a certain knowledge domain (see chapter 2). With regard to green consumption, an ideal member can be understood as a good example of a green product. The prototype itself is only a frame for variables, for knowledge content features such as 'products' and 'product attributes' that facilitate the build-up of knowledge content – *in a proto-typical way*. The prototype does not determine what specific variables are contained in a data structure and what values variables take. In that sense, the prototype is an 'empty' data structure.

Schematic reasoning has to be understood in terms of empty data frames, void even of category headings, such as the variable names 'product', 'product attribute', etc. Such data frames may be compared to empty spread sheets, where columns and rows have not yet been assigned variables (although comparisons to wheel-like structures, such as atomic configurations or patterns in crystal formation, may be more appropriate). Kant's idea of the schema as a pure, a priori mental representation relates to an understanding of schemata at this most basic cognitive level – the data frame that is void of content.

This interpretation leads back to an initial question asked in chapter 2 of how free of knowledge a schema can be: a schema was defined as a configuration of variables that is free of knowledge content. However, what qualifies as a variable at one level in a knowledge hierarchy can be viewed as the value of a variable in a higher level of the knowledge hierarchy. This apparent definitional ambiguity has to be reconciled with the hierarchical nature of schemata: the idea of 'schema' has to be discussed with reference to a *specific level of a knowledge hierarchy*, and here variables and values of variables can be distinguished. On the basis of such a focused discussion, conclusions can be drawn regarding schematic principles of how knowledge is structurally coupled – and how self-organization at the level of the mind works.

In the following, first, findings on the structural nature of knowledge, as made in the analyses of knowledge complexity and knowledge integration, are interpreted regarding schemata and prototypes. Second, suggestions of schema theory on the hierarchical organization of knowledge and, related to it, efficiency advantages of cognition are examined. Third, the question of whether identified categorization patterns could be explained without schema theory is explored. In the concluding parts of this section, the general role of schemata in underwiring cognition is commented on, and implications for the future development of schema theory are outlined.

Schemata and prototypes

The analyses of knowledge complexity and knowledge integration have indicated a number of categorization patterns across the cognitive categories: from the middle cognitive categories onwards, the sequences of recalled products exhibited so-called product class-related grouping. Three, four or five products of the same product class, for example 'detergent and washing-up liquid and cleaners', were recalled in sequence and integrated along the same product attributes, e.g. product ingredients. For the higher cognitive categories, products of the same product class were integrated along more than one or two product attributes. In the top cognitive category, such networking even began to cut across product classes; for instance, milk and shampoo were integrated along the same product attributes. Apparently, categorization developed first with regard to product classes, but not with regard to green consumption in general: only for the very top cognitive category were categorization patterns found that cut across product classes.

The idea of a good example of a green product has been defined on the basis of the PPO analysis (see chapter 3 and Table 3.3). Good examples of green products were, for instance, detergent for the British sample and milk for the German sample. At the knowledge content level, different products qualified as good examples for the British and the German samples, detergent and milk respectively. It was found that recall sequences of products were initiated by such good examples, and also that the integration of knowledge related to good examples of product attributes, especially to product attributes of a product that had been classified as a good example. Product class-related patterns in the organization of knowledge content exhibited a recurring feature: good examples of a certain product class preceded the recall of further products of the same product class; for instance, the recall of dairy products by German consumers reflected such a pattern: milk generally preceded yoghurt in the recall sequence, as yoghurt preceded other dairy products like cream or butter; similarly, for British consumers, the recall of products like detergent and washing-up liquid generally preceded the recall of products like cleaners.

Typical categorization patterns of British green consumers related to product attribute configurations such as 'recycled' and 'product ingredients' for the product class 'paper products'; or 'product ingredients' and 'biodegradable' for washing and cleaning products. For German green consumers, a typical configuration of product attributes consisted of product attributes like 'reusable' and 'packaging material' for dairy products. For the same products, different categorization patterns regarding product attributes were found among British and German consumers; for instance, for the product 'milk', a prototype as found for German interviewees contained product attributes such as 'packaging material', 'reusable' and 'names' (in that order, as reflected by their frequencies), while British interviewees discussed milk with regard to the product attributes 'organic', 'names' and 'reusable' (in general, only the higher cognitive categories applied more than two product attributes for characterizing the greenness of a product). Prototypical variable configurations were apparently first 'transferred' across products within a product class, and only at a later stage in knowledge development across product classes, as found in the higher cognitive categories.

These findings on knowledge complexity and knowledge integration can be explained through the prototype concept. As an organizing structure, the prototype formats knowledge organization by providing a 'place' for a good example of a certain phenomenon. This special 'place' can be thought of as a data structure nucleus that is first filled with knowledge content before other knowledge is associated and integrated with such good instances. If the cognition of British and German green consumers is examined at a level 'below' actual knowledge content, structural patterns of knowledge complexity and knowledge integration are very similar.

Suggestions of the existence of knowledge prototypicality were also supported by certain findings for the lower cognitive categories. The lower cognitive categories knew good examples to a degree that was very similar to that in the higher ones, but there, good product examples were not embedded in product class-related structures. Good examples of products cropped up more or less as singular instances that were barely integrated in the recall sequence along product attributes. In that respect, knowledge prototypicality could not be identified as a *categorization pattern* for the lower cognitive categories. However, 'roots' of prototypical knowledge can be traced in the lower cognitive categories since their knowledge of good product examples was as wide as that in the higher cognitive categories. This indicates that the build-up of knowledge content works by means of good examples. Such a finding is in line with suggestions of schema theory that all levels and all modes of cognitive operations can exhibit schematic characteristics (Abelson and Black 1986: 5, Rumelhart 1984: 162, 169, Brewer and Treyens 1981: 216, Bartlett 1932: 31–3, 201–4).

Schemata and the hierarchical organization of knowledge

Schema theory suggests that schemata are integrated hierarchically (see chapter 2). For the top cognitive categories, especially for cognitive category 5, an integration of products tended to cut across product classes that were 'far apart', e.g. products like shampoo and milk were networked along the same product attribute 'reusable' (regarding their packaging). In the top cognitive categories, one could 'travel' from product to product through the recall sequence: different product class-related prototypes were apparently related to each other along shared product attributes. Such a finding corresponds with the proposition of schema theory that schemata are integrated in hierarchical networks (possibly 'dynamic' hierarchical networks as they were here observed through the recall process). The higher cognitive categories also covered different groups of product attributes – ingredients-, packaging-, LCA- and communications-related product attributes – more comprehensively than the lower cognitive categories.

In the lower cognitive categories, a case for schemata that cut *across* product classes could only be made if product attributes were grouped together more strongly for the purpose of data analysis, e.g. 'product ingredients', 'recycled' and 'biodegradable' were subsumed into one wider variable 'product ingredients-related issues', or product attributes like 'packaging material', 'reusable' and 'amount of packaging' were subsumed into a single variable 'packaging-related issues'. That such a rough grouping (in terms of category headings) was necessary in order to identify categorization patterns for the lower cognitive categories indicated that schematic principles were less developed here.

The suggestion that a knowledge hierarchy exhibited schematic features was also supported by previous findings on abstract shopping maxims. Members of the higher cognitive categories frequently volunteered highly abstract shopping maxims right at the beginning of the interview. For the lower cognitive categories, this was rarely the case. Abstract shopping maxims can be interpreted as 'super-ordinate' schemata that frame thinking from a general perspective, here with regard to green consumption as such (in comparison, prototypes would classify as 'sub-ordinate' schemata that frame thinking with regard to specific issues, e.g. a certain product and its attributes). Super-ordinate and sub-ordinate schemata are expected to relate to each other through hierarchical networks (see chapter 2). Although little can be said about how maxims and prototypes actually related to each other here, it appeared that both maxims and prototypes were far more developed for the higher cognitive categories than for the lower ones.

Partly because of their hierarchical organization, and partly because of their underwiring function, schemata are expected to facilitate cognitive operations and, related to that, the organization and application of knowledge content, thus yielding an 'efficiency' advantage to cognition (see chapter 2). In the higher cognitive categories, such schematic support seemed to exist. Previously, when knowledge content characteristics were compared across the cognitive categories, the build-up of knowledge characteristics, such as knowledge comprehensiveness, knowledge complexity, knowledge specificity and knowledge abstractness, did *not* resemble a saturation process, e.g. a digressively climbing curve. Rather, the build-up of knowledge seemed to occur in a comparatively linear or even progressive fashion (see above). This can be related to the benefits of schematic thinking.

Also, greater 'efficiency' in the recall of knowledge (as expressed by the knowledge comprehensiveness ratios W1/W3 and W2/W4) by the higher cognitive categories can be related to suggestions of schema theory that schemata facilitate the application of knowledge content. Similarly, only members of the higher cognitive categories were able to reveal and express super-ordinate schemata in the form of abstract shopping maxims.

Apparently, schemata were networked in a hierarchical fashion and this seemed to yield certain benefits both for reasoning, such as more efficient recall, and in the application of knowledge. One could speculate tentatively that highly integrated, prototypical knowledge also has a positive impact on behavioural 'consistency' (as diagnosed in chapter 3): interviewees who knew more green product examples bought green products to a proportionally higher degree – more 'consistently' – than those interviewees who knew fewer green products. Such a familiarity effect may relate to schemata. It is discussed in more detail in the next chapter.

Can 'schemata' be explained without schema theory?

A discussion of schematic knowledge is well advised to examine whether patterns in knowledge organization that were identified as 'schematic' could be explained without schema theory: in particular, could the role of good examples in the build-up of knowledge be explained without the schema concept?

A 'schema-free' explanation of a categorizing activity of the mind is provided, for example, by the concept of *associative bridges* (Alba and Hasher 1983: 220; similarly, Alba *et al.* 1991: 5). An associative bridge can be understood as a relationship between knowledge content features. The idea of associative bridges explains cognitive operations, e.g. the integration of knowledge content, on the basis of mere experience effects with no reference to an underwiring, schematic level of cognition. This explanation is rooted in an empiricist tradition to explaining cognition, for instance, in Locke's ideas on how empirical sensations affect reasoning (see chapter 2). The concept of associative bridges assumes less from a conceptual point of view than schema theory does. It is a more parsimonious theory, and if it could explain categorization patterns to cognition as satisfactorily as schema theory, it would be a more attractive theory than schema theory – and hence, schema theory could be dismissed.

An important question for the concept of associative bridges is how a non-random pattern in the building of associative bridges could be explained. Findings on knowledge prototypicality indicated that interrelations between knowledge content features followed a certain, distinctive pattern: good examples of products provided a centre around which other products clustered. And the prototypical good example seemed to affect networking in terms of product attributes that were preferred for knowledge integration. Prototypicality was also present equally for the lower and the higher cognitive categories: if proto-typicality had only been present for the higher cognitive categories, it could have been more easily attributed to an experience effect rather than to innate schemata (that schemata are likely to be of an innate nature has been touched upon in chapter 2; this point is returned to below, pp. 168–70).

In order to explain patterns of knowledge prototypicality, the concept of associative bridges appears to be in need of a conceptual idea such as 'steering principles'. It is difficult to see how non-random patterns of knowledge organi-zation could be explained without such principles. However, if an idea such as steering principles is introduced in the concept of associative bridges, it loses some of its parsimony advantage over schema theory, and it could be asked what differences remain between a concept of associative bridges and schema theory: how would 'steering principles' differ from 'formatting principles' (schemata)?

A basic difference might relate to the way these principles develop and the role actual experience plays in their 'development'. This question of how self-organizing principles to cognition develop can be related to a longstanding debate on the nature of thinking. On the one hand, so-called 'passivists' argue that they develop solely from experience (and related actual behaviour). On the other hand, 'activists' would suggest that patterns in reasoning are only 'activated' but not developed through actual experience.

As indicated, a passivist view is rooted in the empiricist tradition of Locke. The empiricist or passivist would try to explain the prototypicality of knowledge content solely on the basis of experience effects. Naturally, actual experience plays an important role in explaining knowledge content and this is not disputed by an activist approach. Actual experience effects were apparent when different products qualified as good examples of green products for British and German consumers, detergent and milk respectively. A critical question for the passivist position is how experience effects alone could lead to the distinctive patterns that were observed for the lower cognitive categories (and also for non-green interviewees as discussed below with regard to 'stereotyping'), where levels of actual experience were markedly low. In addition, increasing levels of experience across the cognitive categories did not impact on prototypicality negatively: good product examples seemed to be rather robust in the sense that they were not superseded but complemented by further experience. This might indicate a strong 'guiding and shaping influence' on experience effects such as is likely to be exerted by schemata.

An activist view on cognition can be traced back to the works of Kant. Kant's 'a priori understanding' of schemata seems to be close to a view of schemata and schema development as innate. An activist would suggest that schemata are of an innate nature, i.e., that they are only 'developed' in the sense of being activated by actual experience. Schema development would be explained as a genetically determined cognitive ability. It is little disputed that certain cognitive abilities are of an innate nature, e.g. the language learning faculty of small children which diminishes during later childhood.

In general, it appears that it is difficult to explain the knowledge patterns identified solely through a passivist view on cognition, although no final answer can be provided here. The question of innate schemata is likely to touch upon issues of how cognition relates to a physiological, neurological level, which is beyond the reach of this study. However, research findings on the pre-wiring of the brain at a neurological level (see chapter 2) seem to support the idea of an innate cognitive ability at a 'systems software' level of the mind that guides and formats thinking.

In need of stereotypes

The idea of an activist schematic mind was further supported by findings on the non-green interviewees.[16] In contrast to the green interviewees, the non-green interviewees were empirically researched on a hypothetical basis, involving them in a prompting task whereby it had been made sure at the outset of the interview that actual experience with green products was low. Interestingly, among the non-green interviewees certain strong patterns of knowledge integration were observed, but in comparison with the green interviewees the integration of knowledge occurred along a number of rather untypical product attributes, e.g. along the product attributes 'others', 'colour' or 'disposal' (N01, N08, N10). It also appeared that non-green interviewees networked nearly all products for which they were prompted along the same product attributes. The most extreme case in that respect was N10 who had the product attribute 'disposal' very strongly networked and to a lesser degree also the attribute 'others'. In comparison with the green interviewees, the non-green interviewees showed a different pattern of knowledge integration: in a sense, they were more 'consistent' than the green interviewees.

A strong (self-)focusing of reasoning apparently happened during the interview. The non-green interviewees tended to return to the same product attributes they had touched upon initially. They seemed to develop a certain stereotype for one product through hypothetical reasoning or 'rationalizing' and then rather consistently applied and transferred it to other products. It appeared that presently occurring reasoning was strongly bounded by immediately preceding reasoning processes. This indicates that the mind can be highly active in focusing reasoning in the absence of actual experience.

Such a finding was partly already suggested by the correlation analysis, in which knowledge structure variables, such as W1, C1, C3 which were basically *free* from knowledge substance, had had very similar correlation coefficients for the samples of green and non-green consumers, whereas differences in correlation coefficients for knowledge *substance* variables – the abstractness–specificity variables AS1 to AS8 – were observed between the samples of green and non-green consumers.

This stereotypical reasoning pattern of the non-green interviewees also provided a yardstick for assessing whether rationalizing had occurred for the green interviewees. Such self-focusing of reasoning along certain product attributes seemed not to occur for the green interviewees, as reflected in the way one could 'travel' (or not 'travel') through the sequence of freely recalled products. For instance, for the green interviewees in the lower cognitive categories, it was found that very little integration of knowledge had occurred along product attributes, indicating a very different pattern of knowledge recall from that of the non-green interviewees.

In general, explaining a phenomenon like 'rationalizing' or 'stereotyping' poses some problem for a passivist position on cognition. An activist view on cognition has little problem in explaining the easy and quick build-up of stereotypes: stereotyping has been commonly related to schema-based cognitive operations, in particular when experience is lacking (Alba and Hutchinson 1987: 423). The build-up of knowledge in the form of stereotypes or 'naive theories' can be related to the way the human mind works at a 'systems software' level: a schematic underwiring of cognition leaves little room for a 'theory vacuum' at the knowledge content level of the 'theorist' consumer (and for thinking in general). Through stereotypes, sense can quickly and easily be made of new issues. Such a need for quick sense-making is likely to have been favoured by evolutionary processes (Gregory 1990: 330). This, again, seems to hint at innate, genetically determined organizing principles for thinking. Apparently, schemata provide gravity to thinking, and such a 'force' is likely to be inborn. In that sense, stereotyping appears to be in our genes.

Implications for schema theory

A number of issues have been raised for the further development of schema theory (Alba and Hasher 1983: 225, Taylor and Crocker 1981: 125–7). Some of these issues were touched upon in the previous discussion. In the following, implications for schema theory are examined in depth.

One reason for the somewhat controversial status of schema theory is a lack of clarity regarding what is meant and not meant by the schema notion. A narrow definition of the schema notion appears advisable. In this study, the schema notion was restricted to a level of cognition that underwires cognitive operations and knowledge content. Only data structures were referred to as schemata. Notions like 'content schemata' or 'operational schemata' (or 'action schemata' in script research) have to be used carefully: when applied, it should be made clear that they refer to formatting and organizing principles rather than to knowledge content or cognitive operations as such. Related to that, variables and the values of variables, which characterize a data structure, have to be distinguished with regard to a specific level of a knowledge hierarchy.

170

Schema research has to question the existence of a formatting level of cognition. Questions of identifying schematic and non-schematic knowledge structures relate to the possibility of falsifying schema theory. Without the possibility of falsification, schema theory cannot be considered a 'good' scientific theory (however, if one argued that schema theory is only a 'skeletal' theory for organizing explorative research, questions of falsification may not be immediately relevant). Falsification of schema theory has to focus on the formatting level of cognition. Schematic or non-schematic knowledge characteristics have to be inferred from observations of knowledge content. Indications of schemata become much stronger if a distinctive (hierarchical) structure to knowledge integration, such as prototypicality, is observed. By researching knowledge structure *development*, a comparative assessment of knowledge characteristics becomes feasible and certain problems of 'observing' schemata can be reduced (and such a comparative approach was taken in this study).

The specificity of knowledge content has been suggested as a key target for falsifying schema theory (Cohen 1989: 73, Alba and Hasher 1983: 215, Brewer and Treyens 1981: 218). However, falsification approaches that are directed at knowledge content, e.g. the specificity of knowledge content, are likely to be misguided. Highly specific knowledge as such does not pose a conceptual problem for schema theory since it can be underwired by schemata in just the same way as any other knowledge content. A number of schema theorists had little problem in accommodating specific knowledge in schema theory; for instance, the idea of episodic knowledge has been successfully related to the schema concept (Crocker 1984: 473, Taylor and Crocker 1981: 91, Hastie 1981: 41; see also chapter 2).

The choice of a proper empirical research setting is important for knowledge structure research in general, and for schema research in particular. Schemata may be typical 'real-life' phenomena and problems of 'observing' schemata may be aggravated by choosing an inappropriate research setting such as a laboratory (Cohen 1989: 71, Abelson and Black 1986: 3; also Alba *et al.* 1991: 36–7). Important features of empirical research into schemata appear to be, first, a free recall format, and second, the existence of actual experience of subjects with regard to a certain knowledge domain that is investigated (Cohen 1989: 71, Nakamoto 1987: 25, Abelson and Black 1986: 3). Through theoretical sampling, the experience levels of persons can be 'controlled' by the researcher and, as a result, comparative assessments of knowledge structure development, and subsequently schema development, can be made.

Conclusions

The study observed distinctive patterns in the integration of knowledge such as product class-related grouping around good examples and the networking of such knowledge along product attributes. These patterns and how they changed across the cognitive categories provided a first indication of schematic, prototypical knowledge. Such an indication was substantiated by findings on interrelations among prototypes found in the higher cognitive categories: they resembled a hierarchical network.

Advantages in the recall of knowledge by the higher cognitive categories as well as linearly or even progressively increasing knowledge content across the cognitive categories supported the idea that schemata facilitate cognition and lead to 'efficiency' advantages.

The roots of the 'activation' or 'development' of schematic prototypes were traced among the lower cognitive categories who had a knowledge of good examples but showed few signs of integrating such knowledge. Also, the reasoning of the non-green interviewees exhibited schematic knowledge features: in the absence of actual product experience, the mind seemed to play a highly active role in focusing reasoning. Schema theory can explain such findings on stereotyping and on the ease with which stereotypes or 'naive theories' are acquired.

Assessing the schematic principles of reasoning touches upon the self-organizing and self-transforming activities of the mind, and is therefore tricky. Empirical findings made here on the importance of good examples for the build-up of knowledge can stand in their own right, irrespective of whether they are explained by schema theory or by other concepts. The question of whether knowledge prototypicality can be explained by the concept of associative bridges could not be finally resolved here. A possible difference between the concept of associative bridges and schema theory may relate to the question of whether principles in the organization of knowledge are innate.

An understanding of schematic knowledge has a number of practical implications. The success of advertising can be related to its schematic, stereotypical nature, favouring short messages about one or a few product attributes and rehearsing such messages persistently over time, thus fostering the build-up of prototypes. This may indicate a communication problem for complex messages (e.g. for green products) since they are likely to require more complicated communication formats. Knowledge prototypicality may also explain the difficulty of changing (existing) brand images of products. For instance, if 'green' is added to the image of a conventional brand, particularly if 'green' is used to redefine a brand's image (and not just to supplement it on a secondary basis), difficulties in overcoming prototypical product perceptions may arise. Consequently, an attempted image change might fail, possibly even affecting an existing brand image negatively. Also, a widespread failure of (new) product development can be related to schematic knowledge. Knowledge prototypicality research can provide hints regarding product development, and what constitutes a 'good' product. Rather than asking experts to define what a 'good' product objectively is, subjective and deep-rooted consumer perceptions of the good product may hold interesting answers.

Finally, a parallel may be drawn between the idea of scientific research heuristics and the idea of schemata (see also chapters 1 and 2). Heuristics and schemata have in common the fact that they frame and lead thinking. Insights into the working of schemata can inform a debate on the heuristic nature of scientific research. Research heuristics solve the complexity problem of gaining an understanding of our 'infinitely complex world' (Popper 1978: 129) in an apparently *rational* way. But it could be argued that the scientific method is little more than a sophisticated cultivation of stereotyping into a highly abstract mode of thinking. As pointed out, avoiding 'stereotypical' research heuristics is not an option for the scientist. There is a need for complexity reduction, and it is difficult to see how complexity reduction could be achieved without heuristics. What scientists can and should do is to gain awareness of how mind-narrowing research heuristics function. Once the scientist understands the nature of research heuristics, their systematic (rational) handling can be approached. Much social science research seems to be in need of such clarifications (see also Wagner forthcoming/b).

6

EXPERIENCE AND LEARNING: THE PROBLEM SOLVING BEHAVIOUR OF THE GREEN CONSUMER

In the previous chapter, green consumer behaviour was examined from a psychological perspective. Differences in thinking were discussed in terms of the knowledge content and subconscious cognitive activities that underlie the organization, development and application of knowledge. The idea of knowledge structure development was touched upon there: membership in the cognitive categories was interpreted as a reflection of different stages in a process of knowledge structure development or *learning*. This cognitive psychological view on green consumer thinking is extended in this chapter: it is related to the cognitive anthropological perspective on how successful learning occurs.

The idea of experience ('prior knowledge') could be approached from a narrow psychological perspective, e.g. the ability of the green consumer could be assessed on the basis of an IQ-test which may be grounded in life-cycle analysis (LCA). However, for understanding cognition in daily life – how thinking and problem solving of green consumers resulted in membership in different cognitive categories – cognitive anthropological ideas such as practical thinking and bricolage appear highly appropriate. A cognitive anthropological approach lives up to calls to examine cognition as 'lived human experience' (Maturana and Varela 1992: 244-8).

The concept of experience reflects the ongoing and personal-historical nature of knowledge structure development. The concept of experience can be broken down into two different but related aspects: familiarity and ability. Familiarity relates to the quantitative and behavioural side of experience, while ability relates to qualitative, rational aspects of experience. In the following, it is assessed how familiarity and ability related to practical thinking and bricolage and how this reflected on membership in different cognitive categories.

FAMILIARITY AND LEARNING

The concept of familiarity captures quantitative aspects of experience. Familiarity refers to the *number* of behavioural instances of a certain phenomenon (here: green consumption). Familiarity is likely to influence the amount, nature and substance of domain-related knowledge held by a person. On the one hand, familiarity may provide a premature, possibly false sense of successful problem solving: a person may just get used to a certain behavioural routine over time (see chapter 2). On the other hand, it has been pointed out that 'knowing is doing' (Maturana and Varela 1992: 244-8): without actual behaviour ('doing'), the build-up of knowledge is likely to be impaired. Through mere doing, a person develops skills and discovers rules and principles for successful behaviour. For the acquisition of many practical skills, actual doing is essential: for instance, learning to ride a bike requires the acquisition of balancing skills that cannot be taught. Familiarity is also likely to play an important role when it comes to acquiring *conceptual* skills: for instance, learning to play games.

In the following, the relationship between the extent of familiarity and knowledge structure development is examined. How familiarity has contributed to successful green consumer behaviour is discussed. First, the extent of product-related familiarity is assessed in terms of the number of green products that were regularly bought by a consumer. Second, familiarity effects are examined regarding the length of time (number of years) a person had been considering green shopping issues. Finally, findings on the habituation of green consumer behaviour are commented on.

Product-related familiarity

Product familiarity refers to the number of product-related experiences, such as buying, consumption and disposal, a consumer has gone through in the past. It reflects the number of green products that have been regularly bought by a green consumer. In chapter 3, certain differences were already being observed between consumers in the number of green products that were bought. There it was found that interviewees who had recalled many green products also actually bought these many products to a proportionally higher degree than those who knew few green products. For the top quartile of interviewees, the difference between the number of recalled products and the number of products actually bought was proportionally lower than for the bottom one. In terms of actual and regular exposure to green products, quite a large gap in familiarity between highly active and only slightly active green consumers was found (see Appendix 3.4).

A distinction between quartiles does not strictly correspond to the distinction between cognitive categories established by the cluster analysis in chapter 4, but it can be considered an approximation to cognitive categories. Both a high positive correlation of the number of products recalled with knowledge content variables as well as the examination of actual buying frequencies of the paradigmatic subjects and the cognitive categories reflected this (see Appendix 6.1 and Figure 6.1).

The ratio of the total number of products actually bought (NTA variable) to the number of products recalled (NT variable) indicated that the higher

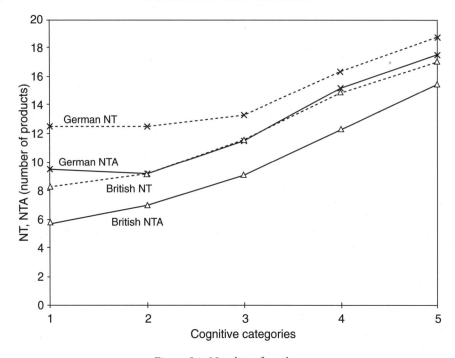

Figure 6.1 Number of products

cognitive categories were more 'consistent' regarding the buying of green products. Adjustments for actual buying behaviour increased from the top to the bottom cognitive categories (see Table 6.1; see also Appendix 3.4).[1]

The emerging picture for the British and German cognitive categories was very similar and it corresponded well to the previous examination of quartiles. Apparently there was quite a variation in product-related familiarity across the cognitive categories. Familiarity in terms of the number of products actually and regularly bought strongly related to membership in the cognitive categories. The higher cognitive categories had a considerably more intensive and regular exposure to green products than the bottom cognitive categories. Differences in knowledge structures, as they were found for the content, operational and schematic levels, can be expected to relate to such variations in product-related familiarity.

It was found earlier that knowledge prototypicality played an important role in knowledge structure development, as reflected by differences in schematic knowledge across the cognitive categories (see chapter 5). The question has been raised of whether schemata develop from repeated interactions, reflecting a familiarity effect, or from particularly good examples of a certain phenomenon (Taylor and Crocker 1981: 127; similarly, Schurr 1986: 498). The findings of this study indicated that no 'either/or' answer can be given. It seems that both

Table 6.1 Adjustments for actual buying

British sample		German sample	
Cognitive category	%	Cognitive category	%
5	−8.9	5	−6.4
4	−17.4	4	−6.7
3	−21.6	3	−13.5
2	−23.0	2	−27.1
1	−31.3	1	−24.0

good examples and product-oriented familiarity play a role, and that they may not be independent of each other: the study found that a knowledge of good examples was to a similar extent available across all cognitive categories. However, the nature and extent of prototypical knowledge – patterns of knowledge integration around good examples – changed and developed from the bottom to the top cognitive categories, as levels of actual interaction (as reflected by actual buying frequencies) also increased steadily from the lower cognitive categories to the higher ones. Apparently, knowledge structures developed around good examples together with increasing familiarity, which points towards the important role of both good examples and actual doing in learning processes. A simple causality-based 'either/or' answer to the question of schema development (and knowledge structure development in general) appears not possible.

Time-related familiarity

Familiarity can also be assessed in terms of the length of time for which green products had been bought. Whether time-related familiarity was reflected by membership in the cognitive categories was examined. It appeared that no such relationship existed between the length of time a person had been involved in green shopping and the development of knowledge structures.[2] For instance, there were consumers with only a few years of green shopping experience in the top cognitive category 5 (e.g. G01), just as there were persons with more than ten years' experience (e.g. G5); similarly wide-ranging levels of familiarity could be found for members of the bottom cognitive category 1, ranging from three to fifteen years.

A comparison of findings on familiarity (in terms of the time a person had been involved in green shopping) with the previous analysis of product-related familiarity showed that some consumers had managed to green their shopping behaviour to a considerable degree (as reflected by being members of the higher cognitive categories 4 and 5) over a relatively short period of a few years, e.g. B01, B03, G01, or G34, while other interviewees who had considered green shopping for over ten years fell into the lower cognitive categories 1 and 2, e.g. B12, B27,

BG37, B55 or G14. This indicated that the length of time a person had been involved in green shopping cannot explain membership in the cognitive categories, at least not on its own. Length of time appears to be neither a necessary nor a sufficient factor for explaining knowledge structure development. Apparently, consumers can learn rather quickly, if 'conditions' are right.

Motivational issues are likely to play an important role in understanding why some green consumers developed a very deep knowledge in a comparatively short period of time, while others had developed little knowledge over a long period of time. As indicated previously, motivational issues were excluded from the research focus of this study. But as a by-product of the open interview approach, certain observations on the motivation of interviewees regarding green shopping were made. It appeared that there was a correlation between membership in the higher cognitive categories and increasing levels of motivation (see the findings from the CI analysis in chapter 3). This can probably explain the inconclusive findings on how time-related familiarity affected learning.

Familiarity and habit formation

Familiarity reflects behavioural habits. Familiarity effects that related to long-established 'habitual' learning-by-doing routines were checked for by the CI analysis (see especially the 'buying frequency' variables of the CI analysis in chapter 3): there seemed to be a strong relationship between membership in the cognitive categories and the detail of the comments on learning-by-doing routines related to green shopping. Members of the top cognitive categories remembered how and when they had changed their buying behaviours from non-green practices to greener ones and often they could also indicate for how long they had been pursuing a certain green shopping practice. In contrast, consumers in the lower cognitive categories only remembered unsuccessful instances of green trial behaviour which had no lasting impact on shopping habits.

It was found that habit effects spilled over from other shopping issues such as vegetarianism or animal rights to green issues. Such 'spill-overs' apparently helped some interviewees to adjust their shopping behaviours more easily with regard to green shopping. For instance B4 stated: 'I used to read the label [of environmentally friendly shampoo] . . . you get very practised in reading labels as a vegan, everything you buy, you have to read the label.' Once habituated, certain shopping-related behaviours, such as 'reading labels', apparently develop a force of their own. After behavioural routines have been established for a specific domain, they seem to facilitate the habituation of behaviour in other, related domains.[3]

Commonly, habitual behaviour is thought to reflect a stimulus-driven mode of cognition which focuses on cognitive operational processes of selection. However, for some interviewees it was apparent that habit formation and habit change did not necessarily reflect such stimulus-driven choice of products. Habit formation and habit change were, to a degree, rather actively and rationally controlled from a level 'above' stimulus-driven product choice; for instance, B15 explained: 'I habitually bought [product A] from [shop A], but now deliberately buy [product A] from [shop B]' in order to achieve a certain ethical purpose; another reference of B15 was: 'I don't think about it [green shopping] on a daily basis, once I've got the concept stuck in my head, I habitually go for it'; B38 reasoned: 'I wouldn't buy [product A] as a routine'; and D10 explained that green shopping was 'gewohnheitssache' [a matter of habit].

It seems that the habituation of shopping behaviour (and product-related familiarity) is to a degree consciously recognized, scrutinized and controlled. No further claims can be made here regarding how widespread or how rare such 'rational' approaches to the habituation of behaviour are, but these findings, even if they are exceptional, point towards a different kind of consumer rationality from that which is usually related to habitual shopping behaviour.

ABILITY AND SUCCESSFUL GREEN CONSUMER BEHAVIOUR

Ability refers to successful problem solving. The ability of the green consumer can be examined through psychological IQ tests, as called for, for instance, by Simon (1992: 272) or SRI (1992: 15). However, IQ tests can assess only certain aspects of ability in which the daily context of behaviour plays little or no role (see chapter 2). This study did not examine the ability of the green consumer from a psychological perspective, through IQ tests. Rather, it applied the anthropological concepts of practical thinking and bricolage to discussing consumer intelligence. Ability was assessed in terms of how skilfully green consumers solved their shopping problem: how they conducted information search and information evaluation in a real-life choice situation.

The ideas of practical thinking and bricolage are closely interrelated. Lévi-Strauss defined practical thinking as task-related practical know-how, while bricolage refers to actual behaviours which are involved in problem solving, namely 'techniques' of doing (see chapter 2). It is difficult to set out absolute and quantitative criteria for assessing the quality of practical thinking and bricolage. Such intelligence assessments have to be conducted on a comparative basis. A comparative approach should be sufficient to contrast different types of consumer intelligence as they can be found in real life. Through comparing the problem solving approaches of different consumers, the skill with which the problem 'green consumption' was solved was examined. A 'higher' or a 'lower' ability regarding practical thinking and bricolage was thus identified. Criteria for a comparative assessment of the quality of practical thinking and bricolage are inventiveness, flexibility, simplicity or efficiency (Scribner 1986: 22-8, Berry and Irvine 1986: 298-300).

In the following, whether and how life-cycle analysis (LCA) considerations were put into practice by green consumers is first discussed. Because of their 'scientific' nature, LCA considerations are particularly revealing regarding how green problem solving works in practice and how it does not. Subsequently, factors other than LCA-related product attributes are examined regarding problem solving skills shown by the green consumer. How the difficulty of green shopping was perceived by consumers is also discussed. Finally, concluding an assessment of the intelligence involved in green consumer behaviour, different ways of practical thinking are outlined.

Practical thinking, bricolage and LCA

LCA considerations provide a good test case for an assessment of the ability of the green consumer. It is possible to examine whether and, if so, how LCA considerations, which are of a somewhat 'scientific' nature, were approached and put into actual shopping practice. As found earlier, LCA considerations were comparatively frequently made by the higher cognitive categories 4 and 5. It seemed that membership in the higher cognitive categories related to a higher degree of LCA-type knowledge. For the lower cognitive categories 1 and 2, LCA-type knowledge was rare (cf. Wild 1995: 5) and, when it was found, LCA considerations were partly mixed up with other shopping considerations (see chapter 5).

It was apparent in the previous analyses that certain LCA considerations received more attention than others: the most commonly attended LCA-consideration was 'locally produced/retailed', which reflects a preference for local goods which were produced and/or retailed 'close by', e.g. regionally rather than coming from far away. About a third of the British and the German inter-viewees referred to the consideration 'locally produced/retailed': nineteen British interviewees (of which none was prompted) and thirteen German interviewees (of which one was prompted) did so. The second most prominent LCA issue that was touched upon by interviewees when characterizing green products was 'production processes': it was referred to by thirteen of the British interviewees (of whom two were prompted) and by six of the German interviewees (of whom one was prompted). Other LCA considerations, such as sourcing, disposal or energy considerations, were rarely attended to. It seemed that LCA considerations were made in a rather *selective* way, strongly favouring the issue 'locally produced/retailed'.

Information taken into account for operationalizing 'locally produced/retailed' was generally of a rather concrete nature: 'made on premises at the end of the road', 'from a local farm that is only twelve miles away', 'comes from England', 'try to go shopping where we live', etc. Rather specific information was available: places like streets, towns, regions, countries or continents were used as *proxy values* for putting a consideration like 'locally produced/retailed' into action. Consumers of the higher cognitive categories 4 and 5 had an ability to 'see' and exploit proxy information that related to 'locally produced/retailed', e.g. the production or retail location of a product, while interviewees from the lower cognitive categories did not see (and thus could not use) such information.

Proxy assessments were made on a *comparative* basis. Consumers did not attempt to consider and optimize actual distances covered by transportation processes when they were looking at 'locally produced/retailed'. A 'better' solution rather than the 'best' solution was aimed for. In general, means of transportation used were neglected in assessing 'locally produced/retailed'. Means of transport from a producer to a retailer were nearly always ignored, while means of transport to and from a retailer, as utilized by consumers themselves, were more often referred to for assessing the product attribute 'locally produced/ retailed'.

The problem solving approach of green consumers to 'locally produced/ retailed' was not very scientific: accuracy in general, and numerical accuracy in particular, did play a small role in practical problem solving. Exact measuring was apparently not regarded as part of the problem.[4] The consumers in the higher cognitive categories had found a way to make selective, approximate and comparative LCA assessments. Apparently, members of the higher cognitive categories had an ability to (subjectively) perceive LCA information once it was (objectively) available. Decision making in the form of selective information search and information evaluation that is based on the comparative assessment of proxy information does not live up to the rigour of a scientifically conducted LCA. Rather, it is pragmatic in its outlook, and it can be judged as skilful practical thinking. The resulting bricolage-type behaviour is likely to be 'better' than behaviour that ignored LCA completely. As Lévi-Strauss (1966: 269) pointed out, practical thinking 'proceeds from the angle of sensible [empirically available] qualities' but not 'formal [scientific] properties'.

When LCA considerations other than 'locally produced/retailed' were attended to, information held on them was generally of a weakly specific and often also of a weakly abstract nature. There appeared to be no easy way to extract from a product, its packaging and its setting reliable proxy information on LCA issues other than the information 'locally produced/retailed'. Knowledge held on the second most common LCA consideration, 'production process', tended to be of a rather vague nature. The strong focusing on 'locally produced/retailed' by the higher cognitive categories in both the British and the German samples reflected the relatively easy availability of such information. It could be speculated that other LCA information, if easily available, would also have been considered by interviewees of the higher cognitive categories.

An examination of LCA considerations and how they were put into practice revealed that the higher cognitive categories had managed to overcome problems of information availability and that they had shown some considerable success in acting upon LCA considerations. Problem solving focused on what was perceived to be possible rather than desirable in terms of a 'scientifically correct' LCA.

'Un-practical' thinking and LCA

Attempts of consumers to conduct a 'scientifically correct' LCA seemed to be counter-productive. Amongst the consumers sampled, there were a few who had a fairly comprehensive knowledge of LCA, but somewhat surprisingly ranked low in terms of membership in the cognitive categories. This was most apparent for interviewee G14, and to a lesser extent also for B53 and G24. G14 had a very well-developed knowledge of LCA which was based on the reading of LCA literature and LCA reports of various companies. A very good argumentative knowledge was shown by G14, in fact the highest of any of the German interviewees. This indicated that some highly complex reasoning was going on, but interestingly the green product-related knowledge of G14 was low, which resulted in this interviewee being classified as a member of the bottom cognitive category 1.

Undoubtedly, G14 had a fairly comprehensive understanding of LCA, but actual consumer behaviour was basically not affected by it. Little pragmatism was shown; for instance, the consideration 'locally produced/retailed', which was focused on strongly by the interviewees of cognitive categories 4 and 5 who had actually managed to put LCA considerations into practice, was not once referred to by G14, and other LCA considerations were only referred to for indicating what was *not* done.[5] Apparently, the attempt to approach green problem solving in the context of daily life scientifically 'from the angle of . . . formal properties' (Lévi-Strauss 1966: 269) failed.

The case of G14 illustrated that a good understanding of the LCA concept alone did not in itself yield *actual* green shopping behaviour. It could be suggested that knowledge – like attitudes and intentions (as discussed in chapter 1 with regard to the Fishbein model) – can only have an impact on actual behaviour if knowledge has developed in relation to certain behaviours: here, the buying of products. Attempts to think context-free with scientific precision about LCA seemed to stifle green behaviour rather than to enable it. Understanding may kill action, and action may depend upon a veil of illusion as Friedrich Nietzsche noted in *The Birth of Tragedy*. For the higher cognitive categories, practical thinking and a bricolage-type approach to LCA considerations enabled pragmatic green behaviour, and it could be said that pragmatism provided here a kind of 'veil of illusion' for green consumer behaviour. To speak of an 'illusion' for the higher cognitive categories 4 and 5 may not be totally appropriate since the 'illusion' was at least partly recognized: pragmatism can be viewed as a non-rational (in the sense of non-scientific) improvisation but a rather consciously negotiated one (which would be in contrast to a subconscious symbolic interpretation).[6]

Other interviewees who had realized the complexities of conducting a 'scientific' LCA tended to use LCA considerations instrumentally in order to distance themselves from green consumption. B53 did so most obviously, and to a degree also G24 and N2. They appeared not to be highly motivated towards green shopping, and this was quite openly stated. The scientific complexity of LCA issues was referred to in order to justify the low priority that they attached to green shopping. It might be speculated that too scientific an understanding of LCA was (partly) responsible for the lowered motivation and for a rather cynical attitude towards green shopping. G14 was highly motivated towards green shopping, which made this case in a way the more puzzling.

Skilful perception of green product attributes

In addition to the examination of how green consumers handled LCA-related product attributes, the skill with which other product attributes were approached and handled was also examined. The paradigmatic subjects were focused on for this assessment. How they defined and solved the green shopping problem in terms of product attributes was assessed:

- *B5* referred most frequently to the product attributes 'product ingredients' and 'locally produced/retailed' as well as 'packaging material' and 'reusable'. Information on ingredients-related issues was derived from the package, e.g. 'low in phosphates', 'non-biological' or 'unbleached'. Most of this information was taken at its face value. Occasionally its meaning was questioned, e.g. 'non-biological', but it was still acted upon despite the ambiguity felt. Some exceptionally abstract knowledge existed for the product attributes 'ingredients' and partly also for 'organic'. This was probably related to B5's background in organic farming. The product attribute 'locally produced/ retailed' was largely related to shopping at local shops. 'Packaging material' was operationalized in terms of a preference for paper packaging, bottles and cans. The use of bottles was subsequently related to 'reusable'; the use of cans was related to 'recyclable'.
- *G5* had the product attributes 'home made',[7] 'reusable' and, if taken together, the packaging attributes 'amount of packaging' and 'packaging material' very strongly developed. The product attribute 'reusable' was highly developed both in terms of the specificity and the abstractness of knowledge content. An extensive knowledge of names was available.
- *B4* had the attributes 'ingredients', 'biodegradable' and 'recycled' strongly developed. Recall focused strongly on information provided on the packaging. The product attribute 'packaging images' was quite prominent. The retailer name 'Co-op' was heavily relied upon and names were generally well specified. For the attribute 'ingredients', information was of a commonsense nature except for the product 'cleaners', which was referred to in a highly abstract way. Ideas like 'biodegradable' and 'recycled' were assessed on the basis of on-package information. B4 could rephrase ideas like 'recycled' and 'biodegradable' in a simple way.
- *G4* had the attributes 'reusable', 'amount of packaging' and 'locally produced/ retailed' strongly developed. 'Reusable' was explained with reference to

returning containers. Also, a detailed and specific knowledge of names was available.

- *B3* had the attributes 'organic' and partly also 'packaging material' and 'amount of packaging' developed to some degree. 'Organic' was not further elaborated on, while the packaging attributes were only weakly developed. Names were highly specific.
- *G3* had the attributes 'reusable' and 'amount of packaging' developed to some degree; certain avoidance behaviours regarding heavily packaged goods were referred to. Names were partly specific, partly only weakly specific.
- For *B2*, names made up the most prominent product attribute. They were volunteered right at the beginning of the interview.
- *G2* had 'packaging material', 'reusable' and 'locally produced/retailed' developed to some degree. As indicated earlier, 'locally produced/retailed' was mixed here with other shopping issues such as a patriotic buying motive.

- It was difficult to assess *B1* and *G1* in terms of how they assessed the greenness of a product since both engaged in green shopping on only a very low level.

In a particular shopping situation, information availability is of a highly subjective nature: it is restrained by the information that is actually 'seen' – that is attended to and sought out of all the information 'objectively' offered by a product, its packaging and its setting. Easily available information, such as product names, on-package information and shopping place-related information, was commonly used. It became apparent that, in general, problem solving and decision making focused on issues for which information could easily be taken into account at the point of shopping in one way or another. 'External memory' seemed to play an important role (see also chapters 2 and 5). Again, the subjective and context-dependent nature of information availability became apparent, as had already been found for LCA considerations. And once more, the higher cognitive categories seemed to be rather more inventive and flexible in retrieving green information from a choice situation.

Perception of task difficulties

Perceptions of task difficulty have an impact on whether and how a shopping problem is solved. How task difficulties were perceived by the different cognitive categories reflects on successful green behaviour. During the interview, task difficulty was discussed at the end of part 1 of the interview. Also, the CI index covered issues relating to task difficulty. In general, the difficulty of solving the green shopping problem was perceived differently across the cognitive categories.

The interviewees voiced a number of reasons for not buying green products (see also Wild 1995: 6, 23-9). The task of buying green products was viewed as difficult (a) because of perceived informational problems in assessing the greenness of a product; (b) because of a perceived clash between the greenness of a product and other product characteristics, such as effectiveness, convenience of use, price, etc.; and (c) because of situational constraints, such as time pressure or the availability of green products. These factors contributed to the perception of a task as difficult and they are assessed in turn in the following.

The paradigmatic subjects experienced the following task difficulties:

- *B5* referred to the lack of information on the production process of supermarket products; issues of information processability, for instance, the meaning of 'non-biological' detergent, were touched upon. The restricted availability of organic food was referred to. Green products were viewed as being only marginally more expensive than non-green ones.

- *G5* perceived time as an important constraint with regard to informing oneself about green products and with regard to the time green shopping takes. The availability of green products was viewed as good. Price was considered as an issue of some but not overwhelming importance that interfered with green shopping.

- *B4* did not discuss task difficulty regarding information problems. Price and the low performance of certain green products, particularly washing and cleaning products, was raised as a main concern.

- *G4* referred to a lack of chemical understanding of certain product ingredients. Also, price was referred to as a main issue. Packaging was raised as another issue. To avoid packaging totally was reckoned to be difficult. The use of certain green products was viewed as inconvenient, but despite such perceptions they were used.

- *B3* referred repeatedly to information problems in terms of not knowing what information to look for. Information diagnosticity or relevance was touched upon here. Difficulties in assessing the benefits of glass recycling were mentioned. A low availability of organic food was referred to.

- *G3* did not discuss task difficulty regarding information problems. Price was raised as an issue that was thought to make green shopping difficult. The availability of green products was generally judged as high.

- *B2* did not discuss task difficulty regarding information problems. Green products were found to be not easily available in supermarkets. Time pressure and the convenience of shopping were raised as important issues.

- *G2* did not discuss task difficulty regarding information problems. Time and convenience were discussed as main issues.

- *B1* discussed the lack of information about global issues and asked 'what green foods looked like'. Price was referred to as a deterrent to buying green products.

- *G1* touched upon informational issues when the use of phosphates in detergents was mentioned. Time and price were discussed as main difficulties. Convenience was raised as another issue.

Perceptions of informational task difficulty reflect problems of how to find, collect and assess information on the greenness of a product. In the previous analyses it had become clear that perceived information availability is of a highly subjective nature. Perceptions of information problems seemed to be in line with previous findings on how perceptions of information availability varied across the cognitive categories. The higher cognitive categories were able to pinpoint information deficits more clearly. They addressed specific information deficits for certain product attributes, while the lower cognitive categories were more concerned with finding out what kind of general information to look for in order to assess the greenness of a product.

Like informational task difficulties, the perceived importance of certain product characteristics of a green product, such as price, performance, convenience, etc., tended to affect the making of a green buying decision negatively. In general, price was touched upon by members of all cognitive categories. Green products were viewed as more expensive than ordinary ones. However, for the higher cognitive categories price was no great deterrence from buying green products (see also Parker 1989: 15): some interviewees accepted higher prices as a matter of fact, which was not further elaborated on. Other members of the higher cognitive categories explained how they had managed to accept higher prices: it was explained that the share of one's total budget given to products consumed on a daily basis was comparatively small in any circumstances and that the buying of green products did not affect that share substantially (G10, G36). Others seemed to have boxed themselves into the acceptance of higher prices through active efforts to ignore price differences between green and non-green products: 'I try not to look at the prices . . . if you find out time and again it's more expensive, it's a deterrence, so I don't look too much' (B06, and similarly G09 and G36). Views of some consumers in the higher cognitive categories (e.g. G36) reflected a changing attitude towards the high prices of green products over time: one of initial 'shock and disbelief' which was later replaced by a growing acceptance. Increasing familiarity with green products and possibly a related change in priorities may have played a role. Such a finding on the weak price sensitivity of green consumers in the higher cognitive categories seems to be in line with life-style categorizations where price was found to be less of an issue for 'true green' consumers (see chapter 1).

Certain performance issues were referred to by all cognitive categories, such as the poor performance of green detergents and cleaning products. A few members of the higher cognitive categories accepted the lower performance of the green product as a direct reflection of the greenness of a product, but, in general, performance problems were a concern for many of the interviewees.

Situational constraints, like time pressure or convenience of shopping, were more often raised as a task difficulty by the lower cognitive categories. Also, perceptions of the physical availability of green products changed from the bottom to the top cognitive categories. Availability problems were less perceived by the top categories. They seemed to know where to get the green products. The higher cognitive categories seemed to have relaxed these situational constraints in line with increasing knowledge and cognitive skills.

In summary, practical problem solving apparently developed in steps. Perceptions of task difficulties, such as information availability, the physical availability of a product, the high price of green products, etc., were of a subjective nature that reflected the personal history of a consumer. In line with increasing experience, perceptions of task difficulty diminished. For example, the higher cognitive categories were capable of describing perceived task difficulties more clearly. Informational problems were more often related to certain individual products than to green shopping in general. The total number of task difficulty issues decreased from the lower cognitive categories towards the higher ones (as found by the CI analysis). If numbers were assessed on a relative basis, e.g. against the total number of products recalled and discussed, perceived problems of task difficulty were even more strongly concentrated in the bottom cognitive categories.

Ways of practical thinking

Conceptual knowledge about green products and cognitive skills for choosing them varied across the cognitive categories. Differently complex and sophisticated systems of sensibility existed for the respective cognitive categories regarding how to define and assess the greenness of a product. Differences across the cognitive categories can be related to the idea that their members were involved in different types of practical thinking.

How a person makes a consumption choice hints at what was perceived as available and possible in a certain situation (Grafton-Small 1993: 42, similarly Campbell 1989: 49). Lévi-Strauss stressed that in the everyday world practical thinking and bricolage constitute a key part of daily life. The construction of reality through practical thinking and bricolage is limited by the way the world is perceived. Such perception develops in line with a person's consumption history: 'We must always do with a finite set of tools and materials, including concepts, which is the contingent result of all the occasions there have been to renew or enrich the stock or to maintain it' (Grafton-Small 1993: 42). Persons are bound to speak through the behavioural choices they made. Over time experience builds up, and hence, the quality of practical thinking and problem solving is likely to rise.

It was found in this study that information availability – both internal and external – was of a highly subjective nature. While the lower cognitive categories concentrated comparatively strongly on information reflecting names, the higher cognitive categories also had access to more conceptual information. Such differences in knowledge substance were reflected by differences in how cleverly members of the respective cognitive categories approached green shopping through practical thinking and bricolage. Also, perceptions of task difficulty became more precise and focused from the bottom towards the top cognitive categories.

Besides its very subjective outlook, the reasoning of the green consumer reflected a highly contextual orientation. The ability to exploit information from the shopping situation in terms of what information could be used for green decision making increased across the cognitive categories: depending upon what kind of knowledge a person brought to a choice situation, information perception and green decision making varied. Such findings can be related to the idea of 'contextual memory' (Gordon and Valentine 1996: 35-7, Warlop and Ratneshwar 1993: 377, 380-1, Ratneshwar and Shocker 1988: 284, Jenkins 1977: 426-7, Bransford *et al.* 1977: 461, 463; see also chapter 7), which seems to play an important role in practical thinking and bricolage.

Across the cognitive categories, different types of practical thinking could be found. They reflected an increase in the quality of practical thinking across the cognitive categories:

- *Pragmatism.* One of the types of practical thinking identified can be labelled pragmatism. It refers to an acceptance of the complexities of green shopping without trying to solve them in their entirety, but only where this can be comparatively easily achieved. Pragmatism can be said to be an enlightened cognitive approach to green shopping. It was especially widespread amongst the higher cognitive categories. As discussed above, for both the German and the British samples, the higher cognitive categories took LCA considerations into account, on a selective and comparative basis, by drawing on proxy information. A better solution rather than the best solution was aimed for.

- *Naivety.* Another mode of practical thinking can be said to be naivety. Certain information was 'believed' in, but not really understood. Behaviour was based on a 'real' illusion; for example, slogans like 'environmentally friendly', symbols like a 'little green tree', or the colour of a packaging, e.g. blue-green, were taken as an indication of a product's greenness. A naive approach to green shopping appeared to be particularly widespread amongst cognitive category 2. For instance, consumers of this category focused nearly exclusively on green names rather than other product attributes for choosing a green product.

- *Cynicism.* A 'mechanism' for *un*successful green problem solving, preventing practical thinking, could be said to be cynicism. Activity levels of green shopping behaviour were negatively affected by views such as knowing too much about green shopping and its effectiveness. It appeared that once a consumer had realized the naivety of initial ideas about green shopping and begun to understand some of the 'scientific' complexities of green shopping, e.g. related to LCA, confusion set in and 'blinded consumers' (Wild 1995: 7, 37, 39, 41, 43-6). This was especially apparent for members of the middle cognitive categories. Confusion seemed to be resolved in two ways over time, either by pragmatism (and a move towards the higher cognitive categories) or by cynicism (and a move towards stagnation or towards the lower cognitive categories). As indicated above, for some interviewees (e.g. B53, G24 and N2) cynicism had prevented further green shopping behaviour.

- *Ignorance.* Another mechanism for *un*successful green problem solving is ignorance: not knowing and not wanting to know about green shopping. Through ignorance, consumers in cognitive category 1 basically avoided green shopping issues. Ignorance cuts short drastically even the attempt to begin practical thinking: there was no attempt to formulate a green shopping problem, mainly due to low motivation regarding green shopping.

These different types of practical thinking reflected different 'veils of illusion', to come back to Nietzsche's term. Pragmatism and naivety had an enabling effect on practical thinking and the bricolage of the green shopping problem, albeit a different one, as indicated above. In contrast, cynicism and ignorance had a disabling effect on actual green consumer behaviour. Pragmatism, naivety, cynicism and ignorance were apparent in all cognitive categories but in rather different degrees: as indicated, ignorance seemed to be particularly widespread for the bottom cognitive categories, as was pragmatism for the higher cognitive categories; naivety and cynicism seemed to be more prevalent in the middle cognitive categories.

These 'ways of practical thinking' do not solely relate to cognitive levels. They are connected to motivational levels, which were excluded from the research conducted here. It is likely that successful green shopping is ultimately enabled or prevented by a combination of motivational, cognitive and behavioural factors. In this study, certain motivational observations, which suggested such an intricate relationship, were only a by-product of the cognitive research undertaken.

CONCLUSIONS

Actual behaviour, as reflected by familiarity, played an important role in successful green consumer behaviour. Product-related familiarity was strongly reflected by membership in the higher cognitive categories. It seemed to be at least a necessary factor for learning. The length of time involved in green shopping did not seem to play a major role in explaining knowledge structure differences between the cognitive categories, which also pointed towards the strong influence of motivational factors. Findings on certain habits of green consumers indicated that familiarity with green products was to a degree consciously recognized and rationally controlled.

In terms of practical thinking, the green consumer exhibited intelligent behaviour to a substantial degree. The higher cognitive categories commanded a considerable amount of LCA-type knowledge, and they put LCA considerations pragmatically rather than scientifically into shopping practice: green buying choices were made on the basis of a comparative and selective assessment of proxy information. The higher cognitive categories showed skilled behaviour in exploiting LCA-type information in a choice context. Members of the lower cognitive categories showed little ability in that respect.

It seemed that extensive product-oriented familiarity, an ability for pragmatic green problem solving as well as high motivation (which was only indirectly touched upon by this study) related to a high level of knowledge structure development. Each of these three factors can be considered necessary for membership in the higher cognitive categories, but none of them appeared to be sufficient on its own. Apparently, knowledge structure development (learning) related to a number of interconnected factors. Whether the idea of causality as the underlying heuristic principle for cognitive research should be given up is an open question. Also, consumption, like most everyday behaviour, is of a personal-historical nature – reflecting experience. An understanding of historical processes of how motivation, cognition and behaviour are interconnected may be difficult to reconcile with the causality principle.

Naive approaches to green consumption were more widespread in the lower cognitive categories. Initial ignorance regarding green shopping seemed to be first replaced by naivety: the greenness of a product was assessed by using information like slogans, names, labels, etc. Once a naive approach was recognized, confusion seemed to set in. Over time, confusion seemed to be replaced either by cynicism regarding green shopping, which had a negative impact on actual behaviour, or by a pragmatic approach to green shopping, which had a positive impact on behaviour.

It appeared that too scientific an approach to green shopping, when applied independently of its real-life choice context, stifled rather than enabled green consumer behaviour. A few 'tragic' figures were found that suffered cognitive frustration because of the perceived complexities of conducting a scientific LCA and, possibly related to that, they showed cynicism regarding green shopping.

The lower cognitive categories perceived task difficulties such as informational problems, quality problems concerning green products, e.g. effectiveness, convenience of use, price, etc., or situational constraints, e.g. time pressure, to a greater degree than the higher cognitive categories. This also reflected on their lack of familiarity and ability, and related to it, a lack of habituation in green behaviour in the lower cognitive categories.

The patterns of practical thinking that were found for successful green consumer behaviour reflected a strong contextual orientation: knowledge was developed and applied through actual behaviour in a certain context. This seems to call for a conceptualization of consumer cognition as 'contextual cognition' which does not treat 'context' as a black box or as an independent variable of behaviour. Depending on what kind of problem a researcher is looking into, a different concept of what a product is is relevant, e.g. being viewed as the output of an industrial process, a status symbol, etc. For understanding consumer behaviour in the everyday world – how a product is assessed and chosen – products are probably best understood as a contextual system of sensibility which is subjectively constructed through practical thinking and bricolage.

7

THE BEGINNING OF
KNOWLEDGE

A NEW APPROACH TO COGNITION

This study undertook a spirited journey through the mind of the green consumer, showing that cognitive research can produce insights that are both theoretically meaningful and practically relevant. It demonstrated that qualitative research into cognition can be conducted on a rigorous scientific basis, yielding interesting and valuable insights into the nature of understanding. For gaining an understanding of cognition, a traditional psychological framework was rejected. Instead, cognition was researched from a comprehensive cognitive psychological and a cognitive anthropological point of view. In that respect, the study returned to the origins of cognitive research, namely the ideas of Frederic Bartlett and Claude Lévi-Strauss.

Reorientation of cognitive research

The idea of cognition relates to a number of concepts, ranging from the organization of knowledge structures and memory processes to intelligence, decision making and problem solving behaviour. Cognition basically refers to understanding – how meaning is 'created', 'applied' and 'stored' in a person's mind.

Sciences like cognitive psychology and cognitive anthropology research cognition differently. They attempt to provide an understanding of *understanding* and they do so from their respective points of view. In its traditional research approach, cognitive psychology has followed in the footsteps of the natural sciences, favouring the research of cognition on a highly fragmented, focused basis and freeing the research into behaviour from its natural context, putting it into a controlled laboratory environment. In contrast, cognitive anthropology approaches the research into cognition on a comprehensive basis, examining the 'whole' cognitive person in her/his natural context, namely daily life.

A main theme of this study has been that cognitive research has to make sure that it provides an explanation of cognition in 'real life'. The study argued that cognitive research, which has traditionally been conducted as psychological research, can gain a lot by incorporating ideas from cognitive anthropology. This is not to say that psychologists should turn into anthropologists. To a degree, it is even irrelevant whether cognitive research is approached from a psychological or an anthropological point of view as long as it is approached from a comprehensive conceptual position that examines the contextual nature of cognition in daily life. This latter consideration does not appear to be a matter of choice regarding the structuring of good cognitive research, whereas a decision to undertake 'psychological' or 'anthropological' research is more or less an arbitrary one. Science that is not capable of producing insights into naturally occurring phenomena risks degenerating into a self-centred intellectual exercise.

A central axiom for a cognitive research programme can be formulated:

Understanding cognition implies understanding cognition in real life;

and, in turn,

understanding cognition in real life implies understanding contextual cognition.

Such an axiomatic basis can be considered a key element of the heuristic framing of cognitive research. It has implications both for the conceptual structuring of a cognitive research problem and for the conducting of empirical research (see Figure 7.1).

A case has been argued that good cognitive research has to be conducted on a more comprehensive conceptual basis than the traditional, highly reductionist

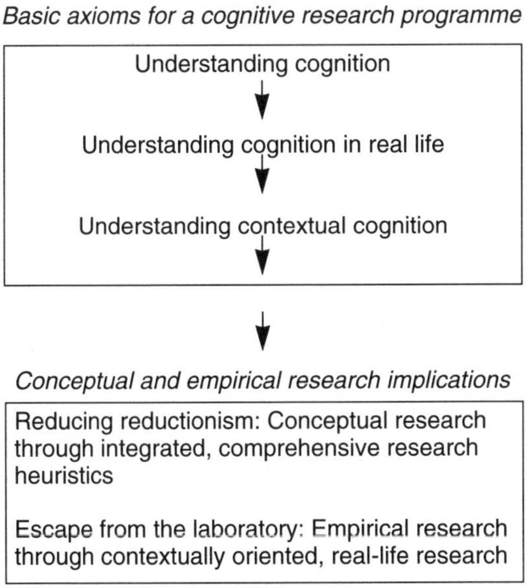

Basic axioms for a cognitive research programme

Understanding cognition

↓

Understanding cognition in real life

↓

Understanding contextual cognition

↓

↓

Conceptual and empirical research implications

Reducing reductionism: Conceptual research through integrated, comprehensive research heuristics

Escape from the laboratory: Empirical research through contextually oriented, real-life research

Figure 7.1 Cognitive research

193

approach of psychology. Psychology isolates its research constructs in an extreme fashion, trying to copy the approach of the natural sciences. This has led to the generation of quantitatively precise and statistically significant research results but results that were often insignificant in terms of relevance and external validity. Kant was sceptical that psychology could ever be a science in the sense of the natural sciences, being based on the causality principle and doing highly focused and controlled research. With the benefit of hindsight after a century of psychological research, Kant's scepticism appears more justified. As Bruner (1979: 28) noted: 'The more rigorously isolated from context and the more tightly controlled the conditions of [laboratory] experiments, the more precise and the more modest have results been [in psychology].' Similar diagnoses have been made by leading psychologists since the very beginning of scientific psychological research. The value of research can be questioned that produces only findings that can be transferred from one laboratory to another but that cannot explain how people think, develop knowledge and solve problems in everyday life. Within psychology, there are a few critical voices who have called for a departure from mainstream psychological research and its treatment of 'context' (Maturana and Varela 1992, Varela *et al.* 1991, Neisser 1978, Jenkins 1977, Bransford *et al.* 1977). Chapters 2 and 3 went into some detail in that respect.

Conceptual comprehensiveness counteracts reductionism. It is achieved through a synthetic analysis of research constructs. In this study, a comprehensive knowledge structure framework was synthesized that covered a knowledge content, a cognitive operational and a formatting level of cognition. Subsequently, findings on knowledge structures were related to an assessment of intelligence and problem solving behaviour in daily life. The framework was put into effect step by step. As a result, a comprehensive understanding of green consumer cognition, and insights into the working of cognition in general, were arrived at.

Besides being comprehensive in conceptual terms, good cognitive research should be contextual in nature. This idea has implications for both the conceptual and the empirical approaches towards cognitive research. Context has to be conceptually integrated into a heuristic framework for understanding cognition. Regarding empirical research, the context in which behaviour naturally occurs has to be examined for cognition to be understood. Laboratory research appears inappropriate as an empirical research method. Actual contact has to be made with the phenomenon under investigation as it 'occurs' in its natural setting. Ideas from case study research as they have been traditionally applied in empirical research in anthropology may prove useful.

Issues of a proper research method for cognitive research lead quickly into a philosophy of science debate which could only be briefly touched upon in this study. The need for a broader philosophy of science for psychology (and psychological consumer behaviour research) that transcends reductionism and the laboratory approach has long been stressed. There seems to be good reason to accept a plurality of methods for psychological research because of their different strengths and potentials for contributions.

Towards a contextual model

A different kind of science is likely to be required for the examination of cognition from that for research on atoms and chemical elements. For cognitive consumer research, such a research approach is outlined in more detail here.

Initially, in the early 1970s, consumer behaviour research was expected to examine problems from everyday life, generating relevant, normative advice for the solution of practical problems. Consumer behaviour research was expected to develop an 'interdisciplinary and pioneering field of study [theory] and practice' (Monroe 1993: n.p.; see also Wells 1993: 489, 500). However, a general accusation of the irrelevance of most consumer behaviour research, e.g. regarding the application of consumer research findings to the solving of marketing management problems, has been upheld over the past decades: 'As we know now ... [c]onsumer research has not "achieved better" than the other social sciences with respect to "richness of thinking, comprehensiveness of theorizing, and testing of theories in naturalistic and realistic settings"' (Wells 1993: 490, referring here to an earlier review of Sheth 1972: 572; similarly Shimp 1994: 1–3, Sheth 1992: 348). Also, the accusation that most consumer behaviour research has been motivated by 'the availability of easy-to-use measuring instruments ... and/or the almost toy-like nature of sophisticated quantitative techniques' is still being made since first voiced in the mid-1970s (Jacoby 1976a: 2; see also Shimp 1994: 5, Wells 1993: 490, Jacoby 1976b). Not surprisingly, a reorientation of consumer behaviour research in general, and cognitive consumer research in particular, has long been demanded; for instance, research into knowledge structure development, and the research of 'real-life' consumer cognition has been called for (Alba *et al.* 1991: 36, Bettman *et al.* 1991: 76, Bettman and Park 1980: 245).

As a consumer research project, this study adhered to such calls for a reorientation, namely to examine 'real problems' and to provide 'real solutions' (Wells 1993: 497-8, 500, Shimp 1994: 5). Likewise, as a psychological research project, the study adhered to calls for a reorientation of cognitive psychological research to 'encompass lived human experience' and to examine the changing nature of human experience over time (Herrmann and Gruneberg 1993: 562, Maturana and Varela 1992: 244-8, Varela *et al.* 1991: xv, Neisser 1978: 13-14, Jenkins 1977: 427, Bransford *et al.* 1977: 461-3; see also Tybout and Artz 1994: 159, Thorngate 1976: 404, 405).

The contextual nature of consumer thinking and behaviour has long been acknowledged, but often this was done as a kind of a lip service: in judgement research, context is ignored altogether (see chapters 2 and 3); other research projects into consumer cognition treated context as a 'black box'; research projects that tried to open the black box 'context' tended to view context – in the psychological research tradition – as being there to be 'manipulated' (Warlop and Ratneshwar 1993).

For an explanation of cognition in daily life, the idea of context has to be integrated into the very explanation of cognition: through the idea of 'contextual knowledge', such integration can be approached. Possible theoretical constructs for operationalizing contextual knowledge are:

- subjectively perceived context constraints
- subjectively perceived context opportunities
- subjectively perceived information availability
- subjectively perceived task difficulty
- subjectively perceived physical availability of products (and of choice alternatives).

The black box 'context' has to be opened and the treatment of context as an independent variable that is there to be manipulated should be avoided, at least in the initial stages of research. In general, a distinction between 'dependent' and 'independent' variables may be unhelpful when it comes to research into contextual knowledge since it draws on the causality principle. And this very principle may have to be challenged when it comes to the reorientation of cognitive research.

The findings of this study stressed the highly contextual nature of consumer choice behaviour. Both familiarity and ability shown by the green consumer reflected a contextual approach to problem solving. For instance, subjectively perceived information availability changed across the cognitive categories: depending on what conceptual knowledge persons brought to a choice situation, objectively available information (through a product, its packaging and its sale setting) was discovered and used by the consumer – or not. The study illustrated how the subjective perception of context aided and enabled consumer choice. Through learning, the perception of context constraints and context opportunities changed. The findings made on the type of information processing shown by green consumers, in particular the understanding gained on the contextual nature of consumer choice, give new meaning to the idea of the consumer 'muddling through' information search and evaluation (Schultz *et al.* 1992: 23). Over time, consumers learned to relax what were initially seen as context constraints and to discover new choice opportunities: old 'veils of illusion' were lifted, while new ones were imposed. Rational or intelligent behaviour can be understood as such subjectively constrained, contextual behaviour.

This study found a few consumers who had apparently tried to approach green shopping through 'scientific thinking' rather than through 'practical (contextual) thinking'. However, their product-related knowledge of green shopping was rather weak. A scientific 'context-independent' approach to green shopping seemed to stifle actual behaviour. These somewhat tragic figures of consumers can be compared to the psychologist who ignores context in the explanation of behaviour.

The study clarified an understanding of 'choice context' and how this construct can be conceptually dealt with in consumer behaviour research. An appropriate conceptual model for contextual consumer research is probably most easily arrived at by opening the psychological approach to anthropological ideas such as 'practical thinking' or 'bricolage'. In cognitive anthropological research, the idea of 'contextual thinking' has generally played a prominent role. Cognitive anthropology examines consumer thinking as 'practical thinking' rather than as 'scientific thinking'. The cognitive anthropological model of the consumer as practical thinker and bricoleur provides a contextual perspective on consumer rationality. It suggests that simple and devious means that are discovered and created in a certain context are used for problem solving. Of key importance is the idea that behaviour is subjectively defined by a person through the perception and construction of the context in which problem solving occurs.

Bricolage-type ability reflects the kind of ability shown by *Homo faber*, the craftsman or handyman who acquires ability through practice and learning in the context of daily life. In a specific problem situation, the creation and application of tools and means for problem solving is up to individual ingenuity, inventiveness and flexibility. In terms of the cultural evolution of man, the ability to use simple tools and ingenious methods appears to be an old form of human intelligence. In contrast, philosophical or scientific reasoning are much more recent forms of intelligence with possibly less immediate relevance for practical problem solving.

An 'anthropological' reorientation of cognitive research appears to be an interesting conceptual route for gaining a deeper understanding of the role of context in consumer behaviour. In the course of such a reorientation, the traditional idea of the consumer as an information processor does not have to be given up, but its heuristic power and conceptual fruitfulness can be greatly extended by linking it to the contextual nature of cognition.

A note on rationality

The debate on cognition and rationality has come some way (Suchaneck 1993, Suchaneck 1992, Langlois 1990, Simon 1987, Simon 1959). In the past decades, the concept of 'bounded rationality' or limited information processing made strong inroads into psychological thinking. An idea of 'bounded' or 'limited' cognition seems to reject a view of cognition that assumes 'unbounded', 'unlimited' cognition. Initially, the concept of bounded rationality was developed as an empirical criticism of the traditional model of *Homo economicus* which apparently applied a concept of 'unbounded' rationality (at least, that is what psychologists claimed). It can be questioned whether such empirically based interdisciplinary criticism is admissible: the basic research heuristic of economics, the model of economic man (*Homo economicus*), is – like any other research heuristic – not constructed as a matter of empirical 'correctness'. Research heuristics frame research on the basis of problem dependence and heuristic power, but not as a matter of empirical accuracy (see chapter 1).

Research heuristics were compared earlier to the 'schemata' of the scientist: by applying research heuristics, scientists can see only what they want to see. As outlined, every research programme requires heuristic 'schemata'. Psychological research that tried to establish and demarcate its research programme through interdisciplinary criticism at an empirical level (as most prominently done by Herbert Simon and his concept of bounded rationality) only points towards a fundamental misunderstanding and an identity crisis within psychological research itself.

The impact of the research programme of bounded rationality on how to conduct cognitive research has been deep and lasting. As suggested and discussed above, cognitive psychologists may be well advised to adapt their research heuristic regarding the idea of 'contextual cognition'. A concept of contextual 'rationality' examines how people actually bind – and also unbind – their cognition through the perception and construction of their behavioural context. For an understanding of problem solving behaviour and how knowledge structures develop in daily life, such a switch in perspectives can be recommended.

CONCEPTUAL FRUITFULNESS OF CONTEXTUAL RESEARCH

This study has explored green consumer knowledge. For that purpose, the cognitive psychological research heuristic was comprehensively developed along three dimensions: a knowledge content dimension, a cognitive operational dimension, and a formatting dimension. The study gave empirical substance to the view that green consumers differ in knowledge structures. A cognitive taxonomy of the green consumer was developed. Through a comparison of knowledge characteristics of different cognitive categories of consumers, conclusions regarding knowledge structure development were drawn. Borrowing ideas from cognitive anthropology, the relationship between experience (familiarity, ability) and knowledge structure development was assessed. Such an interpretation of knowledge structure development was based on the assumption that, historically, the interviewees had been through similar learning processes (see chapter 5). On the basis of such a comprehensive conceptual research design, the study clarified the dimensions of knowledge structure research which yielded a number of implications for the further development of knowledge structure theory.

The structuring of knowledge: trees and staircases

The study provided a detailed picture of how differently and intensively knowledge was concentrated across cognitive categories of consumers. The amount of knowledge increased in a linear fashion, even slightly progressively across the cognitive categories. The higher cognitive categories also had a kind of 'efficiency' advantage regarding the amount of knowledge recalled. Regarding knowledge complexity, the study not only confirmed the view that consumption knowledge is organized in tree-like hierarchical structures, but it also showed in depth what hierarchically organized knowledge looked like and how it varied and built up across the cognitive categories. Regarding knowledge specificity and knowledge abstractness, it was found that knowledge expressed in general terms was comparatively strongly favoured by the bottom cognitive categories. For the middle cognitive categories, abstract knowledge of 'traditional' ideas, e.g. recycled or organic, played an important role. For the top cognitive categories, a comparatively wide knowledge of highly specific, technical ideas, e.g. '100% recycling of old newspapers, but no factory off-cuts', existed.

In general, a high interdependence of specification and abstraction was apparent. Across the cognitive categories, the relationship between specification and abstraction resembled a 'staircase' relation, indicating that the nature and the relative importance of specification and abstraction varied in processes of knowledge structure development. The speculative character of this suggestion was stressed. Similarly implausible appeared, at least at first glance, findings of relatively distinctive clusters of consumers for certain knowledge characteristics, which can be related to the 'staircase' relation and comparatively stable stages in processes of knowledge structure development. If further studies can reproduce such findings, this would have far-reaching implications for understanding knowledge structure development and principles for the self-organization and self-transformation of the mind.

The profoundity of stereotypes: born to be biased

The idea of schemata and prototypes refers to a very basic level of human reasoning that underwires and formats cognition. This study indicated that prototypes hold powerful conceptual promise for knowledge structure research. Research on prototypical knowledge may be deepened by researching prototypes for specific products, e.g. what is perceived to be a prototypical sports car. While experts fail to agree on what characterizes an 'objectively' good product, issues of defining 'good' products may be approached through prototypicality research 'subjectively' – from the point of view of the consumer.

Indications of schematic and prototypical knowledge structures were observed for the green consumer. Certain products and certain product attributes featured prominently when consumers characterized green products. For the British sample, prototypical products were detergent and washing-up liquid, while for the German sample milk and yoghurt were classified as prototypical examples. Interestingly, prototypicality in terms of the extent of good product examples recalled showed up to a very similar degree across *all* cognitive categories for *both* the British and the German samples. This indicated a fundamental role for good examples in the process of knowledge structure development. Progressing knowledge integration related to prototypical knowledge: the higher cognitive categories developed patterns of integrated knowledge around a knowledge structure 'nucleus' that comprised a good example. Indications of the networking of schemata across rather different product categories, such as milk and shampoo, were (only) found in the higher cognitive categories.

Schemata seemed to provide 'gravity' to thinking. Apparently, the mind was highly active in providing a data structure 'nucleus' to format knowledge, thus guiding the structural coupling of knowledge substance. Such a force is probably of an innate nature: the observation of knowledge prototypicality across *all* cognitive categories can be related to a genetically determined (innate) cognitive ability of the mind.[1] In this sense, it appears that a capacity for theorizing and stereotyping is in our genes. Such a suggestion is in line with growing evidence that evolutionary processes favoured 'modern man' rather than some of his biological relatives, like the Neanderthal, because of the capacity of modern man to make sense quickly (Gregory 1990). Schemata enable this by their facilitating effect on categorization.

It is an established fact that thinking is widely influenced and stereotyped by influences external to the individual, such as the social, societal and cultural environment in which a person happens to be. That these influences work so easily can be related to the internal organization of the human mind. Schematic formatting at a 'systems software' level of the mind seems to invite the stereotyping of knowledge substance through environmental influences.

The study pointed out that all theorizing – philosophical, scientific and commonsense – carries a stereotypical element. For manifestations of everyday theorizing, such as proverbs or gossip, this is quite obvious. But to a degree, the same is the case for scientific theorizing, albeit in a slightly different manner. In science, research is 'stereotyped' through the application of research heuristics. It can be suggested that research heuristics are a device for domesticating and cultivating stereotypical 'commonsense' thinking. There are likely to be differences in the way scientific knowledge and proverbial knowledge are generated, but these differences might just be ones of degree rather than dramatic changes in the nature of reasoning. Research heuristics, like gossip or proverbs, aim at the discovery of truth. However, unlike gossip or proverbs, science follows certain principles of methodology which are quite openly discussed and negotiated within the scientific community, namely in a philosophy of science debate.

Familiarity and behaviour: knowing is doing

The study highlighted the importance of actual behaviour for knowledge structure development. Apparently, knowing *is* doing, as Maturana and Varela (1992: 244-8) stressed forcefully. It became apparent that familiarity, as reflected by activity levels for actual behaviour, related strongly to knowledge structure development. In particular, it was found that product-related familiarity increased rapidly across the cognitive categories.

Relationships amongst attitudes, intentions, cognition and actual behaviour are likely to resemble anything other than a simple causal chain. Apparently, there were intricate 'feedback' processes at work between actual behaviour and cognition, as there were between the behaviour and motivation of the green consumer. Motivation seemed to play an important role in getting consumers to start to green their shopping behaviour. But motivation on its own did not appear to be sufficient for a consumer to sustain the greening of shopping behaviour over time. Actual behaviour and the step-by-step mastering of cognitive complexities of green shopping appeared to be equally necessary for the occurrence of green shopping. The Fishbein model stresses the issue-specific nature of attitudes, beliefs and intentions for predicting and explaining behaviour (see chapter 1). Complementary to this, the findings of this study hinted that fairly concrete, issue-specific behaviours are necessary for the development of motivation and cognition.

A conceptual clarification was suggested with regard to the Johnson–Russo debate on how familiarity and learning relate to each other (Wilkie and Dickson 1991, Kardes and Strahle 1986, Johnson and Russo 1984). It was suggested that there is not necessarily a conflict between the 'enrichment hypothesis', which suggests a positive exponential relationship between familiarity and the extent of information search, and the 'inverted U hypothesis' on familiarity and the extent of information search. The study suggested that the relationship between familiarity and the extent of *internal* information search basically reflects the enrichment hypothesis, while the relationship between familiarity and the extent of *external* information search seems to relate to the inverted U hypothesis. This clarification resulted from a comprehensive conceptual approach that could interrelate different research constructs, such as internal versus external information search.

Ability and intelligence: savages are clever

The study assessed intelligence through applying the concepts of practical thinking and bricolage: how skilfully and creatively information problems were solved by the green consumer in the context of daily life. Considerable degrees of intelligent behaviour were observed. The higher cognitive categories approached green shopping rather pragmatically: information was collected selectively; proxy information was used; and information was evaluated on a comparative basis. Even the complex ideas of life-cycle analysis (LCA) were acted upon in this way. Consumers in the middle and lower cognitive categories showed considerably more naivety and cynicism regarding green shopping. Confusion seemed to set in for the middle cognitive categories when their initially naive approach to green shopping was first recognized. For the bottom cognitive category, to a certain extent, ignorance could be diagnosed.

Consumer intelligence was assessed by drawing on ideas from Lévi-Strauss and his reflections on the 'savage mind'. The study resisted the temptation to assess the intelligence and ability of the green consumer in terms of scientific correctness, e.g. on the basis of a psychological IQ-test for green shopping (possibly related to LCA). IQ tests tend to ignore context. They can only examine context-independent abilities such as an ability for numerical calculations or abstract, logical thinking. Hence, they are comparatively unimportant for an assessment of intelligence in daily life. (Besides, IQ tests seem to suffer from further biases such as an ethnic bias, favouring those who have been brought up in the western tradition with its emphasis on 'scientific thinking'.) As the green consumer research demonstrated, intelligence in real life manifests itself especially in the way a problem is formulated and framed. Clever problem formulation incorporated the skilful, creative and flexible usage of context: of information 'tools' and evaluation 'shortcuts' that were developed and applied through a subjectively perceived and constructed context. For an assessment of everyday intelligence, the quality of such problem formulation and problem solving behaviour has to be investigated and 'measured'. In particular, the extent and quality of 'practical thinking' rather than 'scientific thinking' has to be assessed.

PRACTICAL RELEVANCE OF CONTEXTUAL RESEARCH

Scientific research is ultimately justified on the basis that it leads to knowledge that can be (*normatively*) applied to practical tasks (Shimp 1994: 5, Hunt 1991: 31): positive scientific research is expected to provide an input into normative research. For instance, positive research into consumer cognition should yield insights that contribute to the development of a marketing concept or a public policy concept for consumer education. Yet, issues of how to transform positive scientific knowledge into practical concepts have not been explored in any great depth from a methodological point of view.

Consumer behaviour research has been accused of neglecting the translation of positive, theoretical insights into practical knowledge, which may be due to the generally low relevance of (psychologically oriented) consumer behaviour research to practical tasks (Shimp 1994: 1-5, Wells 1993: 498-500; see below). A theory–practice gap can be bridged comparatively easily if a contextual model is applied. Since contextual research develops an understanding of consumer behaviour as it occurs in real life, practical recommendations for how to influence a real-life situation should follow comparatively easily. The theoretical insights generated by this study yielded a number of practical implications for management and public policy (for an overview, see Wagner 1996a: chapter 7, Wagner 1996b, Wagner 1997, Wagner forthcoming/a).

Recommendations for consumer education

Governments were called upon at the Earth Summits in Rio de Janeiro in 1992, in Berlin in 1995 and in New York in 1997 to put more effort into environmental education, in particular the environmental education of consumers (Keating 1993, BUM 1993). A public policy programme could help consumers to make their shopping behaviour less environmentally harmful, but few such governmental programmes have been developed.

The consumer research conducted by this study yielded a number of insights into how green consumers learn successfully. On the basis of these insights, certain recommendations for consumer education can be given: learning should be organized on a step-by-step basis; good examples of green behaviour should play an integral role in educational processes; a learning concept should be built around actual behaviour; the theoretical complexity of green shopping issues should be introduced slowly, especially regarding LCA; the consumer should be supported to overcome naivety and cynicism once they set in; and green consumer behaviour should be directed towards pragmatism, but not scientific correctness.

On the basis of these suggestions, consumers can be guided towards environmentally friendlier practices. A good way of establishing an educational programme appears to be through local schemes: already 'successful' green consumers can work together with interested 'beginners' in green consumption. Such interaction is likely to be important for stimulating green behaviour by setting good examples and encouraging learning-by-doing. The distribution of leaflets or brochures alone appears to be insufficient for achieving green consumer learning, especially in the early phase of learning. Initiatives like the Global Action Plan or the Ethical Consumer movement which train consumers in environmental and ethical practices are likely to benefit from the suggestions made here for educating consumers.

Recommendations for marketing

The insights gained into green consumer cognition can support the development of a marketing communications concept for green products. Environmental marketing communication should aim at the lowering of cognitive barriers that prevent consumers from adopting green products: different consumers are likely to experience different cognitive barriers (as reflected by membership in the different cognitive categories), and hence environmental communication had to be capable of addressing the different information problems of different groups of green consumers (for more details, see Wagner 1996a: chapter 7, Wagner 1996b, Wagner 1997, Wagner forthcoming/a).

Through a layered and phased communications approach, a target audience with a diversity of information needs can be satisfied. In general, messages should be based on facts and they should be pragmatic in their outlook. Communication messages should be tailored to the needs of different cognitive categories of consumers: a layered approach ('message mix') appears most promising in that respect. Messages put forward should vary in terms of their cognitive communication objective, their message substance, message structure, message length and the type of language used, thus accommodating different information needs. The message mix developed should be made accessible to the consumer on a step-by-step basis: through allocating different communication channels, e.g. TV advertising, leaflets, in-house seminars, etc., to the different message layers, a step-by-step access can be established. Different green messages are phased one after another, thus not overburdening consumers who are in an early phase of learning while making sure that those who want and need more information can receive it.

A layered and phased communications approach that is built around a message mix and that can accommodate differences in consumer knowledge may be of a wider interest than just for green communications. It can be thought of as a test case for the communication of complex messages in general. Many firms and many public policy bodies see themselves confronted with difficult communication problems, e.g. the communication of a general overhaul of the tariff system of a telecommunications firm; or the promotion of products offered by a health insurance firm; or the communication of changes to a tax system. In these instances, successful communication has to master the satisfying of highly varied information needs. The communication recommendations made here should help towards such complex communication.

ISSUES FOR FUTURE RESEARCH

This study explored, on its 'substance' level, the fairly new world of green consumption. It shed light on what green consumption looks like in Britain and in Germany. On its conceptual level, the study travelled through the mind of the green consumer. It provided an understanding of how cognition works in everyday life by assessing how the green consumer evaluates and chooses a product. This project also provided the opportunity to address issues of how to conduct proper cognitive research.

Initial ideas for a model of contextual consumer behaviour were proposed here. Future research has to advance such a model, furthering the conceptual integration of 'context' in a model of behaviour. A treatment of context as a black box or as an independent variable should be overcome in this way.

The study explored consumer cognition from a qualitative angle: a comparatively comprehensive theoretical stance was taken at the outset; open interviews were conducted in a real-life setting; a qualitative sample of green consumers was chosen by theoretical sampling; and data analysis went along comparatively interpretative lines, despite some quantification and statistical analysis (cluster analysis and correlational analysis). Future research can try to refine some of the measurements applied here, e.g. a more detailed measurement of knowledge abstractness and knowledge specificity may be attempted, possibly on the basis of a 3×3 or even a 4×4 matrix.

In this study, only one behavioural domain was examined – green consumer behaviour (issues like animal rights or fair trade were excluded from a definition of 'green'). Future research might try to assess the cognition and behaviour of a person across different knowledge domains. An assessment of knowledge in different domains could yield insights into whether and how the general reasoning patterns of an individual might affect domain-related reasoning. Though, if research for different behavioural domains is conducted under real-life conditions, the burden on data analysis is likely to be high since different (domain-related) analytical tools, e.g. bracketing frameworks, would have to be developed.

Despite its comprehensive theoretical focus, the scope of this research project was limited: at the outset, the complexity of green consumer behaviour was heuristically reduced to a *cognitive* investigation. In particular, motivational phenomena were excluded from the research conducted. Future research on the green consumer might address questions such as motivational ones as well as questions from the disciplines of sociology, anthropology, economics, etc.:

- The cognitive research undertaken yielded as a by-product certain motivational insights. The higher cognitive categories apparently had stronger motivation. There were indications of motivational pragmatism for the members of the higher cognitive categories, who freely admitted behavioural inconsistencies, e.g. 'We still go to McDonald's' or 'I am not evangelical about green consumption'. The role of such motivational pragmatism in the face of complex cognitive problems appears worth examining, especially how this relates to successful learning and behavioural pragmatism.

- Certain opinions of green consumers may provide food for thought for a moral philosophy discussion. For many of the green consumers interviewed, green shopping carried an ethical or religious dimension; for instance, the idea of 'ethical treats' was repeatedly voiced by consumers: it reflected that green products, which were viewed as the ethically 'correct' choice, were deliberately bought only from time to time because of certain perceived constraints, e.g. time pressure, lack of funds, taste, etc. An idea of 'ethical treats' raises questions of 'moral inconsistencies' and how they are deliberated on and managed by the individual. From the findings made in this study, it appeared that consumers were not only pragmatic when it came to questions of cognition, but also when it came to ethical reasons for green shopping (and this might relate to 'motivational pragmatism', as discussed above).

- Findings made on certain socio-demographic variables, e.g. pressure group membership, vegetarianism, etc., can be further examined. Such a discussion is likely to lead into sociology, where issues like green life-style extremism, the influence of social networks, e.g. peer group pressure, can also be looked at. Related to that, green products can be examined as status symbols or as symbols of social reassurance.[2]

- Anthropological researchers may want to follow up issues like consumer alienation (but also consumer inspiration) caused by the supermarket shopping culture: how some green consumers have disengaged themselves from society at large, living in autarkic green communities; or how consumption has taken on a mystic dimension (as voiced by some interviewees), e.g. related to astrological principles for biodynamic farming, such as growing vegetables in accordance with the phases of the moon.

- An institutional economic debate can help to clarify how far markets, which are traditionally viewed in economics as morality-free zones, can acquire a moral dimension. Such a debate can address the question of whether and, if so, how morality can successfully enter markets – namely through which market participants (consumers, firms, other parties). In a wider context, this debate can examine the feasibility and theoretical fruitfulness of conceptual projects like business ethics or stakeholder management.

- Further research is necessary on how to bridge systematically a gulf between theory and practice. Such a debate is likely to centre around the concepts of technology and technique (Dasgupta 1991, Suh 1990). At present, there are no clear methodological guidelines for 'translating' theoretical findings into management practice. The lack of understanding of how to apply theoretical knowledge to practical problems has contributed to an image of researchers in management studies (and similarly, in public policy studies, geography, etc.) as 'wild scientists' or 'bricoleurs' who employ their 'own' methods. Shimp (1994: 2) pointed out that management studies researchers started to borrow and to apply sophisticated theories from other disciplines (e.g. psychology) after initial accusations of low standards of research (Gordon and Howell 1959: 6), but by doing so, research became less relevant for the practice of management. The spelling out of general principles of a method for 'social engineering' is likely to be important for counteracting such accusations and for fostering the future development of management studies as a practice-oriented scientific discipline.

APPENDICES

APPENDIX 3.1
INTERVIEW GUIDE

[Examples of questions asked]

Part 1: Collection and discussion of freely recalled products for daily consumption and product attributes/information sources that are thought to indicate 'greenness'

A. Collection of product examples

Do you consider environmental aspects when you buy groceries?
Can you give examples?
For which daily products did you consider 'green' aspects?
Can you think of other products for which you took 'green' considerations into account?
Where do you buy products for daily consumption? Have you changed shopping places in the past few months?

B. Discussion of examples

What 'green' aspects did you pay attention to when you bought product x?
How did you evaluate the environmental friendliness of product x?
What do you think makes product x a 'green' product?
How do you recognise that x is an environmentally friendly product?
For how long have you bought product x for environmental reasons?
Did you always buy product x?
Did you change from another product to x?
Why do you think the buying of x is environmentally sounder than buying another product?
What information do you use for judging x as 'green'?
Do you find it difficult to decide whether [a product of category x] is environmentally friendly?
Do you collect information from other sources than [product x] itself?
Did you come across information about [product x] by chance?

C. Conclusion of part 1:

In general, would you say it is difficult to shop environmentally friendly?
For how long have you considered green issues?

Part 2: Prompting and discussion of product examples

Did you buy [product x from the prompting list] for environmental reasons?
Did you consider 'green' aspects when you bought x?

Prompting list (products already discussed in part 1 are excluded here):

- hair spray & deodorant
- detergent
- toilet paper
- shampoo
- washing up liquid;
- fruit & vegetables;
- soft drinks;
- household cleaners;
- meat;
- milk;
- yoghurt.

Part 3: Further questioning with the help of the prompting list on information sources

Did you consider [issue x] when you bought 'green' products?
Did x play a role for assessing green products?

Prompting list (those issues and information sources that were not focused on by the interviewee in parts 1 and 2 are discussed here in more detail).

- product name and labels;
- product ingredients;
- price of product;
- quality of product;
- amount of packaging;
- type of packaging;
- literature;
- newspaper, TV, radio;
- advertising;
- friends, colleagues;
- shopping place.

Part 4: Concluding questions

Self-rating task

How would you judge yourself overall regarding environmental issues and shopping? Would you be someone who does not consider environmental issues at all? 100 would be an extreme 'green' shopper, here. [Showing ranking scale]

How significant would you rate environmental aspects when you make buying decisions for products you buy every day?

Final question

Did I forget to ask you any important questions? Anything spring to mind?

APPENDIX 3.2
SELF-RATING SCORES

Scores of the British sample   *Scores of the German sample*

B01 75	B21 40	B41 55		G01 65	G21 72.5
B02 70	B22 40	B42 80		G02 70	G22 80
B03 85	B23 75	B43 85		G03 50	G23 90
B04 55	B24 60	B44 75		G04 60	G24 70
B05 25	B25 60	B45 45		G05 40	G25 50
B06 65	B26 60	B46 67.5		G06 40	G26 50
B07 50	B27 40	B47 60		G07 50	G27 80
B08 50	B28 70	B48 90		G08 50	G28 40
B09 60	B29 45	B49 40		G09 70	G29 65
B10 80	B30 90	B50 75		G10 85	G30 75
B11 95	B31 60	B51 65		G11 90	G31 60
B12 70	B32 65	B52 40		G12 90	G32 70
B13 70	B33 75	B53 50		G13 70	G33 75
B14 80	B34 40	B54 70		G14 70	G34 85
B15 35	B35 45	B55 55		G15 80	G35 90
B16 60	B36 80			G16 80	G36 80
B17 60	B37 75			G17 35	
B18 50	B38 75			G18 60	
B19 50	B39 55			G19 50	
B20 50	B40 90			G20 60	

Distribution & distribution function   *Distribution & distribution function*

British				German			
[0,20]:	–			[0,20]:	–		
]20,30]:	1	0.02	0.02	]20,30]:	–		
]30,40]:	7	0.13	0.15	]30,40]:	4	0.11	0.11
]40,50]:	8	0.15	0.30	]40,50]:	6	0.17	0.28
]50,60]:	12	0.22	0.52	]50,60]:	4	0.11	0.39
]60,70]:	9	0.16	0.68	]60,70]:	8	0.22	0.61
]70,80]:	11	0.20	0.88	]70,80]:	8	0.22	0.83
]80,90]:	5	0.09	0.97	]80,90]:	6	0.17	1.00
]90,100]:	1	0.02	0.99	]90,100]:	–		

average 62.3
median 60

average 66.6
median 70

APPENDIX 3.3
OVERVIEW OF PARAMETERS

Variable		Mean	Median	Standard deviation	Minimum	Maximum
Comprehensiveness indicators						
W1	British	59.7	59	29.4	12	163
	German	72.7	65	37.1	15	188
	Non-green	—	—	—	—	—
W2	British	83.4	82	31.7	34	171
	German	98.9	94.5	39.1	48	213
	Non-green	48.1	44	29.4	4	99
W3	British	1493.5	1244	640.7	504	3765
	German	1578.1	1350	704.9	684	4421
	Non-green	94.2	5	136.9	5	409
W4	British	2401.6	2211	793.5	1313	5089
	German	2449.5	2362	670.7	1284	4672
	Non-green	1561.8	1640	380.7	892	2100
Complexity indicators						
C1	British	74.9	64	44.9	9	191
	German	98.5	81	61.2	12	342
	Non-green	—	—	—	—	—
C2	British	100.6	91	47.5	28	206
	German	131.3	118	64.5	54	377
	Non-green	55.6	48.5	42.3	2	134
C3	British	72.8	62	62.4	10	367
	German	125.1	90.5	86.8	8	374
	Non-green	—	—	—	—	—
C4	British	144.2	125	88.8	42	442
	German	244.7	221	136.4	70	594
	Non-green	49.8	42	41.0	2	142
C5	British	62.4	55	39.2	9	186
	German	125.6	113	71.2	34	278
	Non-green	43.7	35	39.3	2	138
Number of products						
NX	British	6.6	6	2.8	2	15
	German	8.5	8	2.8	4	16
	Non-green	—	—	—	—	—
NT	British	11.3	11	3.0	6	19
	German	14.2	14	2.9	9	21
	Non-green	7.5	7	2.4	2	11
Familiarity indicator						
NTA	British	9.0	8.5	/	3.5	16.5
	German	12.4	13	/	6	19
	Non-green	—	—	—	—	—
Specificity & abstractness indicators						
AS1	British	5.8	5	3.2	0	14
	German	8.6	8	4.5	2	23
	Non-green	—	—	—	—	—

APPENDIX 3.3
OVERVIEW OF PARAMETERS cont.

Variable		Mean	Median	Standard deviation	Minimum	Maximum
AS2	British	11.7	10	6.8	2	33
	German	15.7	13	7.6	3	38
	Non-green	—	—	—	—	—
AS3	British	5.6	5	3.7	1	20
	German	6.7	6	5.6	0	27
	Non-green	—	—	—	—	—
AS4	British	1.0	1	1.2	0	5
	German	1.7	1	2.4	0	10
	Non-green	—	—	—	—	—
AS5	British	8.0	7	3.8	0	16
	German	11.8	12	4.6	4	26
	Non-green	7.9	8	3.7	2	13
AS6	British	17.5	17	7.9	7	37
	German	22.7	19.5	8.5	10	44
	Non-green	6.1	7.5	4.0	0	11
AS7	British	8.5	8	3.8	3	20
	German	10.3	9	6.5	1	30
	Non-green	3.5	3.5	2.5	0	8
AS8	British	1.3	1	1.3	0	5
	German	2.5	1	2.8	0	10
	Non-green	0.7	0.5	0.9	0	3

APPENDIX 3.4
QUARTILE DATA

	first quartile	*second quartile*	*third quartile*	*fourth quartile*
	British sample, number of freely recalled products (NX, NXA)			
mean (NX)	43/13	74/14	97/14	147/14
mean (NXA)	29/13	59.5/14	84/14	130.5/14
Relative drop	–33%	–20%	–13%	–11%
	German sample, number of freely recalled products (NX, NXA)			
mean (NX)	48/9	65/9	83/9	111/9
mean (NXA)	36.5/9	57/9	87.5/9	103.5/9
Relative drop	–24%	–12%	–8%	–7%
	British sample, total number of products (NT, NTA)			
mean (NT)	101/13	141/14	164/14	215/14
mean (NTA)	73/13	104.5/14	134/14	181/14
Relative drop	–28%	–26%	–18%	–16%
	German sample, total number of products (NT, NTA)			
mean (NT)	98/9	119/9	130/9	164/9
mean (NTA)	70.5/9	100.5/9	123/9	153.5/9
Relative drop	–28%	–16%	–5%	–6%

APPENDIX 3.5
CONSUMER INTERVIEW INDEX

Acronym	Issue

Knowledge characteristics

Group	Product group relations
Tec	Technical language (terminology)
Arg	Arguments and counter arguments
Dim	Dimensional knowledge
Epi	Episodes

Task considerations

Diff	Task difficulty/complexity
Short	Shortcut to buying 'green'
Choice	Availability of choice
Time	Availability of time
Conv	Convenience considerations
Trust	Availability of credibility/trustworthiness
Cyn	Cynicism/naivety/distrust considerations/admissions
Incon	Inconsistency considerations/admissions

Buying frequency

Trial	Trial buying strategy
Red	Consumption reduction/abstention
Exp	Experience effects/habit references

Errors

Err	Green product property error, availability error, incompleteness error

Other product quality considerations

Price	Price/availability of income
Perf	Performance considerations
Health	Health considerations
Plea	Shopping pleasure 'considerations'
Eth	Ethical considerations (fair trade, animal issues)
Pol	Political considerations (ownership, 'We buy British')
Dur	Durable goods

Non-cognitive issues

Aff	Affect
Mot	Motivation
Cul	Culture, life-style

APPENDIX 3.6
COMPREHENSIVENESS AND COMPLEXITY ANALYSIS OF PA MATRIX

PA matrix for interviewee G38

Products	ingredients	organic	seasonal	smell	taste	home made	pack. material	amount pack.	reusable	biodegradable	recycled	recyclable	pack. images	names	ecolabels	colour	texture	size	sourcing	prod. process	loc. prod./ret.	disposal	energy	word of mouth	pressure groups	advertising	radio/TV/press	literature	others	no. of prod. attributes	squared no. of prod. attributes	no. of words (int. extracts)
detergent (X1-H)	1						1	4	1					6								3								6	36	16
wash.up liq. (X1-M)														7																1	1	7
cleaner (X1-M)	1							2						12						10				1						4	16	16
fruit.,veg. (X1-M)		1						2					2																	4	16	15
wom.san.prod. (X2-N)								2						2											5					2	4	7
shampoo (Y-H)								3						2																2	4	5
toilet pap. (Z1-H)	1										1			1		2														4	16	5
drinks (Z1-M)						2	2					4																		3	9	8
meat (Z1-M)		1																												1	1	1
yoghurt (Z1-M)		1											6																	2	4	7
rice (Y-H)														7																1	1	8:95
no. of X products	2	1				0	0	4		1	0	0	0	4	0					1	1	1		1	1							
squared no. of X products	4	1				0	0	16		1	0	0	0	16	0					1	1	1		1	1							
no. of all products	3	3				1	1	5		1	1	1	1	8	1	1				1	1	1		1	1					31		
squared no. of all products	9	9				1	1	25		1	1	1	1	36	1	1				1	1	1		1	1							

Note: In the cells of the matrix are the number of words (interview extracts) that related to the 'green' characterization of a certain product attribute of a certain product. Indicators of knowledge comprehensiveness and knowledge complexity were derived from this matrix.

APPENDIX 3.7
OVERVIEW OF VARIABLES

Variable	Knowledge comprehensiveness variables
W1	word counts of interview extracts relating to X products
W2	word counts of the free recall part of the interview (part one)
W3	word counts of interview extracts relating to all products
W4	word counts of the total interview

Variable	Knowledge complexity variables
C1	Horizontal complexity relating to X products
C2	Vertical complexity relating to X products' attributes
C3	Horizontal complexity relating to all products
C4	Vertical complexity relating to all products' attributes
C5	C4 adjusted for the product attribute 'names' (excluded)

Variable	Knowledge abstractness–specificity variables
AS1	No. of weakly abstract and weakly specific pieces of knowledge substance (X products)
AS2	No. of weakly abstract and highly specific pieces of knowledge substance (X products)
AS3	No. of highly abstract and weakly specific pieces of knowledge substance (X products)
AS4	No. of highly abstract and highly specific pieces of knowledge substance (X products)
AS5	No. of weakly abstract and weakly specific pieces of knowledge substance (all products)
AS6	No. of weakly abstract and highly specific pieces of knowledge substance (all products)
AS7	No. of highly abstract and weakly specific pieces of knowledge substance (all products)
AS8	No. of highly abstract and highly specific pieces of knowledge substance (all products)

Variable	Product frequency variables
NX	Number of freely recalled products (X products)
NXA	NX adjusted for actual buying frequencies (HMN code)
NT	Total number of products recalled (X+Y+Z products)
NTA	NT adjusted for actual buying frequencies (HMN code)

APPENDIX 3.8
COMPREHENSIVENESS DISTRIBUTIONS

British sample				German sample			
			W1				
[0,10]				[0,10]			
[11,20]	3	0.05	0.05	[11,20]	2	0.06	0.06
[21,30]	7	0.13	0.18	[21,30]	1	0.03	0.09
[31,40]	5	0.09	0.27	[31,40]	8	0.22	0.31
[41,50]	7	0.13	0.40	[41,50]	4	0.11	0.42
[51,60]	7	0.13	0.53	[51,60]	5	0.14	0.56
[61,70]	9	0.16	0.69	[61,70]	4	0.11	0.67
[71,80]	7	0.13	0.82	[71,80]	3	0.08	0.75
[81,90]	1	0.02	0.84	[81,90]	2	0.06	0.81
[91,100]	4	0.07	0.91	[91,100]	2	0.06	0.87
[101,100]	3	0.05	0.96	[101,110]	3	0.08	0.95
[111,120]				[111,120]	1	0.03	0.98
[121,130]	1	0.02	0.98	[121,130]			
[131,140]				[131,140]			
[141,150]				[141,150]			
[151,160]				[151,160]			
[161,170]	1	0.02	1.00	[161,170]	1	0.03	1.01

average 59.7
median 59

average 62.7
median 56
(unadjusted)

British sample				German sample				Non-green sample			
				W2							
[0,10]				[0,10]				[0,10]	1	0.10	0.10
[11,20]				[11,20]				[11,20]			
[21,30]				[21,30]				[21,30]	2	0.20	0.30
[31,40]	5	0.09	0.09	[31,40]				[31,40]	2	0.20	0.50
[41,50]	4	0.07	0.16	[41,50]	6	0.17	0.17	[41,50]			
[51,60]	5	0.09	0.25	[51,60]	6	0.17	0.34	[51,60]	1	0.10	0.60
[61,70]	6	0.11	0.36	[61,70]	4	0.11	0.45	[61,70]	2	0.20	0.80
[71,80]	6	0.11	0.47	[71,80]	1	0.03	0.48	[71,80]	1	0.10	0.90
[81,90]	6	0.11	0.58	[81,90]	4	0.11	0.59	[81,90]			
[91,100]	10	0.18	0.76	[91,100]	3	0.08	0.67	[91,100]	1	0.10	1.00
[101,110]	2	0.04	0.80	[101,110]	4	0.11	0.78				
[111,120]	4	0.07	0.87	[111,120]	1	0.03	0.81				
[121,130]	2	0.04	0.91	[121,130]	5	0.14	0.95				
[131,140]	2	0.04	0.95	[131,140]	1	0.03	0.98				
[141,150]	2	0.04	0.99	[141,150]							
[151,160]				[151,160]							
[161,170]				[161,170]							
[171,180]	1	0.02	1.01	[171,180]							
				[181,190]	1	0.03	1.01				

average 83.4
median 82

average 85.2
median 81.5
(unadjusted)

average 48.1
median 44

APPENDIX 3.8
COMPREHENSIVENESS DISTRIBUTIONS cont.

British sample				German sample			
				W1/W2			
[0.31,0.35]	1	0.02	0.02	[0.31,0.35]	2	0.06	0.06
[0.36,0.40]	1	0.02	0.04	[0.36,0.40]			
[0.41,0.45]	4	0.07	0.11	[0.41,0.45]	1	0.03	0.09
[0.46,0.50]	2	0.04	0.15	[0.46,0.50]	1	0.03	0.12
[0.51,0.55]	5	0.09	0.24	[0.51,0.55]	1	0.03	0.15
[0.56,0.60]				[0.56,0.60]	1	0.03	0.18
[0.61,0.65]	7	0.13	0.37	[0.61,0.65]	2	0.06	0.24
[0.66,0.70]	3	0.05	0.42	[0.66,0.70]	7	0.19	0.43
[0.71,0.75]	12	0.22	0.64	[0.71,0.75]	4	0.11	0.54
[0.76,0.80]	5	0.09	0.73	[0.76,0.80]	6	0.17	0.71
[0.81,0.85]	5	0.09	0.82	[0.81,0.85]	4	0.11	0.82
[0.86,0.90]	4	0.07	0.89	[0.86,0.90]	7	0.19	1.01
[0.91,0.95]	4	0.07	0.96	[0.91,0.95]			
[0.96,1.00]	2	0.04	1.00	[0.96,1.00]			

average 0.70   **average 0.72**

British sample				German sample				Non-green sample			
						W4					
[801,1000]				[801,1000]				[801,1000]	1	0.10	0.10
[1001,1200]				[1001,1200]	1	0.03	0.03	[1001,1200]	1	0.10	0.20
[1201,1400]	2	0.04	0.04	[1201,1400]	2	0.06	0.09	[1201,1400]	2	0.20	0.40
[1401,1600]	3	0.05	0.09	[1401,1600]	3	0.08	0.17	[1401,1600]			
[1601,1800]	7	0.13	0.22	[1601,1800]	6	0.17	0.34	[1601,1800]	4	0.40	0.80
[1801,2000]	13	0.24	0.46	[1801,2000]	6	0.17	0.51	[1801,2000]			
[2001,2200]	2	0.04	0.50	[2001,2200]	4	0.11	0.62	[2001,2200]	2	0.20	1.00
[2201,2400]	9	0.16	0.66	[2201,2400]	3	0.08	0.70				
[2401,2600]	2	0.04	0.70	[2401,2600]	6	0.17	0.87				
[2601,2800]	2	0.04	0.74	[2601,2800]	3	0.08	0.95				
[2801,3000]	2	0.04	0.78	[2801,3000]							
[3001,3200]	1	0.02	0.80	[3001,3200]							
[3201,3400]	4	0.07	0.87	[3201,3400]	1	0.03	0.98				
[3401,3600]	4	0.07	0.94	[3401,3600]							
[3601,3800]	3	0.05	0.99	[3601,3800]							
[3801,4000]				[3801,4000]							
[4001,4200]				[4001,4200]	1	0.03	1.01				
...											
[5001,5200]	1	0.02	1.01								

average 2402   **average 2111**   **average 1562**
median 2211   **median 2036**   **median 1640**
(unadjusted)

British sample				German sample				Non-green sample			
				W3							
[0,200]				[0,200]				[0,200]	8	0.80	0.80
[201,400]				[201,400]				[201,400]	1	0.10	0.90
[401,600]	1	0.02	0.02	[401,600]	1	0.03	0.03	[401,600]	1	0.10	1.00
[601,800]	2	0.04	0.06	[601,800]	4	0.11	0.14				
[801,1000]	10	0.18	0.24	[801,1000]	5	0.14	0.28				
[1001,1200]	9	0.16	0.40	[1001,1200]	9	0.25	0.53				
[1201,1400]	8	0.15	0.55	[1201,1400]	1	0.03	0.56				
[1401,1600]	5	0.09	0.64	[1401,1600]	6	0.17	0.73				
[1601,1800]	3	0.05	0.69	[1601,1800]	5	0.14	0.87				
[1801,2000]	7	0.13	0.82	[1801,2000]	2	0.06	0.93				
[2001,2200]	3	0.05	0.87	[2001,2200]	1	0.03	0.96				
[2201,2400]	3	0.05	0.92	[2201,2400]							
[2401,2600]	2	0.04	0.96	[2401,2600]	1	0.03	0.99				
[2601,2800]				[2601,2800]							
[2801,3000]				[2801,3000]							
[3001,3200]	1	0.20	0.98	[3001,3200]							
[3201,3400]				[3201,3400]							
[3401,3600]				[3401,3600]							
[3601,3800]	1	0.02	1.00	[3601,3800]							
				[3801,4000]	1	0.03	1.02				

average 1494	average 1360	average 94
median 1244	median 1164	median 5
	(unadjusted)	

219

APPENDIX 3.9
COMPLEXITY DISTRIBUTIONS

British sample					German sample			
				C1				
[0,10]	1	0.02	0.02		[0,10]			
[11,20]	4	0.07	0.09		[11,20]	1	0.03	0.03
[21,30]	2	0.04	0.13		[21,30]	1	0.03	0.06
[31,40]	5	0.09	0.22		[31,40]	1	0.03	0.09
[41,50]	5	0.09	0.31		[41,50]	3	0.08	0.17
[51,60]	7	0.13	0.44		[51,60]	5	0.14	0.31
[61,70]	6	0.11	0.55		[61,70]	3	0.08	0.39
[71,80]	5	0.09	0.64		[71,80]	4	0.11	0.50
[81,90]	2	0.04	0.68		[81,90]	3	0.08	0.58
[91,100]	5	0.09	0.77		[91,100]	1	0.03	0.61
[101,110]	3	0.05	0.82		[101,110]			
[111,120]	3	0.05	0.87		[111,120]	2	0.06	0.67
[121,130]	1	0.02	0.89		[121,130]	2	0.06	0.73
[131,140]	1	0.02	0.91		[131,140]	3	0.08	0.81
[141,150]	1	0.02	0.93		[141,150]	3	0.08	0.89
[151,160]					[151,160]	1	0.03	0.92
[161,170]					[161,170]	1	0.03	0.95
[171,180]	1	0.02	0.95		[171,180]			
[181,190]	1	0.02	0.97		[181,190]			
[191,200]	2	0.04	1.01		[191,200]			
					[201,210]			
					[211,220]	1	0.03	0.98
					...			
					[341,350]	1	0.03	1.01

average 74.8
median 64

average 98.5
median 81

British sample					German sample			
				C2				
[0,20]	9	0.16	0.16		[0,20]	1	0.03	0.03
[21,40]	11	0.20	0.36		[21,40]	2	0.06	0.09
[41,60]	7	0.13	0.49		[41,60]	6	0.17	0.26
[61,80]	10	0.18	0.67		[61,80]	5	0.14	0.40
[81,100]	4	0.07	0.74		[81,100]	5	0.14	0.54
[101,120]	5	0.09	0.83		[101,120]	3	0.08	0.62
[121,140]	4	0.07	0.90		[121,140]	1	0.03	0.65
[141,160]	2	0.04	0.94		[141,160]	4	0.11	0.76
...					[161,180]	1	0.03	0.79
[201,220]	2	0.04	0.98		[181,200]	1	0.03	0.82
...					[201,220]	2	0.06	0.88
[361,380]	1	0.02	1.00		[221,240]	1	0.03	0.91
					[241,260]			
					[261,280]	1	0.03	0.94
					[281,300]	1	0.03	0.97
					...			
					[361,380]	1	0.03	1.00

average 72.8
median 62

average 125.1
median 90.5

C3

British sample

Interval	n	freq	cum
[0,10]			
[11,20]			
[21,30]	2	0.04	0.04
[31,40]	3	0.05	0.09
[41,50]	4	0.07	0.16
[51,60]	2	0.04	0.20
[61,70]	4	0.07	0.27
[71,80]	6	0.11	0.38
[81,90]	6	0.11	0.49
[91,100]	5	0.09	0.58
[101,110]	2	0.04	0.62
[111,120]	4	0.07	0.69
[121,130]	2	0.04	0.73
[131,140]	5	0.09	0.82
[141,150]	2	0.04	0.86
[151,160]	1	0.02	0.88
[161,170]	1	0.02	0.90
[171,180]	2	0.04	0.94
[181,190]			
[191,200]	2	0.04	0.98
[201,210]	2	0.04	1.02

average 100.6
median 91

German sample

Interval	n	freq	cum
[0,10]			
[11,20]			
[21,30]			
[31,40]			
[41,50]			
[51,60]	3	0.08	0.08
[61,70]	3	0.08	0.16
[71,80]	3	0.08	0.24
[81,90]	1	0.03	0.27
[91,100]	3	0.08	0.35
[101,110]	4	0.11	0.46
[111,120]	1	0.03	0.49
[121,130]	2	0.06	0.55
[131,140]	1	0.03	0.58
[141,150]	2	0.06	0.64
[151,160]	3	0.08	0.72
[161,170]	3	0.08	0.80
[171,180]	1	0.03	0.83
[181,190]	3	0.08	0.91
[191,200]			
[201,210]			
[211,220]	1	0.03	0.94
...			
[251,260]	1	0.03	0.97
...			
[371,380]	1	0.03	1.00

average 131.3
median 118

Non-green sample

Interval	n	freq	cum
[0,10]	1	0.10	0.10
[11,20]	1	0.10	0.20
[21,30]	2	0.20	0.40
[31,40]	1	0.10	0.50
[41,50]			
[51,60]			
[61,70]	2	0.20	0.70
[71,80]			
[81,90]			
[91,100]	2	0.20	0.90
[101,110]			
[111,120]			
[121,130]			
[131,140]	1	0.10	1.00

average 55.6
median 48.5

C4

British sample

Interval	n	freq	cum
[0,20]			
[21,40]			
[41,60]	7	0.13	0.13
[61,80]	7	0.13	0.26
[81,100]	7	0.13	0.39
[101,120]	6	0.11	0.50
[121,140]	6	0.11	0.61
[141,160]	6	0.11	0.72
[161,180]	5	0.09	0.81
[181,200]	1	0.02	0.83
[201,220]	1	0.02	0.85
[221,240]			
[241,260]	1	0.02	0.87
[261,280]	4	0.07	0.94
[281,300]			
[301,320]			
[321,340]	1	0.02	0.96
...			

German sample

Interval	n	freq	cum
[0,20]			
[21,40]			
[41,60]			
[61,80]	1	0.03	0.03
[81,100]	2	0.06	0.09
[101,120]	4	0.11	0.20
[121,140]	2	0.06	0.26
[141,160]	3	0.08	0.34
[161,180]	3	0.08	0.42
[181,200]	1	0.02	0.44
[201,220]	2	0.06	0.50
[221,240]	2	0.06	0.56
[241,260]	3	0.08	0.64
[261,280]	3	0.08	0.72
[281,300]	1	0.03	0.75
[301,320]	1	0.03	0.78
[321,340]	1	0.03	0.81
[341,360]			

Non-green sample

Interval	n	freq	cum
[0,20]	2	0.20	0.20
[21,40]	3	0.30	0.50
[41,60]	3	0.30	0.80
[61,80]			
[81,100]	1	0.10	0.90
[101,120]			
[121,140]			
[141,160]	1	0.10	1.00

APPENDIX 3.9
COMPLEXITY DISTRIBUTIONS cont.

British sample				German sample				Non-green sample			
				C4 cont.							
[421,440]	1	0.02	0.98	[361,380]	1	0.03	0.84				
[441,460]	1	0.02	1.00	[381,400]	1	0.03	0.87				
				[401,420]							
				[421,440]	1	0.03	0.90				
				...							
				[481,500]	1	0.03	0.93				
				[501,520]	1	0.03	0.96				
				[521,540]							
				[541,560]	1	0.03	0.99				
				[561,580]							
				[581,600]	1	0.03	1.02				
average 144.4				average 244.7				average 49.8			
median 125				median 221				median 42			

British sample				German sample				Non-green sample			
				C5							
[0,20]	6	0.11	0.11	[0,20]				[0,20]	2	0.20	0.20
[21,40]	10	0.18	0.29	[21,40]	3	0.08	0.08	[21,40]	5	0.50	0.70
[41,60]	15	0.27	0.56	[41,60]	2	0.06	0.14	[41,60]	1	0.10	0.80
[61,80]	12	0.22	0.78	[61,80]	9	0.25	0.39	[61,80]			
[81,100]	4	0.07	0.85	[81,100]	2	0.06	0.45	[81,100]	1	0.10	0.90
[101,120]	3	0.05	0.90	[101,120]	3	0.08	0.53	[101,120]			
[121,140]	1	0.02	0.92	[121,140]	6	0.17	0.70	[121,140]	1	0.10	1.00
[141,160]	2	0.04	0.96	[141,160]	1	0.03	0.73				
[161,180]	1	0.02	0.98	[161,180]	3	0.08	0.81				
[181,200]	1	0.02	1.00	[181,200]	2	0.06	0.87				
				[201,220]							
				[221,240]							
				[241,260]	3	0.08	0.95				
				[261,280]	2	0.06	1.01				
average 62.4				average 125.6				average 43.7			
median 55				median 113				median 35			

APPENDIX 3.10
EXAMPLES OF ABSTRACTNESS–SPECIFICITY MATRICES

Product attribute: product ingredients

Low specificity	*High specificity*
1000 (AS1) *(Low abstractness)* 'naturals', 'natural based', 'chemicals', 'harmful chemicals', 'vicious products', 'simple', 'plain', 'pure', 'sprays', 'verseucht'	0100 (AS2) 'plastic', 'tree-free', 'vegetable-based', 'soap-based', 'phosphates', 'cotton', 'lemon thing', 'vinegar', 'bleach', 'CFC', 'pesticides', 'natural chalk', 'enzymes'
0010 (AS3) *(High abstractness)* 'aerosols', 'non-biological', 'non-allergenic', 'low impact stuff', 'baukastenwaschmittel', 'nicht behandelt', 'ingredients list'	0001 (AS4) 'optical whiteners', 'non-chlorine bleached', 'hydrogen chloride', 'CFC-free aerosols', 'no herbicides, pesticides, or fungicides', 'formaldehyde', 'low amount of phosphates and nitrates', 'molke-basis', 'pH-neutral', 'sauerstofftabletten', 'tenside, auf säuen verzichtet', 'milchsäure', 'entkalkungswürfel auf magentischer basis', 'ozonschädliches ersatzhalogen'

Product attribute: organic

Low specificity	*High specificity*
1000 (AS1) *(Low abstractness)*	0100 (AS2)
0010 (AS3) *(High abstractness)* 'organic', 'organic and not treated', 'organic and not sprayed', 'organic and no chemicals', 'biologisch', 'bio-', 'ökologischer anbau', 'unbelastet'	0001 (AS4) 'biodynamic', 'conservation grade organic', 'organic and no fertilizers', 'dynamischer, freier anbau', 'biologisch anerkannte produzenten', 'biologisch kontrollierter anbau', 'Demeterrichtlinie'

APPENDIX 3.10
EXAMPLES OF ABSTRACTNESS–SPECIFICITY MATRICES cont.

Product attribute: biodegradable

	Low specificity	High specificity
Low abstractness	1000 (AS1) 'break down', 'leicht abbaubar'	0100 (AS2) 'zu 99% abbaubar'
High abstractness	0010 (AS3) 'biodegradable', 'biodegradable substances', 'percentage biodegradable', 'biologische abbaubar'	0001 (AS4) 'abbaubar gemäss OECD richtlinie', 'degrades quicker', 'biologisch abbaubar in drei tagen'

Product attribute: recycled

	Low specificity	High specificity
Low abstractness	1000 (AS1)	0100 (AS2) 'made out of newspaper', 'second-hand', 'new ones'
High abstractness	0010 (AS3) 'recycled', 'recycled pulp', 'recycled material', 'recyclingpapier', 'aus altpapier', 'off-cuts'	0001 (AS4) '100% recycled', '80% recycled', 'factory off-cuts', 'virgin pulp', 'low grade recycled waste', 'lowest possible grade paper', '100% post-consumer waste', 'post-consumer waste', 'regurgitated paper'

SPECIFICITY–ABSTRACTNESS ANALYSIS OF PA MATRIX

PA matrix for interviewee G38

Products	ingredients	organic	seasonal	smell	taste	home made	pack. material	amount pack	reusable	biodegradable	recycled	recyclable	pack. images	names	ecolabels	colour	texture	size	sourcing	prod. process	loc. prod./ret.	disposal	energy	word of mouth	pressure groups	advertising	radio/TV/press	literature	others
detergent (X1-H)	100						100	100		10				100							10								0420 (X)
wash.up liq. (X1-M)	100													100															0100 (X)
cleaner (X1-M)	100								10					100										1000					1210 (X)
fruit.,veg. (X1-M)		10							100					1100						110						1100			1320 (X)
wom.san.prod. (X2-N)								100																					1200 (X)
shampoo (Y-H)	100								110					100															0210 (Y)
toilet pap. (Z1-H)	100									10				100	1100														1310 (Z)
drinks (Z1-M)						100	100					100																	0300 (Z)
meat (Z1-M)		10																											0010 (Z)
yoghurt (Z1-M)		10												100															0110 (Z)
rice (Y-H)		10												100															0110 (Y)
'AS1-AS2-AS3-AS4' (X products)	0200					0000	0100	0010	0000		0100	0000		1400	0000					0110	0110			1000		1100			3-12-5-0 (X)
		0010				0000	0310	0000	0100													0010							AS1-AS2-AS3-AS4
'AS5-AS6-AS7-AS8' (all products)	0300					0100	0100	0010	0100		0100	0100		1800	1100					0110	0110			1000		1100			4-22-10-0 (X+Y+Z)
		0040				0100	0420	0010														0010							AS5-AS6-AS7-AS8

Note: In the cells of the PA matrix are the specificity–abstractness codes as they were identified for the kind of 'green' language used to describe a certain product attribute for a certain product.

APPENDIX 3.12
ABSTRACTNESS–SPECIFICITY DISTRIBUTIONS

British sample

AS1

Interval			
[0,3]	13	0.24	0.24
[4,7]	29	0.53	0.77
[8,11]	10	0.18	0.95
[12,15]	3	0.05	1.00

average 5.8
median 5

AS2

Interval			
[0,3]	2	0.04	0.04
[4,7]	18	0.33	0.37
[8,11]	11	0.20	0.57
[12,15]	7	0.13	0.70
[16,19]	12	0.22	0.92
[20,23]	2	0.04	0.96
[24,27]	1	0.02	0.98
[28,31]	1	0.02	1.00
[32,35]	1	0.02	1.02

average 11.7
median 10

AS3

Interval			
[0,3]	21	0.38	0.38
[4,7]	17	0.31	0.69
[8,11]	15	0.27	0.96
[12,15]	1	0.02	0.98
[16,19]			
[20,23]	1	0.02	1.00

average 5.6
median 5

AS4

Interval			
[0,3]	52	0.95	0.95
[4,7]	3	0.05	1.00

average 1.0
median 1

German sample

AS1

Interval			
[0,3]	2	0.06	0.06
[4,7]	15	0.42	0.48
[8,11]	9	0.25	0.73
[12,15]	8	0.22	0.95
[16,19]	1	0.03	0.98
[20,23]	1	0.03	1.01

average 8.6
median 8

AS2

Interval			
[0,3]	1	0.03	0.03
[4,7]	2	0.06	0.09
[8,11]	12	0.33	0.42
[12,15]	5	0.14	0.56
[16,19]	5	0.14	0.70
[20,23]	5	0.14	0.84
[24,27]	4	0.11	0.95
[28,31]	1	0.03	0.98
[32,35]			
[36,39]	1	0.03	1.01

average 15.7
median 13

AS3

Interval			
[0,3]	8	0.22	0.22
[4,7]	17	0.47	0.69
[8,11]	8	0.22	0.91
[12,15]			
[16,19]	1	0.03	0.94
[20,23]			
[24,27]	2	0.06	1.00
[28,31]			

average 6.7
median 6

AS4

Interval			
[0,3]	30	0.83	0.83
[4,7]	4	0.11	0.94
[8,11]	2	0.06	1.00

average 1.7
median 1

British sample

AS5			
[0,3]	6	0.11	0.11
[4,7]	22	0.40	0.51
[8,11]	18	0.33	0.84
[12,15]	6	0.11	0.95
[16,19]	3	0.05	1.00
average 8.0			
median 7.0			

AS6			
[0,3]	2	0.04	0.04
[4,7]	14	0.25	0.29
[8,11]	7	0.13	0.42
[12,15]	13	0.24	0.66
[16,19]	9	0.16	0.82
[20,23]	3	0.05	0.87
[24,27]	3	0.05	0.92
[28,31]	3	0.05	0.97
[32,35]	1	0.02	0.99
[36,39]			
average 17.5			
median 17.0			

AS7			
[0,3]	3	0.05	0.05
[4,7]	23	0.42	0.47
[8,11]	15	0.27	0.74
[12,15]	11	0.20	0.94
[16,19]	2	0.04	0.98
[20,23]	1	0.02	1.00
average 8.5			
median 8.0			

AS8			
[0,3]	50	0.91	0.91
[4,7]	5	0.09	1.00
average 1.3			
median 1.0			

German sample

AS5			
[0,3]	7	0.19	0.19
[4,7]	9	0.25	0.44
[8,11]	14	0.39	0.83
[12,15]	4	0.11	0.94
[16,19]	1	0.03	0.97
[20,23]	1	0.03	1.00
[23,27]			
average 11.8			
median 12.0			

AS6			
[0,3]	1	0.03	0.03
[4,7]	8	0.22	0.25
[8,11]	9	0.25	0.50
[12,15]	3	0.08	0.58
[16,19]	3	0.08	0.66
[20,23]	6	0.17	0.83
[24,27]	4	0.11	0.94
[28,31]	1	0.03	0.97
[32,35]			
[36,39]			
[40,43]			
[44,47]	1	0.03	1.00
average 22.7			
median 19.5			

AS7			
[0,3]	2	0.06	0.06
[4,7]	12	0.33	0.39
[8,11]	9	0.25	0.64
[12,15]	8	0.22	0.86
[16,19]	2	0.06	0.92
[20,23]	1	0.03	0.95
[23,27]			
[28,31]	2	0.06	1.01
average 10.3			
median 9.0			

AS8			
[0,3]	28	0.78	0.78
[4,7]	4	0.11	0.89
[8,11]	4	0.11	1.00
average 2.5			
median 1.0			

ABSTRACTNESS–SPECIFICITY DISTRIBUTIONS cont.

AS5				AS6				AS7				AS8			
						Non-green sample									
[0,3]	1	0.10	0.10	[0,3]	2	0.20	0.20	[0,3]	5	0.50	0.50	[0,3]	10	1.00	1.00
[4,7]	4	0.40	0.50	[4,7]	3	0.30	0.50	[4,7]	4	0.40	0.90				
[8,11]	3	0.30	0.80	[8,11]	4	0.40	0.90	[8,11]	1	0.10	1.00				
[12,15]	2	0.20	1.00	[12,15]											
				[16,19]											
				[20,23]	1	0.10	1.00								

average 7.9   median 8.0   average 6.1   median 7.5   average 3.5   median 3.5   average 0.7   median 0.5

APPENDIX 4.1
SCATTERGRAMS

British sample W1 – C1

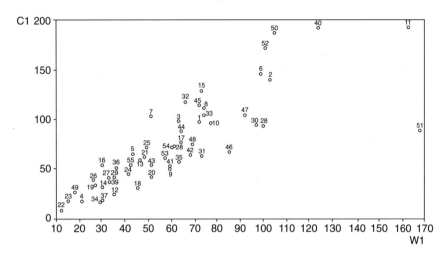

British sample, W1 – AS2

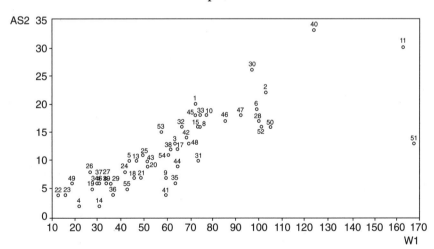

APPENDIX 4.1
SCATTERGRAMS cont.

German sample, C1–C2

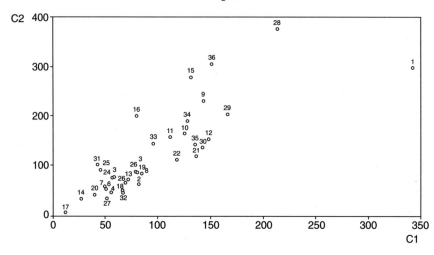

APPENDIX 4.2
DENDROGRAMS

British sample (Z scores)

Dendrogram using Ward's Method: Variable Set 1 (W1, C1, C2)

Rescaled Distance Cluster Combine

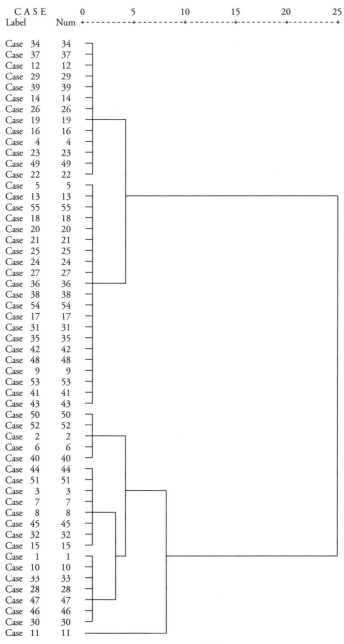

APPENDIX 4.2
DENDROGRAMS cont.

Dendrogram using Group Average Method: Variable Set 2 (W1, C1, C2, AS2)

Rescaled Distance Cluster Combine

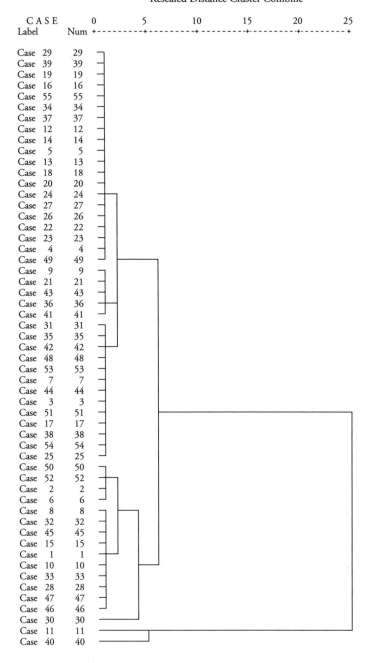

German sample (Z scores)

Dendrogram using Ward's Method: Variable Set 4 (W1, C1, C2, AS1, AS2, AS3, AS4)

Rescaled Distance Cluster Combine

```
      C A S E      0         5        10        15        20        25
      Label      Num  +---------+---------+---------+---------+---------+

Case   3     3    ┐
Case  24    24    ┤
Case  31    31    ┤
Case   2     2    ┤
Case   4     4    ┤
Case  18    18    ┤
Case  32    32    ┤
Case  20    20    ┤
Case  27    27    ┤
Case   7     7    ┤
Case  26    26    ┤
Case   6     6    ┤
Case  25    25    ┤
Case   8     8    ┤
Case  14    14    ┤
Case  17    17    ┤
Case  23    23    ┤
Case   5     5    ┤
Case  13    13    ┤
Case  19    19    ┤
Case  33    33    ┘
Case  15    15    ┐
Case  16    16    ┤
Case  21    21    ┤
Case  35    35    ┤
Case  30    30    ┤
Case  11    11    ┤
Case  34    34    ┤
Case  22    22    ┤
Case  10    10    ┤
Case  12    12    ┤
Case   9     9    ┤
Case  29    29    ┘
Case  36    36    ┐
Case   1     1    ┤
Case  28    28    ┘
```

233

APPENDIX 4.3
EXAMPLES OF CLUSTER SEQUENCES

British sample

Top subjects → ... → Bottom subjects

Variables	Method	Sequence
Set 1	Ward	11 • 2, 6, 40, 50, 52 • 1, 10, 28, 30, 33, 46, 47 • 3, 7, 8, 15, 32, 44, 45, 51 • 9, 17, 21, 25, 31, 35, 38, 41, 42, 43, 48, 53, 54 • 5, 13, 18, 20, 24, 27, 36 • 4, 12, 14, 16, 19, 22, 23, 26, 29, 34, 37, 39, 49, 55
	GA	11 • 40 • 30 • 2, 6, 50, 52 • 1, 8, 10, 15, 28, 32, 33, 45, 46, 47 – 3, 7, 9, 17, 21, 25, 31, 35, 36, 38, 41, 42, 43, 44, 48, 53, 54 • 4, 5, 12, 13, 14, 16, 18, 19, 20, 22, 23, 24, 26, 27, 29, 34, 37, 39, 49, 55
	k = 7	11 o 40 o 2, 6, 50, 52 o 1, 10, 28, 30, 33, 46, 47 o 3, 7, 8, 15, 17, 31, 32, 38, 42, 44, 45, 48, 51, 54, 5, 9, 13, 18, 20, 21, 24, 25, 27, 35, 36, 41, 43, 53, 55 o 4, 12, 14, 16, 19, 22, 23, 26, 29, 34, 37, 39, 49
	k = 10	11 o 40 o 50, 52 o 2, 6 o 1, 10, 28, 30, 33, 46, 47 o 8, 15, 32, 45 o 3, 7, 17, 25, 31, 35, 38, 44, 48, 51, 54 o 9, 21, 36, 41, 42, 43, 53* o 5, 12, 13, 14, 16, 18, 20, 24, 26, 27, 29, 39, 55 o 4, 19, 22, 23, 34, 37, 49
Set 2	Ward	11, 40 • 2, 6, 50, 52 – 1, 10, 28, 30, 33, 46, 47 • 3, 7, 8, 15, 17, 25, 32, 38, 42, 44, 45, 48, 51, 53, 54 • 5, 9, 13, 16, 18, 20, 21, 24, 26, 27, 29, 31, 35, 36, 39, 41, 43, 55 • 4, 12, 14, 19, 22, 23, 34, 37, 49
	GA	11 • 40 • 30 • 2, 6, 50, 52 – 1, 8, 10, 15, 28, 32, 33, 45, 46, 47 • 3, 5, 7, 13, 17, 25, 31, 35, 38, 42, 44, 48, 51, 53, 54 – 9, 21, 36, 41, 43 – 4, 12, 14, 16, 18, 19, 20, 22, 23, 24, 26, 27, 29, 34, 37, 49, 55
	k = 7	11 o 40 o 30 o 2, 6, 50, 52 o 1, 8, 10, 15, 28, 32, 33, 45, 46, 47 o 3, 5, 7, 9, 13, 17, 20, 21, 25, 31, 35, 41, 42, 43, 44, 48, 51, 53, 54 o 4, 12, 14, 16, 18, 19, 22, 23, 24, 26, 27, 29, 34, 36, 37, 39, 49, 55
	k = 10	11 o 40 o 30 o 2, 6, 50, 52 o 1, 10, 28, 33, 46, 47 o 8, 15, 32, 45 o 9, 21, 36, 41, 43 o 3, 7, 17, 25, 31, 38, 42, 44, 48, 51, 53, 54 o 5, 13, 16, 18, 20, 24, 26, 26, 27, 29, 35, 55 o 4, 12, 14, 19, 22, 23, 34, 37, 49
Set 3, 16,	Ward	11 • 6, 40, 50, 52 • 2, 10, 28, 30, 33, 47 • 1, 3, 8, 15, 32, 45 – 7, 17, 36, 41, 42, 44, 46, 48, 51 • 21, 27, 31, 35, 38, 43, 53, 54* • 9, 24, 25, 55 – 5, 13, 14, 18, 19, 20, 29, 39 • 4, 12, 22, 23, 26, 34, 37, 49
	GA	11 • 40 • 50 • 6, 52 • 2, 10, 28, 30, 33, 47 • 1, 8, 15, 32, 45 – 7, 17, 36, 41, 42, 44, 46, 48, 51 – 21, 27, 31, 35, 38, 43, 53, 54 – 3, 9, 25* • 4, 5, 12, 13, 14, 16, 18, 19, 20, 22, 23, 24, 26, 29, 34, 37, 39, 49, 55
	k = 7	11 o 40 o 50, 52 o 1, 2, 6, 7, 8, 10, 15, 28, 30, 32, 33, 41, 44, 45, 46, 47, 48, 51 o 10, 17, 21, 42, 43, 53 o 3, 5, 9, 13, 14, 18, 20, 24, 25, 27, 29, 31, 35, 36, 38, 39, 54, 55 o 4, 12, 16, 19, 22, 23, 26, 34, 37, 49
	k = 10	11 o 40 o 50 o 6, 52 o 2, 10, 28, 30, 33, 47 o 1, 3, 8, 15, 32, 45 o 17, 21, 42, 43 o 7, 9, 25, 36, 41, 44, 46, 48, 51 o 5, 13, 14, 18, 20, 24, 27, 29, 31, 35, 38, 39, 53, 54, 55 o 4, 12, 16, 19, 22, 23, 26, 34, 37, 49

Set	Method	Sequence
Set 4	Ward	11 • 6, 40, 50, 52 • 2, 28 – 8, 10, 30, 33, 45, 47 • 1, 3, 15, 32, 46 – 7, 17, 21, 25, 36, 41, 42, 43, 44, 48, 51 • 9, 13, 14, 20, 31, 35, 38, 53, 54 • 5, 16, 18, 19, 24, 26, 27, 29, 39, 55 • 4, 12, 22, 23, 34, 37, 49
	GA	11 • 40 • 6, 50, 52 • 2, 28 • 30 • 8, 10, 33, 45, 47 – 1, 3, 15, 32* – 42, 46, 48 – 7, 17, 25, 51 – 36, 41 – 21, 31, 35, 43, 53, 54 • 9, 14 – 4, 5, 12, 13, 16, 18, 19, 20, 22, 23, 24, 26, 27, 29, 34, 37, 38, 39, 49, 55
	k = 7	11 o 40 o 6, 50, 52 o 2, 8, 28, 30, 33, 47 o 1, 7, 10, 15, 17, 21, 32, 38, 41, 42, 43, 44, 45, 46, 48, 51, 53, 54 o 3, 9, 13, 20, 24, 25, 31, 35, 36, 41, 55 o 4, 5, 12, 13, 14, 16, 18, 19, 22, 23, 26, 27, 29, 34, 37, 39, 49
	k = 10	11 o 40 o 50 o 6, 15, 46, 52 o 2, 8, 28 o 1, 30 o 10, 32, 33, 42, 43, 45, 47, 48 o 7, 9, 17, 25, 36, 41, 44, 51 o 3, 5, 13, 20, 21, 24, 27, 31, 35, 38, 53, 54, 55 o 4, 12, 14, 16, 18, 19, 22, 23, 26, 29, 34, 37, 39, 49
Set 5	Ward	11 • 2, 28 • 8, 30, 33, 45, 47, 48 • 40, 50, 52* • 1, 3, 6, 15, 46 • 7, 25, 36, 41, 44* • 17, 32, 42, 51 – 10, 43 • 9, 14 – 13, 20, 21, 31, 35, 53, 54 • 5, 16, 18, 19, 24, 26, 27, 29, 38, 39, 55 – 4, 12, 22, 23, 34, 37, 49
	GA	11 • 40 • 50 • 6, 46, 52 • 2, 28 • 8, 10, 30, 33, 45, 47, 48 • 7, 24, 25, 36, 41, 44, 55 • 17, 21, 32, 35, 42, 43, 51 • 1, 3, 13, 15, 20, 31, 53, 54 • 9, 14 – 4, 5, 12, 16, 18, 19, 22, 23, 26, 27, 29, 34, 37, 38, 39, 49
Set 6	Ward	11 • 6, 40, 50, 52 • 2, 28, 30 • 1, 3, 8, 10, 15, 32, 33, 42, 45, 47, 48 • 7, 17, 25, 36, 41, 44, 46, 51 • 9, 13, 14, 20, 21, 31, 35, 38, 43, 53, 54 • 5, 16, 18, 19, 24, 26, 27, 29, 39, 55 – 4, 12, 22, 23, 34, 37, 49
	GA	11 • 40 • 50 • 6, 52 • 2, 28 • 1, 30 • 3, 8, 10, 15, 32, 33, 45, 47 • 42, 46, 48 – 7, 17, 25, 44, 51 – 36, 41 – 21, 31, 35, 38, 43, 53, 54 • 9, 14 – 4, 5, 13, 16, 18, 19, 20, 24, 26, 27, 29, 39, 55 – 12, 22, 23, 34, 37, 49
Set 7	Ward	11 • 6, 40, 50, 52 • 2, 8, 28, 30, 33 • 1, 15, 20, 32, 35, 38, 46, 54 • 10, 21, 42, 43, 45, 47, 48, 53 • 3, 7, 9, 17, 25, 36, 41, 44, 51 • 5, 13, 14, 16, 18, 19, 24, 26, 27, 29, 31, 39, 55 – 4, 12, 22, 23, 34, 37, 49
	GA	11 • 40 • 50 • 6, 52 • 2, 28 • 30 • 1, 8, 15, 32, 33, 45, 46, 48, 53 • 20, 35, 38, 54 • 3, 7, 9, 17, 25, 36, 41, 44, 51 • 10, 21, 42, 43, 47 • 13, 14, 31 – 4, 5, 12, 16, 18, 19, 22, 23, 24, 26, 27, 29, 34, 37, 39, 49, 55
Set 8	Ward	11 – 2, 28, 33 • 1, 30, 32, 40 – 3, 50, 52 • 6, 8, 10, 15, 20, 29, 31, 38, 42, 45, 46, 47, 48, 53, 54 • 7, 17, 35, 41, 43, 44, 55 • 9, 14, 19 – 4, 5, 13, 16, 18, 21, 24, 25, 26, 27, 36, 39, 51•12, 22, 23, 34, 37, 49
	GA	11 • 2 • 28, 33 • 30 • 8 • 1 • 32 • 40 • 3, 52 • 50 • 10 • 6, 15 • 45 • 31, 46, 47, 48, 54 • 20, 29, 38, 42, 53 – 17 • 35 – 43 • 7, 44 • 41, 55 • 9, 14, 19 • 21 • 13, 16, 24, 26, 51 • 4, 5, 18, 25, 27, 36, 39 • 12, 22, 23, 34, 37, 49
Set 9	Ward	11, 40 • 1, 28, 30, 33 • 2 – 6, 8, 32, 50, 52 • 9, 36, 41, 42, 43, 46, 51, 53 – 3, 7, 10, 15, 17, 25, 44, 45, 47, 48 • 20, 35, 38, 39, 54 • 4, 5, 13, 16, 19, 24, 26, 29, 31, 55 – 12, 14, 18, 21, 22, 23, 27, 34, 37, 49
	GA	11, 40 • 2 • 1, 28, 33 • 30 • 6 • 50, 52 • 8, 32 • 38, 54* • 9, 36, 41, 42, 43, 46, 51, 53 • 7, 10, 15, 17, 25, 44, 45, 47, 48 • 20, 35, 39 • 4, 5, 13, 16, 19, 29, 31, 55 – 14, 21, 27 – 12, 18, 22, 23, 34, 37, 49

Key:
– = cluster distance of up to 2 units (sub-group distinction, hierarchical clustering)
• = cluster distance of 3 units or more (group and outlier distinction, hierarchical clustering)
o = group or outlier distinction in K-means clustering
* = no relationship of dominance with previous string

APPENDIX 5.1
KNOWLEDGE VARIABLES OF PARADIGMATIC SUBJECTS

Subjects:	B5	G5	B4	G4	B3	G3	B2	G2	N2	B1	G1	N1
					Comprehensiveness variables							
W1	124	111	100	95	64	59	45	35	—	12	15	—
W2	133	150	119	117	99	78	61	67	73	34	48	25
W1/W2	0.93	0.74	0:84	0.81	0.65	0.76	0.74	0.52	—	0.35	0.31	—
W3	1875	1746	1899	2040	1528	1894	1052	1202	—	504	1136	—
W4	2281	2640	2753	2985	2580	3045	2254	2131	1684	1380	2631	1173
W1/W3	0.066	0.064	0.053	0.047	0.042	0.031	0.043	0.029	—	0.024	0.013	—
W2/W4	0.058	0.057	0.043	0.039	0.038	0.026	0.027	0.031	0.043	0.025	0.018	0.021
					Complexity variables							
C1	191	166	93	136	77	56	31	52	—	9	12	—
C3	209	203	145	120	53	48	35	36	—	11	8	—
C2	206	214	122	175	118	75	41	106	96	32	54	18
C4	278	334	278	261	112	102	72	194	56	54	70	16
C5	157	165	109	140	63	66	30	94	40	18	34	16
NX	12	12	10	8	6	7	4	4	—	3	4	—

Subjects:	B5	G5	B4	G4	B3	G3	B2	G2	N2	B1	G1	N1
Specificity and abstractness variables												
AS1	14	17	5	11	7	5	5	9	—	1	4	—
AS2	33	24	17	22	12	11	7	9	—	4	4	—
AS3	5	9	8	6	10	6	1	1	—	1	0	—
AS4	2	2	5	1	0	1	0	1	—	0	0	—
AS5	15	20	6	13	9	8	7	14	13	3	6	5
AS6	37	34	25	34	17	16	11	20	11	10	14	3
AS7	7	12	12	10	17	8	3	7	6	4	3	2
AS8	2	3	5	1	0	1	0	1	1	0	1	1
Familiarity indicators												
NT	16	17	16	14	12	12	8	12	—	9	11	—
NTA	14.5	15.5	12.5	13	9	7.5	7	9.5	—	5.5	6	—
NT/NTA	0.91	0.91	0.78	0.93	0.75	0.63	0.88	0.79	—	0.61	0.55	—
Constraints indicators												
No. of task constraints	2	7	7	3	6	13	8	7	—	6	14	—
No. constraints/ NT	0.13	0.41	0.44	0.21	0.50	1.08	1.00	0.58	—	0.67	1.27	—

APPENDIX 5.2
KNOWLEDGE VARIABLES OF COGNITIVE CATEGORIES

Cognitive category	Knowledge comprehensiveness				Knowledge complexity				Knowledge abstractness and knowledge specificity								No. of members
	W1	W2	W3	W4	C1	C2	C3	C4	AS1	AS2	AS3	AS4	AS5	AS6	AS7	AS8	
5 British	144	152	2629	1948	191	203	288	360	11–0.18	32–0.53	13–0.22	4–0.07	12–0.18	36–0.55	14–0.21	4–0.06	2
5 German	123	149	3119	2220	177	217	294	460	16–0.26	28–0.46	13–0.21	4–0.07	19–0.25	35–0.46	17–0.22	5–0.07	3
	124	148	3013	2116	169	202	278	410	15–0.25	28–0.47	110.19	5–0.08	18–0.25	33–0.46	14–0.20	6–0.08	4
4 British	88	114	2988	2063	106	133	137	267	4–0.11	20–0.55	9–0.25	3–0.08	6–0.13	27–0.57	11–0.23	3–0.06	7
	85	112	3085	2078	106	135	131	253	5–0.15	19–0.56	8–0.24	2–0.06	7–0.15	27–0.56	11–0.23	3–0.06	9
4 German	93	123	2837	2121	128	165	147	334	11–0.29	19–0.50	7–0.18	1–0.03	14–0.25	28–0.50	11–0.19	3–0.05	7
	93	122	2783	2015	126	160	166	348	10–0.26	21–0.54	7–0.18	1–0.03	14–0.25	29–0.51	11–0.19	3–0.05	10
3 British	62	86	2395	1550	82	114	67	138	8–0.29	12–0.43	7–0.25	1–0.04	11–0.28	17–0.43	10–0.26	1–0.03	9
	59	80	2218	1472	74	102	73	136	7–0.27	11–0.42	7–0.27	1–0.04	10–0.27	16–0.43	10–0.27	1–0.03	13
3 German	63	96	2395	1475	71	109	62	190	4–0.17	11–0.46	8–0.33	1–0.04	8–0.19	20–0.48	13–0.31	1–0.02	4
	62	89	2242	1351	71	101	65	166	5–0.20	11–0.44	7–0.28	2–0.08	8–0.21	18–0.46	11–0.28	2–0.05	6
2 British	43	67	2201	1165	48	70	34	85	5–0.31	8–0.50	3–0.19	0–0.00	7–0.26	14–0.52	6–0.22	0–0.00	7
	40	68	2136	1167	47	74	30	89	5–0.33	7–0.47	3–0.20	0–0.00	7–0.25	15–0.54	6–0.21	0–0.00	10
2 German	39	61	1997	1073	45	74	69	161	7–0.35	10–0.50	2–0.10	1–0.05	10–0.30	17–0.52	5–0.15	1–0.03	4
1 British	23	40	1758	814	19	37	18	61	2–0.20	5–0.50	2–0.20	1–0.10	3–0.17	9–0.50	5–0.28	1–0.06	7
1 German	19	50	2827	1556	20	64	22	94	5–0.42	4–0.33	3–0.25	0–0.00	7–0.25	12–0.43	8–0.29	1–0.04	2

Note: First row in each cell refers to '4 out of 4' demarcation of cognitive categories; second row, where applicable, refers to the '3 out of 4' demarcation of cognitive categories.

APPENDIX 5.3
COMPREHENSIVENESS VALUES

Word counts for interview extracts for freely recalled products (W1):		*Word counts for interview extracts for freely recalled products (W1):*	
Paradigmatic subjects		Cognitive categories (Brit.-Ger.)	
B5: 124	G5: 111	5: 144	5: 123
B4: 100	G4: 95	4: 89	4: 93
B3: 64	G3: 59	3: 62	3: 63
B2: 45	G2: 35	2: 43	2: 39
B1: 12	G1: 15	1: 23	1: 19

Word counts for interview extracts for all discussed products (W2):			*Word counts for interview extracts for all discussed products (W2):*	
Paradigmatic subjects			Cognitive categories (Brit.-Ger.)	
B5: 133	G5: 150		5: 152	5: 149
B4: 118	G4: 117		4: 114	4: 123
B3: 99	G3: 78		3: 86	3: 96
B2: 61	G2: 67	N2: 73	2: 67	2: 61
B1: 34	G1: 48	N1: 25	1: 40	1: 50

Word counts for actual interview for free recall part 1 (W3):		*Word counts for actual interview for free recall part 1 (W3):*	
Paradigmatic subjects		Cognitive categories (Brit.-Ger.)	
B5: 1875	G5: 1746	5: 1948	5: 2220
B4: 1899	G4: 2040	4: 2063	4: 2121
B3: 1528	G3: 1894	3: 1550	3: 1475
B2: 1052	G2: 1202	2: 1165	2: 1073
B1: 504	G1: 1136	1: 814	1: 1556

Word counts for the total of the actual interview (W4):			*Word counts for the total of the actual interview (W4):*	
Paradigmatic subjects			Cognitive categories (Brit.-Ger.)	
B1: 2281	G5: 2640		5: 2629	5: 3119
B2: 2753	G4: 2985		4: 2988	4: 2837
B3: 2580	G3: 3045		3: 2395	3: 2395
B4: 2254	G2: 2131	N2: 1684	2: 2201	2: 1997
B5: 1380	G1: 2631	N1: 1173	1: 1758	1: 2827

Number of freely recalled products (NX):		*Number of freely recalled products (NX):*	
Paradigmatic subjects		Cognitive categories (Brit.-Ger.)	
B5: 12	G5: 12	5: 13.5	5: 14.0
B4: 10	G4: 8	4: 9.4	4: 9.6
B3: 6	G3: 7	3: 6.9	3: 6.3
B2: 4	G2: 4	2: 4.3	2: 4.3
B1: 3	G1: 4	1: 3.7	1: 3.7

APPENDIX 5.3
COMPREHENSIVENESS VALUES cont.

Number of different product attributes recalled (X products):				*Number of different product attributes recalled (X products)*			
Paradigmatic subjects				Cognitive categories (Brit.-Ger.)			
B5:	14	G5:	14	5:	14.0	5:	11.7
B4:	9	G4:	11	4:	11.0	4:	11.0
B3:	12	G3:	8	3:	11.0	3:	9.0
B2:	5	G2:	6	2:	7.9	2:	6.0
B1:	3	G1:	5	1:	5.0	1:	5.5

Number of product attributes over all X products recalled:				*Number of product attributes over all X products recalled*			
Paradigmatic subjects				Cognitive categories (Brit.-Ger.)			
B5:	43	G5:	40	5:	45.0	5:	45.0
B4:	29	G4:	30	4:	28.9	4:	31.2
B3:	21	G3:	18	3:	21.3	3:	19.0
B2:	11	G2:	14	2:	13.6	2:	16.3
B1:	5	G1:	6	1:	7.6	1:	8.5

APPENDIX 5.4
COMPLEXITY VALUES

Horizontal complexity, freely recalled products (C1):
Paradigmatic subjects

B5:	191	G5:	166
B4:	93	G4:	136
B3:	77	G3:	56
B2:	31	G2:	52
B1:	9	G1:	12

Horizontal complexity, freely recalled products (C1):
Cognitive categories (Brit.-Ger)

5:	191	5:	177
4:	106	4:	128
3:	82	3:	71
2:	48	2:	45
1:	19	1:	0

Horizontal complexity, all products discussed (C3):
Paradigmatic subjects

B5:	206	G5:	214
B4:	122	G4:	175
B3:	118	G3:	75
B2:	41	G2:	106
B1:	32	G1:	54

Horizontal complexity, all products discussed (C3):
Cognitive categories (Brit.-Ger.)

5:	203	5:	217
4:	133	4:	165
3:	114	3:	109
2:	70	2:	74
1:	37	1:	64

Vertical complexity, freely recalled products (C2):
Paradigmatic subjects

B5:	209	G5:	203
B4:	145	G4:	120
B3:	53	G3:	48
B2:	35	G2:	36
B1:	11	G1:	8

Vertical complexity, freely recalled products (C2):
Cognitive categories (Brit.-Ger.)

5:	288	5:	294
4:	137	4:	147
3:	67	3:	62
2:	34	2:	69
1:	18	1:	22

Vertical complexity, all products discussed (C4):
Paradigmatic subjects

B5:	278	G5:	334
B4:	278	G4:	261
B3:	112	G3:	102
B2:	72	G2:	194
B1:	54	G1:	70

Vertical complexity, all products discussed (C4):
Cognitive categories (Brit.-Ger.)

5:	360	5:	460
4:	267	4:	334
3:	138	3:	190
2:	85	2:	161
1:	61	1:	94

Number of freely recalled products (NX):
Paradigmatic subjects

B5:	12	G5:	12
B4:	10	G4:	8
B3:	6	G3:	7
B2:	4	G2:	4
B1:	3	G1:	4

Number of freely recalled products (NX):
Cognitive categories (Brit.-Ger.)

5:	13.5	5:	14.0
4:	9.4	4:	9.6
3:	6.9	3:	6.3
2:	4.3	2:	4.3
1:	3.7	1:	3.7

APPENDIX 5.4
COMPLEXITY VALUES cont.

Number of different product attributes
recalled (X products):
Paradigmatic subjects

B5:	14	G5:	14
B4:	9	G4:	11
B3:	12	G3:	8
B2:	5	G2:	6
B1:	3	G1:	5

Number of different product attributes
recalled (X products)
Cognitive categories (Brit.-Ger.)

5:	14.0	5:	11.7
4:	11.0	4:	11.0
3:	11.0	3:	9.0
2:	7.9	2:	6.0
1:	5.0	1:	5.5

Number of product attributes over all
X products recalled:
Paradigmatic subjects

B5:	43	G5:	40
B4:	29	G4:	30
B3:	21	G3:	18
B2:	11	G2:	14
B1:	5	G1:	6

Number of product attributes over all
X products recalled
Cognitive categories (Brit.-Ger.)

5:	45.0	5:	45.0
4:	28.9	4:	31.2
3:	21.3	3:	19.0
2:	13.6	2:	16.3
1:	7.6	1:	8.5

APPENDIX 5.5
GOOD EXAMPLES OF PRODUCTS AND PRODUCT ATTRIBUTES

British sample: first two products mentioned
(in brackets: PPO parameters of the respective products)

Cognitive category 5

B11 milk (>11; –), bread (6; –)
B40 detergent (1; 1), washing-up liquid (1; 2)

Cognitive category 4

B02 bread (6; –), vegetables + fruit (3; 1)
B10 vegetables + fruit (3; 1), meat (8; –)
B28 washing-up liquid (1; 2), detergent (1; 1)
B30 vegetables + fruit (3; 1), eggs (>11; –)
B33 fruit + vegetables (3; 1), drinks (8; –)
B45 detergent (1; 1), washing-up liquid (1; 2)
B47 washing-up liquid (1; 2), shampoo (11; –)

B01 detergent (1; 1), cosmetics (10; –)
B08 cleaners (3; 3), detergent (1; 1)

Cognitive category 3

B03 vegetables + fruit (3; 1), washing-up liquid (1; 2)
B07 washing-up liquid (1; 2), detergent (1; 1)
B17 washing-up liquid (1; 2), detergent (1; 1)
B25 washing-up liquid (1; 2), detergent (1; 1)
B42 washing-up liquid (1; 2), detergent (1; 1)
B44 sugar (>11; –), bread (6; –)
B48 vegetables + fruit (3; 1), oats + grains (>11; –)
B51 vegetables + fruit (3; 1), drinks (8; –)
B54 detergent (1; 1), toilet paper (7; 5)

B21 tissues (>11; –), toilet paper (7; 5)
B41 meat (8; –), vegetables + fruit (3; 1)
B43 washing-up liquid (1; 2), detergent (1; 1)
B53 bread (6; –), detergent (1; 1)

Cognitive category 2

B05 detergent (1; 1), cleaners (3; 3)
B13 vegetables + fruit (3; 1), toilet paper (7; 5)
B18 detergent (1; 1), fabric conditioner (>11; –)
B20 detergent (1; 1), cleaners (3; 3)
B24 meat (8; –), detergent (1; 1)
B27 vegetables + fruit (3; 1), detergent (1; 1)

APPENDIX 5.5
GOOD EXAMPLES OF PRODUCTS AND PRODUCT ATTRIBUTES cont.

B55   vegetables + fruit (3; 1), bread (6; –)

B16   detergent (1; 1), sprays (>11; –)
B29   cleaners (3; 3), toilet paper (7; 5)
B39   soap (>11; –), toiletries (10; –)

Cognitive category 1

B04   detergent (1; 10), toilet paper (7; 5)
B12   toilet paper (7; 5), washing-up liquid (1; 2)
B22   detergent (1; 1), fabric conditioner (>11; –)
B23   detergent (1; 1), washing-up liquid (1; 2)
B34   toilet paper (7; 5), detergent (1; 1)
B37   detergent (1; 1), cleaners (3; 3)
B49   vegetables + fruit (3; 1), nappies (>11; –)

Note: For each cognitive category first '4 out of 4' interviewees, then '3 out of 4' interviewees are listed; for each interviewee the first two products freely recalled are listed; in brackets is the PPO median and the mode for the respective product as calculated for the total sample.

German sample: first two products mentioned
(in brackets: PPO parameters of the respective products)

Cognitive category 5

G28   milk (1; 1), vegetables + fruit (3; 4)
G29   milk (1; 1), bread (2; 3)
G36   cheese (8; –), milk (1; 1)

G09   meat (3; 4), bread (2; 3)

Cognitive category 4

G10   cheese (8; –), vegetables + fruit (3; 4)
G11   vegetables + fruit (3; 4), cleaners (9; 7)
G21   milk (1; 1), yoghurt (3; 2)
G22   meat (3; 1 and 4), fruit + vegetables (3; 4)
G30   vegetables + fruit (3; 4), meat (3; 1 and 4)
G34   toilet paper (>15; –), cream (8; –)
G35   meat (3; 1 and 4), bread (2; 3)

G12   milk (1; 1), drinks (7; 2 and 5)
G15   milk (1; 1), yoghurt (3; 2)
G16   cacao (>15; –), detergent (9; 6)

Cognitive category 3

G02   coffee filters (>15; –), toilet paper (>15; –)

G04   drinks (7; 2 and 5), milk (1; 1)
G23   bread (2; 3), vegetables + fruit (3; 4)
G32   vegetables + fruit (3; 4), coffee milk (>15; –)

G13   milk (1; 1), yoghurt (3; 2)
G26   milk (1; 1), cream (8; –)

Cognitive category 2

G20   fruit + vegetables (3; 4), milk (1; 1)
G25   milk (1; 1), drinks (7; 2 and 5)
G27   butter (>15; –), bread (2; 3)
G31   milk (1; 1), drinks (7; 2 and 5)

Cognitive category 1

G14   milk (1; 1), yoghurt (3; 2)
G17   cleaners (9; 7), vegetables + fruit (3; 4)

Note: For each category first '4 out of 4' interviewees, then '3 out of 4' interviewees are listed; for each interviewee the first two products freely recalled are listed; in brackets is the PPO median and the PPO mode for the respective product as calculated for the total sample.

British sample: first two product attributes mentioned

Cognitive category 5

B11   organic, names
B40   home made, organic

Cognitive category 4

B02   organic, names
B10   names, organic
B28   packaging images, ingredients
B30   names, reusable
B33   organic, names
B45   names, organic
B47   names, biodegradable

B01   names, amount of packaging
B08   names, organic

Cognitive category 3

B03   organic, recycled
B07   ingredients, disposal
B17   names, organic
B25   names, recycled
B42   packaging images, names
B44   production process, energy saving

APPENDIX 5.5
GOOD EXAMPLES OF PRODUCTS AND PRODUCT ATTRIBUTES cont.

B48 locally produced/retailed, organic
B51 organic, locally produced, retailed
B54 names, recycled

B21 recycled, names
B41 organic, recycled
B43 biodegradable, organic
B53 organic, locally produced/retailed

Cognitive category 2

B05 ingredients, amount of packaging
B13 locally produced/retailed, recycled
B18 names, packaging images
B20 names, packaging material
B24 biodegradable, organic
B27 organic, recycled
B55 names, others

B16 packaging images, organic
B29 names, recycled
B39 amount of packaging, home made

Cognitive category 1

B04 ingredients, recycled
B12 recycled, names
B22 recyclable, reusable
B23 recycled, names
B34 recycled, names
B37 ingredients, organic
B49 home made, organic

Note: For each category first '4 out of 4' interviewees, then '3 out of 4' interviewees are listed; for each interviewee the first two product attributes freely recalled are listed.

German sample: first two product attributes mentioned

Cognitive category 5

G28 names, organic
G29 packaging material, names
G36 organic, names

G09 locally produced/retailed, names

Cognitive category 4

G10 reusable, home made

246

G11 names, amount of packaging
G21 names, amount of packaging
G22 amount of packaging, reusable
G30 home made, ingredients
G34 recycled, locally produced/retailed
G35 locally produced/retailed, names

G12 reusable, amount of packaging
G15 packaging material, reusable
G16 names, reusable

Cognitive category 3

G02 ingredients, colour
G04 reusable, packaging material
G23 organic, names
G32 home made, names

G13 reusable, amount of packaging
G26 packaging material, ingredients

Cognitive category 2

G20 names, amount of packaging
G25 packaging material, reusable
G27 names, packaging material
G31 packaging material, names

Cognitive category 1

G14 packaging material, reusable
G17 names, biodegradable

Note: For each category first '4 out of 4' interviewees, then '3 out of 4' interviewees are listed; for each interviewee the first two product attributes freely recalled are listed.

APPENDIX 6.1
PRODUCT FREQUENCIES

Variables (no. of products)	British sample			German sample			Non-green sample		
	Mean	Median	Range	Mean	Median	Range	Mean	Median	Range
NX	6.6	6	[2; 15]	8.5	8	[4; 16]			
NX1	5.4	5	[2; 13]	7.1	7	[0; 7]	(not applicable)		
NX2	1.1	1	[0; 6]	1.4	1	[3; 12]			
NXA	5.5	5	[0.5; 14.5]	7.6	7	[1.5; 14]			
NY	1.1	1	[0; 4]	1.2	0.5	[0; 5]	(not applicable)		
NZ	3.6	3	[0; 8]	4.5	4	[1; 7]	7.2	7.5	[2; 11]
NZ1	3.1	3	[0; 7]	4.1	4	[1; 7]	6.3	6.5	[2; 11]
NZ2	0.5	0	[0; 3]	0.4	0	[0; 2]	0.9	1	[0; 2]
NT	11.3	11	[6; 19]	14.2	14	[9; 21]			
NTA	9.0	8.5	[3.5; 16.5]	12.4	13	[6; 19]	(not applicable)		

Number of freely recalled products (NX):
Paradigmatic subjects

B5:	12	G5:	12
B4:	10	G4:	8
B3:	6	G3:	7
B2:	4	G2:	4
B1:	3	G1:	4

Number of freely recalled products (NX):
Cognitive categories (Brit.-Ger.)

5:	13.5	5:	14.0
4:	9.4	4:	9.6
3:	6.9	3:	6.3
2:	4.3	2:	6.5
1:	3.7	1:	3.5

Number of freely recalled products actually bought (NXA):
Paradigmatic subjects

B5:	11.5	G5:	10.5
B4:	8	G4:	7
B3:	4.5	G3:	3.5
B2:	3	G2:	3.5
B1:	3	G1:	3

Number of freely recalled products actually bought (NXA):
Cognitive categories (Brit.-Ger.)

5:	13	5:	12.8
4:	8.3	4:	8.9
3:	5.8	3:	5.1
2:	3.4	2:	5.4
1:	3.1	1:	3.5

Total number of products discussed (NT):
Paradigmatic subjects

B5:	16	G5:	17
B4:	16	G4:	14
B3:	12	G3:	12
B2:	8	G2:	12
B1:	9	G1:	11

Total number of products discussed (NT):
Cognitive categories (Brit.-Ger.)

5:	17	5:	18.7
4:	14.9	4:	16.3
3:	11.6	3:	13.3
2:	9.1	2:	12.5
1:	8.3	1:	12.5

Total number of products actually bought (NTA):
Paradigmatic subjects

B5:	14.5	G5:	15.5
B4:	12.5	G4:	13
B3:	9	G3:	7.5
B2:	7	G2:	9.5
B1:	5.5	G1:	6

Total number of products actually bought (NTA):
Cognitive categories (Brit.-Ger.)

5:	15.5	5:	17.5
4:	12.3	4:	15.2
3:	9.1	3:	11.5
2:	7	2:	9.1
1:	5.7	1:	9.5

GLOSSARY

AS1 The AS1 variable is one of the abstractness–specificity variables. Knowledge abstractness relates to the degree of technicality of language; knowledge specificity reflects the degree of concreteness of language. The AS1 variable reflects the number of instances of weakly specific and weakly abstract knowledge that were found with regard to freely recalled products (X products).

AS2 The AS2 variable is one of the abstractness–specificity variables. Knowledge abstractness relates to the degree of technicality of language; knowledge specificity reflects the degree of concreteness of language. The AS2 variable reflects the number of instances of highly specific and weakly abstract knowledge that were found with regard to freely recalled products (X products).

AS3 The AS3 variable is one of the abstractness–specificity variables. Knowledge abstractness relates to the degree of technicality of language; knowledge specificity reflects the degree of concreteness of language. The AS3 variable reflects the number of instances of weakly specific and highly abstract knowledge that were found with regard to freely recalled products (X products).

AS4 The AS4 variable is one of the abstractness–specificity variables. Knowledge abstractness relates to the degree of technicality of language; knowledge specificity reflects the degree of concreteness of language. The AS4 variable reflects the number of instances of highly specific and highly abstract knowledge that was found with regard to freely recalled products (X products).

AS5 The AS5 variable is one of the abstractness–specificity variables. Knowledge abstractness relates to the degree of technicality of language; knowledge specificity reflects the degree of concreteness of language. The AS5 variable reflects the number of instances of weakly specific and weakly abstract knowledge that were found with regard to all products (X + Y + Z products).

AS6 The AS6 variable is one of the abstractness-specificity variables. Knowledge abstractness relates to the degree of technicality of language; knowledge specificity reflects the degree of concreteness of language. The AS6 variable reflects the number of instances of highly specific and weakly abstract knowledge that was found with regard to all products (X + Y + Z products).

AS7 The AS7 variable is one of the abstractness–specificity variables. Knowledge abstractness relates to the degree of technicality of language; knowledge specificity reflects the degree of concreteness of language. The AS7 variable reflects the number of instances of weakly specific and highly abstract knowledge that was found with regard to all products (X + Y + Z products).

250

AS8 The AS8 variable is one of the abstractness–specificity variables. Knowledge abstractness relates to the degree of technicality of language; knowledge specificity reflects the degree of concreteness of language. The AS8 variable reflects the number of instances of highly specific and highly abstract knowledge that was found with regard to all products ($X + Y + Z$ products).

B01, B02, . . . , B55 The acronyms B01, B02, . . . B55 are the labels that were assigned in chronological order to the 55 green British interviewees.

Bracketing framework A bracketing framework is an analytical tool for processing and reducing data in qualitative research. In this study, a bracketing framework was developed around three structural axes: the interviewees, products, and product attributes of the green product. Along these three axes, the interview data were analysed.

BUM Bundesumweltministerium (Department of the Environment).

C1 The C1 variable is one of the knowledge complexity variables. It reflects so-called X products only (freely recalled products). C1 was derived by first squaring the number of product attributes per X product, as contained in the PA matrix, and then summing up these squared numbers over all X products of the PA matrix. C1 indicates the extent to which knowledge is integrated across knowledge features such as 'products' and 'product attributes'. In particular, C1 reflects so-called horizontal knowledge complexity – the extent to which freely recalled products are networked across product attributes.

C2 The C2 variable is one of the knowledge complexity variables. It reflects only X products (freely recalled products). C2 was derived by first squaring the number of X products per product attribute, as contained in the PA matrix, and then summing up these squared numbers over all product attributes in the PA matrix. C2 indicates the extent to which knowledge is integrated across knowledge features such as 'products' and 'product attributes'. In particular, C2 reflects so-called vertical knowledge complexity – the extent to which product attributes are networked across X products.

C3 The C3 variable is one of the knowledge complexity variables. It relates to all products discussed by an interviewee (freely recalled and prompted ones). C3 was derived by first squaring the number of product attributes per product, as contained in the PA matrix, and then summing up these squared numbers over all products of the PA matrix. C3 indicates the extent to which knowledge is integrated across knowledge features such as 'products' and 'product attributes'. In particular, C3 reflects so-called horizontal knowledge complexity – the extent to which products are networked across product attributes.

C4 The C4 variable is one of the knowledge complexity variables. It relates to all products discussed by an interviewee (freely recalled and prompted ones). C4 was derived by first squaring the number of products per product attribute, as contained in the PA matrix, and then summing up these squared numbers over all product attributes in the PA matrix. C4 indicates the extent to which knowledge is integrated across knowledge features such as 'products' and 'product attributes'. In particular, C4 reflects so-called vertical knowledge complexity – the extent to which product attributes are networked across products.

C5 The C5 variable is one of the knowledge complexity variables. The C5 variable refers to all products discussed by an interviewee (freely recalled and prompted ones). What distinguished the C5 variable from the C4 variable is that the product attribute 'names' was excluded when C5 was compiled since a probing influence was exerted along this dimension by the interviewer. C5 was derived by first squaring the number of products per product attribute, as contained in the PA matrix, and then summing up these squared numbers over all product attributes – except the name attribute – in the PA matrix (freely recalled and prompted products). C5 indicates the extent to which knowledge is integrated across knowledge features such as 'products' and 'product attributes'. In particular, C5 reflects so-called vertical knowledge complexity – the extent to which product attributes are networked across products.

CA Consumer's Association.

CI analysis 'CI' is an acronym for consumer interview. The CI analysis was discussed in chapter 3. It interprets the distributional information on interview markings as they were made with the CI index and then extracted and put into charts. The CI analysis complemented the main analysis of data, which was organized through the bracketing framework (see bracketing framework).

CI index CI is an acronym for consumer interview. The CI index contained a number of search categories for which the interview data were marked. The number of such markings per search category was subsequently assessed. The search categories of the CI index reflected issues as they were relevant for an assessment of consumer knowledge. The CI index contained six broad search categories: knowledge characteristics, task considerations, buying frequency, errors, other product quality considerations, and non-cognitive issues.

Cognitive categories As a result of a cluster analysis with knowledge content variables, five so-called cognitive categories of consumers were demarcated. The five cognitive categories were labelled cognitive categories 1, 2, 3, 4 and 5 (cognitive category 1 = bottom category, cognitive category 5 = top category).

CSO Central Statistical Office.

G01, G02, . . . G36 The acronyms G01, G02, . . . G36 are the labels that were assigned in chronological order to the 36 green German interviewees.

HMN codes Different codes were used to assess actual buying frequencies of products that were discussed by an interviewee: an H code marked a high buying frequency (H = 1), an M code a medium or low buying frequency (M = 0.5), and an N code a non-buying 'frequency' (N = 0) of a certain product.

IA matrix The IA matrix was organized around interviewees and product attributes, and contained language extracts from the original interview with regard to one product only. All in all there were 39 IA matrices – as many as there were different products or product groups distinguished. The IA matrix was compiled separately for each of the three samples. Each of the IA matrices lists all interviewees vertically in chronological order. For each interviewee the product attributes are listed that this interviewee discussed with regard to one, particular product (the product for which that particular IA matrix was compiled). Product attributes were listed in the order of their occurrence during the interview. For each product attribute discussed by the interviewee, the actual wording of the description of product attributes for a certain product was attached in the IA matrix to the respective product attributes (see chapter 3).

IP matrix The IP matrix was organized around interviewees and products, and contained language extracts of the original interview with regard to one product attribute only. All in all there were 29 IP matrices – as many as there were different product attributes distinguished. The IP matrix was compiled separately for each of the three samples. Each of the IP matrices lists all interviewees vertically in chronological order. For each interviewee the products that this interviewee discussed are listed (with regard to the particular product attribute for which a certain IP matrix was compiled). Products were listed in the order of their occurrence during the interview. For each product discussed, the description of a specific product attribute was attached to the product example given.

LCA LCA is an acronym for life-cycle analysis. Life-cycle analysis is a (scientific) concept used to assess the environmental impact of a product and its related value chain activities, from sourcing, through production, to the distribution and consumption of a product, including its disposal.

LERC Landbank Environmental Research and Consulting.

N01, N02, . . . N10 The acronyms N01, N02, . . . N10 are the labels that were assigned in chronological order to the 10 non-green interviewees.

NSet 1, . . . NSet 8 NSet 1, . . . NSet 8 are acronyms for the eight variable sets, comprising knowledge content variables that were applied to the clustering of the non-green sample.

NT The NT variable reflects the total number of products discussed by an interviewee, comprising all products: X + Y + Z products (see X products, Y products, Z products).

NTA The NTA variable reflects the total number of products discussed by an interviewee that was adjusted for actual buying frequencies in line with the H, M and N codes (see HMN codes).

NX The NX variable reflects the number of freely recalled products discussed by an interviewee, i.e., the number of so-called X products (see X product).

NXA The NXA variable reflects the number of freely recalled products, adjusted for actual buying frequencies (see HMN code).

PA matrix The PA matrix is organized around products and product attributes, and contains language extracts from the original interview. It lists vertically the products that were discussed by an interviewee in the order of their occurrence during the interview. For each product discussed, the respective product attributes are listed in the order of their occurrence, as they were touched upon by the interviewee. For each product attribute, language extracts are contained in the PA matrix. Such information was extracted and put into the PA matrix on the basis of markings on the interview data. The PA matrix was subsequently further condensed.

The condensed PA matrix is organized around products and product attributes. It lists vertically the X, Y and Z products that were discussed by an interviewee in the order of their occurrence during the interviewee. The 'vertical dimension' of the PA matrix consists of the 29 product attributes that were distinguished by the bracketing framework. In the condensed PA matrix, numerical information about an interviewee's description of a product with regard to product attributes is contained. Two types of condensed PA matrices were compiled: one contained word count information (and thus provided the numerical basis for the variables W1 and W2), and one contained language-type information (and thus provided the numerical basis for the language-type variables like AS1, AS2, etc.).

PPO analysis PPO is an acronym for the position of occurrence of products in the sequence of freely recalled products. A PPO analysis was conducted for specific products. The places which certain products occupied in the product recall sequences of the British and the German interviewees were analysed. On the basis of such information, good examples of green products were classified for the British and the

German samples. For instance, for the British sample, products like detergent or washing-up liquid had very good PPO parameters. These products were frequently recalled as the first products a person thought of when asked about green shopping. For the German sample products like milk or yoghurt had very good PPO parameters.

Recall sequence Recall sequence is a technical term for the sequence of freely recalled product examples offered by an interviewee.

SB Statistisches Bundesamt (Statistical Office).

SM Super Marketing [journal].

Variable set 1, . . . variable set 9 Variable set 1, 2, . . . variable set 9 are references to the nine variable sets, comprising knowledge content variables in different combinations, that were applied to the clustering of the green samples.

W1 The W1 variable reflects word counts related to X products (freely recalled products). It reflects word counts of interview extracts as they were put into the PA matrix (product–product attributes matrix). The W1 variable is an indicator of knowledge comprehensiveness – the amount of knowledge held by a person.

W2 The W2 variable reflects word counts related to all products discussed by an interviewee (freely recalled and prompted products). It reflects only word counts related to interview extracts as they were put into the PA matrix (product–product attributes matrix). The W2 variable is an indicator of knowledge comprehensiveness – the amount of knowledge held by a person.

W3 The W3 variable reflects word counts in the first part of the interview, which was the open, free recall part. W3 reflects word counts of the actual interview data. The W3 variable is an indicator of knowledge comprehensiveness – the amount of knowledge held by a person.

W4 The W4 variable reflects word counts in the total interview. It reflects word counts of the actual interview data. The W4 variable is an indicator of knowledge comprehensiveness – the amount of knowledge held by a person.

X products X products are products that were freely recalled by an interviewee in response to an open question. There was no probing or prompting influence exerted by the interviewer.

X1 products X1 products are products that were freely recalled by an interviewee in response to an open question. There was no probing or prompting influence exerted by the interviewer. X1 products refer to product examples given by an interviewee in *direct* response to an open question asked by the interviewer.

X2 products X2 products are products that were recalled by an interviewee during a discussion of green product characteristics of an X1 product. There was no probing or prompting influence exerted by the interviewer.

Y products Y products are products that were recalled by an interviewee where there was a probing influence exerted by the interviewer. The probing influence consisted of a follow-up question that was raised by the interviewer in relation to a product attribute that had previously been freely recalled and discussed by an interviewee.

Z products Z products are prompted products that were remembered by an interviewee in response to prompting. Prompting lists of products and product attributes were applied in parts 2 and 3 of the interview.

Z1 products Z1 products are prompted products that were remembered by an interviewee in *direct* response to prompting. Prompting lists of products and product attributes were applied in parts 2 and 3 of the interview.

Z2 products Z2 products are products that were remembered by an interviewee during a discussion of a Z1 product. Prompting lists of products and product attributes were applied in parts 2 and 3 of the interview.

NOTES

1 A COGNITIVE STUDY INTO ENVIRONMENTALLY ORIENTED CONSUMPTION

1 The issues that need clarification concern *positive* scientific research, which is research that aims at the generation of knowledge about *what there is*. In positive research, a certain naturally occurring phenomenon is analysed and explained. In contrast, *normative* scientific research is concerned with the generation of knowledge about *what there should be*. It develops recommendations regarding how things should be done. Disciplines like the engineering sciences, management studies, or public policy studies have a predominantly normative orientation.

2 The causality principle is a fundamental heuristic principle that unifies scientific research. It also seems to underlie implicitly non-scientific thinking such as 'magical thought' (Lévi-Strauss 1966: 10–11). Whether alternatives to this heuristic principle can be established for scientific research is a critical question in a philosophy of science debate. This question seems to be particularly relevant for research that comes under the headings of 'qualitative', 'interpretative', or 'postmodern' research.

3 Culture is understood as 'the mechanism through which human beings interact or . . . adapt to their [social and natural] environment' (Milton 1993: Ingold 1992: 39, Lévi-Strauss 1985: 6–7, 27, 34–6).

4 Depending on how narrowly or widely one defines the concept of attitude, it can refer to both a motivational and a cognitive level (Foxall and Goldsmith 1994: 93–5, 116).

5 Pilot studies conducted reproduced such an 'attitude–behaviour gap' for environmentally oriented consumer behaviour (see Wagner 1996a: 325–6).

6 In general, the Fishbein model or Theory of Reasoned Action has been found to have a high predictive power (Cohen and Chakravarti 1990: 250). What remains possibly unsatisfactory with the Fishbein model is that it links attitudes, beliefs, behavioural intentions and actual behaviour through their respective classification of being 'issue-specific'. The idea of being issue-specific is a central feature of the Fishbein model. However, the role of general attitudes, i.e. whether and how they link with issue-specific attitudes and subsequent behaviours, and how issue-specific attitudes develop over time, remains unclear.

7 Depending on how one defines 'product', packaging can be considered as a part of a product or as a separate entity that wraps up a product.

8 Surprisingly, in some positive investigations an LCA-type characterization of green consumer behaviour was applied. Research was based on the definition that the environmentally oriented consumer is 'a person who knows that the production, distribution, use and disposal of a product leads to external costs and who evaluates such external costs negatively, trying to minimize them by his own behaviour'

(Grunert and Kristensen 1990: 3, Grunert 1992: 1). Whether and, if so, what kind of methodological considerations were behind such an importation of normatively oriented, LCA-based characterizations of the green consumer into a positive research programme was not made clear. Such an approach does not seem to be fruitful for the conduct of positive research and it is not followed in this study. Most people have only a sketchy knowledge of environmental problems; they may be sensitive to information and to product characteristics that are irrelevant from a normative perspective; and they may lack the ability to employ normative concepts, such as LCA, for the assessment of a product's environmental friendliness (Olney and Bryce 1991: 693, Bänsch 1990: 371, Payne *et al.* 1992: 90, O'Riordan 1981: 219).

9 The term 'supermarket products' is here used only as an illustration. The term is probably too narrow for the purposes of this study since it presumes that products for daily consumption are generally bought at supermarkets, which might not necessarily be the case.

2 COGNITIVE CONSUMER RESEARCH

1 Psychology may successfully develop a theory of knowledge in terms of psychological meaning but it would be likely to fail if it attempted to develop a general theory of meaning, since such an investigation is likely to lead to 'an order of things outside psychology' (Bartlett 1932: 237). And similarly other social science disciplines are likely to fail if they attempt to develop a general theory of meaning (or a general theory of human nature), thus transcending the purpose of their respective research heuristics. For a general theory of meaning, a philosophical framework is likely to be appropriate. There, it can be critically discussed whether the notion of 'meaning' itself should be given up, since this term appears to be geared towards empiricism and nominalism. Such a Wittgensteinian critique at least draws attention to a careful application of the term 'meaning'. Rather than thinking of 'meaning' as something in one's head, the idea of meaning and creating meaning can be closely related to the process of interacting with the world around oneself (see also Ryle 1990, Gardner 1987: 336–8, 353, Polanyi and Prosch 1976). Similarly, Maturana and Varela (1992: 244–8) have stressed the identity between cognition and behaviour – 'knowing is doing'.

2 Where these ends 'come from' is a motivational question which is not further researched here. Motivational issues are basically excluded from the research focus of this study, although certain motivational observations were made as a by-product of the cognitive research conducted and they are briefly commented on in the later chapters.

3 The notion of 'procedural knowledge' is here used in a different sense, e.g. that of Tulving (1983: 9, 28, 1985: 385–8), who applies the notion 'procedural knowledge' to operational modes of cognitive processing; they are discussed here under the heading of 'cognitive operations'.

4 For a distinction between taxonomic categories and goal-derived categories, see Alba *et al.* (1991: 7) and the literature discussed there.

5 The idea of holistic knowledge structures can be related to the concept of attitude (see Foxall and Goldsmith (1994: 94–5) and the literature quoted there).

6 Gregory (1990: 315–16) distinguishes another mode of cognitive processing: a third, 'hybrid' mode that falls in between bottom-up and top-down processing and which is referred to as 'algorithmic processing'. An algorithmic operational mode transcends the largely passive, perceptually oriented bottom-up mode, but it does not reach the high abstractness and complexity associated with top-down processing. An algorithmic mode is meant to provide short cuts for reasoning.

7 Locke 1991: 77, 2.12.1:

> The acts of the mind, wherein it exerts its power over its simple ideas, are chiefly these three: (1) Combining several simple ideas into one compound one; and thus all complex ideas are made. (2) The second is bringing two ideas whether simple or complex, together . . . without uniting them into one; by which way it gets all its ideas of relation. (3) The third is separating them from all other ideas that accompany them in their real existence: this is called abstraction; and thus all its general ideas are made.

8 With regard to the self-organizing properties of the mind, the traditional computer model is quite ill-suited to depict cognition: the components of a computer, such as hardware, systems software, applications software and data files, are clearly separated entities which cannot change and develop themselves over time, and relationships between components are of a fairly static nature. But in another respect, the traditional computer model is a rather good model for exploring cognition: it is a comparatively simple model that is commonly known, and it illustrates the roles of different system components, e.g. the importance of systems software for 'connecting' hardware and applications software.

9 Schema theorists like Bartlett or Rumelhart have stressed the possibility of literal knowledge content being related to schematic operational processing (see the literature quoted above). Similarly, Kant refuted only the view that all knowledge arises out of sensual, literal perceptions. Alba and Hasher's (1983) otherwise excellent review of schema theory suffers from their diagnosis that the observation of concrete, weakly abstract, episodic knowledge represents a problem for or even a contradiction of schema theory (Alba and Hasher 1983: 214–15, 219, 222). If the schema notion is not placed at the knowledge content level which is generally accepted (also by Alba and Hasher), then the observation of literal, concrete knowledge content need not pose a problem for schema theory: concrete knowledge content can be underwired by a schema – a data structure – as any other knowledge content can.

10 Festinger's (1957) theory of cognitive dissonance offers an alternative explanation of how problems related to differing cognitions are resolved by an individual, e.g. by dropping one cognition. Here, the mind is thought to play a more active role than in schema theory when it comes to explaining phenomena such as 'people tend to see what they expect to see'.

11 A 'third' learning route would be to model oneself on another person.

12 Similarly, Bernstein (1992: 48) refers to a Chinese proverb: 'I hear, I forget. I see, I remember. I do, I understand.' This proverb captures an essential piece of wisdom on cognitive development.

13 Lévi-Strauss (1966) nearly equates the notions 'engineer' and 'scientist'. A distinction between basic theoretical science with no immediate practical relevance and an engineering science that tries to apply theoretical knowledge to practical tasks is not made explicit.

14 In judgement research, the framing and constraining of a choice task is conducted by the researcher a priori, thus 'freeing' the subject from problem formulation.

15 Information availability refers to the subjectively perceived availability of information from external and from internal information sources (Spiggle and Sanders 1984: 337). Information availability that is perceived to be low can lead to extended external search and to the substitution of internal search processes. Also, cognitive operations, such as interpretation and integration, may be inhibited by a perception that the task is too difficult, e.g. due to a perceived lack of information (Alba and Hutchinson 1987: 420, 423). The concept of 'external memory', e.g. a product's packaging, illustrates a complementary relationship between external and internal search (Brucks 1986: 62, Newman 1977: 83, 93, Bettman 1979b: 30, 175, 189).

Information processability refers to the perceived ability to process a piece of information cognitively. For instance, highly technical information might be perceived by many consumers as having a low processability.

The relevance of information (or information diagnosticity) for solving a choice problem is subjectively interpreted by a consumer. Consumers devote attention to the information that is perceived to be relevant. Different people may view different pieces of information as diagnostic or salient. In a choice situation, the diagnosticity of information may be subjectively related to the ability of a piece of information to discriminate choice alternatives rather than to its 'objective' quality (Alba *et al.* 1991: 25, 29).

3 EMPIRICAL RESEARCH INTO GREEN CONSUMER BEHAVIOUR

1 Based on the distinction of a subjective and objective epistemology and ontology of research, the empirical research design of this study would qualify as a 'traditional qualitative' approach rather than as an 'interpretive' or 'postmodern' one (Brown 1995: 300–5).

2 Further methodological principles, such as *simplicity, logic* and *construct validity* that refer to the conceptual framing of a research problem have been dealt with in the previous chapters (Yin 1989: 40–1, Weick 1979: 35–6, Thorngate 1976: 406). As further meta-principles for the structuring of scientific research heuristic power, problem dependence and the analytical relevance of research can be distinguished (see chapter 1).

3 Only a small number of quantitative research projects have tried to increase their external validity through avoiding convenience samples, for instance Brucks (1991), Hoyer (1986), Kaas (1984). Due to money and time restraints, many quantitative consumer behaviour research projects have drawn on atypical sampling populations such as undergraduate students, often with a management studies or even marketing background (Wells 1993: 491). For examples of such convenience samples, see MacInnis *et al.* (1992: 261), Park *et al.* (1992: 195), Hastak and Olson (1989: 447), Johnson and Fornell (1987: 219), Alba and Marmorstein (1986: 448), Brucks (1986: 61). For certain products, e.g. trainers, a student population may be considered to be a fairly typical population which should assure a high external validity. For other products, such as those consumed daily, the student consumer may be judged as rather atypical regarding his motivational, cognitive and socio-demographic profile.

4 Besides these two options, consumer cognition can be empirically investigated through so-called 'protocol analysis' which researches presently occurring behaviour at the point of shopping. For a number of methodological reasons this research technique was not applied. Protocol analysis asks consumers to articulate, to 'think out loud', as thoughts occur during shopping. Through protocol analysis the character of a choice situation is considerably influenced. For instance, through the presence of a researcher and the articulation task a consumer is required to perform at the point of shopping, both reasoning and behaviour, as they are usually shown during a shopping trip, e.g. a supermarket visit, may be affected. Cognition and behaviour may be altered subsequently (Payne and Ragsdale 1978: 571–3, Bettman 1979b: 195, 232, Nisbett and Wilson 1977).

5 As noted above, research on motivation was basically excluded from this study.

6 The question of how to organize the empirical measurement of different variables of green consumption – either around green product examples or around green product attributes – can be related to Werner Heisenberg's Uncertainty Relation and

its trade-off implications for the empirical measurement of different aspects of a phenomenon.

7 Regarding the variable 'marital status', a status such as 'cohabiting' (living with a partner without being married) was originally not included in the demographic data sheet. The first few interviewees drew attention to such a 'deficit'. In the course of further sampling, the status 'cohabiting' was checked for by the interviewer when an interviewee indicated the marital status 'single'.

8 Ideally, assessments of over- and under-representation should be made against a typical population of shoppers buying products for daily consumption.

9 This interpretation rests on the assumption that interviewees remained in their respective first, second, third and fourth quartiles after an adjustment for actual buying frequencies had been made. For instance, it is assumed that those interviewees who previously made up the fourth quartile did not become the first quartile after an adjustment for actual buying frequencies. Hypothetically it could be possible that through the adjustment for actual buying frequencies interviewees of higher quartiles could enter lower quartiles; in an extreme case the previously fourth quartile could become the first quartile. For the first quartile this assumption was checked. For the British sample (regarding freely recalled products) it was found that eleven of the thirteen interviewees who made up the first quartile after an adjustment for actual buying had been in the first quartile previously. The two 'newcomers' had entered from the second quartile. The same check was repeated for the German sample. Here six out of nine interviewees remained within their first quartile after the adjustment. The other three had entered from the second quartile, where they previously had been at the very low end of that quartile. These checks support the assumption made: jockeying between quartiles – if it happened at all – appeared to be restricted to 'neighbouring areas'.

4 CLASSIFICATION OF CONSUMERS

1 In the case of *agglomerative* hierarchical clustering, the partitioning process starts with as many clusters as there are individual subjects in a sample, each subject representing 'one cluster'. Step by step, subjects are joined together into new clusters. The partitioning process ends when all subjects have been merged into one cluster (which is identical with the total sample). A *divisive* hierarchical cluster method works the other way round: it starts with the total sample and ends with the division of a sample into as many clusters as there are individual subjects.

2 An analysis of scattergrams through inspection is made easy by SPSS 6.1 since it labels subjects individually with 'subject numbers'. Hence, subjects can easily be identified and traced across different scattergrams.

3 However, in the case that lower dimensional plots, from 2 to n – 1 dimensions, do not reveal any group-related structure, this does not exclude the possibility that a group-related structure exists at an n-dimensional order. The absence of patterns at the level of n – 1 dimensions or lower does not allow for the conclusion that there is no group-related pattern at the level of n dimensions. To test for such a possibility, more comprehensive variable sets with a mix of variables were also subjected to a cluster analysis.

4 This reflects conventional arrangements in cluster analysis (Mitchell 1993: 15, Hair et al. 1987: 306).

5 Alternatively, outliers could first be eliminated from the sample, before sample data are subjected to a cluster analysis. But this requires a decision on what an outlier is, which is not a straightforward issue. If k is large enough, this decision problem is 'solved' by the algorithm.

6 For the German sample, G01 had to be eliminated as an outlier since it did not join the top subject G29 in a top cluster group; rather, as an outlier, G01 'claimed' its own group, thus putting the paradigmatic subjects G21 and G29 into the same group.

5 INTERPRETATION OF KNOWLEDGE STRUCTURES

1 The relationship between familiarity and knowledge structure development is examined in chapter 6 when the role of experience in problem solving is assessed.

2 The product attribute 'names' was excluded from this analysis due to the probing influence that was exerted during the interview with regard to names.

3 In Britain, milk in bottles is a similarly traditional concept that utilizes a returnable container. But British interviewees rarely connected the product 'milk' to environmental thinking.

4 Maxims related to other issues were also touched upon by interviewees, e.g. 'buy the cheapest thing' (B1) or 'animal welfare' (B4).

5 Wenben Lai (1994: 491) integrates in a holistic approach to knowledge structure research the concept of episodic knowledge with product-related knowledge under the heading of 'consumption schemata'.

6 Calculations were here made for *enlarged* cognitive categories to achieve a bigger numerical basis and to reduce outlier effects.

7 If prompted products were included in an analysis of knowledge specificity and abstractness, first the distributional patterns of the abstractness–specificity variables, then the AS5, AS6, AS7 and AS8 variables, became slightly blurred, but they were still discernible.

8 This suggestion is based on the assumption that there was an 'equal distance' between the cognitive categories. Numerical distance information from the dendrograms indicated that the bottom cognitive categories were possibly to some degree closer together than the top cognitive categories.

9 An interpretation of knowledge structure development is of a 'longitudinal' nature: such interpretations have been made here on the basis of a cross-sectional (non-longitudinal) demarcation of cognitive categories. Interpretations of knowledge structure development – here with regard to the development of processes of specification – rest on the assumption that members of the cognitive categories went through very similar processes of learning, e.g. that consumers in cognitive category 5 were, at an earlier period, comparable to consumers in cognitive categories 1 and 2. Obviously, members of the higher cognitive categories had been going through some learning processes. Since findings on knowledge structures (below a knowledge substance level) were replicated to a high degree for the British and the German samples, confidence in the existence of a shared learning process among the cognitive categories increased. Also, members of the higher cognitive categories tended to reflect sometimes on their previous less green approach to consumption; such 'historic' reflections seemed to compare with views voiced by the lower cognitive categories (see, for instance, chapter 6 and the comments of G36 reported there).

10 Like counter-argumentative knowledge, a knowledge of behavioural trade-offs among different types of ethical consumption behaviours reflects complex inferential reasoning. G5 was the only interviewee who touched upon such trade-offs: an ethical trade-off between environmental shopping considerations, e.g. buying locally produced goods, and fair trade considerations, e.g. supporting Third World countries, was discussed. Other trade-offs, namely between green considerations and certain product quality considerations, such as effectiveness or price, were more frequently discussed (see below, pp. 184–7).

11 These differences in how consumers in the respective cognitive categories interpreted green products would have implications for a communications strategy. When it comes to message design, the lower cognitive categories are likely to be in need of a simple message that can be easily interpreted and does not require complicated inferential reasoning, whereas the higher cognitive categories might confront a simple green message with sophisticated, argumentative and counter-argumentative knowledge. They are unlikely to be satisfied by a simple message. This indicates a certain dilemma for communications management which might have to deal with satisfying rather different information needs of green consumers (if information needs of certain groups are not ignored).

12 Since the top-ranking products in terms of their PPO had had relative frequencies of over 80 per cent for the British and the German samples, no separate calculation of PPOs for cognitive categories 1–5 appeared necessary in order to arrive at a yard-stick of what good examples are. Only the first two products recalled were examined since good examples can be expected to show up most prominently at the beginning of recall sequences (see chapter 3).

13 Zeithaml (1991: 33) pointed out that one or a few product attributes might be used by a person as a signal of high product quality. Such a suggestion can be related to the role of a knowledge of good examples (and schematic knowledge prototypicality as it is discussed below).

14 Again, the product attribute 'names' was excluded from an assessment of good examples of product attributes because of the probing influence that was exerted by the interviewer regarding names.

15 Such a finding seems to reflect that people with unconventional life-styles and environmentalist activists were in the British sample. While such interviewees were committed to certain behaviours related to environmental causes, e.g. campaigning, they did not always qualify as members of the higher cognitive categories when it came to consumption behaviour. However, they tended to have access to certain 'specialist' communication sources on green consumption, such as pressure group contacts or pressure group literature (and this was reported in the interview).

16 Nothing can be said about sequential and prototypical aspects of the order of recall of non-green interviewees since they were prompted, and hence the order and type of products that were discussed by them were pre-determined.

6 EXPERIENCE AND LEARNING: PROBLEM SOLVING BEHAVIOUR OF THE GREEN CUSTOMER

1 The calculations are based on the formula $(NTA/NT \times 100) - 100$ [expressed in %].

2 Information on the length of time for which an interviewee had been involved in green shopping was collected at the end of part 1 of the interview. Questions put to the interviewee with regard to the time spent on green shopping were frequently answered in a non-numerical way, e.g. 'some years', which rendered the analysis of this information difficult. In a couple of cases this information could not be collected at all. For an assessment of non-numerical, verbal quantifiers, see Wright et al. (1994: 489, 492–4).

3 Such a transfer of behavioural routines from one domain to another could be related to the cognitive concept of 'scripts', which is related to the schema concept. Scripts are understood as 'action schemata' (see, for instance, Wenben Lai 1994).

4 Similarly, Hull et al. (1988: 18) found that persons who were asked in an experiment to wire plugs ignored the recommended length of cables.

5 It could be suggested that the product-oriented research method applied in this study failed G14. This is true in so far as G14 would have ranked quite high if knowledge

had been 'measured' in a product attribute-oriented way *and* independent of actual behaviour. But this would have been a rather different research project. When it came to product-related actual shopping behaviour, a wide and quasi-scientific LCA-type knowledge did not help G14 to put LCA considerations into practice.

6 Elliott (forthcoming) discusses consumer behaviour which does not aim at the satisfaction of physical, material needs as 'consumption of illusions' and points out that a too rational understanding of consumption illusions may feed back negatively on consumer behaviour.

7 The product attribute 'home made' showed up strongly for the top cognitive categories of the German sample, in general.

7 THE BEGINNING OF KNOWLEDGE

1 Such an ability is likely to relate to a neurological, physiological level of the mind which could not be further examined here.

2 For an interpretation of green products as symbols of social reassurance, see Myburgh-Louw and O'Shaughnessy (1993–4).

BIBLIOGRAPHY

Abelson, R. P. (1976), 'Script Processing in Attitude Formation and Decision Making', in J. S. Carroll and J. W. Payne (eds) *Cognition and Social Behavior*, New York: Lawrence Erlbaum, 33–45.

Abelson, R. P. and Black, J. B. (1986), 'Introduction', in J. A. Galambos, R. P. Abelson and J. B. Black (eds) *Knowledge Structures*, Hillsdale, N.J.: Lawrence Erlbaum, 1–18.

Ackroyd, S. and Hughes, J. (1992), *Data Collection in Context*, London: Longman.

Adams, R. (1990), 'The Greening of Consumerism', *Accountancy* 105, 1162: 81–3.

Ajzen, I. and Fishbein, M. (1980), *Understanding Attitudes and Predicting Social Behavior*, Englewood-Cliffs, N.J.: Prentice-Hall.

Alba, J. W. and Hasher, L. (1983), 'Is Memory Schematic?', *Psychological Bulletin* 93: 203–31.

Alba, J. W. and Hutchinson, J. W. (1987), 'Dimensions of Consumer Expertise', *Journal of Consumer Research* 13, 4: 411–54.

Alba, J. W. and Marmorstein, H. (1986), 'Frequency Information as a Dimension of Consumer Knowledge', in R. J. Lutz (ed.) *Advances in Consumer Research* 13, Provo, Utah: Association for Consumer Research, 446–9.

Alba, J. W., Hutchinson, J. W. and Lynch, J. G. Jr (1991), 'Memory and Decision Making', in H. H. Kassarjian and T. S. Robertson (eds) *Handbook of Consumer Behavior*, Englewood-Cliffs, N.J.: Prentice-Hall, 1–49.

Anderson, J. R. (1976), *Language, Memory, and Thought*, Hillsdale, N.J.: Lawrence Erlbaum Associates.

Anderson, R. C. (1977), 'The Notion of Schemata and the Educational Enterprise: General Discussion of the Conference', in R. C. Anderson, R. J. Spiro and W. E. Montague (eds) *Schooling and the Acquisition of Knowledge*, Hillsdale, N.J.: Lawrence Erlbaum Associates, 415–31.

Antil, J. H. (1984), 'Conceptualization and Operationalization of Involvement', in T. C. Kinnear (ed.) *Advances in Consumer Research* 11, Provo, Utah: Association for Consumer Research, 203–9.

Arabie, L. J. and Hubert, P. (1996), 'An Overview of Combinational Data Analysis', in L. J. Arabie, P. Hubert and G. De Soete (eds) *Clustering and Classification*, Singapore: World Scientific, 5–63.

Bänsch, A. (1990), 'Marketingfolgerungen aus Gründen für den Nichtkauf umweltfreundlicher Konsumgüter', *GfK Jahrbuch der Absatz- und Verbrauchsforschung* 4: 360–79.

Barabba, V. and Zaltman, G. (1991), *Hearing the Voice of the Market: Competitive Advantage through Creative Use of Market Information*, Boston, Mass.: Harvard Business School Press.

Barber, P. (1988), *Applied Cognitive Psychology*, London: Routledge.

Bartlett, F. C. (1932), *Remembering: A Study in Experiential and Social Psychology*, Cambridge: Cambridge University Press.

BBC2 (1994), *One Small Step – Man on the Moon*, 30 July 1994, 9:30–10:30 p.m.

Becker, G. S. (1976), *The Economic Approach to Human Behavior*, London: University of Chicago Press.

Belck, M. A. (1979), 'Identifying the Socially and Ecologically Concerned Segment through Life-style Research: Initial Findings', in K. E. Henion and T. C. Kinnear (eds) *The Conserver Society*, Chicago: American Marketing Association, 69–81.

Berne, E. (1974), *What Do You Say After You Say Hello?*, London: Transworld.

Bernstein, D. (1992), *In the Company of Green: Corporate Communications for the New Environment*, London: ISBA.

Berry, J. W. and Irvine, S. H. (1986), 'Bricolage: Savages Do It Daily', in R. J. Sternberg and R. K. Wagner (eds) *Practical Intelligence. Nature and Origin of Competence in the Everyday World*, Cambridge: Cambridge University Press, 271–306.

Bettman, J. R. (1979a), 'Memory Factors in Consumer Choice: A Review', *Journal of Marketing* 43, 37–53.

—— (1979b), *An Information Processing Theory of Consumer Choice*, Reading, Mass.: Addison-Wesley.

—— (1986), 'Consumer Psychology', in M. R. Rosenzweig and L. W. Porter (eds) *Annual Review of Psychology* 37, Palo Alto, Calif.: Annual Reviews, 257–289.

Bettman, J. R. and Park, C. W. (1980), 'Effects of Prior Knowledge and Experience and Phase of the Choice Process on Consumer Decision Making: A Protocol Analysis', *Journal of Consumer Research* 7, 3, 234–47.

Bettman, J. R., Johnson, E. J. and Payne, J. W. (1991), 'Consumer Decision Making', in H. H. Kassarjian and T. S. Robertson (eds) *Handbook of Consumer Behavior*, Englewood-Cliffs, N.J.: Prentice-Hall, 50–84.

Bettman, J. R., Roedder John, D. and Scott, C. A. (1984), 'Consumers' Assessment of Covariation', in T. C. Kinnear (ed.) *Advances in Consumer Research* 11, Provo, Utah: Association for Consumer Research, 466–71.

Bhaskar, R. (1979), *The Possibility of Naturalism: A Philosophical Critique of the Contemporary Human Sciences*, Brighton: Harvester.

Billig, A. (1994), *Ermittlungen des ökologischen Problembewußtseins der Bevölkerung* 7/94, UBA-FB 93-137, Bonn: BUM.

Bogdan, R. and Taylor, S. J. (1975), *Introduction to Qualitative Research Methods*, New York: J. Wiley.

Bransford, J. D., McCarrell, N. S., Franks, J. J. and Nitsch, K. E. (1977), 'Toward Unexplaining Memory', in R. Shaw and J. D. Bransford (eds) *Perceiving, Acting, and Knowing. Toward Ecological Psychology*, Hillsdale, N.J.: Lawrence Erlbaum Associates, 431–66.

Brewer, W. F. and Treyens, J. C. (1981), 'Role of Schemata in Memory for Places', *Cognitive Psychology* 13, 2: 207–30.

Brown, S. (1995), 'Postmodern Marketing Research: No Representation without Taxation', *Journal of the Market Research Society* 37, 3: 287–310.

Brown, T. J. (1992), 'Schemata in Consumer Research: A Connectionist Approach', in J. F. Sherry and B. Sternthal (eds) *Advances in Consumer Research* 19, Ann Arbor, Mich.: Association for Consumer Research, 787–94.

Brucks, M. (1986), 'A Typology of Consumer Knowledge Content', in R. J. Lutz (ed.) *Advances in Consumer Research* 13, Provo, Utah: Association for Consumer Research, 58–63.

—— (1991), 'The Effects of Product Class Knowledge on Information Search Behavior', in H. H. Kassarjian and T. S. Robertson (eds) *Perspectives in Consumer Behavior*, Englewood-Cliffs, N.J.: Prentice-Hall, 54–74.

Bruner, J. (1979), 'Psychology and the Image of Man', in H. Harris (ed.) *Scientific Models and Man*, Oxford: Clarendon Press, 26–43.

Bryce, D. (1985), 'The How and Why of Ecological Memory', *Journal of Experimental Psychology: General* 114, 1: 78–90.

BUM (1993), *Umweltpolitik. Konferenz der Vereinten Nationen für Umwelt und Entwicklung im Juni 1992 in Rio de Janeiro. Dokumente. Agenda 21*, Bonn: Köllen.

Burnkrant, R. E. (1978), 'Cue Utilization in Product Perception', in H. K. Hunt (ed.) *Advances in Consumer Research* 5, Ann Arbor, Mich.: Association for Consumer Research, 724–9.

Burrell, G. and Morgan, G. (1979), *Sociological Paradigms and Organisational Analysis*, London: Heinemann.

CA (1989), 'Going Green', *Which?*, September, 430–3.

—— (1990), 'Green Labelling', *Which?*, January, 10–12.

—— (1995), 'Lookalike Products', *Which?*, March, 31, 32.

Cacioppo, J. T. and Petty, R. E. (1984), 'The Elaboration Likelihood Model of Persuasion', in T. C. Kenniar (ed.) *Advances in Consumer Research* 11, Provo, Utah: Association for Consumer Research, 673–5.

Campbell, C. (1989), *The Romantic Ethic and the Spirit of Modern Consumerism*, New York: Blackwell.

Campbell, D. and Stanley, J. C. (1966), *Experimental and Quasi-Experimental Designs for Research*, Chicago, Ill.: Rand McNally.

Cassel, L. von (1895), *Sonja Kovalevsky*, London.

Cazeneuve, J. (1972), *Lucien Levy-Bruhl*, Oxford: Blackwell.

Chaiken, S. (1980), 'Heuristic versus Systematic Information Processing and the Use of Source versus Message Cues in Persuasion', *Journal of Personality and Social Psychology* 39, 5: 752–66.

Clifton, R. and Buss, N. (1992), 'Greener Communications', in M. Charter (ed.) *Greener Marketing*, Sheffield: Greenleaf Publishing, 241–53.

Coddington, W. (1993), *Environmental Marketing*, New York: McGraw-Hill.

Cohen, G. (1989), *Memory in the Real World*, London: Lawrence Erlbaum Associates.

Cohen, J. B. (1984), 'Does the Emperor Ride Again?', in T. C. Kinnear (ed.) *Advances in Consumer Research* 11, Provo, Utah: Association for Consumer Research, 367–8.

Cohen, J. B. and Chakravarti, D. (1990), 'Consumer Psychology', in M. R. Rosenzweig and L. W. Porter (eds) *Annual Review of Psychology* 41, Palo Alto, Calif.: Annual Reviews, 243–88.

Cook, T. D. and Campbell, D. T. (1979), *Quasi-Experimentation. Design and Analysis Issues for Field Settings*, Chicago: Rand McNally.

Coolican, H. (1990), *Research Methods and Statistics in Psychology*, London: Hodder & Stoughton.

Cope, D. and Winward, J. (1991), 'Information Failures in Green Consumerism', *Consumer Policy Review* 1, 2: 83–6.

Costley, C. L. (1986), 'Related Theories of Complexity in Information Processing', in R. J. Lutz (ed.) *Advances in Consumer Research* 13, Provo, Utah: Association for Consumer Research, 18–22.

Crabtree, B. and Miller, W. (1992), *Doing Qualitative Research*, Newbury Park, Calif.: Sage.

Craik, F. J. and Lockhart, R. S. (1972), 'Levels of Processing: A Framework for Memory Research', *Journal of Verbal Learning and Verbal Behavior* 11, 671–84.

Crano, W. D. (1981), 'Triangulation and Cross-Cultural Research', in M. B. Brewer and B. E. Collins (eds) *Scientific Inquiry and the Social Sciences*, San Francisco, Calif.: Jossey-Bass, 317–44.

Creswell, J. W. (1994), *Research Design. Qualitative and Quantitative Approaches*, London: Sage.

Crocker, J. B. (1984), 'A Schematic Approach to Changing Consumer Beliefs', in T. C. Kenniar (ed.) *Advances in Consumer Research* 11, Provo, Utah: Association for Consumer Research, 472–7.

CSO (1993), *Annual Abstract of Statistics 1993*, London: HMSO.

Dadd, D. L. and Carothers, A. (1990), 'A Bill of Goods', *GreenPeace* 15, 3: 8–12.

Dahrendorf, R. (1973), *Homo Sociologicus*, London: Routledge & Kegan Paul.

D'Amour, G. (1976), 'Research Programs, Rationality, and Ethics', in R. S. Cohen, P. S. Feyerabend and M. W. Wartofsky (eds) *Essays in Memory of Imre Lakatos*, Dordrecht: D. Reidel, 87–98.

Dasgupta, S. (1991), *Design Theory and Computer Science*, Cambridge: Cambridge University Press.

Day, E. and Castleberry, S. B. (1986), 'Defining and Evaluating Quality', in R. J. Lutz (ed.) *Advances in Consumer Research* 13, Provo, Utah: Association for Consumer Research, 94–8.

Derbaix, C. and Abeele, P. V. (1985), 'Consumer Inferences and Consumer Preferences. The Status of Cognition and Consciousness in Consumer Behaviour Theory', *International Journal of Research in Marketing* 2, 3: 157–74.

Diggins, J. P. (1978), *The Bard of Savagery: Thorstein Veblen and Modern Social Theory*, Hassocks: Harvester.

Douglas, M. and Isherwood, B. (1980), *The World of Goods*, Harmondsworth: Penguin.

Duncan, C. P. and Olshavsky, R. W. (1982), 'External Search: The Role of Consumer Beliefs', *Journal of Marketing Research* 19, 1: 32–43.

Eden, S. (1994-5), 'Business, Trust and Environmental Information: Perceptions from Consumers and Retailers', *Business Strategy and the Environment* 3, 4: 1–8.

Eisenhardt, K. M. (1989a), 'Building Theories from Case Study Research', *Academy of Management Review* 14, 4: 532–50.

—— (1989b), 'Making Fast Strategic Decisions in High-Velocity Environments', *Academy of Management Journal* 32, 3: 543–76.

Elliot, K. M. and Roach, D. W. (1991), 'Are Consumers Evaluating Your Products the Way You Think and Hope They Are?', *Journal of Consumer Marketing* 8, 2: 5–14.

Elliott, R. (forthcoming), 'Existential Consumption and Irrational Desire', *European Journal of Marketing*.

ENDS (1994), 'Public Concern for the Environment', *ENDS Report* 232, 18–20.

Engel, J. F., Blackwell, R. D. and Miniard, P. W. (1990), *Consumer Behavior*, Chicago: Dryden.

Ericsson, K. A. and Oliver, W. L. (1995), 'Cognitive Skills', in N. J. Mackintosh and A. M. Colman (eds) *Learning and Skills*, London: Longman, 37–55.

Everitt, B. S. (1974), *Cluster Analysis*, London: Halsted.

—— (1993), *Cluster Analysis*, London: Edward Arnold.

Eysenck, M. W. (1986), *A Handbook of Cognitive Psychology*, London: Lawrence Erlbaum Associates.

Festinger, L. (1957), *A Theory of Cognitive Dissonance*, Stanford, Calif.: Stanford University Press.

Feyerabend, P. (1993), *Against Method*, London: Verso.

Fishbein, M. and Ajzen, I. (1975), *Belief, Attitude, Intention, and Behavior: An Introduction to Theory and Research*, Reading, Mass.: Addison-Wesley.

—— (1976), 'Misconceptions about the Fishbein Model: Reflections on a Study by Songer-Nocks', *Journal of Experimental Social Psychology* 12, 579–84.

Fletcher, K. (1988), 'An Investigation into the Nature of Problem Recognition and Deliberation in Buyer Behavior', *European Journal of Marketing* 22, 5: 58–66.

Ford, G. T. and Smith R. A. (1987), 'Inferential Beliefs in Consumer Evaluations: An Assessment of Alternative Processing Strategies', *Journal of Consumer Research* 14, 3: 363–71.

Foxall, G. R. (1993), 'Consumer Behaviour as an Evolutionary Process', *European Journal of Marketing* 27, 8: 46–57.

Foxall, G. R. and Goldsmith, R. E. (1994), *Consumer Psychology for Marketing*, London: Routledge.

Frankfort-Nachmias, C. and Nachmias, D. (1996), *Research Methods in the Social Sciences*, London: Arnold.

Friedman, M. (1966), *Essays in Positive Economics*, Chicago, Ill.: University of Chicago Press.

Friedman, R. and Lessig, V. P. (1986), 'A Framework of Psychological Meaning of Products', in R. J. Lutz (ed.) *Advances in Consumer Research* 13, Provo, Utah: Association for Consumer Research, 338–42.

Frost, F. A. and Mensik, S. (1991), 'Balancing Mineral Development and Environmental Protection', *Long Range Planning* 24, 4: 58–73.

Fuller, S. (1993), *Philosophy, Rhetoric, and the End of Knowledge*, Madison, Wis.: University of Wisconsin Press.

Fullerton, R. A. (1990), 'The Art of Marketing Research: Selections from Paul F. Lazarsfeld's 'Shoe Buying in Zurich' (1933)', *Journal of the Academy of Marketing Science* 18, 4: 319–27.

Gardner, H. (1987), *The Mind's New Science. A History of the Cognitive Revolution*, paperback edition, New York: Basic Books.

Glaser, B. G. and Strauss, A. L. (1967), *The Discovery of Grounded Theory: Strategies for Qualitative Research*, New York: Aldine.

Gloria, T., Saad, T., Breville, M. and O'Connell, M. (1995), 'Life-Cycle Assessement: A Survey of Current Implementation', *Total Quality Environmental Management* 4, 1: 33–50.

Goodman, N. (1990), 'Pictures in the Mind?', in H. Barlow, C. Blakemore and M. Weston-Smith (eds) *Images and Understanding*, Cambridge: Cambridge University Press, 358–64.

Gordon, A. D. (1996), 'Hierarchical Classification', in L. J. Arabie, P. Hubert and G. De Soete (eds) *Clustering and Classification*, Singapore: World Scientific, 65–121.

Gordon, R. A. and Howell, J. E. (1959), *Higher Education for Business*, New York: Columbia University Press.

Gordon, W. and Valentine, V. (1996), 'Buying the Brand at Point of Choice', *Journal of Brand Management* 4, 1: 35–44.

Grafton-Small, R. (1987), 'Marketing, or the Anthropology of Consumption', *European Journal of Marketing* 21, 9: 66–71.

—— (1993), 'Consumption and Significance: Everyday Life in a Brand-New Second-Hand Bow Tie', *European Journal of Marketing* 27, 8: 38–45.

Grandy, R. E. (1992), 'Theories of Theories: A View from Cognitive Science', in J. Earman (ed.) *Inference, Explanation, and Other Frustrations. Essays in the Philosophy of Science*, Berkeley, Calif.: University of California Press.

Gray, R. H. (1990), *The Greening of Accountancy: The Profession after Pearce*, London: Certified Accountants Publication.

Gregory, R. L. (1980), 'Perceptions as Hypotheses', *Philosophical Transactions of the Royal Society of London, Series B* 290, 1038: 181–97.

—— (1990), 'How Do We Interpret Images?', in H. Barlow, C. Blakemore, and M. Weston-Smith (eds) *Images and Understanding*, Cambridge: Cambridge University Press, 310–30.

Gross, G. (1974), 'Unnatural Selection', in N. Armistead (ed.) *Reconstructing Social Psychology*, Harmondsworth: Penguin, 42–52.

Grunert, K. G. (1988), 'Research in Consumer Behaviour: Beyond Attitudes and Decision-Making', *European Research*, August: 172–83.

Grunert, S. C. (1992), 'Everybody Seems Concerned about the Environment: But Is This Concern Reflected in (Danish) Consumers' Food Choice?', Working Paper, June, Aarhus: Department of Information Science/Aarhus School of Business.

Grunert, S. C. and Kristensen, K. (1990), 'Factors Influencing Consumers' Demand for Organically Produced Food: Theoretical Notes and Project Outline', Working Paper, November, Aarhus: Department of Information Science/Aarhus School of Business.

Gutman, H. (1976), *Work, Culture, and Society in Industrializing America*, New York: Alfred A. Knopf.

Gutman, J. and Alden, S. D. (1985), 'Adolescents' Cognitive Structures of Retail Stores and Fashion Comprehension: A Means–End Chain Analysis of Quality', in J. Jacoby and J. C. Olson (eds) *Perceived Quality. How Consumers View Stores and Merchandise*, Lexington, Mass.: Gower, 99–114.

Haeckel, S. H. (1987), Presentation to the Information Planning Steering Group, October, Cambridge, Mass.: Marketing Science Institute.

Hair, J. F. Jr, Anderson, R. E. and Tatham, R. L. (1987), *Multivariate Data Analysis. With Readings*, New York: Macmillan.

Haley, R. I. (1968), 'Benefit Segmentation: A Decision Oriented Research Tool', *Journal of Marketing* 32, July: 30–5.

Harre, R. (1974), 'Blueprint for a New Science', in N. Armistead (ed.) *Reconstructing Social Psychology*, Harmondsworth: Penguin, 240–59.

—— (1981), 'The Positivist-Empiricist Approach and Its Alternative', in P. Reason and J. Rowan (eds) *Human Inquiry: A Sourcebook of New Paradigm Research*, Chichester: J. Wiley, 3–17.

Harris, P. (1986), *Designing and Reporting Experiments*, Milton Keynes: Open University Press.

Hastak, M. and Olson, J. C. (1989), 'Assessing the Role of Brand-Related Cognitive Responses as Mediators of Consumers' Responses to Advertising', *Journal of Consumer Research* 15, 4: 444–56.

Hastie, R. (1981), 'Schematic Principles in Human Memory', in E. T. Higgins, C. P. Herman, and M. P. Zanna (eds) *Social Cognition: The Ontario Symposium* 1, Hillsdale, N.J.: Lawrence Erlbaum Associates, 39–88.

Hawes, C. and Murphy, O. (1989), 'Green Issues – Evolution to Revolution', *Conference Paper No. 3*, Market Research Society, 65–81.

Haydock, R., Nichols, P. and Kirkpatrick, N. (1993), *Life Cycle Assessment*, Leatherhead: Pira International.

Head, H. (1920), *Studies in Neurology*, London: Hodder & Stoughton.

Herrmann, D. and Gruneberg, M. (1993), 'The Need to Expand the Horizons of the Practical Aspects of Memory Movement', *Applied Cognitive Psychology* 7, 7: 553–65.

Hirschman, E. C. (1986), 'The Creation of Product Symbolism', in R. J. Lutz (ed.) *Advances in Consumer Research* 13, Provo, Utah: Association for Consumer Research, 327–31.

—— (1993), 'Ideology in Consumer Research, 1980 and 1990: A Marxist and Feminist Critique', *Journal of Consumer Research* 19, 4: 537–55.

Hoch, S. J. (1984), 'Hypothesis Testing and Consumer Behavior: "If it works, don't mess with it"', in T. C. Kinnear (ed.) *Advances in Consumer Research* 11, Provo, Utah: Association for Consumer Research, 478–83.

Hoch, S. J. and Deighton, J. (1989), 'Managing What Consumers Learn from Experience', *Journal of Marketing* 53, 2: 1–20.

Holbrook, M. B. (1987), 'What Is Consumer Research?', *Journal of Consumer Research* 14, 128–31.

Holsti, O. R. (1968), 'Content Analysis', in G. Lindzey and E. Aronson (eds) *The Handbook of Social Psychology: Vol. 2. Research Methods*, Reading, Mass.: Addison-Wesley, 596–692.

269

—— (1994), 'Homo Oeconomicus und Dilemmastrukturen', Working Paper, Ingolstadt: Katholische Universität Eichstätt zu Ingolstadt.

Homann, K. (1988), 'Philosophie und Ökonomik, Bemerkungen zur Interdiziplinarität', *Jahrbuch für Neue Politische Ökonomie* 7, 99–127.

—— (1994), 'Homo oeconomicus und Dilemmastrukturen', in H. Sautter (ed.) *Wirtschaftspolitik in offenen Volkswirtschaften. Festschrift für Helmut Hesse zum 60. Geburtstag*, Göttingen: Vandenhoeck & Ruprecht, 387–411.

Horgan, J. (1996), *The End of Science: Facing the Limits of Knowledge in the Twilight of the Scientific Age*, Reading, Mass.: Addison-Wesley.

Hoyer, W. D. (1986), 'Variations in Choice Strategies across Decision Contexts: An Examination of Contingent Factors', in R. J. Lutz (ed.) *Advances in Consumer Research* 13, Provo, Utah: Association for Consumer Research, 32–6.

Hull, A., Wilkins, A. and Baddeley, A. (1988), 'Cognitive Psychology and the Wiring of Plugs', in M. M. Gruneberg, P. E. Morris and R. N. Sykes (eds) *Practical Aspects of Memory: Current Research and Issues*, Chichester: J. Wiley, 514–18.

Hume, S. (1991), 'Green Marketing: Green Doubletalk Makes Consumers Wary', *Advertising Age* 62, 461: GR4.

Hunt, S. D. (1991), *Modern Marketing Theory*, Cincinnati: South-Western.

Husserl, E. (1950), *Die Idee der Phänomenologie*, W. Biemel (ed.), The Hague: M. Nijhoff.

—— (1952), *Ideen zu einer reinen Phänomenologie und phänomenologischen Philosphie*, M. Biemel (ed.), The Hague: M. Nijhoff.

—— (1954), *Die Krisis der europäischen Wissenschaften und die transzendentale Phänomenologie*, W. Biemel (ed.), The Hague: M. Nijhoff.

Hutchinson, C. (1992a), 'Corporate Strategy and the Environment', *Long Range Planning* 25, 4: 9–21.

—— (1992b), 'Environmental Issues: The Challenge for the Chief Executive', *Long Range Planning* 25, 3: 50–9.

Ingold, T. (1992), 'Culture and the Perception of the Environment', in E. Croll and D. Parkin (eds) *Bush Base: Forest Farm – Culture, Environment and Development*, London: Routledge.

Isen, A. M. (1984), 'Toward Understanding the Role of Affect in Cognition', in R. S. Wyer and T. K. Srull (eds) *Handbook of Social Cognition* 3, Hillsdale, N.J.: Lawrence Erlbaum Associates, 179–236.

Jacobs, E. and Worcester, R. (1991), *Typically British?*, London: Bloomsbury.

Jacoby, J. (1976a), 'Consumer Research: Telling It Like It Is', in B. B. Anderson (ed.) *Advances in Consumer Research* 3, Ann Arbor, Mich.: Association for Consumer Research, 1–11.

—— (1976b), 'Consumer Psychology: An Octennium', in M. R. Rosenzweig and L. W. Porter (eds) *Annual Review of Psychology* 41, Palo Alto, Calif.: Annual Reviews, 331–58.

—— (1978), 'Consumer Behavior Research', *Journal of Marketing* 42, 2: 87–96.

Jacoby, J. and Kyner, D. B. (1973), 'Brand Loyalty vs. Repeat Purchase Behavior', *Journal of Marketing Research* 10, February: 1–9.

Jacoby, J., Troutman, T., Kuss, A. and Mazursky, D. (1986), 'Experience and Expertise in Complex Decision Making', in R. J. Lutz (ed.) *Advances in Consumer Research* 13, Provo, Utah: Association for Consumer Research, 469–72.

Janis, I. L. (1983), 'Groupthink', in J. R. Hackman, E.E. Lawler III and L. W. Porter (eds) *Perspectives on Behavior in Organizations*, New York: McGraw-Hill, 378–84.

Jenkins, J. J. (1977), 'Remember That Old Theory of Memory? Well, Forget It!', in R. Shaw, Robert and J. D. Bransford (eds) *Perceiving, Acting, and Knowing. Toward Ecological Psychology*, Hillsdale, N.J.: Lawrence Erlbaum Associates, 423–9.

Jick, T. (1979), 'Mixing Qualitative and Quantitative Methods: Triangulation in Action', *Administrative Science Quarterly* 24, 4: 602–11.

Johnson, E. J. and Russo, J. E. (1984), 'Product Familiarity and Learning New Information', *Journal of Consumer Research* 11, 1: 542–50.

Johnson, M. D. and Fornell, C. (1987), 'The Nature and the Methodological Implications of the Cognitive Representations of Products', *Journal of Consumer Research* 14, 2: 214–28.

Johnson, M. D., Lehmann, D. R., Fornell, C. and Horne, D. R. (1992), 'Attribute Abstraction, Feature-Dimensionality, and the Scaling of Product Similarities', *International Journal of Research in Marketing* 9, 2: 131–47.

Kaas, K. P. (1984), 'Factors Influencing Consumer Strategies in Information Processing', in T. C. Kinnear (ed.) *Advances in Consumer Research* 11, Provo, Utah: Association for Consumer Research, 585–90.

Kant, I. (1990), *The Critique of Pure Reason*, J. M. Adler (ed.), New York: Encyclopaedia Britannica.

Kardes, F. R. and Strahle, W. (1986), 'Positivity and Negativity Effects in Inferences about Products', in R. J. Lutz (ed.) *Advances in Consumer Research* 13, Provo, Utah: Association for Consumer Research, 23–6.

Kaufman, L. and Rousseeuw, P. J. (1990), *Finding Groups in Data. An Introduction to Cluster Analysis*, New York: J. Wiley.

Keating, M. (1993), *Erdgipfel 1992. Agenda für eine nachhaltige Entwicklung. Eine allgemein verständliche Fassung der Agenda 21 und der anderen Abkommen von Rio*, Geneva: Centre for Our Common Future.

Kidder, L. (1981a), *Research Method in Social Relations*, New York: Holt, Rinehart & Winston.

—— (1981b), 'Qualitative Research and Quasi-Experimental Frameworks', in M. B. Brewer and B. E. Collins (eds) *Scientific Inquiry and Social Sciences*, San Francisco, Calif.: Jossey-Bass, 226–56.

Kinnear, T. C., Taylor, J. R. and Sadrudin, A. A. (1972), 'Socioeconomic and Personality Characteristics as They Relate to Ecologically-Constructive Purchasing Behavior', in M. Venkatesan (ed.) *Proceedings of the Third Annual Conference of the Association for Consumer Research*, Chicago, Ill.: Association for Consumer Research, 34–60.

Kirkpatrick, N. (1994), *Life Cycle Assessment (LCA) – A Tool for Managing Environmental Performance*, Leatherhead: Pira International.

Kotler, P. (1988), *Marketing Management. Analysis, Planning, Implementation, and Control*, Englewood-Cliffs, N.J.: Prentice-Hall.

Küffner, G. (1994), 'Einweg oder Mehrweg. Was Ökobilanzen leisten.', *Frankfurter Allgemeine Zeitung*, 20 September 1994: 7.

Kuhn, T. S. (1996), *The Structure of Scientific Revolutions*, London: University of Chicago Press.

Lakatos, I. (1970), 'Falsification and the Methodology of Scientific Research Programmes', in I. Lakatos and A. Musgrave (eds) *Criticism and the Growth of Knowledge*, Cambridge: Cambridge University Press, 91–196.

—— (1976), *Proofs and Refutations*, in J. Worrall and E. Zahar (eds), Cambridge: Cambridge University Press.

—— (1978), *The Methodology of Scientific Research Programmes* 1, J. Worrall and G. Currie (eds), Cambridge: Cambridge University Press.

Langlois, R. N. (1990), 'Bounded Rationality and Behavioralism: A Clarification and Critique', *Journal of Theoretical and Institutional Economics* 146, 691–5.

LaPiere, R. T. (1934), 'Attitudes vs. Actions', *Social Forces* 13, 230–7.

Laudan, R., Laudan L. and Donovan A. (1992), 'Testing Theories of Scientific Change', in A. Donovan, L. Laudan and R. Laudan (eds) *Scrutinizing Science*, London: Johns Hopkins University Press, 3–44.

Lazarsfeld, P. F. (1933), 'Schuhkauf in Zuerich. Eine Probeerhebung der Wirtschaftspsychologischen Forschungsstelle', research paper, University of Vienna.

—— (1935), 'The Art of Asking Why in Marketing Research', *National Marketing Review*, 1: 32–43.

Leigh, J. H. and Gabel, T. G. (1992), 'Symbolic Interactionism: Its Effect on Consumer Behavior and Implications for Marketing Strategy', *Journal of Consumer Marketing* 9, 1: 27–38.

LERC (1994), *The Phosphate Report*, London: Landbank Environmental Research & Consulting.

Lévi-Strauss, C. (1963), *Structural Anthropology*, New York: Basic Books.

—— (1966), *The Savage Mind*, London: Weidenfeld & Nicolson.

—— (1985), *The View From Afar*, Harmondsworth: Penguin.

Levitt, T. (1980), 'Marketing Success through Differentiation of Anything', *Harvard Business Review* 58, 1: 83–91.

—— (1981), 'Marketing Intangible Products and Product Intangibles', *Harvard Business Review* 59, 3: 94–102.

Levy-Bruhl, L. (1926), *How Natives Think*, London: G. Allen & Unwin.

Lindsay, A. D. (1934), 'Introduction', in I. Kant *The Critique of Pure Reason*, London: J. M. Dent & E. P. Dutton, vii–xx.

Locke, J. (1991), *An Essay Concerning Human Understanding. An Abridgement*, London: J. M. Dent.

Luria, A. R. (1987), *The Mind of a Mnemonist*, Cambridge, Mass.: Harvard University Press.

Lynch, J. G. and Srull, T. K. (1991), 'Memory and Attitudinal Factors in Consumer Choice: Concepts and Research Methods', in H. H. Kassarjian and T. S. Robertson (eds) *Perspectives in Consumer Behavior*, Englewood-Cliffs, N.J.: Prentice-Hall, 101–29.

McClelland, J. L. and Plunkett, K. (1995), 'Cognitive Development', in M. Arbis (ed.) *The Handbook of Brain Theory and Neural Networks*, Cambridge, Mass.: MIT Press.

McClintock, C. C., Brannon, D. and Maynard-Moody, S. (1979), 'Applying the Logic of Sample Surveys to Qualitative Case Studies', *Administrative Science Quarterly* 24, 4: 612–29.

MacInnis, D. J., Nakamoto, K. and Mani, G. (1992), 'Cognitive Associations and Product Category Comparisons: The Role of Knowledge Structure and Context', in J. F. Sherry Jr and B. Sternthal (eds) *Advances in Consumer Research* 19, Provo, Utah: Association for Consumer Research, 260–7.

McIntosh, A. (1991), 'The Impact of Environmental Issues on Marketing and Politics in the 1990s', *Journal of Market Research Society* 33, 3: 205–17.

MacKenzie, D. (1990), 'The Green Consumer', *Business Economist* 21, 2: 31–40.

—— (1991), 'The Rise of the Green Consumer', *Consumer Policy Review* 1, 2: 68–75.

Maloney, M. P. and Ward, M. P. (1973), 'Ecology: Let's Hear from the People', *American Psychologist* 28, 7: 583–6.

—— and Braucht, G. N. (1975), 'A Revised Scale for the Measurement of Ecological Attitudes and Knowledge', *American Psychologist* 30, 7: 787–90.

Mantwill, M., Köhnken, G. and Aschermann, E. (1995), 'Effects of the Cognitive Interview on the Recall of Familiar and Unfamiliar Events', *Journal of Applied Psychology* 80, 1: 68–78.

Markin, R. J. (1974), *Consumer Behavior: A Cognitive Orientation*, London: Collier Macmillan.

Markus, H. (1977), 'Self-Schemata and Processing Information about the Self', *Journal of Personality and Social Psychology* 35, 2: 63–78.

Markus, H. and Zajonc, R. B. (1985), 'The Cognitive Perspective in Social Psychology', in G. Lindzey and E. Aronson (eds) *Handbook of Social Psychology. Vol. 1. Theory and Method*, New York: Random House, 137–230.

Maslow, A. H. (1970), 'A Theory of Human Motivation', in V. H. Vroom and E. L. Deci (eds) *Management and Motivation*, Harmondsworth: Penguin, 27–41.

Massaro, D. W. and Cowan, N. (1993), 'Information Processing Models: Microscopes of the Mind', *Annual Review of Psychology* 44, 383–425.

Maturana, H. R. (1979), *Autopoiesis and Cognition*, Dordrecht: D. Reidel.

Maturana, H. R. and Varela, F. J. (1992), *The Tree of Knowledge*, London: Shambhala.

Mead, G. H. (1934), *Mind, Self, and Society*, Chicago: University of Chicago Press.

Medin, D. L. and Ross, B. H. (1992), *Cognitive Psychology*, Fort Worth: Harcourt Brace Jovanovich.

Meffert, H. (1993), 'Umweltbewußtes Konsumverhalten', *Marketing ZfP* 15, 1: 51–4.

Merton, R. K. and Kendall, P. L. (1945-6), 'The Focused Interview', *American Journal of Sociology* 51, 541–57.

Meyer, M. (1995), *Of Problematology. Philosophy, Science, and Language*, London: University of Chicago Press.

Meyers-Levy, J. and Tybout, A. M. (1989), 'Schema Congruity as a Basis for Product Evaluations', *Journal of Consumer Research* 16, 1: 39–54.

Mick, D. G. (1988), 'Schema-Theoretics and Semiotics: Toward More Holistic, Programmatic Research on Marketing Communications', *Semiotica* 70, 1/2: 1–26.

Miles, M. B. and Huberman, A. M. (1984), *Qualitative Data Analysis: A Sourcebook of New Methods*, Beverly Hills, Calif.: Sage.

Milstein, J. S. (1979), 'The Conserver Society: Consumers' Attitudes and Behaviors Regarding Energy Conservation', in K. E. Henion and T. C. Kinnear (eds) *The Conserver Society*, Chicago: American Marketing Association, 43–50.

Milton, K. (1993), 'Environmentalism and Anthropology', in K. Milton (ed.) *Environmentalism*, London: Routledge, 1–17.

Mintel (1991), *The Green Consumer. Mintel Special Report 1991*, London: Mintel.

—— (1992), *New Product Development News*, November, London: Mintel.

Mitchell, V. W. (1993), 'Using Factor Analysis, Cluster and Discriminant Analysis to Identify Psychographic Segments', *Marketing Working Papers Series*, 9308, Manchester: Manchester School of Management.

Mittelstaedt, R. A. (1990), 'Economics, Psychology, and the Literature of the Subdiscipline of Consumer Behaviour', *Journal of the Academy of Marketing Sience* 18, 4: 303-11.

Monroe, K. B. (1993), Editorial, *Journal of Consumer Research* 19, 4: no page.

MORI (1992), *The Customer Viewpoint. A Quantitative Survey*, London: MORI.

Muncy, J. A. and Hunt, S. D. (1984), 'Consumer Involvement: Definitional Issues and Research Direction', in T. C. Kinnear (ed.) *Advances in Consumer Research* 11, Provo, Utah: Association for Consumer Research, 193–6.

Myburgh-Louw, J. and O'Shaughnessy, N. J. (1993-4), *Consumer Perceptions of Misleading and Deceptive Claims on the Packaging of 'Green' Fast Moving Consumer Goods*, Research Paper in Management Studies No. 10, Cambridge: Judge Institute of Management Studies/Cambridge University.

Nakamoto, K. (1987), 'Alternatives to Information Processing in Consumer Research: New Perspectives on Old Controversies', *International Journal of Research in Marketing* 4, 1: 11–27.

Neisser, U. (1967), *Cognitive Psychology*, New York: Appleton-Century-Crofts.

—— (1976), *Cognition and Reality: Principles and Implications of Cognitive Psychology*, San Francisco, Calif.: Freeman.

—— (1978), 'Memory: What Are the Important Questions?', in M. M. Gruneberg,

P. E. Morris and R. N. Sykes (eds) *Practical Aspects of Memory*, London: Academic Press, 3–24.

Neisser, U. and Hupcey, J. A. (1974-5), 'A Sherlockian Experiment', *Cognition* 3, 4: 307–11.

Nelissen, N. and Scheepers, P. (1992), 'Business Strategy and the Environment: The Need for Information about Environmental Consciousness and Behaviour', *Business Strategy and the Environment* 1, 2: 13–23.

Neurath, P. (1988), 'Paul Lazarsfeld und die Anfänge der modernen psychologischen Markt- und Konsumentenforschung in Wien', *Werbeforschung und Praxis* 33, 2: 29–31.

Newman, J. W. (1977), 'Consumer External Search: Amount and Determinants', in A. G. Woodside, J. N. Sheth and P. D. Bennett (eds) *Consumer and Industrial Buying Behavior*, New York: Elsevier North-Holland, 79–94.

Nickerson, R. S. (1984), 'Retrieval Inhibition From Part-Set Cuing: A Persistent Enigma in Memory Research', *Memory and Cognition* 12, 531–52.

Nisbett, R. E. and Wilson, T. D. (1977), 'Telling More Than We Can Know: Verbal Reports on Mental Processes', *Psychological Review* 84, 231–59.

Olney, T. J. and Bryce, W. (1991), 'Consumer Responses to Environmentally Based Product Claims', in R. H. Holman and M. R. Solomon (eds) *Advances in Consumer Research* 18, Chicago, Ill.: Association for Consumer Research, 693–6.

Olshavsky, R. W. and Granbois, D. H. (1979), 'Consumer Decision Making – Fact or Fiction?', *Journal of Consumer Research* 6, 2: 93–100.

Olson, J. C. (1977), 'Price as an Informational Cue: Effect on Product Evaluations', in A. G. Woodside, J. N. Sheth and P. D. Bennett (eds) *Consumer and Industrial Buying Behavior*, New York: Elsevier North-Holland, 267–86.

O'Riordan, T. (1976), 'Attitudes, Behaviour, and Environmental Policy Issues', in I. Altman and J. F. Wohlmill (eds) *Human Behavior and Environment*, New York: Plenum, 1–36.

—— (1981), *Environmentalism*, London: Pion.

—— (1990), 'Business and Environmental Accountability in the 1990s', *Business Economist* 21, 2: 16–30.

Park, C. W., Feick, L. and Mothersbaugh, D. L. (1992), 'Consumer Knowledge Assessment: How Product Experience and Knowledge of Brands, Attributes, and Features Affects What We Think We Know', in J. F. Sherry and B. Sternthal (eds) *Advances in Consumer Research* 19, Provo, Utah: Association for Consumer Research, 193–8.

—— (1994), 'Consumer Knowledge Assessment', *Journal of Consumer Research*, 21, 1: 71–82.

Parker, L. (1989), *Darker Shades of Green – The Impact of Growing Consumer Concerns*, Leatherhead: Leatherhead Food Research Association.

Patton, M. Q. (1990), *Qualitative Evaluation and Research Methods*, Newbury Park, Calif.: Sage.

Payne, J. W., Bettman, J. R. and Johnson, E. J. (1992), 'Behavioral Decision Research: A Constructive Processing Perspective', in M. R. Rosenzweig and L. W. Porter (eds) *Annual Review of Psychology* 41, Palo Alto, Calif.: Annual Reviews, 87–132.

Payne, J. W. and Ragsdale, E. K. (1978), 'Verbal Protocols and Direct Observation of Supermarket Shopping Behavior: Some Findings and a Discussion of Methods', in H. K. Hunt (ed.) *Advances in Consumer Research* 5, Ann Arbor, Mich.: Association for Consumer Research, 571–7.

Pearce, F. (1990), 'The Consumers Are Not So Green', *New Scientist* 126, 1721, Supplement: Greening of Industry, 13–14.

Peattie, K. (1995), 'A Question of Questions', *Green Management Letter*, June, 5–6.

Petkus, E. (1992), 'Implications of the Symbolic Interactionist Perspective for the Study of Environmentally-Responsible Consumption', in J. F. Sherry and B. Sternthal (eds) *Advances in Consumer Research* 19, Chicago, Ill.: Association for Consumer Research, 861–9.

Petty, R. E. and Cacioppo, J. T. (1984), 'Source Factors and the Elaboration Likelihood Model of Persuasion', in T. C. Kinnear (ed.) *Advances in Consumer Research* 11, Provo, Utah: Association for Consumer Research, 668–72.

Piaget, J. (1959), *The Language and Thought of the Child*, London: Routledge & Kegan Paul.

Pies, I. (1992), 'Normative Institutionenökonomik', Dissertation, Ingolstadt: Catholic University of Eichstätt.

Polanyi, M. and Prosch, H. R. (1976), *Meaning*, Chicago, Ill.: University of Chicago Press.

Popper, K. R. (1978), *Conjectures and Refutations. The Growth of Scientific Knowledge*, London: Routledge & Kegan Paul.

Potter, J. and Wetherell, M. (1987), *Discourse and Social Psychology*, London: Sage.

Price, L. L. and Feick, L. F. (1984), 'The Role of Interpersonal Sources in External Search: An Informational Perspective', in T. C. Kinnear (ed.) *Advances in Consumer Research* 11, Provo, Utah: Association for Consumer Research, 250–5.

Prothero, A. (1990), 'Green Consumerism and the Societal Marketing Concept – Marketing Strategies for the 1990s', *Journal of Marketing Management* 6, 2: 87–109.

Prothero, A. and McDonagh, P. (1992), 'Producing Environmentally Acceptable Cosmetics?', *Journal of Marketing Management* 8, 2: 147–66.

Punj, G. and Stewart, D. W. (1983), 'Cluster Analysis in Marketing Research: Review and Suggestions for Applications', *Journal of Marketing Research* 20, May: 134–48.

Raaij, W. F., van (1991), 'The Formations and Use of Expectations in Consumer Decision Making', in T. S. Robertson and H. H. Kassarjian (eds) *Handbook of Consumer Behavior*, Englewood-Cliffs, N.J.: Prentice-Hall, 401–18.

Ratneshwar, S. and Shocker, A. D. (1988), 'The Application of Prototypes and Categorization Theory in Marketing: Some Problems and Alternative Perspectives', in M. J. Houston (ed.) *Advances in Consumer Research* 15, Provo, Utah: Association for Consumer Research, 280–5.

Reynolds, T. J. and Jamieson, L. F. (1985), 'Image Representations: An Analytic Framework', in J. Jacoby and J. C. Olson (eds) *Perceived Quality: How Consumers View Stores and Merchandise*, Lexington, Mass.: Gower, 114–38.

Robson, C. (1993), *Real World Research*, Oxford: Blackwell.

Robson, S. and Hedges, A. (1993), 'Analysis and Interpretation of Qualitative Findings. Report of the MRS Qualitative Interest Group', *Journal of the Market Research Society* 35, 1: 23–36.

Rosch, E., Mervis, C. B., Gray, W. D., Johnson, D. M. and Boyes-Braem, P. (1976), 'Basic Objects in Natural Categories', *Cognitive Psychology* 8, 382–439.

Ross, W. T., Jr and Creyer, E. H. (1992), 'Making Inferences about Missing Information: The Effects of Existing Information', *Journal of Consumer Research* 19, 1: 14–25.

Rothschild, M. L. (1984), 'Perspectives on Involvement: Current Problems and Future Directions', in T. C. Kinnear (ed.) *Advances in Consumer Research* 11, Provo, Utah: Association for Consumer Research, 216–17.

—— (1987), *Marketing Communications: From Fundamentals to Strategies*, Lexington, Mass: D. C. Heath.

Rowan, J. (1974), 'Research as Intervention', in N. Armistead (ed.) *Reconstructing Social Psychology*, Harmondsworth: Penguin, 86–100.

Rubik, F. (1992), 'Instrumente zur ökologischen Bewertung von Produkten: Methodik und Funktionen der Produktlinienanalyse', *Gfk-Jahrbuch der Absatz- und Verbrauchsforschung* 4, 318–41.

Rumelhart, D. E. (1984), 'Schemata and the Cognitive System', in R. S. Wyer Jr and T. K. Srull (eds) *Handbook of Social Cognition. Vol. 1*, Hillsdale, N.J.: Lawrence Erlbaum Associates, 161–88.

Rumelhart, D. E. and Ortony, A. (1977), 'The Representation of Knowledge in Memory', in R. C. Anderson, R. J. Spiro and W. E. Montague (eds) *Schooling and the Acquisition of Knowledge*, Hillsdale, N.J.: Lawrence Erlbaum Associates, 99–135.

Ryle, G. (1990), *The Concept of Mind*, Harmondsworth: Penguin.

Sacks, O. (1986), *The Man Who Mistook His Wife for a Hat*, South Yarmouth, Mass.: Curley.

—— (1991), *Awakenings*, London: Picador.

Sampson, P. (1986), 'Qualitative Research and Motivation Research', in R. Worcester and J. Downham (eds) *Consumer Market Research Handbook*, London: McGraw-Hill, 29–55.

SB (1992), *Datenreport 5: Zahlen und Fakten über die Bundesrepublik Deutschland 1991/1992*, Munich/Landsberg: Bonn Aktuell.

Schank, R. C. and Abelson, R. P. (1977), *Scripts, Plans, Goals and Understanding: An Inquiry Into Human Knowledge Structures*, Hillsdale, N.J.: Lawrence Erlbaum Associates.

Schiffman, L. G. and Kanuk, L. L. (1987), *Consumer Behavior*, Englewood-Cliffs, N.J.: Prentice-Hall.

Schultz, D. E., Tannenbaum, S. I. and Lauterborn, R. F. (1992), *Integrated Marketing Communications*, Lincolnwood-Chicago, Ill.: NTC Business Books.

Schurr, P. H. (1986), 'Four Script Studies: What Have We Learned?', in R. J. Lutz (ed.) *Advances in Consumer Research* 13, Provo, Utah: Association for Consumer Research, 498–503.

Schwartz, J. and Miller, T. (1991), 'The Earth's Best Friends', *American Demographics* 13, 2: 26–35.

Schwartz, S. H. and Bilsky, W. (1987), 'Toward a Theory of Universal Content and Structure of Values: Extensions and Cross-Cultural Replications', *Journal of Personality and Social Psychology* 58, 5: 550–62.

Scribner, S. (1986), 'Thinking in Action: Some Characteristics of Practical Thought', in R. J. Sternberg and R. K. Wagner (eds) *Practical Intelligence. Nature and Origins of Competence in the Everyday World*, Cambridge: Cambridge University Press, 13–30.

Selnes, F. and Gronhaug, K. (1986), 'Subjective and Objective Measures of Product Knowledge Contrasted', in R. J. Lutz (ed.) *Advances in Consumer Research* 13, Provo, Utah: Association for Consumer Research, 67–71.

Sheth, J. N. (1972), 'The Future of Buyer Behavior Theory', in M. Venkatesan (ed.) *Proceedings of the Third Annual Conference of the Association for Consumer Research*, College Park, Md: Association for Consumer Research, 562–75.

—— (1992), 'Acrimony in the Ivory Tower: A Retrospective on Consumer Research', *Journal of the Academy of Marketing Science* 20, 345–53.

Sheth, J. N. and Gross B. L. (1988), 'Parallel Development of Marketing and Consumer Behavior: A Historical Perspective', in T. Nevett and R. A. Fullerton (eds) *Historical Perspectives in Marketing: Essays in Honor of Stanley C. Hollander*, Lexington, Mass.: Lexington Books, 9–33.

Shimp, T. A. (1994), 'Academic Appalachia and the Discipline of Consumer Research', in C. T. Allen and D. Roedder John (eds) *Advances in Consumer Research* 21, Provo, Utah: Association for Consumer Research, 1–7.

Silverman, D. (1985), *Qualitative Methodology and Sociology*, Aldershot: Gower.

—— (1993), *Interpreting Qualitative Data*, London: Sage.

Simon, F. L. (1992), 'Marketing Green Products in the Triad', *Columbia Journal of World Business*, Fall and Winter: 268–85.

Simon, H. A. (1959), 'Theories of Decision-Making in Economics and Behavioral Science', *The American Economic Review* 49, 253–83.

—— (1987), 'Rationality in Psychology and Economics', in R. M. Hogarth and M. W. Reder (eds) *Rational Choice. The Contrast between Economics and Psychology*, Chicago, Ill.: University of Chicago Press, 25–40.

Sirdeshmukh, D. and Unnava, H. R. (1992), 'The Effects of Missing Information on Consumer Product Evaluations', in J. F. Sherry and B. Sternthal (eds) *Advances in Consumer Research* 19, Chicago, Ill.: Association for Consumer Research, 284–9.

Skretny, J. D. (1993), 'Concern for the Environment: A Cross-National Perspective', *International Journal of Public Opinion Research* 5, 4: 335–52.

Sloan, A. E. (1993), 'Consumers, the Environment, and the Food Industry', *Food Technology*, August: 72–3.

SM (1992), 'Apathy is Tinged with Green', *Super Marketing*, 9 October 1992, 12.

Smith, D. (1992), 'Strategic Management and the Business Environment: What Lies Beyond the Rhetoric of Greening?', *Business Strategy and the Environment* 1, 1: 1–9.

Smith, R. A. and Houston, M. J. (1986), 'Measuring Script Development: An Evaluation of Alternative Approaches', in R. J. Lutz (ed.) *Advances in Consumer Research* 13, Provo, Utah: Association for Consumer Research, 504–8.

Solso, R. L. (1988), *Cognitive Psychology*, Boston: Allyn & Bacon.

Spiggle, S. (1994), 'Analysis and Interpretation of Qualitative Data in Consumer Research', *Journal of Consumer Research* 21, 3: 491–503.

Spiggle, S. and Sanders, C. R. (1984), 'The Construction of Consumer Typologies: Scientific and Ethnomethods', in T. C. Kinnear (ed.) *Advances in Consumer Research* 11, Provo, Utah: Association for Consumer Research, 337–342.

SRI (1992), *Diversity in the Green Spectrum*, Report No. 812/Business Intelligence Program, SRI International.

Srull, T. K. (1983), 'The Role of Prior Knowledge in the Acquisition, Retention, and Use of New Information', in R. P. Bagozzi and A. M. Tybout (eds) *Advances in Consumer Research* 10, Ann Arbor, Mich.: Association for Consumer Research, 572–6.

Stayman, D. M., Alden, D. L. and Smith, K. H. (1992), 'Some Effects of Schematic Processing on Consumer Expectations and Disconfirmation Judgements', *Journal of Consumer Research* 19, 2: 240–55.

Stoecker, R. (1991), 'Evaluating and Rethinking the Case Study', *Sociological Review* 39, 1: 88–112.

Strauss, A. L. (1987), *Qualitative Analysis For Social Scientists*, Cambridge: Cambridge University Press.

Strauss, A. L. and Corbin J. (1990), *Basics of Qualitative Research: Grounded Theory Procedures and Techniques*, Newbury Park, Calif.: Sage.

Strong, C. (1995), 'Are Grocery Retail Buyers Making Greener Puchasing Decisions?', *Greener Management International* 3, 11: 103–12.

Suchaneck, A. (1992), 'Der ökonomische Ansatz und das Problem theoretischer Integration', Dissertation, University of Witten-Herdecke.

—— (1993), 'Der Homo Oeconomicus als Heuristik', *Working Paper No. 38*, Ingolstadt: Wirtschaftswissenschaftliche Fakultät der Universität Eichstätt.

Suh, N. P. (1990), *The Principles of Design*, New York: Oxford University Press.

Sujan, M. and Bettman, J. R. (1989), 'The Effects of Brand Positioning Strategies on Consumers' Brand and Category Perceptions: Some Insight From Schema Research', *Journal of Marketing Research* 26, 454–67.

Taylor, S. E. and Crocker, J. (1981), 'Schematic Bases of Social Information Processing', in E. T. Higgins, C. P. Herman and M. P. Zanna (eds) *Social Cognition: The Ontario Symposium* 1, Hillsdale, N.J.: Lawrence Erlbaum Associates, 89–134.

Thorgesen, J. (1994), 'A Model of Recycling Behaviour, with Evidence from Danish Source Separating Programmes', *International Journal of Research in Marketing* 11, 2: 145–63.

Thorngate, W. (1976), '"In General" vs. "It Depends". Some Comments on the Gergen–Schlenker Debate', *Personality and Social Psychology Bulletin* 2, 404–10.

Troge, A. (1993), 'Lügen die Ökobilanzen?', *Absatzwirtschaft. ZfM* 36, 1: 14–16.

Tulving, E. (1972), 'Episodic and Semantic Memory', in E. Tulving and W. Donaldson (eds) *Organization of Memory*, New York: Academic Press, 381–403.

—— (1983), *Elements of Episodic Memory*, Oxford: Oxford University Press.

—— (1985), 'How Many Memory Systems Are There?', *American Psychologist* 40, 4: 385–98.

Tybout, A. M. and Artz, N. (1994), 'Consumer Psychology', *Annual Review of Psychology* 45, 131–69.

Upsall, D. and Worcester, R. (1995), 'You Can't Sink a Rainbow', WAPOR Conference, 21 September 1995, The Hague.

Urbany, J. E. and Dickson, P. R. (1987), 'Information Search in the Retail Grocery Market', Working Paper, Ohio: Ohio State University.

Vandermerve, S. and Oliff, M. D. (1990), 'Customers Drive Corporations Green', *Long Range Planning* 23, 6: 10–16.

Varela, F., Thompson, E. and Rosch, E. (1991), *Cognitive Science and Human Experience*, Cambridge, Mass.: MIT Press.

Varis, O. (1989), 'The Analysis of Preferences in Complex Environmental Judgements – A Focus on the Analytic Hierarchy Process', *Journal of Environmental Management* 28, 4: 283–94.

Venkatraman, M. and Villarreal, A. (1984), 'Schematic Processing of Information: An Exploratory Investigation', in T. C. Kinnear (ed.) *Advances in Consumer Research* 11, Provo, Utah: Association for Consumer Research, 355–60.

Vinehall, M. (1979), 'Qualitative Research – Summary of the Concepts Involved', *Journal of the Market Research Society* 21, 2: 107–23.

Wadsworth, B. J. (1996), *Piaget's Theory of Cognitive and Affective Development*, London: Longman.

Wagenknecht, H. and Borel, M. J. (1982), 'Cognition', in H. J. Eysenck, W. Arnold and R. Meili (eds) *Encyclopedia of Psychology*, New York: Continuum, 177.

Wagner, S. (1996a), 'Environmentally-Oriented Consumer Behaviour: A Cognitive Study with Implications for Communications Management', unpublished D.Phil. thesis, University of Oxford.

—— (1996b), '"Green" Communications Management: How to Talk Green Sense to Consumers', *Green Management Letter*, May: 7–9.

—— (1997), *Environmental Communication: A Practitioner's Guide*, Haslemere, Surrey: Epsilon Press/Eco-Innovations Publishing.

—— (forthcoming/a), 'Environmental Communication: Insights from Two Cases of Successful European Companies'.

—— (forthcoming/b), 'Images of Man in Organization Theory: How Not to Frame Institutional Man', unpublished D.Phil. thesis, Catholic University of Eichstätt zu Ingolstadt, Germany.

Warlop, L. and Ratneshwar, S. (1993), 'The Role of Usage Context in Consumer Choice: A Problem Solving Perspective', in L. McAlister and M. L. Rothschild (eds) *Advances in Consumer Research* 20, Provo, Utah: Association for Consumer Research, 377–82.

Webster, F. E., Jr (1976), 'Who is the Socially-Ecologically Concerned Consumer?', in K. E. Henion and T. C. Kinnear (eds) *Ecological Marketing*, Chicago, Ill: American Marketing Association, 121–30.

Weick, K. E. (1979), *The Social Psychology of Organizing*, Reading, Mass.: Addison-Wesley.

Weitz, K. A., Smith, J. K. and Warren, J. L. (1994), 'Developing a Decision Support Tool for Life-Cycle Cost Assessments', *Total Quality Environmental Management* 4, 1:23–36.

Wells, W. D. (1993), 'Discovery-Oriented Consumer Research', *Journal of Consumer Research* 19, 4: 489–504.

Wenben Lai, A. (1994), 'Consumption Schemata: Their Effects on Consumer Decision Making', in C. T. Allen and D. Roedder John (eds) *Advances in Consumer Research* 21, Provo, Utah: Association for Consumer Research, 489–94.

Wickelgren, W. A. (1979), *Cognitive Psychology*, Englewood-Cliffs, N.J.: Prentice-Hall.

Wild, H. (1995), *A Study of Awareness, Understanding and Usage of Environmental Claims: Summary of Main Findings*, London: National Consumer Council.

Wilkie, W. L. and Dickson, P. R. (1991), 'Shopping for Appliances: Consumers' Strategies and Patterns of Information Search', in H. H. Kassarjian and T. S. Robertson (eds) *Perspectives in Consumer Behavior*, Englewood-Cliffs, N.J.: Prentice-Hall, 1–26.

Williams, S. M. and McCrorie, R. (1990), 'The Analysis of Ecological Attitudes in Town and Country', *Journal of Environmental Management* 31, 2: 157–62.

Wimmer, F. (1988), 'Umweltbewußtsein und Konsumrelevante Einstellungen und Verhaltensweisen', in A. Brandt, U. Hansen, I. Schoenheit and K. Werner (eds) *Ökologisches Marketing*, Frankfurt: Campus, 44–85.

Winkler, A. R. and Voller, B. (n.d.), *European Consumers and Environmentalism*, Nuremberg: GfK (Gesellschaft für Konsumentenforschung).

Witherspoon, S. and Martin, J. (1992), 'What Do We Mean by Green?', in R. Jowell, L. Brook, G. Prior and B. Taylor (eds) *British Social Attitudes. The 9th Report*, Aldershot: Dartmouth Publishing, 1–26.

Wittgenstein, L. J., von (1967), *Philosophical Investigations, German and English*, Oxford: Blackwell.

—— (1975), *Philosophical Remarks*, New York: Harper & Row.

Wong, V., Turner, W. and Stoneman, P. (1995), 'Marketing Strategies and Market Prospects for Environmentally-Friendly Consumer Products', *Research Paper No. 165*, Coventry: Warwick Business School.

Worcester, R. (1993a), 'Public and Elite Attitudes to Environmental Issues', *International Journal of Public Opinion Research* 5, 4: 315–34.

—— (1993b), *Societal Attitudes and Attitudes to Human Dimensions of Global Environmental Change*, International Conference on Social Values, 28 September 1993, Madrid: Complutense University of Madrid.

——(1994a), 'The Sustainable Society: What We Know about What People Think and Do', 'Values for a Sustainable Future' – World Environment Day Symposium, 2 June 1994, New York.

—— (1994b), 'The Creation of a Corporate Image', John M. Olin Lecture/Friends of Templeton Hilary Term Lecture, 23 March 1994, Oxford: Templeton College.

—— (1995), 'Business and the Environment: The Predictable Shock of Brent Spar', HRH The Prince of Wales's Business and The Environment Programme/University of Cambridge Programme for Industry, 18 September 1995, Cambridge: University of Cambridge.

—— (1996) 'Business and the Environment: In the Aftermath of Brent Spar and BSE', HRH The Prince of Wales's Business and The Environment Programme/University of Cambridge Programme for Industry, 16 September 1996, Cambridge: University of Cambridge.

Worsley, P. (1991a), 'Preface', in P. Worsley (ed.) *The New Modern Sociology Readings*, Harmondsworth: Penguin, 1–7.

—— (1991b), 'Sociology as a Discipline', in P. Worsley (ed.) *The New Modern Sociology Readings*, Harmondsworth: Penguin, 9–12.

Wright, D. B., Gaskell, G. D. and O'Minrcheartaigh, C. A. (1994), 'How Much Is "Quite A Bit"? Mapping between Numerical Values and Vague Quantifiers', *Applied Cognitive Psychology* 8, 5: 479–96.

Wright, P. (1975), 'Consumer Choice Strategies: Simplifying vs. Optimizing', *Journal of Marketing Research* 12, 1: 60–7.

Wyer, R. S., Jr and Srull, T. K. (1981), 'Category Accessibility: Some Theoretical and Empirical Issues Concerning the Processing of Social Stimulus Information', in E. T. Higgins, C. P. Herman and M. P. Zanna (eds) *Social Cognition: The Ontario Symposium* 1, Hillsdale, N.J.: Lawrence Erlbaum Associates, 161–97.

Yin, R. K. (1989), *Case Study Research. Design and Methods*, Newbury Park, Calif.: Sage.

—— (1992), 'The Case Study Method as a Tool of Doing Evaluations', *Current Sociology* 40, 1: 119–36.

Young, K. (1991), 'Shades of Green', in R. Jowell, L. Brook and B. Taylor (eds) *British Social Attitudes. The 8th Report*, Aldershot: Dartmouth Publishing, 107–30.

Zeithaml, V. A. (1991), 'Consumer Perceptions of Price, Quality, and Value: A Means–End Model and Synthesis of Evidence', in H. H. Kassarjian and T. S. Robertson (eds) *Perspectives in Consumer Behavior*, Englewood-Cliffs, N.J.: Prentice-Hall, 27–53.

INDEX

Abelson, R. P. 35, 43, 45, 47–8, 165, 171
ability 50, 52–3, 61; findings on 179–91, 201–2; *see also* intelligence
abstraction *see* cognitive operations
Ackroyd, S. 67
activist mind *see* schema; *see also* associative bridges
actual buying frequencies 86–8; and HMN code 86; and quartiles' analysis 87–8, 99, 175–6
Adams, R. 22
Ajzen, I. 20, 68
Alba, J. W. 12, 28, 31–3, 35–8, 40–1, 43, 45, 47–52, 58, 65, 67, 69–70, 135, 159, 167, 170–1, 195
Alden, S. D. 66, 69
Aldrin, E. 56
Anderson, J. R. 36
anthropology *see* cognitive anthropology
Antil, J. H. 12
Arabie, L. J. 101, 103
argumentative knowledge 121, 151–4, 182; and counter-arguments 154, 156
Armstrong, N. 56
Artz, N. 32, 43, 67, 82, 135, 195
associative bridges 167–8, 172; and passivist mind 168, 170
attitude–behaviour gap 20-1; *see also* Fishbein model

Bartlett, F. C. 29, 31, 34, 45, 47, 62, 64–5, 165, 192
Becker, G. S. 6, 8
Belck, M. A. 22
Berne, E. 57
Berry, J. W. 43, 53–5, 59, 98, 179

Bettman, J. R. 28, 31–3, 36, 41, 43, 48–52, 58, 68–9, 73, 159, 195
Bhaskar, R. 11, 28–9
Billig, A. 1, 72
Bilsky, W. 19
Black, J. B. 35, 43, 45, 47–8, 165, 171
Bogdan, R. 2, 63
Borel, M. 16
bottom-up processing *see* cognitive operations
bounded rationality 197–8
bracketing framework 82–84, 129; and interview guide 82
Bransford, J. D. 49, 54, 188, 194–5
Brent Spar 2
Brewer, W. F. 47, 165, 171
bricolage 50, 55–8, 60, 197, 201–2; and bricoleur 25, 55, 57–9; contextual nature of 55–6; findings on 179–84, 187–8; and *Homo faber* 197
bricoleur *see* bricolage
BBC2 56
Brown, T. J. 36
Brucks, M. 32, 36–7, 40, 45–7, 67–9, 95, 152
Bruner, J. 64–6, 194
Bryce, D. 15, 17, 25, 53, 64, 98
Bundesumweltministerium (*BUM*) (Department of the Environment) 203
Burnkrant, R. E. 58
Burrell, G. 63
Buss, N. 3

Cacioppo, J. T. 33, 43, 50
Campbell, C. 16, 22, 187
Campbell, D. 98
Cassel, L. 66

Castleberry, S. B. 29, 63, 66
causality principle 9–10, 12, 49–50, 177,
190, 194, 196, 201; and alternative
principles 10, 13
Cazeneuve, J. 44
Central Statistical Office (CSO) 81
Chaiken, S. 32
Chakravarti, D. 14, 32, 58
choice model 32–4, 58–9, 66–7, 196–7
classification errors 149, 151, 155; see also
CI analysis
Clifton, R. 3
cluster analysis 97, 101; and cluster
sequences 109–11, 121–2; see also
correlation analysis; and group average
method 102–3, 107–12, 114;
hierarchical 102, 107–15; and
K-means method 102–3, 120;
non-hierarchical 102, 112–14; and
outliers 109; problems in 102–4; and
sub-groups 109; and variable sets 103,
107–8; and Ward's method 102–3,
107–12, 114, 117; see also
scattergrams; sensitivity analysis
Coddington, W. 15
cognition 2, 15–17, 21, 28; definition of
2, 15; research programme for 28–31;
and subjectivity 2, 15–17, 26, 28,
58–9, 199–200; see also cognitive
anthropology; cognitive psychology
cognitive anthropology 4, 17–19, 29,
192, 196; heuristic of 29, 49–50, 193;
see also bricolage; qualitative research;
practical thinking; product
cognitive categories 104, 117–22
cognitive operations 40–43, 60; of
abstraction 41–2, 149–51, 160–2,
199; of bottom-up processing mode
42–3, 160–1; of integration 41–2,
44–5, 156–8, 160, 162, 165, 170,
199–200; of interpretation 41–2,
151–5, 162; levels of 41–2; modes of
42–3; processes of 41–2; and schemata
47; of selection 41–2, 159–60; of
specification 41–2, 147–9, 159–62,
199; subconscious nature of 36, 43; of
top-down processing mode 42–3,
160–1
cognitive psychology 4, 16–17, 29, 192;
criticism of 4, 11–12, 28–31, 33,
49–50, 54, 64–5, 193–4; heuristic of
16, 29, 31–5, 49–50, 192–4; and

information processing paradigm 16,
31, 197; see also knowledge structure
theory; quantitative research; product
Cohen, G. 36, 46–8, 64–6, 79, 171
Cohen, J. B. 14, 32, 58
complexity reduction 8, 10; and
heuristics 8–9, 172–3; limits to 12, 29,
33, 62; need for 9, 12, 14; and
problem dependence 9; and schemata
47–8;
computer analogy 35–6, 41, 44, 48, 123,
162
confusion 3, 188, 190, 201; see also
cynicism
Consumers' Association (CA) 3, 12, 71
consumer behaviour research 11–14; and
anthropology 49–50, 57; criticism of
11–13, 30–1, 65, 195–7, 202; and
definitions 12; and psychology 30–1,
49–50;
consumer education 14, 23; and public
policy 14, 202–3
consumer interview (CI) analysis 90–2,
94, 97, 120–1, 129, 152, 154–5, 187;
and consumer interview index 90
consumer interview index see consumer
interview analysis
contextual cognition 49, 53–59, 181–4,
188, 190–8, 202, 204
Cook, T. D. 98
Coolican, H. 64–5, 75, 81, 98
Cope, D. 15
Corbin, J. 67
correlation analysis 104, 106–7, 121,
140, 169–70
Costley, C. L. 41, 43, 47, 152
Cowan, N. 31
Crabtree, B. 82
Craik, F. J. 41–2, 47, 54
Crano, W. D. 82, 98
Creswell, J. W. 63, 82, 84
Creyer, E. H. 33, 66
Crocker, J. B. 36–8, 45–7, 51–2, 170–1,
176
cynicism 3, 183, 188–90, 196, 201, 203

Dahrendorf, R. 7, 9–10, 21
D'Amour, G. 8
Dasgupta, S. 206
data matrices 84–5, 93–4, 96, 109, 136,
204
Day, E. 29, 63, 66